MANAGEMENT RESEARCH

THIRD EDITION

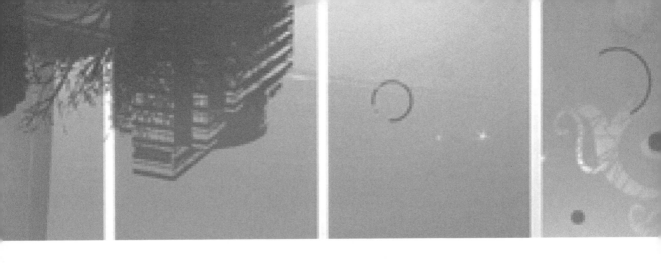

MANAGEMENT
RESEARCH

THIRD EDITION

MARK EASTERBY-SMITH
RICHARD THORPE
PAUL R. JACKSON

$SAGE

Los Angeles • London • New Delhi • Singapore

First edition published 1991. Second edition published 2002. Reprinted 2002, 2003, 2004, 2005.

Third edition published 2008

SAGE Publications Ltd
1 Oliver's Yard
55 City Road
London EC1Y 1SP

SAGE Publications Inc.
2455 Teller Road
Thousand Oaks, California 91320

SAGE Publications India Pvt Ltd
B 1/I 1 Mohan Cooperative Industrial Area
Mathura Road, Post Bag 7
New Delhi 110 044

SAGE Publications Asia-Pacific Pte Ltd
33 Pekin Street #02-01
Far East Square
Singapore 048763

Library of Congress Control Number 2007938693

British Library Cataloguing in Publication data

A catalogue record for this book is available from the British Library

ISBN 978-1-84787-176-3
ISBN 978-1-84787-177-0 (pbk)

Typeset by Cepha Imaging Pvt Ltd
Printed in Great Britain by TJ International Ltd
Printed on paper from sustainable resources

CONTENTS

About the authors ix

Preface to the third edition xi

Acknowledgements xiii

1 Introduction 1

Introduction 2
What is management? 3
Why is management research distinctive? 5
Levels and outcomes of management
   research 8
   Levels of research 9
Conclusion 11
Further reading 12

2 The ingredients of successful research 13

Introduction 14
Motivation 14
Support and supervision 15
Style and creativity 18
   Style 18
   Disciplined imagination 20
   Conceptualization 21
Skills and qualities 21
Getting started 24
Conclusion 27
Further reading 28

3 Doing a literature review 29

Introduction 30
What is a literature review? 30
Search and preparation for the review 31
   Knowing the journals 31
   Exploring potential sources 32

Time devoted to literature searching 33
Focusing the research 33
Learning 33
Getting access to sources of information 33
   Sources 33
   Electronic searches 34
   Alignment with study context and approach 35
Library resources 37
   Books 38
   Journals 39
   *Theses, dissertations and research in
      progress* 40
   Government publications, official statistics 42
   *Reference books, general and specialized
      bibliographic guides* 42
   *Web sites: the Internet as an enabler and an
      adjunct* 43
Organizing your material and being systematic 45
   Organizing 45
   Systematic reviews 46
   Writing reviews 48
Plagiarism 50
   Examples of plagiarism 51
Conclusion 52
Further reading 53

4 The philosophy of management research 55

Introduction 56
Two contrasting traditions: positivism versus
   social constructionism 56
   Positivism 57
   Social constructionism 58
Broadening the philosophical debate 60
   Ontology and epistemology 61
   Epistemology and methodology 62

Research philosophies underlying management
    research practice 64
    Positivist management research 65
    Relativist management research 66
    *Social constructionist management
        research* 68
    Mixed methods in management research 70
    *Strengths and weaknesses of the main
        traditions* 71
Overviews of other philosophies 73
    Critical theory 74
    Feminism 74
    Hermeneutics 75
    Postmodernism 75
    Pragmatism 76
    Structuration theory 77
Conclusion 77
Further reading 78

5 Designing management research 81

Introduction 82
Qualitative and quantitative designs 83
Positivist research designs 84
    Experimental designs 84
    Quasi-experimental designs 86
    Validity of positivist designs 87
Relativist research designs 90
    Survey research design 90
    Validity of research designs 92
Constructionist research designs 93
    Action research and cooperative inquiry 93
    Ethnography 94
    Narrative methods 95
    Validity of constructionist designs 96
Broad-based methods 97
    Case studies 97
    Grounded theory 100
Generic issues 102
    Identifying the unit of analysis 102
    Universal theory or local knowledge? 104
    Theory or data first? 105
    Reductionism versus holism 105
    Verification or falsification 105
Contributing to theory 107

Implications 108
    Contrasting views on validity 108
    Research design template 108
Conclusion 110
Further reading 112

6 The politics and ethics of management research 113

Introduction 114
Political influences on the research question 115
    The experience of the researcher 116
    Academic stakeholders 118
    Corporate stakeholders 123
    The subject of study 125
    Context and models of research 126
Politics of access 129
Ethics 132
Utilization of research 135
Conclusion 138
Further reading 139

7 Creating qualitative data 141

Main methods of qualitative data collection 142
Collecting natural language data 142
    Interviews: how much structure? 142
    In-depth interviews 144
    Interviewing skills 145
    Laddering 146
    Avoiding bias 147
    General interview issues 147
    Critical incident technique 150
    Group and focus interviews 151
    Diary methods 152
    Video recording 153
Ethnographic approaches 155
    Complete participation 156
    Research as the explicit role 158
    Interrupted involvement 159
    Observation alone 160
    Semi-concealed research 160
    Choice of roles 161
Understanding through interaction 161
    Photographs and visual metaphors 162
    Action research 165

General issues in relation to qualitative
   methods 166
Conclusion 168
Further reading 170

8 Making sense of qualitative data 171

Introduction 172
Analysing transcripts 172
   Content analysis 173
   Grounded analysis 175
Discourse analysis 182
   Narrative analysis 182
   Conversation analysis 183
   Argument analysis 183
Using computers and software to analyse
   qualitative data 185
   NVivo in use: evolution of business knowledge
      in SMEs 187
An example of using Atlas.ti 191
   Coding 194
   Network diagrams 194
   Repertory grids 197
   Cognitive mapping 202
   Individual cognitive maps 204
   Group maps 204
Conclusion 208
Further reading 209

9 Creating quantitative data 211

Introduction 212
Sampling design 212
   Principles in designing a sample 212
   Probability sampling designs 216
   Non-probability sampling 217
Sources of quantitative data 219
   Collecting data through surveys 219
   Collecting data through observational
      methods 221
   Using secondary data – databases 223
The process of measurement 227
   Principles in designing structured questions for
      surveys and interviews 227
   Measurement scales for recording responses 228

Conclusion 231
Further reading 231

10 Making sense of quantitative data 233

Introduction 234
   Example dataset for the chapter 235
Summarizing and describing data 239
   Showing the shape of data distributions 239
   Summary measures of location 242
   Summary measures of spread 245
   Comparing summary measures of spread 246
   Importance of symmetry 247
   Formal features of summary measures 247
Going beyond a sample 249
   Rationale of hypothesis testing 249
   Formal steps in hypothesis testing 251
   Testing for group differences – comparing
      groups 257
   Testing association between variables 260
Conclusion 267
Further reading 267

11 Multivariate analysis 269

Introduction 270
   Domain of multivariate analysis 270
   Forms of interdependence in management
      research 271
   Ways of dealing with interdependence within
      quantitative analysis 271
Multivariate analysis of measurement models 275
   Rationale for measurement models 275
   Structure of measurement models 276
   Analysis methods for measurement
      models 277
Multivariate analysis of causal models 279
   Rationale for causal models 279
   Analysis of causal models for observed
      variables 284
   Analysis of observed and latent variables –
      structural equation modelling 296
Conclusion 302
Further reading 303

12 Writing and disseminating management research 305

Introduction 306
The skills of writing 306
  Writing as a habit 307
  Developing structures 307
  Templates for writing papers and research reports 309
  Topping and tailing 310
Outputs and evaluation 313
  Private outputs: reports, dissertations and theses 313
  Public outputs: conferences, journals and books 315
Dissemination strategies 317
Conclusion 319
Further reading 320

Answers to exercises 321

Glossary 326

Bibliography 335

Index 347

ABOUT THE AUTHORS

Mark Easterby-Smith is Professor of Management Learning at Lancaster University Management School. He has a first degree in Engineering Science and a PhD in Organizational Behaviour from Durham University. He has been an active researcher for over 30 years with primary interests in methodology and learning processes. He has carried out evaluation studies in many European companies, and has led research projects on management development, organizational learning, dynamic capabilities, and knowledge transfer across international organizations in the UK, India and China.

He has published numerous academic papers and over ten books including: *Auditing Management Development*, Gower, 1980; *The Challenge to Western Management Development*, Routledge, 1989; *Evaluation of Management Education, Training and Development*, Gower, 1994; *Organizational Learning and the Learning Organization*, SAGE, 1998; and *The Handbook of Organizational Learning and Knowledge Management*, Blackwell, 2005.

At Lancaster he has been Director of the School's Doctoral Programme and Director of the Graduate Management School. Externally he spent several years as a visiting faculty member on the International Teachers' Programme, acting as Director when it was held at the London Business School in 1984. During the early 1990s, he was national co-ordinator of the Management Teaching Fellowship Scheme funded by the UK's Economic and Social Research Council (ESRC) which was responsible for training 180 new faculty members across UK management schools. He is a former member of the ESRC Post-graduate Training Board, and was President of the British Academy of Management in 2006.

Richard Thorpe is Professor of Management Development and Deputy Director of the Keyworth Institute at Leeds University Business School. His early industrial experience informed the way his ethos has developed; common themes within which are: a strong commitment to process methodologies and a focus on action in all its forms; an interest in and commitment to the development of doctoral students and the development of capacity within the sector; a commitment to collaborative working on projects of mutual interest. Following a number of years in industry, he joined Strathclyde University as a researcher studying incentive payment schemes. This led to collaboration on *Payment Schemes and Productivity*, 1986 Macmillan. In 1980, he joined Glasgow University, he widened his research interests to include small firm growth and development as well as making regular contributions to the Scottish Business School's Doctoral Programme. In 1983, he attended the International Teachers' Programme in Sweden where he met Mark and embarked on a PhD under Mark's supervision. Collaboration continued through the 1990s with the ESRC Teaching Fellowship Scheme. In 1996, he was instrumental in establishing the

Graduate Business School at Manchester Metropolitan University and, in 2003, joined the ESRC Training and Development Board. There, he was involved in establishing the training guidelines for both doctorate and professional doctorate provision and more recently in initiatives to address capacity building in management and business. In 2003, he contributed to the ESRCs Evolution of Business Knowledge programme, his research interests including: performance, remuneration, and entrepreneurship, management learning and development and leadership and has published (with others) a number of books including: *Remuneration Systems,* Financial Times/Prentice Hall, 2000; *Management and Language: The Manager as Practical Author*, SAGE, 2007; *The SAGE Dictionary of Qualitative Management Research*, SAGE, 2008; and *Peformance Management; Multidisciplinary Perspectives*, Palgrave, 2008. He was President of the British Academy of Management in 2007.

Paul R. Jackson is Professor of Corporate Communications and Head of the Division of Marketing International Business and Strategy at Manchester Business School. He has a first degree in Psychology from the University of Sheffield and an MSc in Applied Statistics from Sheffield Polytechnic (now Sheffield Hallam University). His first university post was as a research assistant in studies on impression formation, where he decided that it was worth learning how to write programs in Fortran so that the computer could do the tedious work of adding up so that he could do the interesting bits. His research interests have included lab studies of impression formation, large-scale surveys of the impact of unemployment on psychological health, longitudinal field studies of the effects of empowerment and work design on employee health and performance, employee communication and teamworking, mergers and social identity.

He has published widely in journals such as the *Academy of Management Journal, Journal of Applied Psychology, British Medical Journal, Human Relations, Journal of Occupational Health Psychology and British Journal of Management*. His books include: *Developments in Work* and *Organisational Psychology: Implications for International Business*, Elsevier, 2006; *Psychosocial Risk Factors in Call Centres*, HSE Books, 2003; *Change in Manufacturing: Managing Stress in Manufacturing*, HSE Books, 2001; and *Organisational Interventions to Reduce the Impact of Poor Work Design*, HSE Books, 1998.

He has been Director of Doctoral Programmes at the University of Sheffield and at UMIST, and designed the doctoral training programme which formed the basis for the programme that now runs at MBS. He has been teaching research methods to undergraduate, masters and doctoral students since 1975 and has contributed to books on research methods teaching as well as workshops for students and teachers on behalf of the British Academy of Management.

PREFACE TO THE THIRD EDITION

The first edition of this book appeared in 1991, at a time when there were very few management research methods books on the market. It quickly became established as the leading text because it covered all of the essential ground, yet was not too long or intimidating. Students and staff liked it because it tackled difficult issues, but avoided either trivializing them, or making them unnecessarily complex.

The second edition was published in 2002, and this included a substantial updating of the material since methodology had become a hot topic during the intervening years, and there were therefore many new methods and approaches to management research that needed to be covered. The market had also begun to change significantly, since research methods were starting to be taught at undergraduate levels. This resulted in a modest repositioning of the book, but also stimulated the appearance of strong competitors, which also provided comprehensive overviews of methods and techniques.

This third edition maintains continuity in the sense that it provides comprehensive treatment of philosophies and methods, plus coverage of both qualitative and quantitative techniques; but it also introduces some radical departures both in terms of content and design. The most important change is that we have significantly strengthened the treatment of quantitative methods, which now runs from basic techniques for collecting and analysing quantitative data, up to multivariate analysis and structural equation modelling. In keeping with our belief that research methods should not be overcomplicated, we have emphasized understanding of the principles of analytic methods without the unnecessary addition of complicated algebra. We would like to claim, therefore, that this part of the book now provides advanced statistics without tears! In addition, we have extended and updated our treatment of research philosophies, ethics, qualitative analysis, ways of conducting literature reviews and approaches to writing up the results.

The design of this edition is also quite different from its predecessors. In addition to the inevitable introduction of colour, we have added boxed examples both from our own experiences and those of our students. We also provide a number of exercises, which we have used in our own methodology teaching for many years and which can be used either for individual study or for group work in the classroom, and we have added a glossary to the end of the book, for which all items are picked out in bold on their first appearance in the text. And as final proof of our technological competence, we (and SAGE) have provided a companion web site www.sagepub. co.uk/managementresearch that contains further guidance for teachers, plus exercises and tests for students. All this has added somewhat to the length of the book, so it is no longer pocket size; but it is still readable and should fit easily into a small bag. We hope that it becomes a useful companion to you!

ACKNOWLEDGEMENTS

Although this book is based on the personal research experience of the authors but thanks should also go to a number of students and colleagues. Both have contributed to this edition in a number of ways, through their encouragement as well as their ideas. We have tried to reflect their suggestions as far as possible in the text.

Our students have taught us a great deal and we have included a number of their examples. We would like to thank, Chavi Chen, Ray Forbes, Suzanne Gagnon, Jean Clarke, Anya Johnson, Mohamed Mohamud, Marie Norman, Allan Macpherson, Joanne Scammell, Anna Zueva, Brian Simpson and Susan Baker, who sadly is no longer with us.

To the colleagues who have also assisted us by reading through the transcripts, making comments, and suggesting ideas, we are extremely grateful. These include, Lisa Anderson, Joep Cornelissen, Ardha Danieli, Ashish Dwivedi, David Holman, Robin Holt, Jeff Gold, Krslo Pandza Ossie Jones, Efthimios Poulis and Christine Reid. Jean-Claude Usunier provided a valuable critique of the first edition of the book from a European perspective, and this led to a French translation of the book, which is now in its second edition. Joanne Larty helped with the references, and Mirjam Werner has provided extensive assistance with the general editing and organizing of the book.

Our editor at SAGE for the first edition of the book was Sue Jones. She provided us with the initial inspiration, and since then Rosemary Nixon, Kiren Shoman and most recently Natalie Aguilera and Delia Alfonso offered encouragement, and occasionally hectored us – this third edition has been no exception.

We would like to acknowledge the contribution of Dr Andy Lowe to the first and second editions of this book, and are grateful for his continuing support with this venture.

The authors are grateful to SAGE for permission to include extracts from Thorpe, R. and Cornelissen, J. (2003), 'Visual media and the construction of meaning', chapter 4 in *Management and Language*, Holman, D. and Thorpe, R. (Eds).

Finally, we would like to thank our families for their tolerance while this book was being written and re-written – we hope they will consider the outcome to be worth the effort.

GUIDED TOUR

Welcome to the guided tour

of *Management Research*.

This tour will take you through

the main sections and special

features of the text.

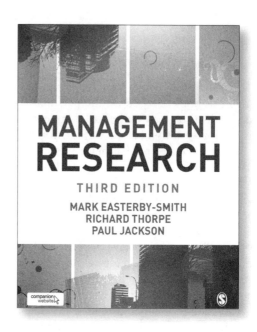

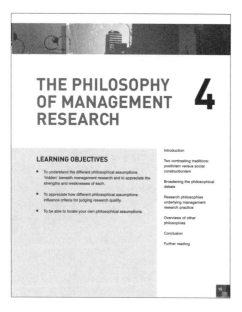

Learning objectives: A clear set of key learning
objectives are provided for each chapter.

Introduction: The introduction acts to set the
scene for what will be discussed over the course of
the chapter.

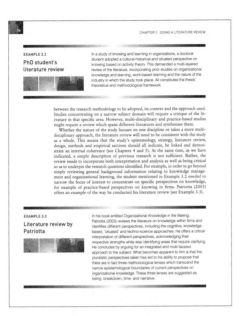

Examples: Concepts and theories are given context through the inclusion of 'real-life' examples that will assist in overall understanding and awareness of the topics covered.

Exercises: Each chapter is accompanied by a range of practical exercises, ranging from individual work to group activity.

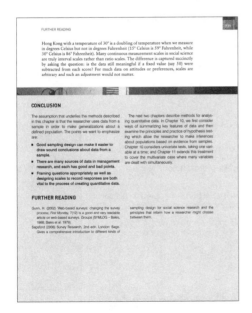

Conclusions and Further readings: Drawing together and summarizing the chapter discussion, Conclusions also re-emphasize the most important points. Suggestions and information on further readings to provide deeper understanding on the issues raised in the chapter

Glossary Through out the text **bolded** words signify key terms and phrases that can be looked up in the glossary.

THE COMPANION WEB SITE

Be sure to visit the companion web site (www.sagepub.co.uk/managementresearch) to this text where you will find a number of resources, both for students as well as instructors.

FOR INSTRUCTORS

Password-protected instructor resources are provided on the companion web site

- *Tutor's notes:* Helpful notes for tutors using the text in their teaching.
- *PowerPoint® slides:* Slides are provided for each chapter and can be edited as required by the instructor for use in lectures and seminars.
- *Extra case studies:* Extra cases are provided to support the material in the book and to provide fresh and helpful examples that will aid classroom teaching and discussions.

FOR STUDENTS

- *Online readings:* We have selected a number of interesting and relevant journal articles that we hope will add to your understanding and awareness of the topics covered in the book.
- *Links to relevant web sites:* Useful links are provided for each chapter.
- *Practice datasets:* Helpful for you to practice and establish your familiarity with this type of research material.
- *Online glossary:* Key terminologies are covered.

Homepage
About the Book
Description
Table of Contents
Lecturer Resources
Instructors' Manual
PowerPoint Slides
New Case Studies
Student Resources
Online Readings
Web links
Data sets
Glossary
Book Details

Authors
Mark Easterby-Smith,
Richard Thorpe and
Paul Jackson

Pub Date: 03/2008
Pages: 384

Click here for more
information.

Management Research
Third Edition

Easterby-Smith, Thorpe and Jackson

Welcome to the companion website for Management Research 3e

This website provides additional material and resources for both lecturers and student using Management Research.

About The Book

This section contains details about the book.

Lecturer Resources

This section contains resources that are available free of charge to lecturers who adopt Management Research authored by Mark Easterby-Smith, Richard Thorpe and Paul Jackson. The material within the Lecturer Resources section comprises of Instructors' Manual, PowerPoint slides and additional case studies.

This are of the site is password-protected. To request and inspection copy, please contact inspectioncopies@sagepub.co.uk. You will be sent a password on adoption.

For lecturers based inside North America, please contact Nichole Angress at the Sage California office at nichole.angress@sagepub.com to request a complimentary copy and password.

Student Resources

This section provides material students can draw on when working with the book. The material within the Student Resources section comprises of Online Readings, Web Links, Datasets and a Glossary.

© Sage Publications Ltd.

INTRODUCTION

1

Introduction

What is management?

Why is management research distinctive?

Levels and outcomes of management research

Conclusion

Further reading

LEARNING OBJECTIVES

- To appreciate the link between models of management and different types of research.

- To understand what is distinctive about management research.

- To see how research may contribute both to the understanding and practice of management.

INTRODUCTION

This book is written for people wishing to study management and organizations, either as part of formal courses, or as part of funded research projects. It covers both the practical techniques for conducting research, and the philosophies and assumptions underlying these techniques. Our aim, therefore, is to draw together the main threads of management research and to provide a bridge between theoretical and practical issues. We start this chapter by sharing some of our assumptions about management and research.

First, we regard management research as an everyday activity for people who work, or live, in organizations, and certainly not the exclusive preserve of 'experts'. Most people spend a lot of time trying to make sense of their experiences, whether in their personal lives or at work. Managers are paid to innovate new products and processes, to determine actions in uncertain circumstances, to organize the work of others and, more generally, to create order out of chaos. In this context research can be seen as a way of accelerating the process of understanding, and hence it should lead not only to a better knowledge about management, but also to better practical guidance about how management should be conducted.

Second, management research fashions have swung back and forth over the last few decades between the use of qualitative and quantitative methods. When the first edition of this book was published, in 1991, quantitative methods were in the ascendancy, with an emphasis on coding and counting events, often at the expense of understanding *why* things are happening. We therefore tried to redress the balance by providing an emphasis on qualitative methods in the second edition. Now that there is a wider appreciation of the use of qualitative methods, however, we feel it is appropriate in this third edition to extend our treatment of quantitative methods to a more advanced level.

Third, we believe it is very important to have a good appreciation of the philosophical foundations to management research. The decision to study a topic in a particular way always involves some kind of philosophical choice about what is important. For example, we can study corporate performance either by tracking profit figures and other public data across a range of companies, or we can see the idea of 'performance' as unique to each company and the product of numerous internal discussions between managers about which messages to provide for outside consumption. In the former case it is the numbers that are important, providing a definite and objective view of reality; in the latter case it is discussions and perceptions which are important, suggesting a subjective and negotiated view of reality. It is important for the researcher to be aware of the potential choices, and then to decide where the emphasis should lie.

Fourth, we give emphasis to political factors in management research. Access to companies can be obstructed by managers if they consider a piece of research to be harmful to their own, or their company's, interests; and there is always the danger of research data and results being used out of context to strengthen the case of one group against another. Researchers can also come under pressure to provide positive stories about the companies they study, often as a condition for being allowed further access. This means that the researcher should be prepared to confront ethical issues and to navigate complex relationships. In this book, we provide guidance on these matters.

The issues, or prejudices, described above have given rise to this book. They have influenced both the overall structure and our choice of content in the subsequent chapters. However in this first chapter we begin by considering the nature of management and the different forms that research may take in this context.

WHAT IS MANAGEMENT?

There are many views about what constitutes 'management', and clearly the notion of management as an activity is not new: the Egyptians built the pyramids, the Chinese built the Great Wall and the Mesopotamians learned to irrigate the land and wall their cities. All these feats required a high degree of co-ordination, and although many had captive labour forces, there must have been sophisticated organization of their work. Formal records of production management techniques can be traced back to Mencius (372–289 BC). This Chinese philosopher dealt with models and systems, and pointed to the advantages of the division of labour, putting the concepts redis-covered over 2000 years later into perspective.

A common distinction is between management as a 'cadre' of people, and manage-ment as an activity. Management as a cadre are those members of an organization who carry the title of manager and who commonly share similar beliefs about their status and right to manage. Usually the title of manager is given to people in the organization hierarchy who are at one or more levels above 'first-line' supervision. This definition can be applied most easily in a traditional manufacturing company. However, with the growth of the service sector, the move from hierarchical to mul-tiple matrix structures, and the development of virtual teams and global corpora-tions, the traditional means of defining a manager is becoming increasingly problematic (Castells, 2000). Handy (1996) has noted this change, when he says that in new organizations, everyone must have management skills. It is not just the tradi-tional resources such as people, capital and technology that need to be managed nowadays; an increasing emphasis is being placed on the management of intangibles, such as learning and knowledge, and many authors (e.g. Moingeon and Edmondson, 1997; Easterby-Smith and Lyles, 2003; Scarbrough, 2008) now believe that these factors hold the secret to competitive advantage.

The modern use of the term 'management' derives from the USA, with the require-ment for business and entrepreneurial skills in the early 20th century when American industries and railroads were developing very rapidly (Lawrence, 1986). From these beginnings, management was put forward as an important subject that could, and should, be taught in business schools. The establishment of business schools led to greater sys-tematization of techniques and knowledge, although much of this was based on the principles that managers had distilled from their own experiences. Two of the dominant figures during this period were Taylor (1947), who developed rational systems to sim-plify the organization of work and link rewards directly to effort, and Fayol (1916/50) who classified the main functions that managers should perform, such as: planning, organizing, co-ordinating and controlling. Although this **classical management theory** has much face validity, later researchers were to show that these functions did not resem-ble what managers actually did in their work (Mintzberg, 1973), nor did it provide an adequate account of how they might get the best results out of their subordinates.

An early critique of the classical view was the **human relations** school, which demonstrated that workers were not necessarily motivated by rational incentives and that they were more likely to be productive if managers took personal interest in them (Roethlisberger and Dickson, 1939), or if they were given more responsibility in their jobs (Herzberg et al., 1959). Moreover these researchers suggested that a key role for managers was to get employees to accept changes and improvements in the workplace, and this would be accomplished most easily if they involved them closely in decision-making processes (Coch and French, 1948). The focus of this work was therefore on the non-rational aspects of human behaviour in organizations.

During the 1960s, a view was developed that the key to effective management was the ability to take rational decisions, even under conditions of uncertainty (Simon, 1959; Cyert and March, 1963). This **decision theory** approach emphasized the techniques that could be used to analyse the impact of external factors on corporate strategy, and ways of reaching adequate decisions under conditions of uncertainty, even if they were not completely ideal. This led to the development of quantitative methods of analysis and model-building, which still dominate the curricula of many business schools, especially in the USA and France.

The classical view has also been attacked by researchers such as Stewart (1967), Mintzberg (1973), Kotter (1982) and Hales (1986) who, as we have indicated above, found almost no evidence of managers behaving as they are supposed to behave. Instead of standing back and directing enterprises strategically, most managers spend most of their time talking to people; they work long hours at an unrelenting pace; their work patterns are varied, fragmented and reactive; and there is rarely any time for planning and anticipating crises. Consequently, those who follow the **work activity** view argue there is little point in trying to get them to behave according to the classical text books. Rather, managers should be helped to deal with the realities of their jobs through management of their own time and development of better leading and negotiating skills.

The second line of attack came from employers, and has been readily assisted by a number of academics (Hayes and Abernethy, 1980; Peters and Waterman, 1982; Bennis and O'Toole, 2005; Mintzberg, 2005). The main argument is that the emphasis on analytic techniques is of limited value, and may even be harmful to companies. It is more important for managers to exhibit leadership, to provide collective visions, and to mould the culture and values of the organization in appropriate directions. This line has given rise to a view of management as a set of **competencies** that represent the skills that need to be demonstrated in the course of effective managerial work (Boyatzis, 1982; Silver, 1991; Evers and Rush, 1996). Even the academic establishment in the USA has begun to accept that the content and process of management courses may not be fully appropriate to the needs of the modern manager. Following the publication of a mildly critical report about how the system should adapt to meet the challenges of the future (Porter and McKibbin, 1988), there was a rapid growth in courses and research into topics such as leadership, entrepreneurship and international management.

There has also been a relaxation in the strict accreditation criteria of US business schools, and they are now allowed more freedom to determine the content of their MBA courses provided they are able to justify it against their own objectives. But there may well be too much inertia in a system that produces over 100,000 MBAs per annum. Academics complain that research into topics such as international manage-ment is still seen as less prestigious than research into mainstream disciplines such as strategy or marketing (Boyacigiller and Adler, 1991; Steers et al., 1992) and, moreover, the changes to curricula still treat 'management' as a subject that can define clear answers to problems that can then be taught to students who will subsequently apply them in their management work. Changes have been incremental rather than radical.

The last decade has seen the rise of much literature that takes a **critical** view of management. This has come from various sources, including postmodernism that rejects the rationality which is so strongly embedded in the idea of management (Hassard and Parker, 1993), social constructionism that emphasizes that the most important part of management involves making sense of ambiguous and complex situations through conversations and dialogue (Weick, 1995; Cunliffe, 2002) and critical theory that tends to see management as an agent in maintaining wider power differences in society (Fournier and Grey, 2000; Alvesson and Deetz, 2000).

The final view has developed in parallel with the critical view, and emphasizes the importance of **learning** processes and the management of organizational knowledge. It includes the idea that managers should seek to create learning organizations (Senge, 1990; Easterby-Smith 1997), facilitate knowledge creation (Nonaka and Takeuchi, 1995), absorb ideas from external sources (Todorova and Durisin, 2007), and ensure that both codified and personalized knowledge is distributed appropriately around the organization (Scarbrough, 2008). Increasingly this perspective is becoming combined with some of the other views, such as the focus on change leading to dynamic capabilities (Winter, 2003), and the importance of power and politics under-lying knowledge legitimation (Lawrence et al. 2005; Buchanan and Bryman, 2007).

The seven views summarized in Table 1.1 are by no means the only views about what management is, or should be; but they are important historically. It should also be apparent that these include different types of theory. Some are **normative**, in the sense that they specify what, or how managers should do their work; some are **descriptive**, because they try to describe what managers do in practice, and some are **analytic** because they take a particular theoretical perspective which emphasizes some aspects of work, at the expense of others.

In the context of the present book, the implications should be self-evident: the procedures for management research are likely to vary considerably according to the view that the researcher takes of the nature of management. If they are interested, for example, in the decision theory school, they will be interested in manipulating quan-titative data that can simulate processes or predict the best courses of action; if they are influenced by the work activity view of management, then they will be interested in observational methods that provide a structured description of managerial activities and roles within real organizations; and if they are interested in manage-ment as a socially constructed activity, then they are more likely to be interested in gathering stories, narratives and conversations about management.

WHY IS MANAGEMENT RESEARCH DISTINCTIVE?

Despite the maturation of management as an area of study, the majority of books on management and organizational research still rely heavily on cognate disciplines such

TABLE 1.1 Seven perspectives on management

Views of management	Period of dominance	Key features	Type of theory
Classical	1910—1950	Functional activities	Normative
Human relations	1940—1970	Motivating people and managing change	Normative
Decision theory	1950—1970	Optimising decisions	Analytic
Work activity	1970s	What managers do	Descriptive
Competencies	1980s	Skills required for effective performance	Normative
Critical	1990—present	Social construction and politics	Analytic
Learning	1990—present	Managing knowledge and learning	Analytic and normative

as sociology, education and psychology. We agree that many of the methodology books coming out of the social sciences are very good indeed, and we make full use of both recent and classic texts in this volume. However, we also believe that management research poses some unusual problems which are not often encountered in the broader social sciences, and there is a need to rethink some of the traditional

EXERCISE
1.1

Management perspectives and research foci

For each of the seven perspectives of management described in the test, summarize in one sentence the way that research is most likely to be conducted. Work in small groups. We have already provided hints above for three of them.

A Classical

B Human relations

C Decision theory

D Work activity

E Competencies

F Critical

G Learning

techniques and methods that can be easily borrowed from other fields. These unusual challenges provide opportunities to develop new research methods and traditions, which might have applications outside the field of management; at the same time management researchers need to have the confidence to adapt or reject advice from other disciplines where it is not appropriate. For example, there are very good opportunities to develop new forms of collaborative research, and it is always important to consider how methodologies like 'grounded theory' and computer-based analytic software may need to be adapted for the specific contexts of management research.

In our view there are four main features that make management research distinctive. First, despite the progress towards creating distinct disciplines within management, the practice of management is largely *eclectic*: managers need to be able to work across technical, cultural and functional boundaries, and they need to be able to draw on knowledge developed by other disciplines such as sociology, anthropology, economics, statistics and mathematics. The dilemma for the researcher, then, is whether to examine management from the perspective of one discipline, or whether to adopt a trans-disciplinary approach (Burgoyne and James, 2006). The former is often seen to be the safer course for those who wish to gain respectability from academic peers, whereas the latter is more likely to produce results that are of use to practising managers. Moreover, the danger of eclectic approaches to research is that they may incorporate underlying assumptions which are incompatible with each other, which is why we devote the whole of Chapter 4 to reviewing the philosophical underpinnings of research approaches and methods.

Second, managers tend to be *powerful* and busy people. They are unlikely to allow research access to their organizations unless they can see some commercial or personal advantage to be derived from it. This means, as we shall see in Chapter 6, that access for fieldwork can be very difficult and may be hedged with many conditions about confidentiality and publication rights. So feasible research questions may be determined more by access possibilities than by theoretical considerations, and the overall uncertainty means that neat research designs may be very difficult to achieve. Managers are usually under a lot of pressure and generally have to be careful about the use of time, and therefore short interviews, fitted into busy schedules, will be much more feasible than unstructured observations and discussion, which can take a lot of time. Even when conducting questionnaire surveys, for example about the views of senior managers, there is no guarantee that responses will not be drafted by assistants or secretaries, rather than the managers themselves.

Third, managers are increasingly *educated*. Most managers have undergraduate or MBA degrees, and many specialists, particularly in research-oriented companies, have PhDs – thus they have similar educational backgrounds to the researchers who would study them. This means that they will be more likely to appreciate the value of research-based knowledge and have clear views about the appropriate directions of research. It also means that researchers cannot assume that they have the premium on expertise, and this opens up the possibility of the joint production of knowledge – combining the insights and expertise of both managers and researchers. Of course, this challenges traditional assumptions about the objectivity of researchers and intriguing problems about the ownership of scientific knowledge.

TABLE 1.2 Implications of distinctive features of management research

Key features	Implications for management researchers
Management research methods are eclectic	Researchers need to be aware of different underlying assumptions.
Managers are powerful	Research depends on support of managers, and researchers are much less in control than in 'normal' social science.
Managers are educated	Managers will have academic interest in research process/ results and may want to contribute to direction of work.
Action is a frequent outcome of management research	Research results may both derive from, and lead to, practical action. Both traditional analytic research and action research are legitimate activities.

Fourth, there is often an expectation that research will lead directly to *action*. The expectation comes both from managers in exchange for offering access and support, and from funding agencies that look for potential economic benefits from management research. This has led to a variety of ways whereby researchers engage with both practice and practitioners, as will be discussed in the next section.

We summarize the features that make management research distinctive in Table 1.2. Admittedly each is not unique to management research: the problem of multiple disciplines exists in educational research; the access problem is very evident in organizational sociology; and the wider dissemination of higher education means that the expertise of lay people must be recognized in many fields, including health research. But the combination of all four at the same time within management research suggests that some of the traditional assumptions and practices in social research may well need rethinking. This is what we do in this book, and it is something that is being taken further in the Sage Series on Management Research.

LEVELS AND OUTCOMES OF MANAGEMENT RESEARCH

As suggested at the outset, this book is intended to aid research at several different levels, and this includes undergraduate, postgraduate and doctoral degrees, and funded research projects. In this section we start with some of the main classifications of research - pure, applied and action – and then discuss how they may apply to different levels of research.

A central question is that of whether management research should lead to developments in academic theory or whether it should lead to solutions of practical problems. This debate has been neatly captured in the work of Gibbons et al. (1994) who describe two forms of research: **mode 1 research** concentrates on the production of knowledge by detached scientists focusing on theoretical questions and problems; and **mode 2 research** is characterized by the production of knowledge through direct engagement with social practice and problems. Some management scholars argue that management research should follow the latter approach with an emphasis on practical application (Tranfield, 2002) – others suggest a compromise position where both theoretical and practical work is required, which is sometimes characterized as **mode 1½ research** (Huff, 2000).

Modes 1 and 2 are similar to pure and applied forms of research. The former is intended to lead to theoretical development, and there may, or may not, be any practical implications. One of the key features of **pure research** is that its results are openly disseminated through books, articles, conference papers or theses, addressed mainly at an academic audience. Dissemination is seen as a major responsibility for the researcher, and career progress for academics depends on getting the fruits of their work placed in the most prestigious journals, which is seen as proof of the quality of the work. **Applied research** is intended to lead to the solution of specific problems, and usually involves working with clients to identify the important problems and decide how best to tackle them. It may involve the application of existing theory to deal with these problems; or it can sometimes take the form of **best practice research**, where other 'leading' companies are surveyed in order to assess how they have tackled, or solved, the same problem (Burgoyne and James, 2006).

The results of applied research always need to be reported to the client, who is likely to evaluate the quality of the research in terms of its usability. But there is always the potential to publish the results of applied research in practitioner or professional journals provided the results can be shown to have wider significance, although this possibility often raises questions of commercial confidentiality and the need to maintain good relationships with the initial client. In Chapter 6, we discuss in more detail issues such as ethics, confidentiality and the control of information.

A number of research approaches have developed in management which do not fit neatly into either of the above categories, and we have grouped these under the heading of **action research**. A classical definition is provided by Rappoport: 'Action research aims to contribute both to the practical concerns of people in an immediate problematic situation and to the goals of social science by joint collaboration within a mutually accepted ethical framework' (1970: 499). Thus the researcher no longer tries to maintain a distance from the thing that is being researched. Action research starts from the idea that if you want to understand something well you should try changing it, and hence change should be incorporated into the research process itself. Because of the collaborative features of action research, participants (the researcher and the researched) are likely to learn a lot from the process itself, and their interest may be on what happens next rather than on any formal account of research findings. But it may still be worth writing up action research as a narrative, so that a record is maintained of how understanding changes and develops over time.

Levels of research

As indicated earlier we are addressing four main research levels in this book: undergraduate, postgraduate, doctoral degrees, and funded research projects. At *undergraduate* levels, research is likely to be specific and bounded, either as an assignment from tutors or as a question posed by a client. Common tasks include small market research studies, or interview-based studies of employee attitudes, and hence an emphasis on applied research is most likely. In most cases a single method will be used and this may also be specified in advance. The opportunities for choice are mainly around how methods are used and how results are interpreted and communicated. In most cases undergraduate research projects are conducted in teams because this creates economy of scale from a teaching point of view, it also means that significant projects can be undertaken in a short period of time, and students should benefit from combining their skills when working as teams.

Research conducted as part of a *masters* degree will normally have greater scope, and more time will be available. Again, applied research is likely to predominate, with evaluation research being one of the easiest options. This involves looking at some system or practice that already exists and making recommendations for how it might be changed and improved. If the project seeks to create or learn from organizational change it will assume features of action research. Involvement in change can lead to rich and interesting results, and it may be a valuable experience for people seeking work in consultancy.

Doctoral dissertations need to produce theoretical contributions with some degree of originality, and this suggests that there needs to be a significant element of pure research in these cases. Although doctoral studies may include both applied and action research elements, the theoretical contribution is a necessary condition for the award of a doctorate. These contributions may include the discovery of new ideas, the invention of new procedures and methods, the replication of existing studies in new contexts, or the application of new theoretical perspectives to existing research questions.

Funded projects are usually conducted by experienced researchers, but face many of the same choices as projects conducted for university degrees. Required outputs will depend on the expectations of the funding body: if it is a company there may be an emphasis on applied research and if it is a research council then there will be an emphasis on pure research. But all forms of output are possible in this case, including action research.

We summarize in Table 1.3 the main links between types and levels of research. We will discuss in more detail in Chapters 4–6 the many factors, both political and philosophical, which can influence the way research is designed and conducted in practice.

TABLE 1.3 Types of research most likely to be associated with different levels

	Undergraduate level	Postgraduate level	Doctoral level	Funded projects
Applied research	**	*	*	**
Action research	*	**	*	*
Pure research		*	***	**

We also review, in Chapter 12, both strategies for demonstrating a 'contribution', and how the evaluation criteria might vary with different contexts.

The examples in Table 1.3 have all assumed that research will involve the collection of **primary data** directly by the researchers. The value of primary data is that it can lead to new insights, and greater confidence in the outcomes of the research which is very useful for students wishing to use their research experiences as a basis for subsequent careers in management or consultancy practice. Consequently, it is normally expected that dissertations at undergraduate, postgraduate and doctoral levels will include some primary data. However, some subjects such as economics and finance rely more on public or corporate financial data and statistics. This is known as **secondary data,** and the skill of the researcher is demonstrated by exploring new relationships and patterns within this existing data. Another form of secondary data is represented by published literature, and all research studies need to demonstrate familiarity with existing literature both to ensure that the research is not merely repeating something that has already been done, and to provide an opportunity to build on what has been done before. In Chapter 3, we discuss both sources and strategies for using secondary data especially in the form of literature surveys which are commonly used to underpin primary data collection.

CONCLUSION

In this opening chapter we have discussed a number of ways of understanding management, and some of the implications for the conduct of management research. In particular, we suggest that:

- management research is not necessarily the preserve of experts, and can be an 'everyday' activity for managers and students of management;

- there are many different views about the nature of management and these have implications for both the content and process of management research; and

- management research has unusual features which make it distinctive both in form and content, especially in comparison with other social science disciplines.

There are two obvious implications of this distinctiveness: first, we suggest that when social science research methods are applied in the field of management research there needs to be careful consideration of underlying assumptions; and, second, that the methodological challenges of management research mean that there is good potential for developing new research methods which may eventually have application in other fields. Thus we would like to see the management field becoming a net exporter of research methodologies!

This volume is intended to be self-sufficient in a number of ways. It provides extensive coverage and guidance in relation to: philosophical and political perspectives (Chapters 4 and 6); reviewing literature and designing studies (Chapters 3 and 5); choosing and using both qualitative (Chapters 7 and 8) and quantitative methodologies (Chapters 9–11); and writing up research (Chapter 12). This coverage should be sufficient for most research projects at undergraduate and postgraduate levels – and has been approved by the UK's Economic and Social Research Council as the basis for research training in management and business studies. Naturally, additional techniques may be appropriate in some specialized areas of research and we provide guidance on further reading about these. The book also provides basic grounding for the first year of doctoral training, although doctoral students will also need to refer back to original sources, and to develop their *own* critiques of methods and underlying philosophies.

The book is furthermore intended to be self-sufficient pedagogically. That is, we provide a range of examples and exercises across all the chapters which can be used for individual review and for group discussion in classrooms. There are additional exercises in the accompanying web site (www.sagepub.co.uk/managementresearch), and this provides further guidance to teachers in using these exercises with different groups of students. Finally, we have tried not to flinch from tackling research concepts and problems that are complex and intractable, but we do so with simple language, and make use of our extensive research experience over many years.

In conclusion, although we give a lot of advice about research methods in this book, it should not be seen as definitive. The researcher must be prepared to use his or her own judgment continually – and this, as Buchanan (1980) suggests, is one of the most important outcomes from the use of research projects in management development programmes. Research is always hedged about with uncertainty and risk. Those who learn to work effectively and independently with this uncertainty will find they possess a skill that can be transferred very easily into roles outside the academic world.

EXERCISE
1.2

Schools of thought about management

We have described seven views of management above, but there are others, such as 'mushroom management' (where you keep everyone in the dark and every now and then you open the door and drop a pile of shit on them!). Working in small groups share your experiences of managing or being managed: use this to invent a new label, or school of thought, about management. Be prepared to explain and justify to other groups.

FURTHER READING

Grey, C. (2005) *A Very Short, Fairly Interesting and Reasonably Cheap Book about Studying Organizations*. London: Sage. As it says on the label, this book provides a succinct overview of theories of management and organization, and it is reasonably cheap (£13.99). It adopts a critical view in the sense that it has a slight preference for the perspectives of those who are managed, rather than the managers themselves.

Mintzberg, H. (2005) *Managers Not MBAs: A Hard Look at the Soft Practice of Managing and Management Development*. San Francisco: Berrett-Koehler.

Henry Mintzberg made his reputation from demonstrating the inadequacy of classical views of management and the nature of managerial work. This book continues his argument that managers are less in need of the analytic skills taught on traditional MBAs, and more in need of process and intercultural skills. In particular, it looks at ways in which managers can best learn these skills and abilities.

THE INGREDIENTS OF SUCCESSFUL RESEARCH

2

Introduction

Motivation

Support and supervision

Style and creativity

Skills and qualities

Getting started

Conclusion

Further reading

LEARNING OBJECTIVES

- To gain insights into the factors that affect the relative success of doing research.

- To appreciate the need for a research focus from the outset of any research.

- To consider a number of issues that will assist in getting the research started.

INTRODUCTION

There is no simple way of ensuring that research will be successful. The types and contexts of research vary so widely that 'ideal' strategies will differ from situation to situation. Moreover, it is often difficult to chart the ideal course of any investigation in advance with precise certainty. Nevertheless there are a number of factors that seem to increase the chances of research being successful – all things being equal. Four such factors are discussed in this chapter: motivation; support; style and creativity; and personal qualities. The chapter concludes with some thoughts about one of the biggest problems of all: getting started.

MOTIVATION

Determination and single-mindedness are essential to completing any significant piece of research. There is so much uncertainty about the processes and outcomes of any research project, with the work invariably expanding beyond anything considered reasonable at the outset, that it is not an activity for the faint-hearted. Here we distinguish between three apparent motives for (management) researchers: as a vehicle for learning; as a basis for personal growth and advancement; and as a means of enhancing managerial skills.

It is now very common for management courses, particularly if they lead to qualifications, to contain an element of research as a primary vehicle for learning. Many taught courses use a research project or dissertation as a kind of 'capstone', as a way of integrating the different functional disciplines such as accounting and marketing which are often taught separately in business schools. Projects are also a popular way of enabling students to *learn* from direct engagement with the outside world. They can provide them with greater confidence in their own opinions as well as an opportunity to test out the validity of the theories offered by the text books.

Students react differently to research projects. Some will treat them instrumentally, as a way of achieving a pass on the course; some may use them to obtain contacts, experience and credibility which will help with job-hunting; yet others find themselves getting absorbed by their projects and excited at the novel possibility of studying something in depth.

This links to the second main source of motivation, *personal growth and career development*. There are many possibilities here. People may register for research degrees because they want to be given an external discipline for examining something in which they have long held a passionate interest. Perhaps they want to prove to themselves that they can do research, or they may simply want to belong to a research 'community' for a few years. For those wishing to develop careers as academics a research 'identity' is essential. This means that a consistent thread to an individual's research interests is sought when assessing candidates for academic appointments, and it is easiest to achieve this consistency when one is driven by strong personal interest. With the growth in interest in faculty with strong research credentials in most business schools, gaining a PhD, which indicates that the person is a fully trained researcher, has very much become a *sine qua non* for anyone who is intent on an academic career.

The third source of motivation comes from a recognition that research experiences may lead to the *enhancement of managerial skills* and the solution of problems at work. As we suggested in the first chapter, research may help to develop the skills of judging what information is important, how and when to obtain it, and how best to communicate results. It is also likely to strengthen independence, because of the lack of prior rules, and the need to initiate structure and monitor progress on one's own for most of the time. But most of all it develops an individual's critical faciluties in relation to judging the quality of evidence used to support particular courses of action. These skills are likely to become more important for managers as the business environment becomes more complex and unpredictable. Over recent years the professional doctorate (usually a DBA within the management and business field) has become a vehicle for doing this (see Chapter 6).

As this section has shown, there are different reasons for doing research. It can be viewed as a vehicle for learning, as a basis for personal growth and advancement, or as a means of enhancing managerial skills. Some people may well have all three of the above reasons for doing research. Whatever the prime reason for opting for a research career may be, at the very least it helps if one has a combination of 'internal' and 'external' pressures, such as a strong interest in a particular topic and clear expectations and deadlines from a sponsor, or one's family. And when embarking on research, especially where it involves a long term commitment, it is worth considering one's motives carefully.

SUPPORT AND SUPERVISION ·

Research work can be very demanding on the individual; there are many uncertainties, doubts and crises that enter into research projects. Here we concentrate primarily on doctoral research because it lasts a long time and relationships with supervisors are often critical. Many of the issues discussed are also relevant to other levels of research. From her interviews with students, Phillips (1984) identified seven main stages in the process of conducting a PhD. These were: enthusiasm; isolation; increased interest; increasing independence; boredom; frustration; and a job to be finished. Not every research project necessarily goes through precisely the same seven stages, but ups and downs are inevitable. The emotional cost of these crises can be quite high, and hence it is important to consider the support, both technical and emotional, that can be obtained.

When the research is part of an academic degree the most obvious source of support is the supervisor or tutor. However, the quality and different styles of supervision may vary considerably. The following points are based on a combination of our, and others', experiences about the behaviour of supervisors who seem most successful at the task of supervising doctoral degrees. These points might be taken into account by those who are able to influence their choice of supervisor. First, he or she must possess some technical expertise, although some would argue that a general knowledge of the research area and of relevant methodologies is perhaps more useful than a very deep knowledge of the subject to be investigated. As the field of management develops, however, specialist knowledge of debates and recent literature in the chosen area is increasingly important. Moreover, the supervisor who is personally active as a researcher is also likely to belong to the international networks that control the leading journals and conferences. These networks provide a source of external examiners for doctoral candidates and also act as gateways into academic careers. With regard to the practical aspects of the relationship, Phillips (1984) found that the better supervisors tend to set regular, and realistic, deadlines, although they do not interfere too much with the detail of the work. A 'responsive' style seems most appropriate if the researcher is to be encouraged to become autonomous and independent. It also helps if the supervisor is prepared and willing to respond quite rapidly to any problems or to written work. Ideally the supervisor should be prepared to 'turn round' draft chapters and reviews within a week or two, despite the growing pressures on academics. Availability is very important, and for this reason the guru with a string of brilliant publications but who is never available for consultations, may not necessarily be the best supervisor.

The relationship between supervisor and student is also important because it must be strong enough to cope with the different stages of the research process (Deem and Brehony, 1997). Ideally there should be mutual commitment between the two parties, and this should, if possible, result from the initial choice and negotiation process. It should also be recognized that the role of the supervisor can be difficult at times. A very eminent colleague of ours Tom Lupton, who supervised 35 PhDs to completion, had a model for supervisory support that encompassed five phases of the process (see Table 2.1).

From our own experiences as supervisors there is often a nagging doubt that the advice one is giving may be wrong, and in most cases students will move beyond the existing knowledge of the supervisor during the course of the project. In the case of a doctoral thesis this is almost an inevitable consequence of the requirement for originality in a doctoral thesis. But also in postgraduate and undergraduate dissertations which involve tackling broad-based problems the research is likely to fall outside the specialist area of the supervisor who therefore has to rely on 'generic' supervisory skills such as asking challenging questions or pointing the student(s) to alternative sources of expertise. There is, moreover, a delicate balance required between providing feedback, which highlights weakness in a piece of work, and providing praise and encouragement to try harder. The way out of this dilemma is to put across the message: 'this is fine in the following respects . . . but it could be made even better in these areas . . . and the way I'd go about it is. . .!'

Not everyone is lucky enough to have a supervisor, and even when they do, especially at the beginning of a piece of research when both parties are learning to work together, there are likely to be elements of ambiguity in the relationship. Hence it is always worth considering alternative sources of support. If things do go wrong then all universities have guidelines of what to do in cases such as this and these need to be consulted and followed. One of the best forms of support can come from colleagues, either through naturally occurring friendships, or through constructing a 'support set' – a group of four or five researchers committed to meeting regularly every few weeks to discuss their research progress and problems. It helps if the members of this set are working in related fields, but they should not be too close because this can sometimes generate conflict and competition. The set may have a tutor (or set advisor) who can help it to organize itself, and possibly, provide specialist advice and support. The members of the set should be able to use it to 'bounce' ideas off

TABLE 2.1 Five stages in the supervisory support process

Phases of the process	Main focus of attention
1. Getting started and finding a topic	At this stage Tom considered it essential for there to be a close supervisory relationship. Students need support in searching the field and formalizing their perspectives. Supervisors can help shape the direction of the research by being on hand so that students can test out their ideas.
2. Finding out what was already known about a topic through a review of the literature and scanning the field	At this point he saw the supervisor's role as not being quite so intense, rather the supervisor should move into a position of guidance and facilitation.
3. Out in the field collecting data	During data collection he saw the supervisory responsibility as being on tap, but not on top. Tom considered that it was beneficial for students to make mistakes and perhaps even have an adventure but someone should also be available to help them should any problems arise.
4. Writing up	At this stage he considered it very important for supervisors to reengage with the research project. In particular, there is a need to check the quality of the work, the writing style and to give constructive (often detailed) feedback.
5. Preparing for the oral defense	Tom identified that students often need more support in preparing for the oral defence than they realize. They are often so close to their work that they don't recognize the contributions that they had made and they often need help to stand back and see what they have achieved in perspective.

each other and, particularly for those who are researching part-time, to provide contact with others who may be going through similar experiences of doubt, confusion and disillusionment.

Furthermore, it is important to recognize the potential for support outside one's immediate institution. Those wishing to develop academic careers will need to develop links within the broader community working in a particular area, and, as we have pointed out above, this should be regarded as a crucial responsibility for the supervisor. Many of the better academic conferences will also organize doctoral days where doctoral students get the chance to present their ideas informally with leading figures in their field. By the second year of a doctoral thesis one should be submitting papers to conferences, possibly in conjunction with the supervisor initially. It is through presenting papers at such conferences that one can develop contacts with other collaborators and potential sponsors. It forms an induction into the academic community which can be both reassuring and motivating for one's own research.

Those carrying out research as part of taught courses work under different time pressures and may be supervised both by an academic and a client/practitioner. In this case group supervision may be the norm, as with action learning sets or group-based projects. Though there is an important distinction here in that within an action learning set the members will be looking at different topics, while members of a group project team will be focusing on the same issue. The downside of group projects is, of course, that they now have to work as a team and this provides the added complication of having to work effectively in a group situation. For those planning careers as practitioners it can also be important to attend professional conferences. The opportunities for instant visibility and fame are less, simply because presentation platforms are normally reserved for people who already have established reputations. Nevertheless, such conferences can put one in touch with what are considered to be the hot issues and fashionable ideas, and these may lead to the establishment of personal contacts which have direct career implications. In addition, the rise of the Internet has created considerable networking opportunities for people on a global scale both via public conferences and through private e-mail exchanges.

STYLE AND CREATIVITY

In the previous section we explained why emotional support is a key factor in the successful completion of research work. Here we focus more on ways of ensuring that the research will be of good quality and will contain some originality. We argue that this is determined largely by the personal style and approach adopted by the researcher. In all research there is a need to understand that the success of the research, and the extent to which it will be accepted or not, will relate to the degree to which it is coherent and contains within it a strong argument that is supported by data, whether this be quantitative or qualitative. This means that the researcher has to understand the issue that they wish to address in their research and that this needs to emerge from the way the research is conducted. There is a whole range of ways in which a person's creative processes can be stimulated so that resulting ideas can be captured and analysed, but we believe that a person's attitude towards preparing and doing research is crucial.

Style

A fascinating study into the personal factors that contribute to discoveries in medicine is provided by Austin (1978), an American neurosurgeon who had become dissatisfied by the trite explanations provided by scientists about how great discoveries whether in the natural or social sciences, come about. He differentiated between four factors, or forms of 'chance', which seem to underlie many discoveries.

- Chance 1 is simply *blind luck*. Although this may often be important, it is unlikely to be the only reason for a breakthrough. Relying on blind luck can take a long time. Austin reminds us that in bridge if you wait for 13 spades to turn up in a hand of cards, the odds are 635 million to one against.
- Chance 2 derives from the researcher being *in motion*. Nobody, it has been said, trips over anything while sitting down. The greater the curiosity,

resilience and persistence of the researcher, the more likely he or she is to find something of significance.

- Chance 3 comes from having a *prepared mind* and being ready to see new relationships and solutions. This means being aware of past research that has been conducted through searching the literature and talking to other researchers, while at the same time being prepared to think outside existing frameworks and knowledge.

- Chance 4 is a product *of individualized action*, which links to absorptive capacity. This means encouraging distinctive, even eccentric, hobbies and lifestyles. In particular, the researcher should try to take a broad interest in people and other disciplines. Creativity is often born from associations and links made across traditional boundaries. There are many examples of scientific research where the above elements of 'chance' are demonstrated.

The illustration that Austin uses, is Fleming's discovery of penicillin in 1928. In an interview after World War II, Fleming commented that the discovery of penicillin was almost entirely a matter of luck: 'like winning the Irish Sweepstake'. But Austin shows that this was not just a matter of blind luck. Fleming, by all accounts, was a tireless researcher; his great aim being to discover a new antiseptic, and even after the penicillin discovery he was extremely busy making and selling antibacterial vaccines. Thus he was a man who was continuously *in motion*.

It was his *prepared mind* which enabled him to note the effect on colonies of bacteria when a stray spore of a rare mould fell by accident onto his culture dish. Nine years earlier he had discovered the bacterial enzyme Lysozyme when . . . 'whilst suffering from a cold, his own nasal drippings had found their way into a culture dish. He noted that the bacteria round the mucus were killed and astutely followed up the lead' (Austin, 1978: 74). The parallels between these, and other experiences would be easy to perceive. *Individualized action* enters into the story because Fleming was a keen swimmer and water polo player. He had chosen to train and work at the old St Mary's hospital not because of the excellence of its scientific facilities, but because it had a good swimming pool. The laboratories were basic, badly equipped, cold and 'contaminated by organisms swirling in and out of the London fog' (Austin, 1978:92). This made them a particularly good breeding ground for bacteria and stray spores! In this example it is possible to see all four forms of chance at work, and Austin suggested that major discoveries are most likely to take place when several forms coincide. This is what he calls the 'unifying observation' of the Fleming effect.

Unfortunately not all researchers are destined to make major discoveries. Indeed it is wise to content oneself with, what we call, invention or reflection; discovery is but a bonus, which may be made more likely if one follows Austin's prescriptions. The bulk of research is much more humdrum. This is true both for the social and natural sciences. Many sociologists have carried out detailed studies of the way in which the natural sciences progress, and the consensus is that it is a gradual process, with much hard graft and very few genuine breakthroughs. Latour and Woolgar (1979) demonstrated in a classic study of a biological laboratory how scientific 'facts' emerged through a process of debate which was linked to the career strategies and progress of individual researchers. More recently, the study by Law (1994) into the management and organization of a particle physics research laboratory shows the impact of factors such as funding, politics and status hierarchies on the way scientific knowledge is produced and recognized. He also commented self-reflexively on his debates with colleagues and various changes of heart in the course of doing his own research study. These issues will be considered in more depth in Chapters 4 and 5.

Disciplined imagination

Building on some of the above ideas on how to stimulate creativity which may lead to conceptual breakthroughs, Karl Weick, a well-known organization theorist, views the way in which a researcher forms ideas about a subject as a process of disciplined imagination. When a researcher thinks about a subject or problem, he or she imagines various ways of viewing and operationalizing the subject (the 'imagination' element) before making a decision on one or a range of perspectives (the 'discipline' element) that are adopted and elaborated on in the research. Weick likened this process to artificial selection as 'theorists are both the source of variation and the source of selection' when they imagine and select theoretical perspectives and ideas in relation to a particular subject or problem (Weick, 2001: 520). Weick also suggested that 'disciplined imagination' is characterized by simultaneous rather than sequential thinking and revolves around three components: problem statements, thought trials and selection criteria. These components represent reference points in the process where researchers can act differently and produce theories of better quality. As Weick remarks; '... theory construction can be modified at the step where the problem is stated (make assumptions more explicit, make representation more accurate, make representation more detailed), at the step where thought trials are formulated (increase number of trials generated, increase heterogeneity of trials generated), and at the step where criteria select among thought trials (apply criteria more consistently, apply more criteria simultaneously, apply more diverse criteria)' (2001: 529).

The important implication of Weick's notion of 'disciplined imagination' is that researchers should engage in a number of mental experiments or thought trials where they iterate between reviewed literature, preliminary analyses, background assumptions and their own intuition to consider a variety of metaphors, ideas and models as representations of the subject or problem in hand ('imagination') before selecting and deciding upon one metaphorical image that serves as a starting point for a further inquiry into it ('discipline'). Research in this sense includes a combination of both deductive reasoning, based upon a reading of the available literature on the topic, and inductive reasoning through intuitive and creative thinking, rather than a focus on either one (Weick, 1989). Another implication of Weick's thinking is that it suggests an active role for researchers who imagine or construe theoretical representations, rather than seeing such theoretical representations as deductively or naturally following from a literature review. 'Disciplined imagination' is rooted in the view that the 'logic' of research and the process of theory construction is creative and psychological. It is a matter of heuristics and associative thinking. In Weick's words, research and theorizing is therefore more like artificial selection than natural selection as 'the theorist rather than nature intentionally guides the evolutionary process' of selecting new ideas and theoretical representations (1989: 519).

Conceptualization

A last thing to keep in mind, is that all researchers imagine and construe theoretical representations in their own way, and this means that different researchers will come up with different theoretical representations even though the general topic of the research may be the same. One's educational and cultural background, as well as previous research experiences, all affect the way in which a researcher views a research topic conceptually.

An example of someone who has gone through a process of conceptualizating of their research topic is offered by Joanne, a doctoral student at Cardiff Business School in Example 2.1 (see overleaf). Having a conceptual model is not meant to restrict the student, merely to guide and align their thinking into more productive channels. The student from the example above says that she found many new and different avenues to follow in her research, but it did help to have a guiding model that kept the project focused.

Three further characteristics of good research, whether it be grand or humble, and which distinguish it from activities such as decision-making or consultancy, are identified by Phillips and Pugh (2005). First, good research is based on an *open system of thought*. This requires continual testing, review and criticism of others' ideas, and willingness to hazard new ideas, even if one can't find half a dozen references to support one's view. Second, one must always be prepared *to examine data critically*, and to request the evidence behind conclusions drawn by others. Third, one should always try to *generalize the research*, but within stated limits. This means attempting to extract understanding from one situation and to apply it to as many other situations as possible.

The first two of these characteristics may require researchers to be aware of their own preconceived views, or to be self-reflexive, as Law (1994) describes it, and to be willing to look for information that will disconfirm what they already believe to be the case. This willingness to have current beliefs disproved is important if new ideas are to be developed, and it also has a strong philosophical justification. The requirement for generalization may be either descriptive, where one wishes to demonstrate that the characteristics of one setting are similar to those in other settings, or it can be theoretical, where one demonstrates that the ideas developed within one context are relevant and useful in very different contexts. These issues are developed further in Chapter 5.

SKILLS AND QUALITIES

The qualities that are needed to make a good researcher are not easy to define. Turner (1988) compares the researcher to an expert cook, who finds it difficult to explain what he or she does but claims that the end result is evidence of his or her proficiency. There are many tacit skills involved in research. Although it is possible to develop formal skills and knowledge through training, these tacit skills can only be fully acquired through experience, and this necessarily implies working with others who are able to pass on the tacit skills that they have previously acquired. This is where the relationship with the supervisor is very important, and if one gets the chance to work on a project with experienced researchers, this can be very valuable.

EXAMPLE 2.1

A PhD student reflects on conceptualization

When I initially embarked on the PhD program I thought that I was quite fortunate, already having an idea of what subject area I wanted to explore 'the family in business'. This feeling of security quickly changed to a state of anxiety when I was told by my supervisor that I would have to have some kind of 'conceptual model' to frame my research. Despite initially trying to hope this requirement would disappear I eventually came to accept that I have to have a basis from which to work and as a consequence I would need to have to look for a 'model' which justified my chosen approach. My salvation was my supervisor who proposed I use his model on networking and 'systems of exchange'. It took some time for me to see how this model would fit with my research area – family business – while making a contribution to organization theory, but, after reading more of the literature, connections began to emerge between these two aspects which I incorporated into the conceptual schema. Social capital literature made a good bridge and other links became apparent and began to fall into place. It was the identification of the linkages that led to the building of the conceptual model below. This was aided by the fact that I was able to use my masters as a pilot study for the PhD, and this really helped me get a sense of how I could apply the features of the model. It also highlighted to me elements that could be included in the model that currently were not, such as trust and the differing orientations to action of the different actors in a relationship.

The diagram below represents my thinking of 'if that, plus that, are taken into account, then maybe we may end up with a model looking something like that…'. This has meant that the initial conceptual development is something like a hypothesis or research question which will serve to guide my research and help me stay focused.

Conceptual Development

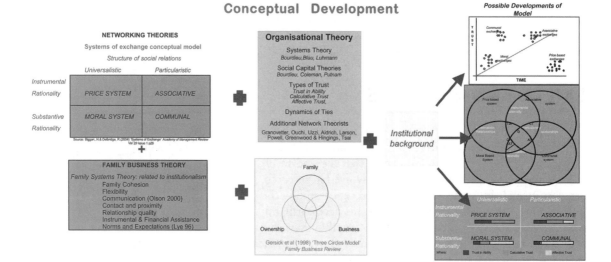

In this section we have listed what we believe to be the important qualities of researchers. These are based partly on our own experiences and partly on external sources such as the ESRC Guidelines for Management Research Training (ESRC, 2005). The resulting personal qualities we have classified according to whether they comprise knowledge, skills or personal attributes. This classification is based substantially on Burgoyne and Stuart's (1976) work into the attributes of effective managers, and it is here that we think the greatest transferability lies between managing and researching. The skills and knowledge areas are progressively more specific to the conduct of research. These are 'core' qualities, which are important in any form of research, and are listed in Exercise 2.1

EXERCISE

2.1

Rating skills and qualities

Rate yourself on each quality using the following 1–4 scale:

1. Have virtually none of these

2. Possess to a limited extent

3. Possess to a moderate degree

4. Possess to a high degree

Knowledge/ awareness of	Skills and abilities	Personal qualities
1. Different assumptions about the world ☐	**7.** Planning, organizing and managing one's own time ☐	**13.** Self Awareness ☐
2. Qualitative and quantitative research methods ☐	**8.** Searching libraries and on-line data sources ☐	**14.** Clarity of thought ☐
3. Range of research designs ☐	**9.** Interviewing and observation ☐	**15.** Sensitivity to events and feelings ☐
4. Immediate subject of study ☐	**10.** Structuring and arguing a case in writing ☐	**16.** Emotional resilience ☐
5. Related subjects and disciplines ☐	**11.** Defending and arguing views orally ☐	**17.** Creativity ☐
6. Key networks and contacts in chosen research area ☐	**12.** Gaining support and cooperation from others ☐	**18.** Learning from experience ☐
Total ☐	*Total* ☐	*Total* ☐

If you have managed to rate yourself on the qualities in Excersise 2.1, then any ratings below three may be cause for concern (with the possible exception of item 5). What to do about any apparent deficiencies is, of course, a different matter. As a generalization: 'knowledge' can be acquired by reading and talking, or by attending courses; 'skills' can be acquired through practicing them, either in a simulated or a real environment; and 'personal qualities' can be acquired, with much difficulty, through life or educational experiences. This book certainly cannot offer everything. It provides a reasonable coverage of items 1, 2, 3, 8, 9 and 10; and it touches on 6, 7, 12, 13 and 18. As for the rest, they may be acquired most easily by working with other researchers, in the form of apprenticeship suggested by Turner (1988).

Beyond a certain point, however, specialization begins to creep in. One form of specialization depends upon whether the researcher is following a primarily quantitative or qualitative path. Thus if someone is carrying out analytic research into financial markets, they may not need to use any qualitative data in their research, and training in qualitative methods may seem a great irrelevance. But we still feel that it is important that they are able to appreciate and evaluate qualitative data and the inferences made from them by others, because it could still have some bearing on their own research. In addition, there is a trend towards more mixing of subjects and methodologies as will be explained further in later chapters. Thus quantitative subjects may be tackled with qualitative methods, as in behavioural accounting; and qualitative subjects can be tackled with quantitative methods, such as frequency counts in textual analysis.

Researchers need to be skilled in the use of different methods for such things as seeking information, analysing data and presenting research results. Those following the quantitative path will need to have high levels of skill in areas such as survey design, sampling methods and statistical analysis; those following the qualitative path may need to be skilled at conducting 'in-depth' interviews, making field notes, coding and interpreting transcripts, and so on. In Chapters 7–11, we give extensive guidance on the choice and application of qualitative methods, and provide a review of possible quantitative methods.

GETTING STARTED

It is very rare for students to have a clear focus at the outset of their research, and yet many find the lack of a clear focus is a major impediment to getting started. It often takes doctoral research students a whole year to find an acceptable focus, and this may include false starts, drifting, and moments of despondency and elation. Indeed, the whole research project may be seen as a continuous process of focusing and refocusing.

Whatever one's situation, it is worth getting started as quickly as possible. This means defining a provisional area of interest, reviewing relevant literature and gathering some data relevant to the focus. One way of thinking about a topic is to produce a model or **mind map** of the issues involved (see also Chapter 12). An example of such a scheme developed in relation to a project by Mark Easterby-Smith on international organizational learning is shown in Figure 2.1.

In a postgraduate project time is short and one may then need to launch directly into the main study. In a doctoral project there is usually time to carry out a pilot investigation to test methodologies and to assess the feasibility of initial ideas, which might then lead into a larger study, or be completely jettisoned at a later stage.

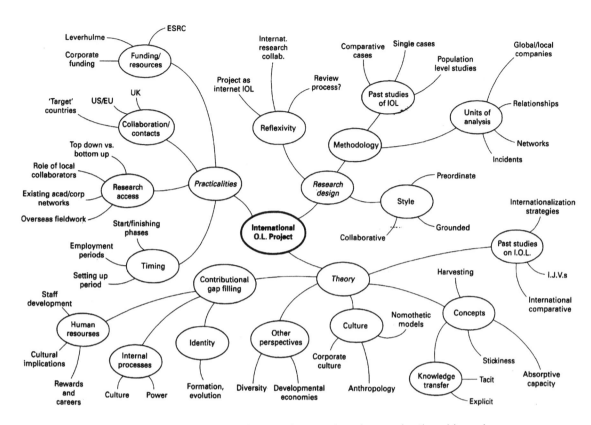

FIGURE 2.1 Initial mind map for a project on international organizational learning

Even if data and reading subsequently needs to be discarded it does not necessarily mean that time has been wasted. There are most likely to be indirect benefits in terms of the contacts, ideas, or techniques one encounters on the way, and at the very least one is invoking Austin's (1978) second principle of being 'in motion' (see page 18, above). Once possible topics have been identified it might be worth considering them against four criteria defined by Huczynski (1996) for why certain management ideas and theories become successful and gain popularity at the expense of equally well researched and valid alternatives:

1 It must be *timely* and address a problem that is seen as important at that moment.

2 It has to be *promoted* effectively via academics, consultants and the business media.

3 It must *relate* to the needs and concerns of the managers to whom it is addressed.

4 It must be *presented* in an engaging way.

Sooner or later it is worth writing a research proposal that summarizes what the project is about and how it is to be investigated. Most institutions require a proposal from prospective research candidates before registration, they also require a more extensive proposal after 12–15 months if a decision is required about upgrading registration from MPhil to PhD levels. Research councils require detailed (but concise!) proposals before they will allocate money to major research projects; shorter proposals may also be required at the beginning of postgraduate projects. Even if there is no formal external requirement to produce a proposal, the exercise of producing one is a very good discipline for drawing together half-formed ideas in the early stages of research.

The main items that should go into a *research proposal* are as follows:

1 A statement of the focus of the research and the main questions to be investigated. It is useful here to produce a series of between four or five aims that the research will address. These can be quite short but should be real aims in the sense that each has an outcome. For example:

- Conduct a literature review in the fields of knowledge management, management learning and small business development.

- Conduct research in a sample of firms in the North West of England in the manufacturing sector to understand the way in which owner managers acquire knowledge to tackle significant business related problems.

- Locate the findings of the study within the literatures of knowledge management and management learning.

- Develop training for business support agencies so that they can provide more appropriate assistance.

2 An explanation of how it relates to, builds on, or differs from previous work in that field, and hence how it will constitute a 'contribution' (see Chapters 3, 5 and 12). The references used in this section need to be from research sources rather than textbooks and as up-to-date as possible.

3 A summary of the research design including a description of what and how data will be collected (see Chapter 5 for more details).

4 An explanation of how data will be interpreted and how this will relate back to the initial questions posed (see Chapters 8, 10 and 11 for more details).

5 Comments on the practical value of the research, and any problems that may be encountered in its conduct.

Our view is that the document should not normally exceed 2500 words although the amount of detail required will depend on the scale of the project and the time available. Likewise the emphasis and structure of the proposal will vary according to such things as the intended audience, the style of research and the methods to be used – and we extend the discussion further in Chapter 5 when discussing research designs. As we suggested at the beginning of this chapter, there is no single formula for ensuring that research will be successful. One must always exercise judgment according to the particular circumstances that prevail. The rest of this book will explain many of the factors that shape and constrain research, and thus to assist the researcher in making informed choices as he or she progresses.

CONCLUSION

In this chapter, we have discussed the different elements that contribute to the (relative) success of a research project. The key points/lessons that we emphasize in this chapter are:

- **The need to negotiate and maintain adequate support.**

- **Self awareness including your own drivers and motives for doing research.**

- **Having patience/confidence that you'll find your own unique angle.**

- **Being willing to keep searching although being aware it may not come easily.**

A research project can only be a success if it is sufficiently embedded in existing literature and knowledge on the subject. This can be achieved by doing a complete and coherent literature review. The next chapter will go into the way in which researchers can find important data and write a comprehensive literature review.

Problems with supervision

EXERCISE

2.2

Find out the procedures you have to follow in your institution if you are having difficulties with your supervisor. This information should be easily accessible on your institution's intranet. Remember supervisory problems are matters of serious concern and should be dealt with as soon as possible to avoid the situation escalating.

Motivations for conducting research

EXERCISE

2.3

In small groups, discuss your own motivations for undertaking your research. Take into account the support you have, both emotional and financial at your disposal. How did this support impact on your decision to undertake research?

Mapping the different perspectives on your research question

EXERCISE

2.4

In pairs set out in diagrammatic form the various approaches that different disciplines or fields have taken to explain the issue related to your research. Argue for the approach you are taking and how it will lead to new understandings.

FURTHER READING

Cryer, P. (2000) *The Research Student's Guide to Success*. Buckingham: Open University Press.

A useful guide for PhD students, written in a conversational style this book is full of practical and useful tips to help you plan, execute and complete your research successfully.

Rugg, G. and Petre, M. (2004) *The Unwritten Rules of PhD Research*. Maidenhead: Open University Press.

This book aims to give an insight into the day-to-day life of a PhD student and aims to highlight the 'unwritten rules' of research and academic writing. It will be useful both for students considering doing a PhD and those already engaged in doctoral research.

Weick, K. E (2001) 'Theory construction as disciplined imagination', *Academy of management Review*, 14 (4): 516–31.

This is a highly innovative and interesting paper relevant for students who aim to construct new theory from their research. Weick proposes imagination in an attempt to free theorists' thinking from restrictive ideas and develop new understandings.

DOING A LITERATURE REVIEW

3

LEARNING OBJECTIVES

- To appreciate what a literature review in management research entails and why it is necessary.

- To understand and evaluate different sources of information.

- To know how to conduct and write literature reviews.

Introduction

What is a literature review?

Search and preparation for the review

Getting access to sources of information

Library resources

Organizing your material and being systematic

Plagiarism

Conclusion

Further reading

INTRODUCTION

This chapter considers how one can discover what is already known about a particular field of study and how this information can help with one's own research. It deals with published texts such as books and journal articles, and also how knowledge can be gained from other communities of practice such as consultants and official bodies. It is important for (management) researchers to be familiar with a range of perspectives and sources, whether these are internal or external, public or private.

The first part of the chapter reiterates the importance of being familiar with the literature in the researcher's field of study. The second part outlines how to get access to the information required and how to undertake a bibliographical search to find the data needed for a literature review. The third part discusses how the material collected can be recorded and organized and the electronic aids that have emerged to assist in this. The fourth part indicates how a search activity might be framed, using examples from a systematic review, while the final part offers some conclusions and tips for undertaking a literature review.

WHAT IS A LITERATURE REVIEW?

Reviewing the literature is a research activity all in itself and a contribution can be made to knowledge on a particular subject through the literature review. It is not unusual to see published reviews of literature, notably in journals such as the *International Journal of Management Reviews*, *Academy of Management Review* or *Psychological Review*, that act as invaluable resources for those wanting to gain an overview of existing studies in a particular field. Literature reviews undertaken as part of a thesis invariably focus on the topics that relate to the main research questions that have been raised and highlight the influential conceptual or empirical studies that have been conducted in the field.

As indicated above, a literature demonstrates knowledge about the extant literature of the field, but it is more than simply describing other authors' perspectives, it is expected to include a critical evaluation of those studies. A good review, furthermore, gives a novel synthesis of existing work, which may lead to new ways of looking at a subject or identifying gaps in the literature. One of the common criticisms made by external examiners is that students undertaking research use literature in a very accepting way, often with very little comment and without critiquing it or explaining its limitations or contexts. It is our view that research students need to be critical not only of their own work, but should also be critically reflective of other literatures. Such a level of understanding helps the final research outcome to be located back into the literature and shows how a contribution to knowledge is made (Mauch and Birch, 1983). Moreover, as mentioned above, the review process involves identifying gaps in prior studies, with a view to locating one's investigation in a broader context. Silverman identifies the contents of a literature review as:

- What do we already know about the topic?
- What do you have to say critically about what is already known?

- Has anyone else ever done anything exactly the same as what is proposed?
- Has anyone else done anything that is related?
- Where does your work fit in with what has gone before?
- Why is your research worth doing in the light of what has already been done? (2000: 227)

A literature review has a number of discernible features and imperatives as its characteristics. The first imperative is the need for the reviewer to give a rigorous yet pragmatic account of what is being reviewed. By engaging with and critiquing previous studies, the researcher needs to strike a balance that simultaneously displays criticality through inquisitive and considered arguments with regard to the assumptions, theories and methods used while at the same time acknowledging the validity of and insights and strengths made by the study. Second, literature reviews ought to supersede a descriptive re-run of what had been written and incorporate a thread – a train of thought – that progressively builds towards the very research topic for which the review is being conducted. This includes identifying gaps in the extant literature. A third feature, and one that attracts little attention, is that reviews go on throughout the duration of a research project rather than the conventional understanding that it is conducted at the beginning of a study and ends there. The review remains an ongoing project, which requires refinements and modifications as the study progresses. This is due in part to empirical findings that might lead the research in a new direction and therefore require adjustments to initial arguments and also because new findings emerge all the time and the research needs to reflect these and be as up-to-date as possible.

SEARCH AND PREPARATION FOR THE REVIEW

Knowing the journals

You will probably already have read something about your topic in a book or in a book chapter. You will be becoming familiar with the language used and the issues that appear important. You now need to know the studies already conducted in the field so that researchers avoid re-inventing the wheel and can identify what the contribution of your own ideas might be to the existing body of knowledge. Looking at journals that deal with these topics will give you either useful insights directly from the articles studied or, at the very least, clues or leads to follow from the references cited. This can lead to a significant saving of time and possibly save a good deal of unnecessary work.

An even more important purpose (and this links closely to the writing of research proposals) is for a researcher to be able to position his or her own topic in the context of what has already been looked at in prior research. If this position proves a difficult thing to do, it does at the very least give an opportunity to follow a theme or idea over a number of years and the literature can be collated, re-conceptualized or otherwise brought up to date. There is a great sense of satisfaction to be gained from knowing the journals, the recurring names of authors and the conferences where your topic is most often presented or discussed.

Exploring potential sources

There are numerous ways in which a literature search can be done. Perhaps the most obvious is to begin with the library. JAI Press, for example, publishes a series of editions on research in various disciplines. These are updated regularly as new material is published. It is also important to take note of seminal works in the area, particularly those that offer an overview of the approaches to and extant literature upon a particular topic. For example, Mark Easterby-Smith published a review of Organizational Learning from the perspective of six different disciplines (Easterby-Smith, 1997) and a systematic review of knowledge in SMEs can be seen in Thorpe et. al. (2005). Both can be used as starting points for more specific investigations in these areas.

Another way of getting started is to begin with the relevant studies written on the topic over the years. These texts often provide interesting references, but this does have the drawback that it very quickly broadens the field of research and this can work against the need for research focus. Some publications offer a systematic précis of the articles published in editions of that volume year. For example, the *Journal of Marketing* offers such a précis. Over several pages it covers all types of significant articles and publications in all aspects of marketing (e.g. distribution, publicity, sales or strategy) for that volume year.

It is also an excellent strategy to see what subject-specific networks exist for researchers so that they may become part of a wider research community in a particular research area. This can be a very fruitful way of getting to know like-minded colleagues who are working in a similar field or on a similar topic not just in a researcher's own country but all over the world. An example of such a network is the British Academy of Management (http://www.bam.ac.uk/groups). It has special interest groups that now cover more than 14 different fields in management and related activities. Many useful leads and references can come from participating in e-mail discussion groups. Contacts for such groups are often found at conferences or similar academic associations. For doctoral candidates this kind of networking is perhaps even more important than for those simply engaged on an individual research topic, as it will bring them in touch with other researchers who are or have been undergoing the same experience. Research workshops and colloquia are organized by most of the big UK and USA and European conferences such as the British Academy of Management (BAM), European Group of Organisational Studies (EGOS), the American and European Academies of Management (AoM and EURAM), the European Doctoral Network (EDEN) and the European Institute for Advanced Studies in Management (EIASM). All these groups enable doctoral candidates to meet and submit their current research for discussion and debate with fellow doctoral candidates and senior academics. In addition, there are conferences organized by disciplines within management and these again often have their own doctoral provision, for example the BAM and the Institute for Small Business and Entrepreneurship. Both the AoM and EURAM both have also special interest groups which cover a range of disciplines and cross-disciplinary topics, they hold regular seminars and workshops and are very welcoming to new researchers. Perhaps it is also worth noting here that researchers often publish their most recent work as working papers, published through their own universities or through symposia. It is therefore important to know where research groups are based, their research focus, and how to get hold of their most recent working papers (there is usually a small cost attached).

Time devoted to literature searching

The time that researchers can devote to searching for literature will vary according to the stages of development of their research. Certainly at the beginning a great deal of time will be needed – some estimates suggest three quarters of a researcher's time at the beginning stage of research will be absorbed in this activity. But the activity should not become obsessive. It should be a means to an end with the study of the literature producing meaning and a concrete focus for the research. Although continuous studying in the library might sometimes be appealing, in a rather pragmatic way researchers will need to make the transition into the field. Too much information can be paralysing and research can lack focus or move in a fruitless direction.

Focusing the Research

As has been discussed in Chapter 2, focusing one's research often is a major problem and remains so at many stages of the research process. It is, though, of particular importance in respect to reviewing the literature. The literature review, and particularly the way that it is presented in a report or thesis, presents a major challenge. Conceptualizing a broad field can be difficult; bringing together a broad cross-section of papers and articles can be a gargantuan task and sometimes even insurmountable. However, having a focus to the research will make the research clearer and to the point, rather than chaotic but all-covering.

Learning

Doing a literature search can be a significant learning experience for researchers. Connecting what is read to what is already known, critiquing the literature and conceptualizing and re-conceptualizing prior work into new patterns and themes can be a major contribution to a research study in its own right. Further, students should be encouraged to examine the ontological, epistemological and methodological assumptions, which will be further explained in Chapter 4, made in prior research so as to better understand what they regard as knowledge. Researchers undertaking research projects, whether they be funded for theses, dissertations or for undergraduate projects are expected, amongst other things, to display knowledge of the literature in their chosen field.

GETTING ACCESS TO SOURCES OF INFORMATION

Sources

The library represents the obvious source for obtaining published material. Most readers who have experience with libraries sometimes feel that using a library gives rise to a mixture of frustration when books are not on the shelves, vital inter-library loan articles are delayed in the post or Internet search engines are 'down'. But whatever one's impressions, behind the library shelves are trained and professional information managers who keep on top of an ever increasing quantity of information, whether it is in Britain, France or the USA (10,000 publishing outlets in Great Britain, – 125,000 items in print in the area of social sciences alone, – 8000 available journals and 5 million entries in the British Library Catalogue www.bl.uk/catalogue).

In addition to simply housing information, the British Library performs a role in making information accessible. It is possible, for example, to obtain photocopies of articles or research papers and it will assist in locating PhDs completed within the UK, Europe more generally though is somewhat behind the USA and Canada in this information dissemination role where information on research is more easily available.

The very important aspect of using a library is to establish a rapport with one or a number of librarians, preferably one who is familiar with your field of study, and once the contact has been established, never neglect it. Such contact effectively means that researchers have a 'go-between' in someone who can communicate with the library system on their behalf. This is particularly important, as undertaking research can require a high level of specialized information as well as particular library skills that are not normally required; working with a librarian who has the inside knowledge and skills can thus be invaluable.

At present, although with new technology things are continually changing, the main types of support for bibliographic information are:

- Traditional 'hard copy' support; books and journals.
- Electronic databases, which can be accessed online via the library's web site, and increasingly offer full text electronic journals and at the very least abstracts.
- Other information; for example company accounts and market data.

When beginning any research 'search' it is always useful to weight the advantages and disadvantages of the support likely to be available. Issues that perhaps researchers ought to consider are availability, cost and time to gain access. There are two main ways of tackling a literature search; either the researcher has and needs a wide overall review of the literature in a specific field or they know exactly the articles that they want and simply need to collect these. Selvin and Stuart (1966) refer to this as 'trawling' (when it involves a wide sweep to see what can be brought in) and 'fishing' (which involves a more targeted search). Trawling and fishing should not be seen as opposites, more as different starting points, independent of the extent of the researcher's prior knowledge and focus.

Electronic searches

Before going to the library on a trawl, that is, sweeping up what information that exists on a topic, time can be saved by a researcher in deciding and being selective in what he or she is after. Before preparing for a search researchers should identify the types of information that they require. They can then prepare searches for the different resources, i.e. searches on the catalogue will be more general than those on a database and so on. Try to think a little bit about what you are attempting to look for so you limit what you get from the search and can be more confident that what you do retrieve relates to what you want to know more about. More specifically, a researcher needs to think about the keywords that can be used to identify a field of study.

Using keywords, operators such as AND, OR and NOT can be combined to create search statements and refine searches. Most articles carry keywords beneath the abstract that identify themes addressed in the study. These can be invaluable filters when looking to focus one's literature review. It is useful to remember, however, that being too broad in terms of the keywords used will lead to too many references (often thousands) to handle, whereas being too focused may produce limited and orthodox returns.

Alignment with study context and approach

A review of the literature may be in a single disciplinary area or in several areas, depending on the nature of the research and its subject area. Regardless of the setting and the issue being investigated, it is paramount that there is some kind of alignment

EXAMPLE 3.1

A keyword search using Web of Science

An example of too broad a keyword might be 'knowledge'. There will literally be hundreds of thousands of articles using this term, in many different disciplines, with different meanings and linked to different concepts. It may refer to knowledge as a configured resource, or to a skill to be developed, or to the knowledge of researchers themselves. It might also be linked to a firm's performance, or to psychological needs, or even to non-humans such as machines. Too narrow a keyword might be 'patent'. The noun is a very specific form of knowledge asset, and whilst used internationally in no way does it capture the entire range of activity associated with new product development and exploitation. The point that we make here is that terminology is very important. In order to find out what one wants from the mass of information in the library, a researcher needs to identify his/her interests clearly. An example of a search and the number of hits returned is shown below.

Focus of the search	Search term	Number of hits
Web of Science	Knowledge	100,000+
Web of Science	Management	100,000+
Web of Science	Knowledge or Management	100,000+
Web of Science	Knowledge and Management	27,564
Web of Science	Knowledge Management and Small Firms	115

EXAMPLE 3.2

PhD student's literature review

In a study of knowing and learning in organizations, a doctoral student adopted a cultural-historical and situated perspective on knowing based on activity theory. This demanded a multi-layered review of the literature, incorporating prior studies on organizational knowledge and learning, work-based learning and the nature of the industry in which the study took place. All constituted the thesis' theoretical and methodological framework.

between the research methodology to be adopted, its context and the approach used. Studies concentrating on a narrow subject domain will require a critique of the literature in that specific area. However, multi-disciplinary and practice-based studies might require a review which spans different literatures and synthesises them.

Whether the nature of the study focuses on one discipline or takes a more multi-disciplinary approach, the literature review will need to be consistent with the study as a whole. This means that the study's epistemology, strategy, literature review, design, methods and empirical sections should all indicate, be linked and demonstrate an internal coherence (see Chapters 4 and 5). At the same time, as we have indicated, a simple description of previous research is not sufficient. Rather, the review needs to incorporate both interpretation and analysis as well as being critical so as to underpin the research questions identified. For example, in order to go beyond simply reviewing general background information relating to knowledge management and organizational learning, the student mentioned in Example 3.2 needed to narrow the focus of interest to concentrate on specific perspectives on knowledge, for example of practice-based perspectives on knowing in firms. Patriotta (2003) offers an example of the way he conducted his literature review (see Example 3.3).

EXAMPLE 3.3

Literature review by Patriotta

In his book entitled *Organizational Knowledge in the Making*, Patriotta (2003) reviews the literature on knowledge within firms and identifies different perspectives, including the cognitive, knowledge-based, 'situated' and techno-science approaches. He offers a critical interpretation of different perspectives, acknowledging their respective strengths while also identifying areas that require clarifying. He concludes by arguing for an integrated and multi-faceted approach to the subject. What becomes apparent to him is that the pluralistic perspectives taken has led to his ability to propose that there are in fact three methodological lenses which transcend the narrow epistemological boundaries of current perspectives on organizational knowledge. These three lenses are suggested as being: breakdown, time, and narrative.

A subject-search then demands as a pre-condition the *identification of keywords* of one's subject area. A researcher should not think, though, that he or she has to find an exact match with those words used in the library to name a subject. Any classification system provides for alternative 'labels' to identify a category, and the researcher's part is to be aware of the most likely alternatives. It might be helpful to write a list of the different ways that a subject area might be described. An alternative term might be as straightforward as changing the word slightly, for example when using 'organizational knowledge' as keywords, it would also useful to try typing in 'knowing'. Most databases allow the researcher to use a 'wildcard' when a term can have several endings, for example 'know*' would search for 'knowledge' and 'knowing' in some databases. Check the individual databases for the different forms these wildcard symbols take.

Three of the pitfalls that might be encountered in conducting a literature search need to be borne in mind:

1 Do not be afraid to change the concept or label of the subject you are investigating. For example, returning to our search under organization knowledge – the wrong keywords can give some surprising titles, e.g. 'the organization of bees: knowledge of cellular structures'. Keywords clearly work better in some fields than others, but even these outlying titles can sometimes help to refine your objectives. If your search reveals many works on apiaries then you may be prompted into using hives and worker bees as at least appropriate metaphors for organizational knowledge; your conception of what's included in your subject expands. If no matches can be found, then other different keywords, sometimes broader, will need to be used. If on the other hand the research is too wide, more specific keywords will need to be used.

2 Equally, do not be fooled into thinking that an existing detailed analysis of research literature will substitute for your own analysis. Researching, as we have discussed before, is not exclusively about refining what has been said by others, it is also in part an act of synthesis. A detailed analysis of the subject will provide the keywords to commence the search but will not do it all for you!

3 Do not expect to find a single document that answers the essential points you are searching for. For example, a complex group of keywords such as: consumer, culture, scale, measure, psychometric, will not automatically lead to specialized articles in the marketing literature dealing with problems of cross-cultural equivalence of the scales of measures used in commercial consumer marketing research. It is even less likely to lead to a specific book on the subject! Consequently, when entering a library be willing and ready to consult a selection of materials.

Having considered the above, you are now ready to enter the library and switch on the computer.

LIBRARY RESOURCES

As we have discussed in the examples of the literature used, management comprises a wide range of subjects and is continually expanding as a discipline and body of knowledge. Fortunately there are a number of bibliographical publications and document services that can assist in searches. General literature and bibliographical publications which are the key to information searching fall roughly into seven broad groupings:

1 Books
2 Journals
3 Theses
4 Government publications and official statistics
5 Reference works, general guides to the literature and guides to the literature in particular subject areas (compendium catalogues)
6 Conference and working papers of research in progress
7 Web sites

Each of these will be dealt with in detail separately but a good strategy for a researcher is to begin by fully exploiting the stock and bibliographical publications in your own library. If necessary the research can be extended through borrowing books from other libraries through the inter-library loan system (bear in mind that this can take several weeks!). Electronic resources are now extending to include books and many journals have a service referred to as 'online early', which offers advanced sight of articles accepted for publication in future editions. These electronic versions of the article are identical to those that will eventually be published (apart from the fact they have no date) in the journal and cannot be altered or changed.

Books

Most libraries classify books in subject themes according to one of the major published classification schemes (for example, the Dewey Decimal System), often with some modification to suit local requirements. Browsing among books can be a useful way of providing an overview but it is always likely to be a partial one. If all aspects of literature were grouped in a single place, literature searching would be a simple undertaking. Often, however, the subjects are scattered around and range, for example, from economics to industrial sociology to psychology. The logic of this stems from the general structure of knowledge that is far from being immediately obvious. Sometimes it can be difficult to know where to classify a book, for example, the consequences to business after UK entry into the single European market. The online catalogue is, therefore, the best place to start a search for books. If the subject is a fairly specific one, it could be the case that there are no books on the topic and there may be a need to look under a wider heading in the subject or keyword index. Here you are likely to find several references and if there is a bibliography, it will refer to other works such as books and papers in journals. This should point the way to other potentially useful material.

The subject index and catalogue can also point to bibliographies that exist in the library's stock. If it is obvious at this stage that there are other published bibliographies which are relevant to the research then the next step is to consult one of the guides that list bibliographies. The *Bibliographic Index Plus* (www.hwwilson.com/

Databases/biblio.htm) is a list of both separately published bibliographies and ones occurring in books and articles. By examining this, it should be possible to find references to promising bibliographies including books that are in stock in the library.

The output of published material has become so great that it is unlikely that any library, however large, will be able to meet all of a researcher's needs from its own resources. So, once the stock of books available in one's university library has been reviewed, you may want to take things further and see what else has been written. To do this, the appropriate national bibliographies need to be consulted listing the book output of individual countries. Copac provides free access to the merged online catalogues of 19 of the largest university research libraries in the UK and Ireland (http://www.copac.ac.uk). The British Library Public Catalogue (BLPC) offers free online access to over 10 million records of items in the British Library Collection, and includes a document ordering link (http://opac97.bl.uk). Similarly the Bulletin Board for Libraries (BUBL) provides access to online public access catalogues by region (http://link.bubl.ac.uk:80/libraryopacs).

A comprehensive list of links to world libraries is usually available on most university web sites. To undertake an effective search you will need to know the foreign equivalents of the subject keywords being searched and access to a translator or interpreter may also be necessary. For the non-linguist, there are information sources that refer to works that have been translated, such as the Index Translationium and the British Lending Library's BLL Announcement Bulletin.

Before concluding this section about books, it is worth mentioning the existence of catalogues from other libraries that can be a very useful source. These printed or online catalogues are, of course, restricted to the holdings of the library concerned, but are not limited to the output of any particular country. Very large libraries such as the British Library or the Library of Congress (USA) contain almost all publications in the English-language and a large percentage (although on the decline) of foreign-language publications. In addition, there are such online national/international catalogues as Copac, Bibliotheque Nationale (Paris), Deutsche Bibliothek (Germany) and Biblioteca Nacional (Spain). Specimens of more specific catalogues can be supplied by such institutes as: the Institute of Chartered Accountants, which goes under the name of Current Accounting Literature and also by the Baker Library from the Harvard Business School, entitled Core Collection – An Author and Subject Guide (http://www.library.hbs.edu).

Journals

For research, perhaps the most important area is the stock of periodicals or journals. These hold the key to the most up-to-date research and are the sources that researchers need to make sure they cite on proposals; they also represent the means by which the most recent research is placed in the public domain, and because of the screening employed (through the refereeing process adopted by the highest ranked journals) they represent quality. There are a number of ways in which articles on relevant topics are to be found. For example, the researcher could simply leaf through some of the best-known business journals in order to spot how journals deal with particular topics or themes by using their annual indices which usually produces a subject and author guide but usually a student would register with Zetoc. Zetoc provides access to the British Library's electronic table of contents of around 20,000 journals and 16,000 conference proceedings annually. Zetoc also allows you to keep abreast of what is coming out as it sends out emails to alert you of new publications in the area you have specified.

Some libraries keep up-to-date summary catalogues to be consulted on the spot, i.e. content pages of everything new in a particular month. And, it is often also possible to sign up with publishers to be informed of new issues. However, a far more effective way of locating articles is to use the appropriate abstracting and indexing services, since by doing this a researcher can scan as many as several hundred journals at one time, where articles appear useful the expectation now is for them to be able to offer a full text service. As you are able to view the abstracts first it will help you decide whether an article is worth downloading or not. Using this approach, it is possible to discover references that a researcher would not normally come across. The abstracts give the precise reference for an article and offer a summary, while the 'index' is limited to simply the bibliographic details. Some of these abstracting and indexing databases also offer access to the full text article directly from the database, though where this is not the case use the library catalogue of your home institution to see if the library subscribes to this journal either in print, or electronically.

Most business school libraries as well as several universities offer a wide range of abstracts and indices covering a range of management themes, the majority of which are now in electronic format. Perhaps the two most useful general services are ABI Inform and Business Source Premier. Emerald is also a full text data base of journals although it only covers emerald's own journals.

In addition to the general 'abstracts and indices' there are several others which focus on specialized fields, such as for example, International Abstracts of Human Resources, International Abstracts in Operations Research, Marketing Information Guide, Packaging Abstracts, Psychological Abstracts, Training Abstracts and many more. Others such as Public Affairs Information Service Bulletin (PAIBS) are very useful for retrieving information on affairs connected with the international public environment, while the current Technology Index, although being on the boundary of management studies can also be very useful.

The service is free to all those in higher education institutions. What you get is not full text but instead table of contents, however once a issue has been identified of interest, links enable you to access the full text. Complete Exercise 3.1 to register with Zetoc (zetoc.mimas.ac.uk).

Theses, dissertations and research in progress

For those undertaking higher degree research as well as those who are undertaking research generally, it is often important to know what theses have already been completed, if only to identify the individuals to make contact with. There are several ways of knowing just what research is being conducted. In Britain theses are available through the *Index to Theses with Abstracts Accepted for Higher Degrees by the Universities of Great Britain and Ireland* (published by Aslib). Dissertation

EXERCISE

3.1

Setting up your Zetoc Alert

To set up a Zetoc Alert you should first log into homepage of Zetoc (http://zetoc.mimas. ac.uk). You should then enter your username and password which you should be able to get from your central library. Your institution may use Athens logins or individual institutional logins but your librarian should be able to give you this information. Once logged in follow the instructions on the site. More detailed information about setting up a Zetoc Alert may be found at http://zetoc.mimas.ac.uk/alertguide.html

Abstracts International provides electronic access to international dissertation abstracts by library subscription, or free on the web for two years (http://wwwlib. umi.com/dissertations/). In France, there is a national register of current theses managed by the Université Paris IO Nanterre. There is also DOGE, an abstract of the underground literature on management in France, mainly research papers and theses and in Germany the Jahresverzeichnis der Deutchen Hochshulschriften.

In the USA, Dissertation Abstracts International offers one of the largest and up-to-date lists. It is divided into several parts: Humanities & Social Sciences (Section A); Physical Sciences & Engineering (Section B); and the European Abstracts (Section C). Dissertation Abstracts covers most theses produced in North America; copies of which can be borrowed within a few weeks at a very reasonable price from the British Library Document Supply Centre at Boston Spa. Management is contained in Volume 8 of the index. A check needs to be made under the keyword. If there are no titles of interest listed, then the individual volumes will need to be checked. If no theses are found, it should not be considered a waste of time since it is helping to ensure that there is no duplication of research. As the cost (in time) of duplication of research is high, searches of this kind can be a very worthwhile exercise. There is currently an initiative under way through Je-S to make this process all electronic.

Information on research actually in progress is not easy to come by and it is here that experienced researchers, who tend to build up contacts over the years have a considerable advantage. Being members of a British Academy of Management Special Interest Group or one of the American Academy of Management Divisions can give access to a vibrant network. The Economic and Social Science Research Council's newsletter (*The Edge* from the ESRC) brings the latest and most topical social science research to key opinion formers in business, government and the voluntary sector. Other possible sources of information include the registers of current research published by several leading Business Schools. In France there are newsletters such as *Courier du CNRS*.

Government publications, official statistics

On a case by case basis, libraries choose to classify official publications either separately or include them within the general catalogue. In Britain, researchers should refer to the Annual List of Government Publications or, if necessary, to the monthly or daily lists. This involves first looking at the index at the back of each list for headings that appear to be of interest or 'fit' the keyword describing the subject. There are many published introductions to government publications and official statistics and many libraries produce their own guides to their stocks. For more comprehensive information on what official statistics are available, the Central Statistical Office's Guide to Official Statistics is an invaluable source (http://www.statistics.gov.uk). An online resource of the British Publications Current Awareness Scheme is available online (http://www.bopcas.com/).

Some international organizations also offer important statistical information. The Organisation for Economic Co-operation and Development (OECD), for example, provides information on the economic indicator statistics on international trade and statistics on products (http://www.oecd.org/statistics). The FMI sums up the main economic and financial data for all EU member states. The ONU statistical directory and the Communantes European (Official Statistics Bulletin for the EU members) are both useful sources. An online catalogue for The Stationery Office (formally the HMSO) can be found at http://www.thestationeryoffice.co.uk.

Reference books, general and specialized bibliographic guides

The final group of publications which a researcher needs to know about are a group of publications that are general guides to the literature or subject areas. New researchers can use reference works, for example to become aware of any organizations relevant to their interests and these can indeed be fertile sources of information.

In Great Britain, there are publications such as A.J. *Walford's Guide to Reference Material*, *Current British Directories* or its European counterpart, the *Current European Directory*. Directories such as *Kompass* and *Who Owns Whom* (the FT500 is now only available through the FT web site) also constitute useful sources of business information. In France, researchers could use, for example, *Sources d'Informations Statistiques*, published by Editions Ytem or the *Bottin Administratif*. For those who need detailed financial information on a company, services such as FAME (Bureau van Dijk, http://www.bvdep.com) or Global Business Browser (OneSource, http://www.onesource.com/index.htm) supply financial data on most sizable businesses as well as the main European companies as the DAFSA does in France. Data is also held for unit trusts. Other sources are the *International Stock Exchange Yearbook* and a specialized journal published by the Financial Times Business Service, Mergers and Acquisitions, which includes relevant information on mergers and acquisitions. Services such as Datastream and Exstat give direct access to financial data. In France, Diane supplies, electronic data on French businesses. Share prices can be consulted on Datastream, and on similar products such as Perfect Analysis and Hemscott, or on the financial pages of the *Financial Times* or the *Wall Street Journal* depending on the financial market being analysed. For up-to-date press comment on individual companies there are databases, the most useful are Lexis-Nexis or Factiva.

Web sites: the Internet as an enabler and an adjunct

One method of undertaking research that has become much more of an everyday facet of both doing business and conducting management research is the Internet. From its beginnings in the late 1960s as a means of networking the US Defence Agency, through the introduction of the World Wide Web, to the current Internet information structure, the Internet has had a high input on the ways in which information flows and where information resides. Its impact is also felt in the way research is conducted.

Raymond Lee (2000) has outlined the potential uses of the Internet as an 'unobtrusive' way of gathering data for social research. He argues that the wide availability of personal computers now affect the researcher in a new way to acquire, store and manage data. The advantages are fourfold; first, access to 'unusual' groups has become easier, due to their increased visibility and the lessening of time and space constraints. Second, it is possible to trace patterns of social interaction and social trends through a record of Internet usage and perhaps through the tracing of Internet trends. Third, researching through the Internet may well provide a very reliable means of guaranteeing anonymity both to respondents and the researcher during research projects, which could be useful in researching sensitive topics. Fourth, the Internet may enable social researchers to trace social processes more easily than through face-to-face interaction.

One of the themes that we have touched on in this book is the importance of play. The Internet could encourage both respondents and researchers to be more playful in research projects. There are also the issues of ease and relative low cost (both in terms of time and resources) which research via the Internet provides. Surveys could be distributed more easily than through the post; email may provide a way both of making initial contact and conducting adhoc interviews; and the Internet itself provides an enormous documentary resource for the researcher to exploit.

However, these advantages should perhaps be balanced with a number of obvious problems. First, the reliability of the data (as with any data) must always be considered; bluntly, is the source to be trusted? Data made available through governmental web sites, for example, may be much more reliable than data posted by someone from a lobby group. (This of course, does not imply that state-sponsored web sites are somehow value-free or neutral and should not be considered critically!) Second, the use of the Internet to conduct empirical data collection must also be considered in the light of the huge increase in electronic traffic over the last few years. Just as a survey may end up in the bin of a manager who receives it in the post, so might the email and attachment! Perhaps this is becoming even more likely with the increase in viruses and the care with which people are reminded to open attachments. Response rates therefore, may be at least as low as for postal surveys. Third, the lack of physical contact needs to be considered (what Lee calls the 'disembodied' nature of Internet interaction) as it may lessen the richness of the data collected. Fourth, and relatedly, the impact of the 'asynchronous' nature of the majority of Internet interaction.

This relates to the relatively small opportunity to communicate with respondents in 'real time' and is an interesting aspect to consider when assessing data collection electronically.

The enormous information resource that is potentially available is both, as Lee (2000) suggests, a blessing and a curse. The sheer volume of information makes finding what you are looking for both more likely and more difficult. This is where search engines play their part. Lee has some suggestions when deciding which search engines to use, particularly the choice between the active and the passive. Active engines search (or 'crawl') through the Internet pages themselves, cataloguing by vocabulary used or by sites visited. Passive engines on the other hand, depend on the page 'owner' forwarding a description to the search engine administrator. Each has inherent advantages and disadvantages: active searching may generate more contemporary links, and a larger number; passive engines may however, be more relevant in the 'hits' presented to you.

Of course as with any data collection, the best way of moving forward is to try out different approaches. In this way experience will help the user decide between alternatives. The now ubiquitous Google does have a very useful offshoot called Google Scholar which if used in the advanced search mode provides the most relevant links, is easy to use, often the quickest, and has no advertising! Others search engines with similar offerings include:

- Webcrawler: http://www.webcrawler.com
- InfoSeek: http://www.infoseek.com
- Yahoo: http://www.yahoo.com
- Lycos: http://www.lycos.com
- Altavista: http://altavista.com

Wikis can also be useful sources of information. They are online databases that allow users to add and edit content – the most well know of these is Wikipedia. As a range of users can change the content of the database, researchers should use their common sense and verify anything they are taking from a Wiki source. Therefore if approached with caution, a Wiki can be a useful way of gathering preliminary information.

Finally, a *caveat*. Lee notes, that there may be some form of change for the increasing amount of the information and data that is available through the Internet. The initial ethos of the Internet, based on sharing information and ideas in a safe academic forum, has become commercialized through both online trading and the sale of data. As a rule of thumb, it may be best to work with the idea that the Internet will not provide 'something for nothing' in terms of data. Often your library will subscribe to journals allowing you direct access to articles, but equally often you will be asked to pay a fee to get access. It is often worth checking alternative sites to check whether what costs through one site is free through another. The Internet is undoubtedly of great use in identifying and honing research questions and issues, and in facilitating communication and it will continue to grow in importance.

In connection with getting hold of specific material of relevance, it is important to know something about a bibliographical aid known as 'citation indexing'. Briefly, a citation index brings together all the other papers that have subsequently made reference to a given paper, and is the only indexing method that enables a researcher to search forward in the literature. This type of indexing is based on the concept that an author's references to previous articles identify much of the earlier work that is relevant to his or her present paper, and are themselves the best indicators of its subject. The Science Citation Index has been available to researchers in the sciences and technologies since 1963. In 1973, the Social Sciences Citation Index was launched, with a coverage of 1000 journals. This was a major development in literature searching for social scientists, as its value increases as the database grows in size with the passage of time. To begin searching for articles on a particular subject in the Social Sciences Citation Index, a researcher only needs to know the name of one author who has written something on or related to the chosen topic; he or she can then find all the articles up to the present that have cited the earlier article.

ORGANIZING YOUR MATERIAL AND BEING SYSTEMATIC

Organizing

To avoid being flooded with references whose contents and quotations are difficult to control, mechanisms for organizing become essential. We therefore recommend devising a system of storing your results, either an electronic database or something much simpler. There are both low-tech and high-tech options here. The low-tech option is to use standard hand-written record cards in subject and alphabetical order: do not dismiss these just because we live in an electronic age! Having things permanently visible can be an advantage as we will see in Chapter 8 when we examine the various merits of different methods of data analysis. The high-tech option involves using a computer database. There are many database packages available which can easily deal with this type of information handling. They range from the rudimentary to the exotic. In attempting to discover which system to purchase, it is worth giving some real data to a system to see how 'easy' or complex it is to use. Never purchase any software without trying it out first. Universities and colleges often subscribe to a specific package such as the Endnote or ProCite, which are packages specifically designed to help students keep track of their references. They can be set up in such a way that the reference can be linked through to your institution's electronic library and so in effect an electronic copy of all your references can be held at the touch of a button. Remember though that this usually only works from the university's main site, and off-site use of this link can be difficult. These do not have to be used in conjunction with bibliographic databases, and can be used as an electronic catalogue of those studies you have deliberately and personally chosen. The advantage of these packages is that in addition to being widely available, and often accessible simply through registering as a student, they are also compatible with the growing number of bibliographic databases.

It might appear an obvious point to make, but one tip is to make sure all references are recorded. No one will believe it but once books have been read and returned to the library shelves or radio programmes have finished and the day they were broadcast forgotten, it is extremely difficult and very time-consuming to find references unless the researcher has developed some kind of systematic cataloguing system.

If the researcher has a personal style that precludes systematically writing on cards or typing them into a database as the literature is being read, then at the very least go for a low-tech option of using a cardboard box or a shopkeeper's spike for their references. This way they are in one place and can be retrieved later! Using a software package goes a long way to alleviating this problem. Once stored and backed up they can be used again and again. As time goes on, you can build up your own library of references, with associated abstracts and keywords. This software also enables you quickly and accurately to create your own bibliographies when writing and to do so according to the dictates of all manner of citation styles (typically these will be Harvard or Chicago styles).

Whatever system you use there is a need to build bibliographies from the start of a research project. The bibliography must not be written at the end of research work. One can simply use a text organizer such as Word allowing material to be sorted alphabetically. What follows is how you might approach a review of a particular area or field. First you need to consider the type of review that is to be undertaken. Remember, the aim you are trying to achieve is how the findings and concepts of what has gone before help the argument that you are trying to develop. The review is seeking to identify themes, patterns and contradictions that help you to take a position and locate your own work.

Systematic reviews

In essence, a systematic review involves two processes. First, defining review protocols and mapping the field by accessing, retrieving and judging the quality and relevance of studies in your research area. Second, reporting the findings to identify where gaps in the current research exist and so indicate where your research might make a useful contribution very much in the way we have already discussed, and many doctorate programme directors are now requiring students to both know of (but in some cases be able to complete) the systematic review process and know the protocols that are required to be followed.

Typically, systematic reviews are restricted to published peer-reviewed, academic articles that exist within management and organization studies fields, because it is through such peer reviews that quality of the research and its relevance can be judged and maintained. It is recognized that there is a lack of searchable databases for book chapters and reports, though currently there are a number of national and university libraries working to increase the number of books available online. The choice of bibliographic databases will depend upon what access is available although as we have discussed universities often subscribe to a number of them.

The objective of a systematic review is to identify a manageable number of studies, without excluding important key studies. To further assist in limiting the search, exclusion criteria can be used which have been discussed earlier in this chapter. The point behind systematic reviews (i.e. why they are systematic rather than simply personal choice) is that each filtering decision is noted down and is transparent for others to see what you have done and so to judge the relevance and substantive nature of your review. Articles that are returned are not seen to have been selected on the basis of personal preference.

Each database will yield a list of potentially useful studies using search strings alone. These can then be exported to referencing software such as Endnote or Procite. The advantage of doing this is twofold. First, if the lists are still too large they allow for further filtering using features like keyword and journal searches. They also allow the researcher to collate the different lists from the different databases, and so remove duplicate studies. Second, once the relevant studies have been reduced to a manageable size, they allow the researcher the opportunity to read through each of the abstracts. It is at this stage that the studies can be divided into: relevant, partially relevant and less relevant. The review being systematic means the criteria for judging which study goes into which list have also to be identified and justified. So again a degree of self reflection might also be useful here. The reflection might cover, for example, concerns such as: data quality; access; theory development and ambition; links to research question and so forth. Remember that at this stage it is only abstracts that are being examined so a great deal depends upon the coverage and clarity of the abstracts concerned and journal style does vary enormously. With some studies there may be wholly inadequate abstracts and this may mean that the introduction and/or conclusions of the article need to be examined – what is sometimes referred to as examining in detail.

Once the final relevant list has been drawn up, they then need to be read and summarized so that they can be classified. The categories chosen will be yours and they will reflect the sense that you make of what has gone on already in your research, which areas have been covered and in what depth so you can more confidently see the relevance and contribution your work makes to the whole. The analysis of the studies may look to group those studies by types of methodology used, by titles of journals, in which they are published, by types of firm studied, and by the conclusions reached; each of these being further classified where common themes can be discovered. To assist in this process (especially if the number of studies to be read covers 100 or more), coding software such as NVivo might need to be considered, which will be further discussed in Chapter 8. The resultant categorization then forms the basis of the structure for writing up your literature review; the conclusion of which will be a discussion of where your own work will relate, compliment and/or challenge existing studies. To help with this, reference should be made to 'organizing a draft' in the section below.

A good way to familiarize yourself with the systematic review method is to read a few recent editions of the *International Journal of Management Reviews* or consult the Advanced Institute of Management's web site (www.aimresearch.org) and to then begin to design and follow your own search protocols and criteria. Tranfield et al. (2004) have drawn up several phases that suggest what a systematic review might consist of. These range from preparation for the review to the final documentation and use of the results, as shown in the Table 3.1.

One of the problems with systematic reviews is that they often encourage the widespread use of citations based simply upon a reading of abstracts. Some academics have made cutting remarks about researchers who are happy to quote material that they have not actually read (but instead have assimilated concepts and ideas from other articles). We must be clear here and point out that if the material is a quotation from a secondary source, for example an author cited by another author and this is the only way in which the reference can be cited then that is one issue, but quite another is when reference is made that stretches beyond what we do not

TABLE 3.1 The systematic review process

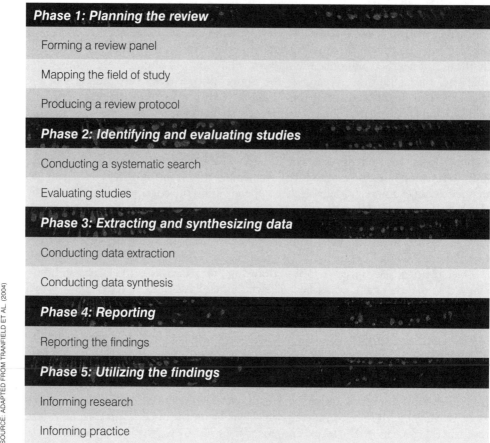

SOURCE: ADAPTED FROM TRANFIELD ET AL. (2004)

Phase 1: Planning the review
Forming a review panel
Mapping the field of study
Producing a review protocol
Phase 2: Identifying and evaluating studies
Conducting a systematic search
Evaluating studies
Phase 3: Extracting and synthesizing data
Conducting data extraction
Conducting data synthesis
Phase 4: Reporting
Reporting the findings
Phase 5: Utilizing the findings
Informing research
Informing practice

physically possess or know and what we have not read. It is probably advisable to avoid quoting this kind of material as it can lead to difficulties concerning comprehension and interpretation, and dangerous even if the citing or quotation is not entirely proper. The risk lies in revealing an author's thought without having recourse to one's own reasoning.

There is value in presenting a concrete example where a systematic review was used in a study. One such review is illustrated here in Example 3.4, which is the work of Thorpe et al. (2005) who conducted a systematic review of how small and medium enterprises (SMEs) create and use knowledge.

Writing reviews

Having read critically and produced analytical summaries of the literature, it is then important to synthesize an interpretation that both reflects and demonstrates comprehension and familiarity with the literature reviewed. There are several ways in which this can be achieved. One approach advocated by Buzan (2004)

EXAMPLE 3.4

Systematic review by Thorpe et al. (2005)

The study by Thorpe et al. (2005) had a number of key stages. *Background preparation:* a review panel was first formed consisting of the study's authors. The panel considered prospective sources of information, deciding on using peer-reviewed journals – both practitioner and academic. Books, reports and book chapters were excluded on the grounds that they did not provide the opportunity for searchable bibliographical databases. The team then used terms relevant to the study as keywords to determine the most appropriate databases given the peculiarities of the research. Thus, words such as know* and learn* were employed. The asterisk (*) helps retrieve variations and related words to the items entered in the search. For example, searching for the word know* encapsulates knowledge and its derivatives, including 'knowing'. The returns were analysed and used as guides in narrowing down the type of databases. In this case the databases with the most returns were chosen, which were ABI Proquest, Business Resource Premier, and Ingenta (incorporating Science Direct). Up to this point the process involved identifying relevant databases. The next step was to do detailed keyword searches.

Keyword search: since the topic was knowledge and learning within SMEs, the team's principal keywords and search strings included know*, learn*, SME or small firms and Entrepreneur*. When keywords were deemed to complement one another the word AND was used to enable the retrieval of a comprehensive result (for example know* AND learn*). Where they were seen to be substitutes OR was used instead (an example here is SMEs OR small firms). Of course know* and learn* may also be viewed as substitutes, and this was reflected in searches, with keyword searches alternating between the formats know* AND learn*, and, learn* OR know*.

Exporting results: the results were downloaded into the Procite software program. This gave each paper's keywords and abstracts. In the first instance, the team sifted through the abstracts determining each article's relevance to the subject of study. Those articles considered irrelevant were excluded as were those from other fields such as education and engineering. The key guiding idea at this stage was relevance and not the depth of the articles.

Further exclusions: with the articles put together, the next step was to interrogate them based on a number of criteria: theory robustness, implications for practice, coherence between data and arguments put forward, theory, relevance to SME knowledge (on account of findings, methods, and theories), and contributions made. The result of this exercise was the identification of papers that dealt with SME knowledge while meeting the set criteria.

Themes and conceptualizations: the study portrayed a landscape of studies into SME knowledge and produced broad themes as well as sub-themes about the subject. These findings were eventually published as an academic paper.

involves creating an idea map. A mind map of a research project is shown in Chapter 2. But wherever the researcher begins he or she will need to be able to construct a literature review intelligently, clearly and interestingly. Reviewing the literature is a difficult art as it often contains a variety of diverse materials that needs synthesis. In our view, it is the following that needs emphasizing:

1 The basic questions at the heart of the particular piece of research. These can sometimes best be illustrated by the questions posed by those currently working in the field. They often have a legislative authority to suggest the research questions that ought to be answered.

2 The genesis of the thinking at different periods of time in the study of a topic or phenomenon.

3 Relating the hypothesis and theoretical perspectives to the early stages of the research methodology explaining how the methodologies adopted might lead to new or more valid insights from the research.

4 Conceptualizing different dimensions from the literature review, for example, fundamental theories that relate to specific contexts.

5 Preparing the reader for the argument that they might be making as a result of having conducted the literature review. That is to say, compiling a literature review that makes clear just where a researcher's own contribution will be made later in the research.

In the example shown above (Thorpe et al. 2005) two aspects were highlighted from the review as being significant. One related to the importance of social capital, the other to absorptive capacity. Both these concepts formed a major focus of investigation. Examples of how to structure and write a literature review are dealt with in Chapter 12.

PLAGIARISM

Over the years there has been a steady growth in cases of plagiarism and discussions about plagiarism among students often reveal uncertainty and doubt regardless of the attention it receives. Generally, plagiarism involves presenting the work and ideas of other people and passing them off as your own, without acknowledging the original source of the ideas used. Although plagiarism is not a new issue, its existence has been less easy to detect and it is only through the advent of information technology and packages such as Turnitin (www.turnitin.com) that plagiarism can be detected. While Internet search engines may make information easier to acquire, they also serve to provide students with endless sources of material from which to 'cut and paste'. What were once cases of minor infringements have become a problem of epidemic proportions (Duggan, 2006). Similarly, while there maybe naïve use and sloppy referencing, Leask (2006) observes that there is a growth in deliberate plagiarism, especially as it relates to the Internet. He draws attention however to ambiguities that can exist between interpretations, arguing that plagiarism has different meanings, depending on the context. For example whether plagiarism relates to a research in the context of a report or exam, issues are raised about the variation in cultural norms and traditions in respect of citing material. All this is not helped by researchers who appeared to find no problem in 'borrowing', without referencing, large chunks of material from a US PhD student in order to compile material to support a particular position on Iraq, without reference to the original source, which the then UK prime minister went on to present more widely. But for the purposes of this book, discussions on plagiarism centre around conscious attempts by individuals to steal the work of others. Also under this heading are those researchers who, without due recognition or reference, memorize ideas that originate from other sources, and, after a degree of assimilation then go on to prefer these ideas as their own and as a consequence fail to add an appropriate acknowledgement (Park, 2003).

Examples of plagiarism

The recurring themes as to what constitutes plagiarism includes as we have already identified copying another person's material without proper acknowledgement or reference, paraphrasing others with out acknowledgement, thereby giving others the impression that the work represents your own original formulation, and of course buying ready-made material from professional writers. There is an increasing number of web sites that offer such services and some of those being offered are extremely sophisticated. Payment relates to the level of degree but individual topics can be specified. Of course for those who have to undergo an oral defence of their work the fact they are not attached to the literature soon means they are caught out, while references that are not in the university libraries also raise suspicion. In preparing this book, use has been made of the work of others, but references or acknowledgement will be seen in the text. Where researchers have provided data or material for incorporation or critical feedback obtained from colleagues they have been acknowledged by name at the front of the book. Park synthesized four different forms of plagiarism found to be common among students:

1 *Stealing material from another source and passing it off as your own, for example:*
   a *buying a paper from a research service, essay bank or term paper mill (either pre-written or specially written);*
   b *copying a whole paper from a source text without proper acknowledgement;*
   c *submitting another student's work, with or without that student's knowledge (e.g. by copying a computer disk).*
2 *Submitting a paper written by someone else (e.g. a peer or relative) and passing it off as their own.*
3 *Copying sections of material from one or more source texts, supplying proper documentation (including the full reference) but leaving out quotation marks, thus giving the impression that the material has been paraphrased rather than directly quoted.*
4 *Paraphrasing material from one or more source texts without supplying appropriate documentation. (2003: 475)*

In order to avoid plagiarism students should ensure that they have clearly referenced where others' words and concepts have been used but also where others' ideas have influenced their thought process. This involves keeping up-to-date and precise references about where you have accessed material from, as even accidental plagiarism is considered a serious issue. Given the increase in plagiarism, universities are employing a zero-tolerance policy and students are increasingly being penalized over this issue. In an attempt to combat this problem, institutions are beginning to run courses which aim to educate students to ensure that they are aware of what constitutes plagiarism. Given that plagiarism is a difficult and confusing area, it may be worthwhile checking if any such courses are available at your institution, where you will be most likely be given clear examples of both deliberate and accidental plagiarism to ensure you are aware of the potential perils of careless referencing.

CONCLUSION

In this chapter, we have aimed to provide insights into where to find relevant literature and other sources for a research project and what aspects are important when actually writing a literature review. The key points of this chapter, therefore, are:

- The literature review is a continuous process, requiring writing and re-focusing throughout the research project.

- The literature review should be used as a tool to strengthen your personal argument, rather than blindly repeat what has been said before.

- As with research in general, the review is about crafting and arguing for your contribution through demonstrating a thorough knowledge of what has gone before.

Which literature researches use for their literature review is, of course, influenced by the questions they want to answer in their research projects. The questions that researchers ask in their research projects are in turn affected by the philosophical assumptions that underlie the way they see the world. Which different philosophical assumptions there are, and in what way these may direct a research project will be discussed in the next chapter.

EXERCISE

3.2

Being organized and deciding on a bibliographical format

If you don't know what bibliographical format you are going to use, Endnote or ProCite are flexible and will enable changes to be made later. Examine a number of bibliographical formats and decide which you are going to use. If you are going to use a computer package such as one of the above, book yourself on a course from your training support unit.

EXERCISE

3.3

Pros and cons of searching systematically

In pairs, discuss the advantages and disadvantages of using systematic searches compared to a more personally directed approach to the identification of appropriate sources.

EXERCISE

3.4

Experience of doing a literature review

Select two journal articles relevant to your topic. The first should have been published within the last two years and the second should have been published before 1990. You should identify the following themes in each paper:

- What was the research question?
- What theoretical approach underpins each paper?
- What methodology was adopted for the collection of data?
- How were the data analysed?
- What was the nature and the size of the sample?
- What were the key findings?
- How many times has the article been cited?

FURTHER READING

Tranfield, D., Denyer, D. and Smart, P. (2003) 'Towards a methodology for developing evidence-informed management knowledge by means of systematic review,' *British Journal of Management*, 14 (3): 207–22.

This article examines the case for making reviews of the literature more systematic. The authors criticize traditional 'narrative' approaches to reviews for their lack of thoroughness and their failure to take account of evidence that might provide insights and guidance for practitioners and policymakers. They compare management to medicine, another applied discipline and evaluate the extent to which the process of systematic reviews in management also produces reliable knowledge that enhances practice. The challenges in such a methodological approach are also discussed.

Hart, C. (1998) *Doing a Literature Review: Releasing the Social Science Research Imagination*. London: Sage.

This book has been written for students from across the social sciences and humanities. It offers a practical and comprehensive guide to writing a literature review. It takes the reader through the initial stages of an undergraduate dissertation or postgraduate thesis.

THE PHILOSOPHY OF MANAGEMENT RESEARCH

4

LEARNING OBJECTIVES

- To understand the different philosophical assumptions 'hidden' beneath management research and to appreciate the strengths and weaknesses of each.

- To appreciate how different philosophical assumptions influence criteria for judging research quality.

- To locate your own philosophical assumptions.

Introduction

Two contrasting traditions: positivism versus social constructionism

Broadening the philosophical debate

Research philosophies underlying management research practice

Overviews of other philosophies

Conclusion

Further reading

INTRODUCTION

It is a capital mistake to theorise before one has data

ARTHUR CONAN DOYLE

The relationship between data and theory is an issue that has been hotly debated by philosophers for many centuries. Failure to think through philosophical issues such as this, while not necessarily fatal, can seriously affect the quality of management research, and they are central to the notion of research design. The aim of this chapter is therefore to consider the main philosophical positions that underlie the designs of management research – in other words, how do philosophical factors affect the overall arrangements which enable satisfactory outcomes from the research activity?

There are at least three reasons why an understanding of philosophical issues is very useful. First, it can help to clarify research designs. This not only involves considering what kind of evidence is required and how it is to be gathered and interpreted, but also how this will provide good answers to the basic questions being investigated in the research. Second, knowledge of philosophy can help the researcher to recognize which designs will work and which will not. It should enable him or her to avoid going up too many blind alleys and should indicate the limitations of particular approaches. Third, it can help the researcher identify, and even create, designs that may be outside his or her past experience. And it may also suggest how to adapt research designs according to the constraints of different subject or knowledge structures.

Arguments, criticisms and debates are central to the progress of philosophy. But it is unfortunate that within the social sciences such debates sometimes take the form of denigrating the other point of view, or of completely ignoring its existence. We believe that it is important to understand both sides of an argument because research problems often require eclectic designs, which draw from more than one tradition. Thus we try to provide here a balanced view of the different philosophical positions underlying research methods and designs, and to do this we have had to return to some of the original sources of these positions. The chapter therefore starts by reviewing some key debates among philosophers of the natural sciences and social sciences. We then dig a little deeper into these philosophies, and review a number of distinct philosophical alternatives.

TWO CONTRASTING TRADITIONS: POSITIVISM VERSUS SOCIAL CONSTRUCTIONISM

We start here with a straight debate between two contrasting views of how social science research should be conducted, and we will then broaden out the discussion in the following section. The two traditions are **positivism** and **social constructionism**.[1]

---

[1]We use this term, rather than the expression of 'social constructivism', which is preferred by Guba and Lincoln (1989) and Knorr-Cetina (1983).

In the red corner is constructionism; in the blue corner is positivism. Each of these positions has to some extent been elevated into a stereotype, often by the opposing side. Although it is now possible to draw up comprehensive lists of philosophical assumptions and methodological implications associated with each position, it is not possible to identify any philosopher who ascribes to all aspects of one particular view. Indeed, occasionally an author from one side produces ideas which belong more neatly to those of the other side.

Also when one looks at the practice of research, as we shall see below, even self-confessed extremists do not hold consistently to one position or the other. And although there has been a trend away from positivism towards constructionism since the early 1980s, there are many researchers, especially in the management field, who adopt a pragmatic view by deliberately combining methods drawn from both traditions. We elaborate on these two traditions below.

Positivism

The key idea of positivism is that the social world exists externally, and that its properties should be measured through objective methods, rather than being inferred subjectively through sensation, reflection or intuition. The French philosopher, Auguste Comte (1853), was the first person to encapsulate this view, as he said: 'All good intellects have repeated, since Bacon's time, that there can be no real knowledge but that which is based on observed facts'. This statement contains two assumptions: first, an ontological assumption, that reality is external and objective; and second, an epistemological assumption, that knowledge is only of significance if it is based on observations of this external reality. There follow from this a number of implications, although not all of them were proposed by Comte (see Table 4.1). It is worth repeating that these propositions are not simply the view of any single philosopher; they are a collection of points that have come to be associated with the positivist viewpoint. Some 'positivists' would disagree with some of these statements. Comte, for example, did not agree with the principle of reductionism. Wittgenstein, for example, argued strongly in his early work that all factual propositions can be reduced into elementary propositions which are completely independent of one another. But in his later work he challenged his earlier view on the grounds that elementary propositions, such as colours, could still be logically related to each other (Pears, 1971). So philosophers within one school not only disagree with each other; they may also disagree with themselves over time.

The view that positivism provides the best way of investigating human and social behaviour originated as a reaction to metaphysical speculation (Aiken, 1956). As such, this philosophy has developed into a distinctive **paradigm** over the last one and a half centuries. This term 'paradigm' has come into vogue among social scientists, particularly through the work of Kuhn (1962) who used it to describe the progress of scientific discoveries in practice, rather than how they are subsequently reconstructed within text books and academic journals.

Most of the time, according to Kuhn, science progresses in tiny steps, which refine and extend what is already 'known'. But occasionally experiments start to produce results that do not fit into existing theories and patterns. Then, perhaps many years later, a Galileo or Einstein proposes a new way of looking at things, which can

TABLE 4.1 Philosophical assumptions of positivism

- *Independence*: the observer must be independent from what is being observed.

- *Value-freedom*: the choice of what to study, and how to study it, can be determined by objective criteria rather than by human beliefs and interests.

- *Causality*: the aim of the social sciences should be to identify causal explanations and fundamental laws that explain regularities in human social behaviour.

- *Hypothesis and deduction*: science proceeds through a process of hypothesizing fundamental laws and then deducing what kinds of observations will demonstrate the truth or falsity of these hypotheses.

- *Operationalization*: concepts need to be operationalized in a way which enables facts to be measured quantitatively.

- *Reductionism*: problems as a whole are better understood if they are reduced into the simplest possible elements.

- *Generalization*: in order to be able to generalize about regularities in human and social behaviour it is necessary to select samples of sufficient size, from which inferences may be drawn about the wider population.

- *Cross-sectional analysis*: such regularities can most easily be identified by making comparisons of variations across samples.

account for both the old and the new observations. It is evident from these examples, and from the illustrations given in Chapter 2, that major scientific advances are not produced by a logical and rational application of scientific method. They result from independent and creative thinking which goes outside the boundaries of existing ideas. The result of this is a 'scientific revolution' which not only provides new theories, but which may also alter radically the way people see the world, and the kind of questions that scientists consider are important to investigate. The combination of new theories and questions is referred to as a new paradigm.

Social constructionism

The new paradigm which has been developed by philosophers during the last half century, largely in reaction to the application of positivism to the social sciences, stems from the view that 'reality' is not objective and exterior, but is socially constructed and given meaning by people. The idea of social constructionism then, as developed by authors such as Berger and Luckman (1966), Watzlawick (1984) and Shotter (1993), focuses on the ways that people make sense of the world especially through sharing their experiences with others via the medium of language. Social constructionism is one of a group of approaches that Habermas (1970) has referred to as interpretive methods. We will touch on these, and a number of other approaches, in the course of this and the following chapter.

What, then, is the essence of social constructionism? First, is the idea, as we have mentioned above, that 'reality' is determined by people rather than by objective and external factors. Hence the task of the social scientist should not be to gather facts and measure how often certain patterns occur, but to appreciate the different constructions and meanings that people place upon their experience. The focus should be on what people, individually and collectively, are thinking and feeling, and attention should be paid to the ways they communicate with each other, whether verbally or non-verbally. We should therefore try to understand and explain why people have different experiences, rather than search for external causes and fundamental laws to explain behaviour. Human action arises from the sense that people make of different situations, rather than as a direct response to external stimuli.

The methods of social constructionist research can be contrasted directly with the eight features of classical positivist research. They are summarized in Table 4.2. Again, it should be emphasized that these represent a composite picture rather than the viewpoint of any single author. Some of the distinctions in the table should be self-evident, but others require more explanation. We will therefore elaborate further on issues such as interests, units of analysis, theoretical generalizations and sampling as the stories of Chapters 4, 5 and 6 unfold.

TABLE 4.2 Contrasting implications of positivism and social constructionism

	Positivism	*Social constructionism*
The observer	must be independent	is part of what is being observed
Human interests	should be irrelevant	are the main drivers of science
Explanations	must demonstrate causality	aim to increase general understanding of the situation
Research progresses through	hypotheses and deductions	gathering rich data from which ideas are induced
Concepts	need to be defined so that they can be measured	should incorporate stakeholder perspectives
Units of analysis	should be reduced to simplest terms	may include the complexity of 'whole' situations
Generalization through	statistical probability	theoretical abstraction
Sampling requires	large numbers selected randomly	small numbers of cases chosen for specific reasons

The implications of holding these different views may be seen, for example, in the way researchers might study managerial stress. The social constructionist would be interested in the aspects of work that managers consider 'stressful', and perhaps in the strategies that they develop for managing these aspects. He or she would therefore arrange to talk with a few managers about their jobs, about the aspects they find more, or less, difficult, and would attempt to gather stories about incidents that they had experienced as stressful. The positivist, conversely, would start with the assumption that occupational stress exists and then would formulate measures of stress experienced by a large number of managers in order to relate them to external causes such as organizational changes, interpersonal conflicts, negative appraisals, etc. Measures of stress could be based on standardized verbal reports from the managers, or on physiological factors such as blood pressure.

BROADENING THE PHILOSOPHICAL DEBATE

In the discussion above we have referred to debates among natural scientists as well as social scientists, and we have also mentioned in passing the links between terms such as **ontology** and **epistemology**. This is because methodological choices for social scientists can be located within broader debates on the philosophy of science. Unfortunately, some philosophical terms are used interchangeably and consequently there is confusion about their meaning. So, although these wider issues are not central to the design of management research some clarification seems in order, and hence in this section of the chapter we expand on them before returning to management research per se.

We start in Table 4.3 with some definitions that are our own distillation of common usage among researchers. Since the second half of the book is concerned with the choice and application of individual methods we will concentrate on the first three terms now.

TABLE 4.3 Ontology, epistemology, methodology and method[1]

Ontology	Philosophical assumptions about the nature of reality.
Epistemology	General set of assumptions about the best ways of inquiring into the nature of the world.
Methodology	Combination of techniques used to enquire into a specific situation.
Methods	Individual techniques for data collection, analysis, etc.

[1]This framework is similar to the hierarchy used by Crotty (1998). His terms are, in order: epistemology, theoretical perspective, methodology and method. His use of theoretical perspective equates to our use of ontology, but we think that his ordering of terms leads to confusion because ontological concerns are more fundamental, and epistemological decisions follow from the determination of ontology.

Ontology and Epistemology

The first term, ontology, is the starting point for most of the debates among philosophers. Although there have been strong parallels between the debates within the natural sciences and the social sciences there have also been differences. Thus among philosophers of *natural science* the debate has been between **realism** and **relativism**. Realists come in several varieties. Traditional realists start with the position that the world is concrete and external, and that science can only progress through observations that have a direct correspondence to the phenomena being investigated. This extreme position has been modified by philosophers of science in recent decades who point out the difference on the one hand between the laws of physics and nature, and on the other hand, the knowledge, or theories, that scientists have about these laws. This position is labelled by Bhaskar as *transcendental* realism, which assumes that 'the ultimate objects of scientific inquiry exist and act (for the most part) quite independently of scientists and their activity' (1989: 12). Internal realists concentrate more on the processes of observation (epistemology) which have emerged in response to advances in physics. They point out that whether or not phenomena are concrete, it is only possible to gather indirect evidence of what is going on in fundamental physical processes (Putnam, 1987). The classical example is the Indeterminancy Principle, formulated by Werner Heisenberg in 1927, which states that: 'The more precisely the position is determined, the less precisely the momentum is known in this instant, and vice versa.' Thus it is never possible to obtain full and objective information about the state of a body because the act of experimentation itself will determine the observed state of the phenomenon being studied. Any attempt to measure the location of an electron will, for example, affect its velocity.

Internal realists do accept, however, that scientific laws once discovered are absolute and independent of further observations. The relativist position goes a stage further in suggesting that scientific laws may not be quite so immutable. It has been strongly influenced by the work of Latour and Woolgar (1979) who have studied the evolution of scientific ideas within research laboratories and noted how ideas only gain acceptance as being 'true' after much debate and discussion which is also tied in to the personal careers and statuses of the main protagonists. Furthermore, Knorr-Cetina (1983) points out that the acceptance of a particular theory, and hence the 'closure' of a scientific debate, may be highly influenced by the politics of business and commercial resources.

Realist scientists have responded vigorously to the relativist challenge by arguing that even if scientists work through social and political networks, the truth of scientific laws is quite independent of the process of discovery. Richard Dawkins, the biologist, famously comments that even the most dedicated relativist does not believe, when flying at 40,000 feet in a Boeing 747, that the laws of physics which hold the jet in the air are mere constructs of the imagination (Irwin, 1994).

The arguments among *social scientists* can, in some respects, be mapped onto the natural science debate. Here we expand on the view developed in the previous section by looking at three main ontological positions: **representationalism, relativism** and **nominalism**. The first two correspond roughly to the internal realist and relativist viewpoints of science, although the subject matter of social science is people rather than physical objects. The position of nominalism includes the view that it is the labels and names we attach to experiences and events which are crucial. The strongest debate occurs between the two more extreme positions with the sharpest attacks coming from the nominalist end (Cooper and Burrell, 1988; Cooper, 1992). The relativist position, in both science and social science, assumes that different observers may have different viewpoints and that, 'what counts for the truth can vary from place to place and from time to time' (Collins, 1983: 88).

Another variant of the relativist position is the idea of **critical realism**, which starts with the realist ontology of Bhaskar and then incorporates an interpretative thread (Sayer, 2000). Critical realism makes a conscious compromise between the extreme positions: it recognizes social conditions (such as class or wealth) as having real consequences whether or not they are observed and labelled by social scientists; but it also recognizes that concepts are human constructions. There are also differences in the way the quality of types of research should be judged. For example, the representationalist asks whether the research results are an accurate reflection of reality; the relativist will want to ensure that a broad sample of viewpoints has been taken into account; and the nominalist will be interested in where the labels came from and who influenced their acceptance. We will return to this point in Chapter 5 when we discuss different forms of **validity**.

In Table 4.4 we summarize the ontological positions in the social sciences, and indicate the link to corresponding epistemological positions. Although different terms are used for the extreme positions, in the middle position, the term 'relativism' tends to be used to refer either to ontology or epistemology. In the next section we look further at the methodological implications of each epistemological position.

Epistemology and methodology

The acceptance of a particular epistemology usually leads the researcher to adopt methods that are characteristic of that position. Conversely, where a given range of methods is employed in a particular study it is possible to infer that the researcher

TABLE 4.4 Ontologies and epistemologies in social science

Ontology of social science	Represent-ationalism	Relativism	Nominalism
Truth	requires verification of predictions.	is determined through consensus between different viewpoints.	depends on who establishes it.
Facts	are concrete, but cannot be accessed directly.	depend on viewpoint of observer.	are all human creations.
Epistemology of social science	**Positivism**	**Relativism**	**Social constructionism**

holds, perhaps implicitly, a corresponding epistemology. Table 4.5 summarizes the likely correspondence between the three main epistemologies and methods in the social sciences.

We comment briefly on a few of these concepts here since this will help to clarify the epistemological distinctions and their links to ontological positions, and we shall return to a number of them later in Chapter 5. In both the positivist and relativist positions it is assumed that there is a reality which exists independently of the observer, and hence the job of the scientist is merely to identify, albeit with increasing difficulty, this pre-existing reality. From the positivist perspective this is most readily achieved through the design of experiments that eliminate alternative explanations and allow key factors to be measured precisely in order to test predetermined hypotheses. From the relativist position, the assumed difficulty of gaining direct access to 'reality' means that multiple perspectives will normally be adopted, through both **triangulation** of methods and the surveying of views and experiences of large samples of individuals. Even so, it is only a matter of probability that the views collected will provide an accurate indication of the underlying situation.

The story from the constructionist perspective is different again. The researcher starting from a viewpoint that does not assume any pre-existing reality aims to understand how people invent structures to help them make sense of what is going on around them. Consequently, much attention is given to the use of language and conversations between people as they create their own meanings. Furthermore, the recognition that the observer can never be separated from the sense-making process means that researchers are starting to recognize that theories which apply to the subjects of their work must also be relevant to *themselves*. Such reflexive approaches to methodology are recognized as being particularly relevant when studies are considering power and cultural differences (Anderson, 1993; Easterby-Smith and Malina, 1999; Cunliffe, 2002).

TABLE 4.5 Methodological implications of different epistemologies within social science

Social science epistemologies Elements of methodologies	Positivism	Relativism	Social constructionism
Aims	Discovery	Exposure	Invention
Starting points	Hypotheses	Propositions	Meanings
Designs	Experiment	Triangulation	Reflexivity
Techniques	Measurement	Survey	Conversation
Analysis/interpretation	Verification/ falsification	Probability	Sense-making
Outcomes	Causality	Correlation	Understanding

These three philosophical positions are, of course, the 'pure' versions of each paradigm. Although the basic beliefs may be quite incompatible, when one comes down to the actual research methods and techniques used by researchers the differences are by no means so clear and distinct. Moreover, some management researchers deliberately use methods which originate in different paradigms, and there is something of a debate as to whether this is an acceptable strategy. We will come back to this debate later, but in the meantime we shall look at some classic examples of management and organizational research which are widely acknowledged as representing one or other of these points of view. As we shall see, none of them can be considered as completely pure applications of their assumed paradigms.

EXERCISE

4.1

Spot the epistemdogy!

Researchers normally betray their epistemology in the language they use. Here are four brief statements of the aims of different papers. Which is which? What clues did you spot?

A '… we advance research on absorptive capacity by extending and empirically validating the conceptual distinction between potential and realized absorptive capacity … To date, corresponding measures for dimensions that forms potential and realised absorptive capacity are still lacking.' (Jensen et al., 2005: 1000)

B 'This paper develops a holistic model of the overall process, by integrating knowledge oriented, routine oriented, and social/context perspectives.' (Hong et al., 2006: 1027)

C 'This article contributes to the study of managerial agency in the absorption of new knowledge and skills … Empirical data are drawn from a longitudinal study of a mature manufacturing firm in North Wales.' (Jones, 2006: 355)

D 'We (also) examine the influence of tacit and explicit knowledge on IJV performance. We find that relational embeddedness has a stronger influence on the transfer of tacit knowledge than it has on the transfer of explicit knowledge'. (Dhanaraj et al., 2004)

RESEARCH PHILOSOPHIES UNDERLYING MANAGEMENT RESEARCH PRACTICE

In this section we will review a number of 'classic' research studies that have ostensibly adopted one or other of the three philosophical positions identified for social science research in Tables 4.4 and 4.5. In each case we will consider to what extent the studies have been consistent with the principles of the respective paradigms.

Positivist management research

The first example of positivist research is the work of Pugh and his colleagues at Aston University into organizational structure. These studies achieved international fame when the results were written up in a series of articles that appeared in *Administrative Science Quarterly*, and which were subsequently collected together in a book (Pugh and Hickson, 1976). Possibly their main significance is the way they highlight the authority structures within organizations as key factors to consider when attempting to change, or understand, organizational behaviour. Pugh (1988) feels that this provides a useful counterbalance to the prevailing emphasis on individual and group-related factors.

EXAMPLE 4.1

Aston University studies on organizational structure

From 1961 onwards, Pugh's research team conducted a number of major studies of organizations in the West Midlands of England, and in other parts of the world. Their initial, and best-known, study involved a sample of 46 organizations with manufacturing or service operations in Greater Birmingham, each one employing at least 250 people. Organizations were selected to provide a good range of sizes and product types. The researchers used a highly structured interview schedule in order to gather data on a total of 132 measures which characterized the structure and context of each organization. From an analysis of the data across their sample, they came up with a number of general conclusions, for example, that size is the most important determinant of organizational structure, and that organizations which are closely dependent on other organizations tend to centralize as many decisions as possible.

In a separate account of the ideas and methods behind this work, Pugh (1983) describes himself as an 'unreconstructed positivist'. The key principles that he applies to his work include: focusing on hard data rather than opinions; looking for regularities in the data obtained; and attempting to produce propositions that can generalize from the specific example to the wider population of organizations. He states his view that facts and values can be clearly separated, but he also adopts a 'systems' view, which attempts to examine the full complexity of the data, rather than simply reducing it to its simplest elements. This latter point is perhaps a modification of the positivist view which has arisen partly as a result of developments in the natural sciences (Von Bertalanffy, 1962), and partly as a result of the ability of modern computers to enable researchers to conduct very sophisticated multivariate analysis of data, provided it is expressed in quantitative terms. Thus Pugh, by his own admission, sticks fairly closely to the positivist paradigm described above, although in his own research programme he also found it necessary to conduct more detailed case studies of individual organizations in the later stages of his research in order to give a fuller understanding of what was taking place inside (Pugh, 1988).

The second example of positivist research is the classic study of Hofstede (1984, 1991) into the effect of national cultures on social and work behaviour. This was based on 116,000 questionnaires completed between 1967 and 1972 by approximately 88,000 employees of IBM. Hofstede's data was totally quantitative and it was processed through a factor analysis to yield four dimensions indicative of national culture (see Table 4.6). Each of these dimensions was statistically independent in the sense that a high score on one would imply neither a high nor a low score on any of the other dimensions. Hofstede, as the researcher, was also distanced and independent from the respondents of the questionnaires. Thus, in terms of how it is presented, Hofstede's highly quantitative research appears to conform closely to the positivist paradigm.

But in the light of his own account of the research process (Hofstede, 1984), the degree of fit with the positivist paradigm is much less clear. For example, first he accepts that he is dealing with mental constructs rather than hard objective facts. The four main dimensions of national culture were not formulated as initial hypotheses, but only after considerable post hoc analysis of the data and much reading and discussion with other academic colleagues. Second, the labels attached to the dimensions were his words; they did not emerge through some disembodied process from the data. Third, he is fully aware of the importance of avoiding making assumptions about culture which imply that any one culture is superior to another; and therefore he accepts that his results are not necessarily value-free. Fourth, he recognizes that different methods will provide different perspectives on what is being studied, and therefore it is worth 'triangulating' where possible by using a combination of both quantitative and qualitative methods. Thus, in practice, some of Hofstede's methods show signs of the relativist paradigm.

Relativist management research

The first example we offer here comes from an international study into human resource management (HRM) practices in 10 different countries for which the authors published a detailed review of the methodology, both as intended and as it worked out in practice (Teagarden et al., 1995).

TABLE 4.6 Cultural dimensions

Dimension	Features resulting in high score
Individualism	Whether a society emphasizes individual autonomy as opposed to responsibility to the group
Masculinity	How far roles in society are differentiated between men and women
Power distance	The extent to which inequality is accepted by the less powerful people in society
Uncertainty avoidance	The need for rules and concern about 'law and order' in a society

EXAMPLE 4.2

International study of human resource management

The study by Teagarden and colleagues (1995) was co-ordinated in the USA, but implemented through collaboration with academics based in each of the countries covered by the survey. The main aims were: to identify which HRM practices were most commonly used in a range of companies, countries and industrial sectors; to establish which HRM practices were linked to organizational performance; and to determine to what extent both practices and their effectiveness were situation-specific, or whether there were some universal principles that could be applied. To this end the researchers devised a standard questionnaire which was to be mailed to a random sample of approximately 800 companies in each country. Completed questionnaires were to be returned to the project coordinators for analysis and interpretation.

In Example 4.2 we can see most of the features of the relativist position as characterized in Tables 4.4 and 4.5. It starts with the ontological assumption that there are 'HRM practices' within companies, and that with a bit of ingenuity the researcher will be able to identify and group these practices both within and across countries. Some ingenuity will be required because the HRM practices are not immediately evident, hence the need to conduct surveys across substantial samples of companies in order to be able to describe the typical patterns and to have a good understanding of the likely degrees of variation. There is also the suggestion that correlations will be required in order to establish relations between particular patterns, their assumed outcomes in terms of organizational effectiveness, and a range of contextual variables.

That was how the project was intended to work. In practice, the researchers found that they had to make a number of substantial adjustments to cope with the problems of cross-national empirical research. Translations of the core questionnaire not only had to deal with linguistic equivalence (through using back-translations), but they also had to be adapted for local cultural differences – for example, the German managers felt insulted by the range of salary levels provided from the translation of the US version, and these had to be adapted accordingly. The researchers also found that they could not achieve random sampling of companies because in some countries, such as the UK and Mexico, companies would not respond to anonymous questionnaires. Hence the local contacts had to use their personal networks to obtain responses, which meant that the samples were, by definition, not going to be random.

Teagarden and her colleagues saw these factors as threats to the overall quality of the project, and felt caught in the dilemma of wanting to present the project as a rigorous, positivistic study, and yet recognizing the practical limitations on this aspiration. They question themselves as follows: 'How far can a study deviate from the normal rules of scientific rigor and still make a contribution? Is it advisable to strive for positivistic methods, or should alternative approaches be granted more legitimacy? How can researchers compensate for such disadvantages?' (1995: 1276).

This suggests that the relativist position can be uncomfortable for researchers, especially when they operate within an academic tradition which gives primacy to positivistic methods.

Another study, still within the relativist tradition, but on a smaller scale than the above study is provided by Tsang (1997, 1999, 2002). The researcher aimed to discover what and how Singaporean companies learn from foreign direct investments (FDIs) in China and from conducting international joint-ventures (IJVs) with Chinese companies. His gained access to 19 Singaporean companies with business experience in China, and then carried out approximately 80 interviews with both Singaporean and Chinese managers working for these companies. In addition he examined records of meetings and reports of visits by members of these companies whenever he could gain access to them. On the basis of his data he was able to conclude that Singaporean companies rarely learn much from their business links in China, although in most cases there was evidence of considerable transfer of technological and managerial systems to the Chinese partners. He was also able to infer a number of reasons for this one-way traffic. First, most Singaporean managers felt that their systems were superior to those in China, and therefore they did not have much to learn from Chinese partners. Second, although managers seconded to the Chinese operations generally learnt a lot during their stay (especially if they were assigned full-time for a substantial period of time) it was hard for them to transfer this learning back to the parent company because no institutional structures were set up for this purpose.

This study has a number of features of the relativist tradition. First, there is an ontological assumption that specific practices and structures exist which will lead to organizational learning taking place, and that it is possible for the researcher to map these out. The methodology involved semi-structured interviews, which meant that, as far as possible, the same questions were asked in each of the interviews. This provided a structured and standardized set of data from which associations between variables could be investigated. There was also a questionnaire which was analysed using probabilistic statistics which was described in the earlier publication but was not mentioned in the later publication (Tsang, 1999). Together it is therefore possible to see a number of methods and viewpoints being used in order to be able to identify and represent, as accurately as possible, the phenomena under investigation. This form of triangulation is another hallmark of a relativist design.

Social constructionist management research

Finally, we consider two examples of social constructionist research here, both focusing on what managers do in practice, but separated by a period of over 30 years. The reason for choosing studies that look at the same substantive topic is to show that this general type of research is by no means a new invention, and that nevertheless ideas and methods have evolved significantly over this period. First we will look at the pioneering work of Melville Dalton (1959), and then at a study by Tony Watson (1994).

Dalton studied managerial work from the perspective of an insider. This was published as a major book in 1959, and he then followed it up with a paper reviewing his methodology (Dalton, 1964). In the review he describes the ideas and philosophies that guided his work, and discusses some of the ethical dilemmas that were encountered. For a start Dalton rejects the classical 'scientific method' as inappropriate to his work (in this case, the sequence of hypothesis, observation, testing and confirmation or disconfirmation of hypotheses). He points out that not only is this method rather idealistic in the sense that natural scientists do not usually follow it themselves (except in the school laboratory), but it was also not feasible to use it in the situation he had chosen. He is opposed to the tendency to quantify and to reduce variables to their smallest components on the grounds that this loses most of the real meaning of the situation.

EXAMPLE 4.3

Melville Dalton's study of managerial behaviour

Dalton decided to study the behaviour of managers while he was working as a manager in the same organization. Curiously enough, although he is quite open about his methods and some of the dilemmas this caused, he does not say precisely what his role was, but remarks that this allowed him 'much unquestioned movement about the firm'. While working in the company he gathered data from his own observations and from those of a number of informants. The informants were clearly aware to some extent of Dalton's purposes, but the rest of the people in the company were largely ignorant of what he was doing – his role was therefore partly overt and partly covert. This clearly meant that he was not in a position to establish any formal experiments to test his ideas, although he comments that some of his informants who were aware of his general purpose, occasionally deliberately set up situations for Dalton to observe. Thus in no way was Dalton an independent observer of what was taking place; his presence certainly had some impact on the company, even though he does not speculate much about the nature of that impact.

Although much of his data was qualitative, in the form of observations by him and comments from his informants, he was not averse to collecting a certain amount of quantitative data such as the salaries of managers in the company. This he obtained informally from a secretary in the personnel department in exchange for counselling about whether or not she should marry her boyfriend (in the end she did marry him, against Dalton's advice!). It is quite clear that Dalton did not start the research with any clearly preconceived set of hypotheses and theories to test; his research grew out of his own 'confusions and irritations'. Rather than trying to formulate explicit hypotheses and guides for his work, he contented himself with framing simple questions about things that were taking place and which he did not clearly understand. After looking at a number of specific topics such as the reasons for conflict between different groups of people or the way people accounted for the success of some managers, he finally settled on the overall scheme of attempting to understand the distinction and relationships between official and unofficial action within the organization.

Dalton was also aware that having looked at only one organization in depth this could limit the generalisability of his conclusions. To counter this he supplemented his work with studies through other contacts in several other organizations in the same area, which gave him the confidence that the things he had observed in his own company, Milo, were quite likely to be taking place in most other organizations, at least in that part of the USA. Dalton follows many of the precepts of the social constructionist paradigm, in the sense that he took an open minded view of what he wanted to find out, and then engaged in extensive conversations with people backed up by observations and access to documents. Conceptually, he was trying to make sense of what he had observed and to link this to existing theories, such as the distinction between the formal and informal organization. But there are a number of subtle differences between Dalton and the more recent study of managerial behaviour conducted by Tony Watson (1994), who starts by acknowledging his debt to Dalton.

Watson entered his host company, ZTC Ryland, overtly as an academic researcher, although he also agreed to conduct a project for his sponsors at the same time. He thus had a mixed agenda, which was reasonably explicit. The official project was to develop a listing of competencies required of managers who would be able to function effectively in the company's new business environment. Unofficially, he was interested in several things including the impact of modern management theory on a company which had gone to considerable lengths to introduce topical ideas like total quality management, team working, performance related pay, etc.

His book differs from Dalton's in several ways, particularly in the degree of reflexivity that he offers about his motives and methods. Here he is influenced by ideas from ethnography and comments on the importance of 'reveal(ing) the hand behind the text' (Watson, 1994: 7). This is done by offering portions of transcripts which show his contribution to discussions, which demonstrate his personal relationship with informants, and which occasionally discuss explicitly why informants give him stories that are different to those offered to their bosses. This enables him to develop theoretical observations about the differences between 'official' and 'unofficial' discourses in the company, and the way that exchanges are strategically shaped. Also, in contrast to Dalton he does not seek additional sites for his observations, recognizing the distinction that has arisen between theoretical and empirical generalizations.

The two studies by Dalton and Watson are classic examples of how to conduct observational studies from a social constructionist perspective. In example 4.4 we summarize a project conducted by an postgraduate student at lancaster that follows this tradition. As we will see from Chapter 5, some contemporary researchers have extended the method, for example by commenting systematically on their own roles (reflexivity), or by involving members of the host organization in the direction and interpretation of observations (collaborative research). But the fundamental building blocks remain the same.

Mixed methods in management research

The above studies were selected as relatively pure examples, but as we have shown, in practice the researchers involved do not hold scrupulously to any single approach. Although the distinction between paradigms may be very clear at the philosophical level, as Burrell and Morgan (1979) argue, when it comes to the choice of specific methods, and to the issues of research design, the distinction breaks down

EXAMPLE 4.4

Student research based on personal observations

Neil was a training manager in a hospital which was about to merge with another (more prestigious) hospital and started to keep a diary where he kept notes of meetings he attended and conversations he had (or overheard) with other managers. A year after starting the diary he joined the part-time MA in Management Learning at Lancaster, and when looking for a subject for his dissertation suddenly realized that he had a rich and longitudinal set of data about organizational change. On reviewing his diary he noticed that the quality and strategies of leaders were critical to the success and failure of post-merger integration in different parts of the two hospitals. He therefore based his (successful) dissertation on observations and quotes from his diary supplemented by formal interviews with key managers and their subordinates.

(Punch 1986; Bulmer, 1988). However, authors and researchers who work in organizations and with managers argue that one should attempt to mix methods to some extent, because it provides more perspectives on the phenomena being investigated. Fielding and Fielding (1986) used both quantitative and qualitative methods to good effect in researching organizations such as the National Front, in Britain. Cresswell (2003) suggests that qualitative and quantitative methods may be mixed either simultaneously or sequentially, although in the latter case he assumes that qualitative methods should precede quantitative methods.

We have reservations about mixing methods when they represent very distinct ontologies. And although the researcher may get away with using mixed methods where the overall direction and significance of the two sources are fairly similar, there are difficulties when different kinds of data say contradictory things about the same phenomena. A personal illustration is provided in Example 4.5.

Strengths and weaknesses of the main traditions

Before we leave the discussion of how paradigms may underlie practical examples, it is worth summarizing from a pragmatic view what are seen as some of the strengths and weaknesses of each position (Table 4.7). This should help the researcher to choose which methods and aspects are most likely to be of help in a given situation. In the case of quantitative methods and the *positivist* paradigm, the main strengths are that they can provide wide coverage of the range of situations, they can be fast and economical and, particularly when statistics are aggregated from large samples, they may be of considerable relevance to policy decisions. On the debit side, these methods tend to be rather inflexible and artificial; they are not very effective in understanding processes or the significance that people attach to actions; they are not very helpful in generating theories; and because they focus on what is, or what has been recently, they make it hard for the policy-maker to infer what changes and actions should take place in the future. And much of the data gathered may not be relevant to real decisions even though it can still be used to support the covert goals of decision makers.

EXAMPLE 4.5

A problem with mixed methods

Morgan Tanton and Mark Easterby-Smith carried out a comparative evaluation study of two executive management programmes (Courses A and B), held in two different business schools (respectively, Institutions A and B). Observations during the course, and qualitative data obtained from follow-up interviews, showed quite clearly that Course A was superior to Course B, but the quantitative data in the form of student ratings about the two courses showed to a high level of significance that Course B was preferred to Course A. Was this discrepancy caused by the methods used, or could it highlight some unusual features of the two courses being examined? To resolve this dilemma we showed the data to participants on a later course, and asked for their explanations. First, participants commented that they tended to be rather cautious when filling in multiple choice rating forms, because they could never be sure what the data would be used for; therefore, they usually avoided extreme responses in either direction. Second, the course designs and institutional settings affected the criteria that participants used for evaluating the two courses. In Institution A the emphasis was on the longer term application of what had been learnt; in Institution B the emphasis was on the immediate quality of sessions conducted within the classroom. Thus it was not surprising that the rating forms that were completed at the end of the course showed one pattern; whereas follow-up interviews conducted some months later showed another pattern. Ironically, it was only through talking further to some of the participants (i.e. through using qualitative methods) that we were able to come up with a satisfactory explanation of the discrepancy. The moral of this story is to be wary of mixing methods simply for the sake of getting a slightly richer picture, because you may get more than you bargained for. The reality of what is being investigated may be considerably more complex than any one data collection method, and hence sharply contradictory positions are very possible when different methods are combined. These will need further exploration and explanation, which will take more time than expected.

The strengths and weaknesses of the *social constructionist* paradigm and associated qualitative methods are fairly complementary. Thus they have strengths in their ability to look at how change processes over time, to understand people's meanings, to adjust to new issues and ideas as they emerge, and to contribute to the evolution of new theories. They also provide a way of gathering data which is seen as natural rather than artificial. There are, of course, weaknesses. Data collection can take up a great deal of time and resources, and the analysis and interpretation of data may be very difficult, and this depends on the intimate, tacit knowledge of the researchers. Qualitative studies often feel very untidy because it is harder to control their pace, progress, and end points. And there is also the problem that many people,

TABLE 4.7 Strengths and weaknesses of different epistemologies

	Strengths	Weaknesses
Positivist	Can provide wide coverage. Potentially fast and economical. Easier to provide justification of policies.	Inflexible and artificial. Not good for process, meanings or theory generation. Implications for action not obvious.
Relativist	Accepts value of multiple data sources. Enables generalizations beyond present sample. Greater efficiency including outsourcing potential.	Requires large samples. Cannot accommodate institutional and cultural differences. Problems reconciling discrepant information.
Social Constructionist	Good for processes, and meanings. Flexible and good for theory generation. Data collection less artificial.	Can be very time consuming. Analysis and interpretations are difficult. May not have credibility with policy makers.

especially policymakers, may give low credibility to studies based on apparently 'subjective' opinions.

It is tempting, then, to see the relativist position as a useful compromise that can combine the strengths, and avoid the limitations, of each. But life is not that simple: the *relativist* position is distinct and has its own strengths and weaknesses. The main strengths are that: it accepts the value of using multiple sources of data and perspectives; it enables generalizations to be made beyond the boundaries of the situation under study; and it can be conducted efficiently, for example, through outsourcing any survey work to specialized agencies. The weaknesses are that: large samples are required if results are to have credibility, and this may be costly; the requirement for standardization means it may not be able to deal effectively with the cultural and institutional differences found within international studies; and it may be hard to reconcile discrepant sources of data that point to different conclusions.

OVERVIEWS OF OTHER PHILOSOPHIES

Up to this point, we have reviewed the fundamental philosophical positions which underlie the practice of management research. We have discussed and evaluated them in an open sense in order to provide options which the researcher can choose depending on the situation and his or her interests. However, there are also a number of philosophical positions which have been worked out as coherent schools of thought, and which, to some extent, exclude other positions. We have already mentioned critical realism in passing, and this will be one of a number of positions to which numbers of social researchers will adhere. Hence it seems important to explain a little more about these philosophical frameworks since they represent relatively coherent ways of thinking which are promoted by influential proponents. In this section, we cover, in alphabetical order: critical theory, feminism, hermeneutics, postmodernism, pragmatism and structuration theory.

Critical theory

Critical theory started as an intellectual movement, also known as the Frankfurt School, which sought to critique the effects of society and technology on human development. The key figure in this movement was Habermas (1970) who argues that society leads to inequalities and alienation, yet this is invisible to people who do not realise what is taking place. He therefore argues that there is a degree of irrationality in capitalist society that creates a false consciousness regarding wants and needs. Thus people are seduced into wanting consumer products that they do not really need.

Habermas also identifies clear differences between the natural and social sciences: the former being based on sense experiences, and the latter on communicative experiences. This means that although understanding in the natural sciences is one-way (monologic), where scientists observe inanimate objects; in the social sciences communication should be two-way (dialogic), with both researchers and the researched trying to make sense of the situation. Hence he suggests that only through dialogue will social scientists be able to work effectively. Another important point introduced by Habermas (1970) is the idea that knowledge is determined by interests and very often it is the more powerful people in society who determine what is regarded as 'true'. Consequently, truth should be reached through discussion and rational consensus, rather than being imposed by one group on another.

Critical theory has several implications in management and organizational research. It casts a sceptical eye on the motives and impact of powerful groups and individuals, which in an emancipatory way shows a concern for the interests of the least powerful members. And of course there is increasing relevance to being aware of the way that knowledge is determined by political processes – especially within the so-called knowledge intensive organizations.

Feminism

Feminism is critical of the status quo, but from a very specific angle: that women's experiences have been undervalued by society and by scientific enquiry. From a philosophical view it contains a strong critique of science on the grounds that women's perspectives have been ignored by most scientific enquiry, in at least five aspects (Blaikie, 1993): (1) there a very few women employed within science; (2) there is gender bias in the definition of research problems; (3) there is bias in the design and interpretation of research; (4) there are too many rigid dualisms in male-dominated science; and (5) science is not as rational and objective as it claims to be. Furthermore, it is claimed that similar processes operate in the social sciences especially with structured interviews which create a status difference between the interviewer and respondent, even when the interviewer is a woman (Cotterill, 1992). In particular it is emphasized that external knowledge is impossible and we must therefore understand human behaviour from within, through understanding the experiences of women themselves.

There is also an emancipatory agenda to feminism, although in relation to (social) science, there is a split between epistemologies known as 'feminist empiricism' and 'feminist standpoint'. The former assumes that the problem is not with science itself, but with the way it is conducted, therefore there is a need to rectify the norms and procedures of the natural sciences and the social sciences so that they incorporate a gendered perspective. The feminist standpoint, on the other hand, is more radical. It suggests that social science and its methods are fundamentally flawed, and it needs to be completely rethought. In particular, it needs to include issues of power dynamics and gender differences, and should make a far greater use of subjective experiences and the procedures of reflexivity. Its relevance to management research is not only that it provides a spotlight on the historical and continuing inequalities of women working in most organizations, but it also provides sensitivity to other areas of discrimination within organizational life, which may be caused by other factors such as race or age.

Hermeneutics

Although **hermeneutics** were originally developed by Protestant groups in 17th-century Germany as a means of interpreting the Bible, it still has some relevance to management research. Essentially it provides insight into ways of interpreting textual material which can comprise both formal written texts and spoken words which can be recorded. Two of the best known proponents of hermeneutics are Gadamer (1989) and Ricoeur (1981).

Gadamer is particularly concerned about the context within which texts are written. He points out that contemporary interpretations of earlier texts are influenced by the culture in which the interpreter is located, so in order to understand a particular text one must try to understand what is going on in the world of the writer at the time that the text is written. Ricoeur argues that when reading any text there is bound to be a gap between the author and the reader due to temporal differences – which he refers to as 'distanciation'. Ideally, there needs to be some kind of discourse between the author and the reader at the same point in time, but in the case of historical texts this is no longer possible. We therefore have to be aware that there may be no single, and correct, interpretation of a particular text, because both the writing and the reading will be context dependent.

From the viewpoint of management research, some of the insights from herme-neutics have obvious relevance if the researcher wishes to analyse corporate docu-ments such as annual reports. In this case, instead of, for example, conducting a content analysis of statements about the environment in annual reports for 1980, 1990 and 2000, one would need to analyse references in each report separately in relation to the social, economic and political context at each point of time. Thus the analysis would the between context based observations, rather than simple additions and enumerations of mentions.

Postmodernism

Postmodernism first came to wide academic attention with the English publication of Jean-François Lyotard's (1984) book, *The Postmodern Condition*, although the term had been used intermittently in relation to literary criticism since 1926 (Chia, 2008). A loose cluster of other, mainly French, philosophers have been associated with the development of ideas around postmodernity, including Derrida and Foucault.

There are three key ideas to postmodernism. First, it provides a critique of scientific progress as being linear and continuous, suggesting that it is discontinuous and contested. Lyotard, for example, examines the impacts of computerization on the control of knowledge, and the relationships between large corporations and states. Second, it is associated with a somewhat experimental movement in architecture and the arts, which seeks to redress the excesses of modernism, for example the bleak concrete architecture of the 1960s. Thus postmodern architecture tends to be very eclectic, drawing upon different traditions and ideas, and therefore avoiding the large scale regularity of a modern architecture. Third, as we have discussed above it contains an ontological position which is opposed to realism, though it is sometimes dismissed as supporting relativism and mere nihilism.

There are several implications for organizational research. First, the opposition to systematic control and regularity leads to an emphasis on flux and flexibility. Thus, postmodernists do not see organizations as static and monolithic, and this makes their perspective particularly sensitive to organizational dynamics and change. Second, the opposition to realism places an emphasis on the visible elements and processes of organizations, including tacit knowledge and the informal processes of decision-making. Finally, postmodernism retains a critical edge and is sceptical about the role and motivation of large industrial organizations, and questions whether they are of lasting value to society.

Pragmatism

Pragmatism originated in the writings of 19th-century American philosophers, particularly William James and John Dewey. A central theme of pragmatism is that in the social world there are no pre-determined theories or frameworks that shape knowledge and understanding. Essentially, any meaning structures, which get developed, must come from the lived experience of individuals. John Dewey (1916), in particular, talks about the need to balance concrete and abstract on one hand, and reflection and observation on the other.

Perhaps it is no coincidence, since Dewey was an educationalist, that pragmatism has had a significant impact on theories of learning within organizations. The Kolb Learning Cycle (Kolb, 1984) adopts a pragmatic approach, suggesting that learning takes place as a continual movement from concrete experience, to reflective observation, to abstract conceptualization, to active experimentation and back to concrete experience. Some organizational theorists have adopted elements of pragmatism because it offers a synthesis between features often regarded as irreconcilable dualisms, such as positivism/anti-positivism (Brandi and Elkjaer, 2008). And the impact of pragmatism on management research methods can be seen particularly in the tradition and methods of grounded theory – which we will discuss in some detail in the next chapter.

Structuration theory

Structuration theory is most associated with the work of Anthony Giddens (1984), where he develops the idea of 'duality of structure', in that structure and agency should not be regarded as pre-ordained. Instead, he suggests that structures are created and recreated through social action and the agency of individuals, and structure then guides and constrains individual agency. Hence, there is a continual interaction between social structure and social action.

Philosophically he is at pains to point out that the laws of science and social science are fundamentally different, because the former are potentially universal, while the latter depend upon the context (including both structure and action) in which things are taking place. He is also concerned about the use of language, pointing out that words are not precisely 'representational', and their use depends on agreement about their meaning which may be the product of debates and reinterpretations. Because language is essentially problematic he therefore advocates that social scientists should try to avoid specialist language, because it potentially obscures and creates confusion to outsiders. In order to communicate insights from social science he suggests that social scientists in the normal course of their work should attempt to use common-sense language.

From the viewpoint of management research, structuration theory has relevance to understanding the relationships between employees and the organizations within which they work, or between communications and the information systems which are supposed to facilitate them. In other words, it can throw light on aspects of organizations where there is some kind of structural duality.

CONCLUSION

In this chapter we have concentrated on the philosophies that underlie management research. Our main aim has been to help the reader identify philosophical assumptions underlying other people's work and to understand how they might influence and assist our own research endeavours. The key points of this chapter are:

- All researchers hold philosophical assumptions, whether or not they are aware of them.

- The strongest philosophical contrast is between realist and interpretative ontologies.

- There is often correspondence between ontologies, epistemologies and methodologies.

- Researchers need to be aware of their own philosophical assumptions.

- Although philosophies are normally expounded in pure form, their application to research practice often involves compromise.

So far, the discussion has been inevitably theoretical. In the next chapter we will start to work on how these philosophical positions influence specific research methods, and will provide a number of illustrations, and practical exercises to assist in developing research plans, or designs.

EXERCISE
4.2

Identifying your own philosophical positions

Write down a very brief description of some research that you are planning to do, or might do, including a title, the main question, and how you would do it (one sentence for each). Consider (1) what ontology you are adopting (i.e. how far do you consider the thing you are investigating real/objective, or social/subjective), and (2) what epistemology you are likely to adopt (positivist, relativist, or social constructionist).

Share/exchange with two colleagues and try to challenge the analysis that each provides.

EXERCISE
4.3

A balloon debate

The idea of a 'balloon debate' is that contestants have to imagine that they are travelling in a hot air balloon that is running out of fuel and is about to crash into a mountain. In order to save the lives of the majority, it is decided that one person must be tipped out of the basket. Each person in the basket therefore has to argue why they would represent the greatest loss to society if they were to be sacrificed.

Within the balloon debate each person normally has to argue the case for a famous person or an ideology. In this case we suggest each group argues the case for one of the philosophical positions outlined above. So, divide into groups of 4 or 5 people. Each group should:

- Pick one general philosophical position described in the penultimate section (i.e. critical theory, feminism, hermeneutics, etc.).

- Summarize its main features.

- Draw out methodological implications for researching a question or issue.

- Make the case to the rest of the class for why this is a valuable philosophy/method and why it should not be thrown out of the balloon.

After each group has presented, groups are to identify one of two philosophies that should remain in the balloon (no self nominations or tactical voting!)

FURTHER READING

Blaikie, N. (1993) *Approaches to Social Enquiry*. Cambridge: Polity Press.

This book provides an excellent overview of different philosophical approaches to social research, with particular attention to the question of whether the research methods in the natural sciences are appropriate for the social sciences. It is quite comprehensive and very useful, provided you are prepared to put in the effort!

Hassard, J. and Parker, M. (eds) (1993) *Postmodernism and Organizations*. London: Sage.

Since postmodernism is such a wide and disparate field, it is probably best to start with edited collections. This book is one of a number of edited works on postmodernism, but has the advantage that it focuses on the relevance and application of postmodernism to organization and management theory. Contributors include many of the leading European management scholars with expertise in postmodernism.

Sayer, A. (2000) *Realism and Social Science*. London: Sage.

An important book which explains the origins of critical realism, discusses its application to research methods, and examines how it fits in with wider philosophies of social science. Although well written, it tackles complex ideas, so can be hard going at times – so perhaps not an ideal bedtime reading companion.

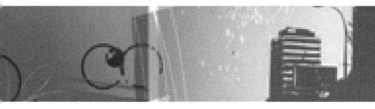

DESIGNING MANAGEMENT RESEARCH

5

LEARNING OBJECTIVES

- To appreciate how research philosophies impact on research designs.

- To understand what is regarded as (good) theory within each tradition.

- To develop and critique research designs.

Introduction

Qualitative and quantitative designs

Positivist research designs

Relativist research designs

Constructionist research designs

Broad-based methods

Generic issues

Contributing to theory

Implications

Conclusion

Further reading

INTRODUCTION

As suggested in the previous chapter, research designs are about organizing research activity, including the collection of data, in ways that are most likely to achieve the research aims. Imagine you wish to conduct empirical research (i.e. gathering your own data) into the changes in corporate accounting practices following the Enron scandal. Following the three philosophical positions outlined in the previous chapter, you might choose (1) to conduct a review of new legislation and accountancy practices published over the period 2002–2005, or (2) to send out a postal questionnaire to 200 members of the Chartered Institute of Management Accountants, or (3) to get a job for a year in the accounting department of a US energy company.

Each of these brief statements includes at least three decisions about research designs. In (1) there is a decision to focus on two categories of written documents published over a specific period of time; in (2) the decision is to design a questionnaire that will be mailed to a specific number of people who belong to one professional association; in (3) the decision is to invest personal time in observing accountancy practices in a US company within a specific industry. Each of these decisions specifies courses of action in preference to other options. For example, the focus on published sources precludes internal corporate documents; the decision to mail the questionnaire precludes face-to-face interviews; and the decision to work in one company precludes obtaining direct data from other companies.

This is the start of research design: it is about making choices about what will, and will not, be observed. But each of these designs is incomplete, and there are many other choices to be made, and features to be specified. A research design is a statement written, often before any data is collected, which explains and justifies what data is to be gathered, how and where from. It also needs to explain how the data will be analysed and how this will provide answers to the central questions of the research.

In this chapter we explain what a research design is, what are the main choices that need to be made, how research designs vary according to the underlying philosophical position, and how the quality of research designs can be judged. In the later chapters of the book we will be looking in detail at methods for gathering and analysing qualitative and quantitative data; but questions of research design need to be resolved before gathering (much) data.

QUALITATIVE AND QUANTITATIVE DESIGNS

There are many factors that affect research designs. As discussed in the previous chapter the philosophical position, particularly the ontology or epistemology, has a major impact on the way research is conducted and evaluated. In this chapter we maintain the distinction between three epistemological positions – positivist, relativist and social constructionist – as background to understanding the different methods and choices available.

However, there is also an important surface distinction, between so-called qualitative and quantitative methods. The former involves collecting data that is mainly in the form of words, and the latter involves data which is either in the form of, or can be expressed as, numbers. Many textbooks use this distinction as the key to understanding different research designs. In our view, this apparent simplification can lead to confusion, because qualitative and quantitative methods may be used according to both constructionist and positivist epistemologies, and be underpinned by both nominalist and realist ontologies.

For that reason, we have decided to use the three basic epistemologies as the framework of this chapter – although later in the book we use the qualitative–quantitative distinction when discussing how to gather and analyse different forms of data. Later in the chapter, we discuss a number of dilemmas and choices, which repeat in each area. These include: identifying the unit of analysis, choices about whether the research should generate theories or test theories; and whether the researcher is seeking to generate universal theory, or locally relevant knowledge; whether theory or data should come first; the tension between reductionism and holism; and the relative value of verfication and falsification.

In Table 5.1 we have plotted the location of different methodologies in relation to different epistemologies. We use one star to indicate potential links, but two stars to indicate the position with which each methodology is primarily associated. As can be seen from the spread of stars, some methods can be used in very different ways, and so can cover a range of epistemologies. In the following sections we concentrate on positivist, relativist and constructionist epistemologies, and these are illustrated by the methodologies that are primarily associated with them: experimental methods,

TABLE 5.1 Research methodologies mapped against epistemologies

	Positivist	Relativist	Constructionist
Action research	*		**
Case method	*	*	*
Collaborative research			**
Cooperative inquiry			**
Ethnography			**
Experimental methods	**	*	
Grounded theory	*	*	**
Narrative methods			**
Quasi-experimental research	**	*	
Survey feedback	*	*	*
Survey research	*	**	*

survey research and ethnography. There also a lot of other methodologies associated with different epistemological positions, especially in the case of constructionism. In addition, we will look in some depth at two other methodologies – case method and grounded theory – because they are notable for spanning epistemologies, and this is often a cause of confusion for students and researchers.

POSITIVIST RESEARCH DESIGNS

As we noted in the previous chapter, positivist methods usually incorporate the assumption that there are true answers, and the job of the researcher is either to start with a hypothesis about the nature of the world, and then seek data to confirm or disconfirm it, or the researcher poses several hypotheses and seeks data that will allow selection of the correct one. The ideal methodologies for doing this are experimental and quasi-experimental methods, and we will describe the key principles of each below.

Experimental designs

Classic experimental method involves **random assignment** of subjects to either an experimental or a control group. Conditions for the experimental group are then manipulated by the experimenter/researcher in order to assess their effect in comparison with members of the control group who are receiving no unusual conditions. This approach dominates natural science and medical research. For example in agriculture, if researchers want to know the effect of a new fertilizer compared to existing products they will divide the same batch of seed into two, or more, equal groups. The seeds are then planted on the same day in separate sections of the same field. The new fertilizer is spread on Section A, the old fertilizer on Section B, and perhaps no fertilizer is spread on the Section C.

From that day on, all sections are treated identically in all respects, and on the day of harvesting the yields from each section are compared. If the yield from Section A is significantly different from the other two, say 8 tonnes per hectare compared to 6 and 4 tonnes respectively, we may conclude that the difference is only due to the new fertilizer. Of course, this raises the question of how big the difference needs to be in order for it to be considered as 'significant', and this is one of the issues that we tackle later in Chapter 10. Exercise 5.1 reports on a piece of agricultural research, and then asks some questions about this research design.

Medical research has a preference for experimental designs when testing the use and effectiveness of new drugs or treatments – although this is not always possible. Typically, new drugs are tested through four distinct phases. In the first phase, the drug is administered to a small group of healthy volunteers in order to establish things such as the safe dose range, possible side-effects, and how the body handles and reacts to the drug. In the second phase, the drug is administered to a number of patients who have the condition in order to establish whether it works well enough for trials to continue, and to gather further information on dosages and potential side-effects. The third phase is conducted on a much larger scale and is the only phase which involves full experimental design: patients are randomly assigned to the

EXERCISE

5.1

Experimental research design

Triticale breaks the '10-tonnes-per-hectare' barrier. 26 April 2005

Agronomists at the University of New England have broken the elusive barrier of '10 tonnes per hectare' for the yield of a wheat-related grain crop. 'We've done what we set out to do,' said Associate Professor Robin Jessop (pictured here), who leads the UNE team that has been working towards that goal for the past 25 years. 'It's a heck of a step up'.

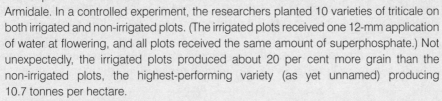

Dr Jessop has always suspected that triticale, a hybrid cross between wheat and rye, had the potential to yield more than 10 tonnes per hectare. 'For comparison, Australia's average wheat yield is only two tonnes per hectare, and even in Europe the yield does not exceed six to eight tonnes per hectare', he said.

The record-breaking result was achieved on experimental plots at UNE's Laureldale Research Station near Armidale. In a controlled experiment, the researchers planted 10 varieties of triticale on both irrigated and non-irrigated plots. (The irrigated plots received one 12-mm application of water at flowering, and all plots received the same amount of superphosphate.) Not unexpectedly, the irrigated plots produced about 20 per cent more grain than the non-irrigated plots, the highest-performing variety (as yet unnamed) producing 10.7 tonnes per hectare.

Dr Jessop emphasized the point that these yields were from experimental plots, and that commercial yields would be expected to be lower (except under irrigated conditions where more than 12 mm of water could be applied). He admitted that, during the experiment 'conditions were in our favour'. 'We've shown that, given the best conditions, triticale has the potential to produce very high yields', he said.
http://tinyurl.com/2mdeew

Questions

A What is the primary question/ hypothesis of the researchers?

B What are the key features of the research design?

C What are the strengths and weaknesses of this design?

experimental and control groups, who are respectively administered the new drug, the old drug and/or a placebo, in order to demonstrate the differential benefits of the new drug. Finally, in the fourth phase, and after the drug has been licensed for general usage, longitudinal trials are carried out on normal patients who have the drug prescribed by their doctors in order to assess long-term risks and benefits.

In studies of social and human life, such experiments still remain quite popular amongst psychologists, particularly where there is a ready supply of undergraduate students upon whom to conduct the experiments. They are very much harder to conduct within real organizations, or where one does not have a captive population from which to draw volunteers. Occasionally, if one is as lucky as Melville Dalton (1964) was (see Chapter 4), the researcher might find people who are prepared to set up small artificial experiments for them when they are studying within organizations, but this is obviously a rarity.

The main *advantages* of experimental research designs are that they encourage clarity about what is to be investigated, and should eliminate many alternative explanations because the random assignment ensures that the experimental and control groups are identical in all respects, except for the focal variable. It is also easier for another researcher to replicate the study, and hence any claims arising from the research can be subjected to public scrutiny. The *disadvantages* are practical and ethical. With medical research there is always the danger that volunteers will be harmed by drug tests; hence stringent ethical guidelines have been developed, which are now filtering into social science and management research (see Chapter 6). Also, when dealing with people and business situations it is rarely possible to conduct true experiments with randomization. For example, if a company wants to assess the value of an elite highflier career development scheme, it cannot simply assign managers at random to the scheme because the managers themselves will be aware of what is happening, and there will also be strong ethical, performance related and employment law objections to this arbitrary assignment. For this reason, quasi-experimental methods have been developed in order to circumvent the problem of random assignment.

Quasi-experimental designs

The classic exposition of quasi-experimental design advocates using multiple measures over time in order to reduce the effects of control and experimental groups not being fully matched (Shadish et al., 2002). Individuals are not allocated randomly to the treatment group and the control group, but rather allocation takes place on some other criterion, usually by using intact groups. As a result, the validity of inferences from this type of design depends critically on how equivalent the two groups actually are. Since equivalence cannot be guaranteed in this type of design, some statisticians insist that they be called **non-experimental designs**; though the reality is that many forms of quasi-experimental design can allow relatively strong inference in settings where true experiments would be impossible to achieve.

One of the most common methods is the 'pre-test/post-test comparison design'. For example, the effects of a leadership course on a group of managers might be evaluated by measuring the managers' attitudes and behaviour before and after the course, and by comparing the differences with those from a similar group of managers who did not attend the course but who completed identical tests at the same times.

This design is illustrated in Figure 5.1, although there are substantial problems when using it in real organizations. For example, the design assumes that 'nothing' happens to the control group during the period that the treatment (course attendance) is being given to the experimental group. This is a naive assumption, as Easterby-Smith and Ashton (1975) found, when attempting to evaluate a project-based management

FIGURE 5.1

Quasi-experimental
research design

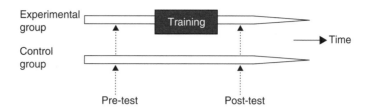

development programme held at Durham University Business School. While the 'chosen few' were away on the course, several members of the control group seized the opportunity to improve relationships with their bosses and strengthen their political standing in the company, thus effectively shutting out a number of managers who had attended the course.

Quasi-experimental methods share some of the advantages of full experimental methods such as clarity, transparency and repeatability. However, as we have indicated above, they have problems accommodating the politics and agency of human beings in work settings. And there are also other subtle problems with pre/post-test designs because changes over time may be a consequence of measurement itself (a **testing effect**). The first measurement may get respondents to reflect on their initial answers, and this can lead to them answering differently the next time – not because of the intervention itself, but because they have been measured before. Thus, the process of measurement itself becomes a kind of intervention, but one which cannot easily be directly assessed.

Validity of positivist designs

Positivist methods are particularly concerned to ensure that results provide accurate reflections of reality. They distinguish between internal and external validity with the former relating to *systematic* factors of bias and the latter being concerned with how generalizable a conclusion is across all types of person, settings, and times.

The aim of positivist research designs is to maximize **internal validity**, and this requires the elimination of plausible alternative explanations for any differences observed between groups. That is why full experimental designs require random assignment to control and experimental groups, and efforts are then made to ensure that the subsequent experiences of the two groups are identical in all respects, except for the focal variable. But there are many threats to internal validity including history (experiences of the two groups diverge in some unexpected way), maturation (group members get older or other life changes take place) or mortality. The latter can be a problem in medical research where people literally die before the experiment is completed, and in organizational studies people may vanish from the research because they move jobs, leave the company or lose interest. Threats to internal validity are systematic rather than random; and they tend to focus on factors which cloud the interpretation of differences between groups in change over time.

External validity is about generalisability of results beyond the focal study. In the physical sciences we assume that Newton's Laws of Motion will have equal validity whether applied in New York, Bogota, Xi'an or in other worlds. If they do not apply in the same way everywhere, then there should be a clear way of understanding how they vary in different circumstances. Thus Albert Einstein predicted through his Theory of Relativity that bodies do not follow Newton's Laws when they are moving at relative velocities near to the speed of light, and that light does not travel in straight lines when subject to strong gravitational forces. The latter prediction was confirmed by observations of the total eclipse of the sun in 1919 (see Example 5.1).

EXAMPLE 5.1

Relativity and the 1919 total eclipse of the sun

Probably the most important eclipse in the history of science occurred on 29 May 1919. Just six months after the end of World War I, British astronomers used it to test a new idea that came from Germany in 1915. Expeditions of astronomers photographed the eclipse in difficult tropical conditions in Brazil and on the African island of Principe. At the time, the Sun was in front of a useful cluster of stars, the Hyades. The astronomers compared the relative positions in the sky near the Sun with the positions of the same stars as previously photographed in the night sky.

The proposition was that gravity affected light, space and time itself, and as a result the Sun would deflect starlight passing by it. Changes in the apparent direction of stars in the sky, seen close to the Sun during a total eclipse, could confirm the idea. Even for stars almost in line with the Sun, the shift in apparent position is less than two seconds of arc, or a few ten-thousandths of a degree. The 1919 measurements confirmed that the Sun bent the light rays by roughly the right extent – less than predicted in Principe, more than predicted in Brazil (http://tinyurl.com/2jawv3).

However, in order to demonstrate external validity, management research designs need to demonstrate a number of features. First, they need to demonstrate that the results observed are not just a product of the selection of individuals or organizations. Sometimes the people who volunteer to take part in research are open minded and keen to help; sometimes they will put themselves forward because they have strong opinions or 'axes to grind'. Managers will often 'volunteer' employees to take part in research because they believe they will show the organization in a positive light, and will not offer individuals who are critical of the organization; or they will allow access to the organization because they hope research will add legitimacy to a new innovation or policy that they wish to promote. These issues of access and sampling are discussed further in later chapters (Chapters 6 and 8), but the key point to remember is that selection should avoid sources of bias as far as possible.

Other threats to external validity come from the setting and history. In the first case, the results of a piece of research in the health service may be difficult to generalize to an automobile manufacturer. Similarly, research conducted in large organizations may not apply to small organizations; and there is also increasing awareness that research conducted in one national setting may not apply to other national settings. With regard to history, it is important to note that patterns and relationships observed in one era may not apply in another era. For example at the present time, with the emergence of China as a global economic force, the theories about the behaviour of financial markets which were developed during the era of US dominance are now having to be rewritten. Similarly, a study on reward systems conducted in one country where the supply of skilled labour is plentiful might not be relevant in another country where there is a marked shortage of skilled labour.

Quasi-experimental study on autonomous workgroups

Wall et al. (1986) conducted a quasi-experimental study of the long-term effects of implementation of autonomous workgroups on job satisfaction in a manufacturing environment, and this study serves to illustrate ways in which strong inferences can be drawn by utilizing natural comparisons within an organization.

Research Design

There were four conditions and three measurement occasions, as shown in the table below. Condition A, the main experimental group, included all day-shift employees in a new factory who from the outset of production worked under a system of autonomous workgroups. Within the overall research design, Condition B served initially as a non-equivalent control group and later as a second experimental group. It included all employees on the evening shift at the new factory who made the same products using the same machinery as their day-shift colleagues. For the first 12 months of the study their work was conventionally organized: employees were allocated to particular tasks, and a supervisor who reported to a shift manager had control over all aspects of production. After 12 months of production at the new factory, however, the company decided to extend autonomous group working to this evening shift, largely at the request of the employees themselves. At this point, condition B became a second experimental group.

Conditions C and D were two further non-equivalent control groups, representing day and evening shifts in a factory elsewhere in the organization where jobs had conventional designs. The products and technology were very similar to those in the Greenfield site: the same overall company policies were in force, and pay levels were equivalent.

Three measurement occasions were planned for the Greenfield site after 6, 18 and 30 months of production, and two measurement occasions for the conventional site corresponding to the first two occasions at the first site. However, the final data collection for Condition D was rendered impossible as the evening shift at the conventional factory was discontinued.

Summary of Research Design

				$Time_1$	$Time_2$	$Time_3$
Condition A	Greenfield	Day shift	x	O	O	O
Condition B	Greenfield	Evening shift		O	x O	O
Condition C	Conventional	Day shift		O	O	-
Condition D	Conventional	Evening Shift		O	-	-

x indicates the introduction of autonomous group working; O indicates measurement under conventional working; O indicates measurement under autonomous group working.

Continued

EXERCISE
5.2

Discussion Questions

A What are the main threats to validity in this design, and how have the researchers tried to deal with these?

B What additional checks would you carry out to ensure that the four groups are, and remain, as equivalent as possible throughout the study?

C What general pattern of results would lead you to conclude that autonomous work groups lead to higher job satisfaction?

D Can you see other potential comparisons that can be made with this set of data (the authors identified six)?

RELATIVIST RESEARCH DESIGNS

As explained in the previous chapter, the relativist epistemology assumes that there are regular patterns in human and organizational behaviour, but these are often difficult to detect and extremely difficult to explain due to the number of factors and variables which might produce the observed result. Consequently, relativist research tends to use cross-sectional designs which enable multiple factors to be measured simultaneously and hence potential underlying relationships to be examined. Since the research involves multiple factors, and needs to make approximations of reality, relatively large samples are usually required, and hence surveys are the preferred methodology in this area.

Survey research design

There are three main types of survey: factual, inferential and exploratory. Inferential surveys predominate in academic management research, particularly in the fields of strategy, marketing and organizational psychology, and for that reason we will concentrate in this section on inferential surveys, although we will briefly describe and illustrate each of the other two types. Further information on the technical design of surveys can be found in Chapter 9.

Factual surveys are most often associated with opinion polls and market-research, and involve collecting and collating relatively 'factual' data from different groups of people. Thus, in order to assess market share or loyalty we might be seeking to identify what percentage of the population of Southampton entered either a Sainsbury's or Tesco's supermarket at least once in the previous week. This is reasonably factual data that could be gathered by a postal questionnaire or **structured interviews**; however, it could be affected by people's ability to recall what they did in the previous week, and possibly by **social desirability** factors where they claim loyalty to one supermarket over another in anorder to project a particular image of themselves to the researcher.

Inferential surveys are aimed at establishing relationships between variables and concepts, whether there are prior assumptions and hypotheses regarding the nature of these relationships. The usual starting point is to isolate the factors that appear to

be involved, and to decide what appears to be causing what. This means that researchers have to identify the main **dependent** and **predictor**[1] variables: it is the latter which
are assumed to be causing the former.

In Figure 5.2, we are suggesting (hypothesizing) that the predictor variables of
salary, leadership and responsibility have an impact on the dependent variable:
motivation at work. In order to test this hypothesis it would be necessary then to
define ways of measuring each of these variables, generally through a small number
of items in a questionnaire, and this would need to be completed by a sample of
employees in one or more places of work. Naturally, this requires that the measures
of the four variables are accurate, and that the sample is appropriate in terms of size
and constitution in order to test the hypothesis: we discuss how to do this in more
detail in chapter 9. Moreover, the four factors identified in Figure 5.2 could be examined in more detail. For example, one might be interested in the interactions between
some of the variables, such as whether some forms of leadership lead to greater
responsibility being distributed around the workforce; or one might be interested in
whether some of the arrows might work in other directions, so that a highly motivated workforce would lead to particular styles and strategies of leadership. These
are some of the relationships that can be analysed, particularly with more complex
models, through the use of structural equation modelling (see Chapter 11).

Studies of this kind are often known as **cross-sectional surveys** because they involve
selecting different organizations, or units, in different contexts and investigating how
other factors, measured at the same time, vary across these units. The classic
Aston studies used cross-sectional design to identify general relationships between
organizational structure and other variables such as size and technology.

Similarly, Lyles and Salk (1996) were interested in the conditions that led to greater
transfer of knowledge from foreign parents into international joint ventures. So
they selected a sample of 201 joint ventures that were regarded as being small or
medium-sized across four manufacturing industries in Hungary. Through comparing
indicators of performance across the whole sample, they were able to conclude first
that there was a strong link between knowledge transfer and performance, and second
that this transfer was most likely to take place when the foreign and domestic parents
had equal (50/50) equity stakes in the new venture. The sample size of 201 was
sufficient for them to demonstrate that the results were statistically significant,
although one of the key problems for researchers using cross-sectional designs is to
know how large the sample needs to be (see Chapter 9).

FIGURE 5.2 Possible
predictors of motivation at
work

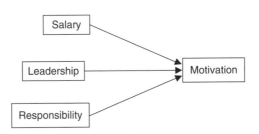

---

[1]The term 'independent' variable is often used instead of 'predictor' variable. We prefer the latter term
because in practice, even 'independent' variables tend to be related to each other, and therefore use of
the term is misleading.

We discussed Geert Hofstede's (1984) study in the previous chapter, and this is an example of an **exploratory survey**. He attempted to develop a universal set of principles against which any culture can be measured – in the hope that this would provide a basis for predicting the behaviour of individuals and organizations in almost any country. However, he did not start with an explicit set of hypotheses; rather, he had a large number (about 216,000) of questionnaires completed by employees of IBM with regard to their views and values, and he was looking for patterns in the data. This he did by using cluster analysis and factor analytic techniques (see Chapter 11). The four dimensions, which we have discussed in the previous chapter, emerged from his data, and by demonstrating that they fitted reasonably well with prior research into this topic, he was able to substantiate his claim to the importance of his four dimensions.

EXAMPLE 5.2

Which variable is which?

Chen's doctoral thesis examined how workers in virtual teams doing different tasks used instant messaging to support their work. Her respondents were all Chinese-language speakers in China or Taiwan; and some of them worked with people in the same location (building or city) while others worked with colleagues in other countries (such as Canada, USA, Germany).

Instant messaging is not a variable because everyone in the study uses it; but other communication technologies (such as email, video-conferencing and face-to-face meetings) are variables because some people use them while others do not. Similarly dual language use (Chinese and English) is not a variable because the whole sample spoke both languages.

The focus of the study became on what led people to switch communication media or languages, and this therefore was the *dependent* variable. The *predictor* variables were task characteristics, indices of relationship quality (how well people knew each other), and whether they worked in the same or different locations.

Validity of relativist designs

Since relativist studies are informed by internal realist ontology, the issues of validity are quite similar to those of positivist studies. Thus, there is a major concern about whether the instruments and questionnaire items used to measure variables are sufficiently accurate and stable. Most of this is done through pre-testing instruments before the actual research is carried out, and hence measures of **reliability** are important because they assess how far each instrument can be relied upon to produce the same score for each occasion that it is used. There is also the question of external validity: whether the patterns observed from the sample data will also hold true in other contexts and settings. And again, the technicalities of assessing reliability and validity with survey data will be discussed further in Chapter 9.

CONSTRUCTIONIST RESEARCH DESIGNS

Constructionist research designs start from the assumptions that there is no absolute truth, and the job of the researcher should be to establish how various claims for truth and reality become constructed in everyday life. Hence it is not surprising that, in contrast to the two previous epistemologies, there is quite a wide range of methodologies which fit within the constructionist paradigms. Here we cover some of the main methodologies – action research and cooperative inquiry, ethnography and narrative methods – which are primarily based on constructionist designs. Two other methods, case study and grounded theory, which are often associated with constructionist designs will be considered in the subsequent section. The reason is that there are quite significant differences of opinion among academics regarding the correct way of conducting case based or grounded theory research. In those two instances, the differences in perspectives and prescriptions can be quite problematic for researchers, because they are rooted in ontological assumptions, and are therefore often unconscious.

Action research and cooperative inquiry

One of the key assumptions of positivism, and of natural scientific methods, is that the researcher should be objective, maintaining complete independence from the object of study. In the social sciences, where claims of the researcher's independence are harder to sustain, many people have tried to turn this apparent 'problem' into a virtue. This is the tradition of **action research** which, as we have explained in Chapter 1, assumes that social phenomena are continually changing rather than static. With action research, the researchers are often part of this change process itself. The following two beliefs are normally associated with action research designs:

1 The best way of learning about an organization or social system is through attempting to change it, and this therefore should be an objective of the action researcher.

2 The people most likely to be affected by, or involved in implementing, these changes should as far as possible become involved in the research process itself.

Some forms of action research appear to follow the principles of positivism, for example by attempting to change the organization from the outside and then measuring the results. Kurt Lewin (1948) who originated the action research tradition, used experimental designs when investigating the efficacy of different ways of getting housewives to change their nutritional habits during World War II (see Example 5.3).

Kurt Lewin's studies were, however, different from traditional experimental research because there was an emphasis on changes in behaviour, and his housewives were active participants in deciding whether or not to change. The weakness with his experimental design was that it did not allow him to discover *why* the changes took place. This required subsequent experiments and qualitative studies to build up deeper understanding of why behaviour changed under these different circumstances.

EXAMPLE 5.3

An early example of action research

During World War II, Kurt Lewin and his associates experimented with groups of American housewives to see if they could be persuaded to serve unpopular types of meat, such as beef hearts, sweetbreads and kidneys to their families. They used two methods to try to persuade them to change their habits. In the first case, a lecturer gave an attractive talk to members of the group on the dietary and economic value of using these meats, and offered some good recipes. In the second case, the same information was provided to the housewives; but they were invited to discuss the information and at the end to indicate by a show of hands whether they intended to serve the new meats. In a follow-up study it was found that only 3 per cent of the members of the lecture groups served one of the meats, compared with 32 per cent for the discussion/decision groups.

Similar results were obtained when persuading mothers to give orange juice and cod liver oil to their infants, although in these cases the discussion/decision method was only found to be twice as effective as the lecture method.

(Source: Krech et al., 1962: 229 – 30)

Involvement in the research process is taken a stage further in what has come to be known as cooperative inquiry (Reason, 1988; Heron, 1996). This has been developed for researching human action mainly at individual and community, rather than at organizational levels. It starts with the idea that all people have, at least latently, the ability to be self-directing, to choose how they will act and to give meaning to their own experiences. It rejects traditional positivist methods where people are studied as if they were objects under the influence of external forces. Cooperative inquiry not only focuses on the experiences and explanations of the individuals concerned, it also involves them in deciding in the first place what questions and issues are worth researching. Thus the 'subjects' become partners in the research process.

Ethnography

The key principle of **ethnography** is that the researcher should 'immerse' himself or herself in a setting, and become part of the group under study in order to understand the meanings and significances that people give to their behaviour and that of others. Most outsiders who are new to an organization or group will encounter things that they do not understand. These are what Agar (1986) calls 'breakdowns': events or situations where the researcher's past experience gives no help in understanding what is going on. This breakdown therefore represents something unique about that organization, and previously unknown to the researcher. For example, most groups have 'in-jokes', based on experiences shared only by members of the group. In order for an outsider to make sense of the breakdown provided by an in-joke it will be necessary to track back to the original experiences (Roy, 1952; Collinson, 2002). The breakdown provides a kind of window into exploring aspects of the experiences and meaning systems of groups and organizations. It will only be possible to resolve the breakdown when the researcher has understood these meaning systems.

Another important distinction is between what are known as **emic** and **etic** perspectives. These two terms were first coined by the American linguist Kenneth Pike (1954): emic refers to the sounds within a language that could only be distinguished by speakers of that language; and etic refers to features of a language that are easily identified by outsiders, but are largely inaudible to people who spoke that language. For example, the four Chinese tones are emic because they cannot easily be distinguished by a non-Chinese speaker, yet are absolutely critical to understanding the language. In contrast, most speakers of English are unaware that their speech is seen (from an etic perspective) as tight-lipped and monotonic by French and Italian speakers.

The emic and etic perspectives are now used in a wider way, referring to researching a culture or context from the inside out (emic) or from the outside in (etic). The distinction has also led to the view that better insights can be gained into management and organizations through combining insider and outsider perspectives. Thus, Bartunek and Louis (1996) advocate methods that involve research teams which combine one or two people working inside the organization with one or two people working from the outside. Using methods like this the ethnographer has the opportunity to challenge and extend conventional wisdom, and to generate new insights into human behaviour.

Narrative methods

Another group of constructionist research designs have been given the general label of **narrative** methods (Boje, 1995, 2001; Czarniawska, 1998; Daiute and Lightfoot, 2004). These contain both ontological and epistemological elements. The ontological view suggests that stories and myths form a central element of organizational reality, and therefore organizational research that ignores stories is necessarily incomplete. The epistemological position is that by collecting organizational stories the researcher will gain insights into organizational life which could not be reached by more conventional means. This may involve participant observation where the researcher can become part of the process of constructing and transmitting stories, or they may be collected through interviews by asking people for the stories that they have heard about particular events (see Example 5.4). In essence, the method relies on literary theory (Hatch, 1996), and hence both the position of the narrator and the role of the analyst are very important.

One of the criticisms of narrative methods is that they do not offer much that is distinctive or additional to 'normal' qualitative research. Nevertheless, they do have a number of strengths: they provide a holistic perspective on organizational behaviour; they are particularly useful in developing social histories of identity and development; they are useful in helping to examine relationships between individuals and the wider organization; and they introduce values into the research process.

EXAMPLE 5.4

A narrative-based study

Humphreys and Brown (2008) investigated the way corporate social responsibility (CSR) was introduced as an important function within a financial services company. The authors, consistent with our definition above, considered stories and narratives to be central to the way managers and employees make sense of what was going on in the company. But their research design also involved the collection of stories from key actors involved in the establishment of corporate social responsibility within the company. From the analysis of semi-structured interviews with 64 employees they identified three major themes/narratives associated with CSR: idealism and altruism, economics and expedience, and ignorance and cynicism – which summarized the conflicting perspectives on CSR in that company.

Validity of constructionist designs

There is much concern about how to assure and demonstrate the quality of construc-tionist designs, although authors rarely use the term 'validity'. In a classic paper Golden-Biddle and Locke (1993) identify three key criteria: authenticity; plausibility; and criticality. *Authenticity* involves convincing the reader that the researcher has a deep understanding of what was taking place in the organization; *plausibility* requires the research to link into some ongoing concern/interest among other researchers; and *criticality* encourages readers to question their taken-for-granted assumptions, and thus offer something genuinely novel. More recently Amis and Silk (2008), in discussing 'non-foundationalist' qualitative research, suggest that good research within the constructionalist tradition should be partisan, taking the side of the less powerful members of society and organizations, and supporting a 'moral-sacred' philosophy. Thus quality would be indicated by the presence of the audience in the text, the sharing of emotional experience, stressing political action, taking sides, moving people to reflect and even act – all of which builds collaborative, reciprocal, trusting and friendly relations with those studied.

Another perspective is provided by David Silverman (2000) who argues for a more objectivist stance because there are few safeguards to prevent researchers from picking evidence out of the mass of data to support their particular prejudices. In order to defend themselves against charges of 'anecdotalism' he suggests several principles, including refutability, constant comparison, comprehensive data treatment and tabulations. *Refutability* involves looking for examples that might disconfirm current beliefs; *constant comparison* follows the principles of grounded theory (see below) in looking for new cases and settings which will stretch the current theory; *comprehensive data treatment* involves carrying out an initial analysis of all of the data available before coming up with conclusions; and *tabulations* imply greater rigour in organizing data, and accepting that it can also be useful to add up the occurrence of phenomena sometimes.

Our own view is that the results of constructionist research should be believable, and they should be reached through methods that are transparent. Thus it is very important for the researcher to explain how she gained access to the particular organization, what processes led to the selection of informants, how data was created and recorded, what processes were used to summarize or collate it, how the data became transformed into tentative ideas and explanations, and how she felt about the research. These are some of the procedures that will be considered more fully in Chapter 8.

BROAD-BASED METHODS

Several methods, which have a single label, may be used in quite different ways by different proponents. This is particularly true with case method and grounded theory. Although the dominant texts about case method come from the positivist end, the method can also be designed in ways consistent with relativist and constructionist perspectives. Conversely, grounded theory was designed as a constructionist alternative to positivist methods, yet some respected versions now contain positivist elements.

Case studies

Although case studies are extensively used for teaching purposes, our interest here is in their application to *research*. Essentially the case study looks in depth at one, or a small number of, organizations, events, or individuals, generally over time. There is a very extensive literature on the design, use and purposes of case studies. In the management field authors tend to coalesce around those who advocate single cases and those who advocate multiple cases. Advocates of single cases generally come from a constructionist epistemology; those who advocate multiple cases usually fit with either a relativist or positivist epistemology.

Robert Yin (2002) is the best known exponent of case method in the social sciences. His concern is that case studies are vulnerable to a number of criticisms from more *positivist* researchers. In particular, it is suggested that they do not have the rigour of natural scientific designs. They rarely allow generalizations to be made from specific cases to the general population; and they produce huge piles of data, which allow researchers to make any interpretations they want. In response to these criticisms, he suggests that all case studies should have clear designs produced before any data is collected, and these designs should cover: the main questions or propositions, the **unit of analysis**, links between data and propositions, and procedures for interpretation of data. His main concern is to demonstrate that case studies may contain the same degree of validity as more positivist studies and therefore his exposition of the method contains both rigour and the application of careful logic about comparisons.

The contrasting position, which is informed by a *constructionist* epistemology, is much less concerned with issues of validity, and more concerned with providing a rich picture of life and behaviour in organizations or groups. Robert Stake (2006) writes about qualitative case studies, and distinguishes between instrumental and expressive studies. The former involves looking at specific cases in order to develop general principles; the latter involves investigating cases because of their unique features which may, or may not, be generalizable to other contexts. An example would be Andrew Pettigrew's (1985a) research into Organization Development within ICI during the 1970s and early 1980s. In those days ICI was the most powerful manufacturing company in Britain, so there was naturally a lot of interest in understanding how they were managing and developing themselves. In that respect, the study was expressive, but there was also an instrumental element since Pettigrew was interested in understanding the phenomenon of organization development, and ICI was regarded as one of its leading proponents. His research involved numerous interviews with key actors in the company over several years, and this provided a longitudinal element to his research which enabled him better to understand both the contextual and historical settings of the company.

From a similar perspective, Nikkolaj Siggelkow (2007) provides a spirited defence of cases arguing that they are particularly valuable for demonstrating the importance of particular research questions, for inspiring new ideas and for illustrating abstract concepts. He also points out that even single cases can provide very convincing tests of theory by quoting the famous 'talking pig' example. Thus we only need to produce one example of a talking pig to demonstrate the error of the popular idea that pigs are incapable of intelligent speech. The logic being that we only need a single example of an anomaly to destroy a dominant theory – as in the case of Einstein's refutation of Newton's theory. And although we are unlikely to identify a 'talking pig' organization, there are many examples where single cases can be uniquely interesting – for example, the company that does significantly better (or worse) than all others in the same industry, or the entrepreneur who builds a fortune from small beginnings.

EXERCISE
5.3

A longitudinal case study

A recent study conducted by Prieto and Easterby-Smith (2006) explored the links between dynamic capabilities and knowledge management through a case study of the evolution of a single company over several years. Because the researchers were interested in dynamic capabilities – which are by definition about continuous change – it made sense to observe processes over time so they could examine how, for example, the introduction of knowledge sharing routines led to greater strategic flexibility. Accordingly, the researchers spent time observing management meetings, talking with participants at meetings and interviewing other managers. They also followed information exchanges with partner organizations by conducting visits to their sites; repeating interviews with key informants; and feeding back emerging insights to senior managers to 'validate' their interpretations and to stimulate further insights.

Questions

A How would you justify that this research was 'valid'?

B What possibilities are there for generalizing the findings from this research?

C Do questions about validity and generalisability make any sense in this instance?

TABLE 5.2 Key features of case method informed by different ontologies

	Realist (Yin)	*Relativist (Eisenhardt)*	*Constructionist (Stake)*
Design	Prior	Flexible	Emergent
Sample	Up to 30	4–10	1 or more
Analysis	Across	Both	Within case
Theory	Testing	Generation	Action

A few points are important about constructionist studies. First, they are based on direct observation and personal contacts, generally through interviews. Second, they take place within single organizations, but then involve sampling from numbers of individuals. Third, the collection of data takes place over a period of time and may include both live observations and retrospective accounts of what has happened. Thus the unit of analysis is either the individual, or specific events such as the exchange of a piece of knowledge, or strategies employed to transfer or retain control of knowledge.

There is a third, *relativist*, position which has been developed particularly through the work of Kathy Eisenhardt (Eisenhardt, 1989; Eisenhardt and Graebner, 2007). This view, which draws inspiration from both the positivist and constructionist positions, has been adopted widely by researchers using case method, particularly in North America. She is eclectic in her advice about methodology: using designs that are established at the outset, but then being flexible about their adaptation; recommending data collection through using multiple methods; and conducting both within case and across case analysis.

Above all, Eisenhardt is concerned about building theory from case based research, and this takes the form of developing hypotheses. She recommends that hypotheses can be formed, or 'shaped' through three main stages. The first stage involves sharpening up the basic constructs, and this is essentially an iterative process of moving back and forth between the constructs and the data. The second stage involves verifying that emergent relationships between constructs fit with the evidence from each case. In this respect she comments that: 'Each case is analogous to an experiment, and multiple cases are analogous to multiple experiments' (1989: 542). The third stage involves comparing the emergent theory/concepts/hypotheses with the existing literature. In particular, she suggests paying attention to literature that is contradicted by the evidence, both because any evidence of having ignored contradictory findings is likely to reduce confidence in the final conclusions, and because the highlighting of contradictory conclusions is likely to make the original contribution from the research most explicit.

Although the variations in case study design and application are complex and sometimes blend into each other, we summarize in Table 5.2 some of the main distinctions in the use and application of case method according to each of the three basic ontologies.

EXAMPLE 5.5

Comparative case study design

In a comparative study of investment decisions in Chinese and UK companies (Lu and Heard, 1995) case studies of 16 decisions in eight companies were compared and contrasted in order to establish the cultural and institutional variations in business decision-making between China and the UK. The study involved collecting both qualitative and quantitative data, including extensive site visits to companies in both China and the UK. Each UK company was matched, in terms of size and industry, with the equivalent Chinese company. This allowed for a number of comparisons, between different industries, and between China and the UK which led to a number of emergent insights. For example, in the latter case the researchers noticed that the mean time between the inception and implementation of a major investment decision (approximately £100 million) was virtually identical in both China and the UK (approximately 3.4 years). This significantly contradicted theory of that time which suggested that decision-making in China was far slower than in the UK. Of course, with the benefit of hindsight it is possible to now see how fast Chinese companies have been developing over the last two decades; but this study was one of the first to demonstrate the speed of economic development in China.

Grounded theory

Grounded theory was first formulated by Glaser and Strauss (1967). They saw the key task of the researcher as being to develop theory through 'comparative method', through looking at the same event or process in different settings or situations. For example, the researcher might be interested in the workings of performance appraisal interviews and would therefore study a number of interviews handled by different managers, in different departments, or in different organizations. As a result of the studies it might be noticed that most appraisal interviews either focus on reviewing performance in relation to last year's objectives, or they focus on future goals and how the subordinate may be helped to achieve these. They might then be labelled as 'judgemental' or 'developmental' interviews, and the distinction would represent a *substantive theory* about appraisal interviews.

However, the theorizing could be taken further. For example it might be observed that neither form of interview has much effect on individual performance, nor on the relationships between the managers and their subordinates. Then we could conclude that both forms of interview are simply organizational rituals, which have the function of demonstrating and reinforcing hierarchical power relations. This would be the beginning of a more generalized *formal theory* about power and organizational rituals. Glaser and Strauss consider both substantive and formal theory to be valuable, and they propose two main criteria for evaluating the quality of a theory. First, it should be sufficiently *analytic* to enable some generalization to take place; at the same time it should be possible for people to relate the theory to their own experiences, thus *sensitizing* their own perceptions.

TABLE 5.3 Agreed features of grounded theory

Grounded theory	
Must	Fit the substantive area
	Be understandable and useable by actors
	Be sufficiently complex to account for variation
Key analytical operations are	Cycle of theoretical sampling
	Constant comparisons
	Evolving theory, *leading to …*
	Theoretical saturation

It is important to note that 'I'm doing grounded theory', should not be used as a justification for doing some vaguely qualitative research without any clear view of where it is supposed to lead. Grounded theory contains precisely articulated methods and presuppositions. The problem is, as Locke (1997) explains, that methods have evolved and developed since their initial exposition, and at the heart of this was a rather acrimonious debate between Barney Glaser and Anselm Strauss.[2] In essence, Glaser now believes that researchers should start with no presuppositions, and should allow ideas to 'emerge' from the data (Glaser, 1978, 1992); whereas Strauss recommends familiarizing oneself with prior research and using structured, and somewhat mechanistic, processes to make sense of the data (Strauss, 1987; Strauss and Corbin, 1998). The implication is that the researcher should be aware that there are different versions of grounded theory, and hence needs to articulate his or her own position when writing up the research. These differences are summarized in Table 5.4.

The debate is extended further by Kathy Charmaz (2000), who characterizes the methods of both Glaser and Strauss as 'objectivist'. Her complaint is that both authors

TABLE 5.4 Points of disagreement between Glaser and Strauss

	Glaser	Strauss (and Corbin)
Researcher roles	Maintain distance and independence	Active interrogation of data
Theory	Emerges from data itself	Arises from theorist/data interaction
Ontology	World is 'out there'	Reality and experience are constructed
Pre-understanding	Avoid literature from immediate area	Flexible approach, insights from many sources

[2]We understand that Glaser and Strauss did meet up and resolve their differences shortly before the untimely death of Anselm Strauss (personal communication).

separate the researcher from the experiences of the subjects of the study. She also feels that the recommendations from Strauss and Corbin (1998) about detailed analysis of transcripts, including line by line analysis and 'fracturing of data' reduces the ability to represent the whole experience of individuals involved. In her view, a constructivist should recognize, 'that the viewer creates the data and ensuing analysis through interaction with the viewed' (2000: 523). As such she is located a little further in the constructionist direction than Strauss because she emphasizes the interaction between the researcher and the researched, rather than between the researcher and the data.

In order to make sense of these differences, we need to look both at the ontology and epistemology of the authors. Ontologically, Glaser comes across as a realist, or possibly a relativist; whereas both Strauss and Charmaz have a more nominalist ontology, because they assume that the social world is created through the interaction of actors. Epistemologically Strauss, who was significantly influenced by Corbin (pers. comm.), adopts a more relativist position, which emphasizes systematic and reductionist approaches to the analysis of data. Glaser, in contrast, promotes a more relaxed epistemology, insisting that the data should be analysed in its entirety, and should not be reduced to discrete elements. In some respects this is similar to the constructionist perspective of Charmaz, though she goes further in emphasizing the primacy of the stories and experiences of her research subjects.

Before completing this section, it is important to note that the methods of grounded theory have been developed mainly within educational and health settings where the 'white coat brigade' can have relatively easy and flexible access to data and cases. But access is far more difficult within commercial organizations, and researchers are rarely given the freedom to select their samples on theoretical grounds – hence some of the assumptions of grounded theory have to be amended further to deal with this kind of situation (Locke, 2001). Organizational researchers have to accept the interviewees assigned to them by powerful organizational members who act as gatekeepers (see the discussion on strategies for gaining research access in the following chapter); there are also limits imposed in terms of timing, topics and the use of data. This often requires a number of compromises to be made in terms of research design, as can be seen from the reflections of Suzanne Gagnon in Exercise 5.4 about her study of identity formation among highflying managers in two different international organizations.

GENERIC ISSUES

In this section we identify five generic issues which require clarification and choices to be made when formulating research designs, irrespective of the ontology or epistemology that informs the study.

Identifying the unit of analysis

The **unit of analysis** is the entity that forms the basis of any sample. Thus, samples may be formed from one or more of the following: countries, cultures, races, industrial sectors, organizations, departments, families, groups, individuals, incidents, stories,

How grounded is this? A letter from a doctoral student

Hi Mark

Here is my attempt to explain in concise fashion the degree to which I am using grounded theory.

- I started with a general area for study – the interplay of personal and organizational identities in multi-nationality, multicultural organizations (how important is organizational culture in such settings and how and why? What identities do people see themselves as having in these settings, and why?).

- Once having been in the sites for some time and gathered some data through interviews, I found that <u>identity regulation</u> was a term (perhaps even a central category' in Strauss' and Corbin's words) that had explanatory power; I got this term from the literature, having continued to iteratively study the literature and the data, while continuing to gather data.

- My 'sample' was more or less set from the beginning (all participants on two management development programmes), so in this sense I did not use theoretical sampling. However I did add questions and change emphases in the interviews as I proceeded.

- Whether I reached theoretical saturation, I am not fully sure. In a sense it was more a question of talking to everyone, and then sampling the data (with some follow-up and changes to subsequent questioning and focus, as above).

- I have not been guided solely by the data but also by literature – to an extent I am using some existing concepts as heuristic devices to make sense of the data.

- I see this as a kind of 'theory elaboration' rather than deduction per se. But there is definitely a deductive side to it.

- It may also be the case that I come up with my own theory (hope so), especially, perhaps, in comparing results across the two cases.

That's as far as I can go at the moment. What do you think?? (How grounded is this?)

Suzanne

Questions

A How grounded is this?

B Should she be sticking more closely to GT, principles, and if not, why not?

accidents, innovations, etc. In positivist and relativist forms of research it is important to be clear about the unit of analysis in advance, because this is the basis for collating data, which will subsequently be analysed. In constructionist forms of research, especially case studies, it is also critical because of the potential 'seeing the wood from the trees' problem which arises from the complexity of qualitative data. In the Example 5.5 from our research that compared decision-making between China and the UK, the unit of analysis was the company, but there was a subsidiary unit of analysis (what is sometimes referred to as an **embedded case**) which was the investment decision. Hence it is possible to have more than one unit of analysis provided the theoretical aims of the research justify this, but it is not advisable to have too many.

Universal theory or local knowledge?

One of the key principles of scientific methods and positivist knowledge is that theories and observations made in one context should be applicable to other defined contexts. As we have discussed above, being able to provide assurances of **generalizability**, or external validity, are critical features both of experimental designs and the statistical procedures that are employed to interpret relativist research data. In these cases, as with the guidance of Kathy Eisenhardt on case method, the objective is to produce **universal theories**.

Conversely a number of scholars argue that **local knowledge** is more significant. For example, according to post-colonial theory many theories of race, economic development and culture are constructs of scholars in Western countries, which typically cast non-Western culture and institutions as being somehow inferior to their own (Said, 1978). Similarly, from feminist theory there is a strong view that many of the dominant theories of social behaviour are blind to the effects of gender and patriarchy which may have far greater significance (Ahmed, 1998). In both cases the argument is that any generalized statement about the social world is likely to contain within it assumptions that mask relations of power between those who formulate theories and those to whom they are applied. Moreover, there is a strong view that significant social theory should be understood in relation to the context whence it is derived.

Local knowledge is also important for management and organizational research. First, it is suggested that the practical knowledge used by managers is essentially contextually bound, and is learnt through engaging in practice (Cook and Brown, 1999; Rouleau, 2005). If this is the case then it follows that for research to have theoretical value it should focus on these local practices – which may well be unique to that situation. Second, some people argue that managerial behaviour is culturally relative, and these include both national and organizational cultures (Boyacigiller and Adler, 1991). Hence researchers should formulate their ideas separately within each cultural context, and should not try to generalize across cultures.

For example, there is a growing literature on 'transitional economies' and one of the key areas of interest in these cases is in privatization processes. But there are two main groups of literature on transitional economies, one dealing with Eastern European countries and the other dealing with China. Although there are superficial similarities in context, in that they were all in centrally planned economies, there are much deeper differences between China and Eastern Europe which mean that both the issues and the ideal procedures are very different in the two cases. Moreover, as Nor (2000) found in his study of Malaysia, theories of privatization drawn either from transitional economies, or from Western countries such as the UK, were largely irrelevant because of Malaysia's unique cultural, political and institutional circumstances.

Theory or data first?

The third choice is about which should come first: the theory or the data? Again this represents the split between the positivist and constructionist paradigms in relation to how the researcher should go about his or her work. The Straussian view of grounded theory assumes that pre-conceptions are inevitable. After all, it is common sense to assume that someone will not be interested in a research topic or setting without knowing something in advance about it. Hence he argues that the researcher should make him- or herself aware of previous work conducted in the general field of research before starting to generate his or her own theory.

Recent developments in organizational research have led to a wide range of designs, some of which extend the range of fieldwork methods, and others which provide intermediate positions between the two extremes. In a recent research project looking at absorptive capacity within European companies Easterby-Smith et al. (2008) became increasingly aware that the relationship between theory and data needs to be an interactive process. When researchers observe something in a company which seems surprising or novel it is important to go back to the literature in order to see whether anybody else has remarked on it. Similarly, when a new paper gets published it may have a direct impact on the ongoing collection and interpretation of data.

Reductionism versus holism

Cross-sectional designs, particularly those which include questionnaires and survey techniques, belong either to the *relativist* or *positivist* traditions. As we have noted earlier, they have undoubted strengths in their ability economically to describe features of large numbers of people or organizations. But a major limitation is that they find it hard to explain *why* the observed patterns are there. Thus, although Lyles and Salk (1996) were confident that balanced equity stakes led to the highest chance of knowledge transfer, their study itself could not explain what mechanisms or processes led to knowledge being transferred.

So there are some similarities between apparently in-depth and cross-sectional studies in that they all look at multiple instances, but that the unit of analysis is at a 'higher' level in the latter cases. Even still, the number of observations will differ between the two types since cross-sectional studies will typically require hundreds of instances, whereas in-depth studies may only require tens of observations. The reason why different sizes of sample are appropriate is linked to the processes of generalization which employ different forms of logic for positivist and constructionist research, as will be explained below.

Verification or falsification

This final choice is slightly different from the three preceding ones since it is not linked to resolving the broader debate between positivist and constructionist views, but it is very important both for researchers and for managers. The distinction between **verification** and **falsification** was made by Karl Popper (1959) as a way of dealing with what has become known as Hume's 'problem of induction'.

This is the philosophical problem that, however much data one obtains in support of a scientific theory it is not possible to reach a conclusive proof of the truth of that law. Popper's way out of this problem is to suggest that instead of looking for confirmatory evidence one should always look for evidence that will *disconfirm* one's hypothesis or existing view (as in the 'talking pig' example above). This means that theories should be formulated in a way that will make them most easily exposed to possible refutation. The advantage then is that one only needs one instance of refutation to falsify a theory; whereas irrespective of the number of confirmations of the theory it will never be conclusively proven.

The example often given to illustrate this approach takes as a start the assertion that: 'all swans are white'. If one takes the verification route, the (non-Australian) researcher would start travelling around the country accumulating sightings of swans, and provided that he or she did not go near a zoo, a very high number of white sightings would eventually be obtained, and presumably no black sightings. This gives a lot of confidence to the assertion that all swans are white, but still does not conclusively prove the statement. If, conversely, one takes a falsification view, one would start to search for swans that are *not* white, deliberately looking for contexts and locations where one might encounter non-white swans. Thus, our intrepid researcher might head straight for a zoo, or perhaps book a flight to Western Australia where most swans happen to be black. On making this discovery, the initial hypothesis would be falsified, and it might then have to be modified to include the idea that 'all swans have either white or black feathers'. This statement has still what Popper calls high 'informative' content because it is expressed in a way that can easily be disproved; whereas a statement like 'all swans are large birds' would not be sufficiently precise to allow easy refutation.

Much of the debate about verification and falsification fits within the positivist view because ideas of 'truth' and 'proof' are associated mainly with that paradigm. But there are also important lessons that the constructionist might take from this discussion. For example, Alvesson and Deetz (2000) advise 'critical sensitivity', and Reason (1988) advocates 'critical subjectivity', which involves recognizing one's own views and experiences, but not allowing oneself to be overwhelmed and swept along by them. If the idea of falsification is to be applied more fully to constructionist research then one should look for evidence that might confirm or contradict what one currently believes to be true.

This advice not only applies to researchers but also to managers who are concerned to investigate and understand what is taking place within their own organizations. Most managers are strongly tempted to look for evidence which supports the currently held views of the world. This is not surprising if they are responsible for formulating strategies and policies within a context that is very uncertain, and hence they will be looking for evidence that demonstrates that their strategies were correct. The logical position that follows from the above argument is that, even if *disconfirmatory* evidence is unpopular, it is certainly both more efficient and more informative than confirmatory evidence. Moreover, if managers adopt the falsification strategy and fail to come up with evidence that disconfirms their current views, then they will be able to have far more confidence in their present positions.

CONTRIBUTING TO THEORY

Good research designs need to have some link to theory. In the case of student projects and dissertations it is generally necessary to *use* theory, whereas for doctoral theses and papers in academic journals it is necessary to demonstrate a *contribution* to theory. This is not as daunting as it might seem, and in this section we elaborate on the types and purposes of theory, and explain how it can be incorporated into research designs.

The term 'theory' often has negative connotations. Someone might report back on a lecture saying, 'It was all a lot of theory!' meaning that it was either difficult to understand, or just plain boring. Or someone might react to a new idea saying, 'Well that's all right in *theory*, but ...', meaning that although the idea sounds plausible, it would not work in practice. So, in this case theory is seen as the opposite of practice. In contrast, there is the well-known saying, 'There is nothing so practical as a good theory' (Lewin, 1948). In order to unscramble this confusion we offer distinctions between everyday and academic theory, the latter subdivides further into middle-range and grand theories.

Everyday theory refers to the ideas and assumptions we carry round in our heads in order to make sense of everyday observations. For example, if you observe an old man walking down the street arm in arm with a young woman you might conclude that they were grandfather and granddaughter. In order to reach this conclusion you might hold two assumptions about family relations – that grandparents often live close to their family members and that grandparents often have very close relations with their grandchildren. If the man is leaning slightly on the woman, then it would strengthen the grandfather-daughter hypothesis; but if the man's walk was very unsteady this might suggest a new theory, that they are patient and nurse. Further, if the man is well dressed and the woman is conspicuously glamorous, an alternative hypothesis might suggest itself: that the man is a wealthy philanderer and the woman is a mistress or 'trophy' wife.

Although everyday theories enable people to make sense out of specific events or situations, **academic theories** tend to look for higher levels of generalization. Following the above example for just a moment, in order to explain what was going on, a sociologist might draw on theories about the power of male patriarchy, palliative care for the elderly or the evolution of the institution of marriage. The distinction between **middle-range** and **grand theories** is a matter of scale and formality. An example of the former would be the key idea of absorptive capacity: that the ability of a organization to absorb new external knowledge depends on whether it already possesses related knowledge (Cohen and Levinthal, 1990). It is middle-range because it is a generalizable proposition which can potentially be tested empirically. Conversely, grand theories tend to be more abstract and contain whole edifices of assumptions which are often not testable. The theory of psychoanalysis is one example, because it provides a self-contained set of ideas to explain human behaviour. Similarly personal construct theory (PCT) contains a set of propositions starting with the 'fundamental postulate' that, 'A person's processes are psychologically challenged by the way they anticipate events', which is linked to a series of corollaries about human sensemaking and communications (Kelly, 1958; Bannister and Fransella, 1971). In the management field, elements of PCT have been used to make sense of group decision-making and strategy formulation. A number of the integrated philosophies summarized at the end of the last chapter, such as critical theory or structuration theory, are grand theories in the way we have described them here.

Where researchers are seeking to build theory, this is normally at the level of middle-range theory, and is an incremental process. Thus recent work on absorptive capacity has argued that Cohen and Levinthal's model of absorptive capacity is too rational and unduly focused around R&D, and consequently more attention needs to be paid to political and systemic processes (Todorova and Durisin, 2007). This leads to a question about how we can evaluate the quality of theories, or theoretical contributions, and how we can distinguish a good contribution from one that is less good? The answer is that some criteria are fairly obvious: good theories need to be simple, have good explanatory power, and be relevant to issues that need explaining. But beyond this the evaluation of contribution is largely a matter of judgement among people who already know the field quite well, which is why peer review is normally used to evaluate the theoretical contributions of research proposals and academic papers. We will be returning to these issues at various points later in the book, especially in Chapter 12.

IMPLICATIONS

In this penultimate section we summarize first the implications for different views of validity, then provide a checklist for research designs under different epistemological regimes.

Contrasting views on validity

There is an underlying anxiety amongst researchers of all persuasions that their work will not stand up to outside scrutiny. This is very understandable since research papers and theses are most likely to be attacked on methodological grounds, and one of the key claims of 'research' is that it is more believable than common everyday observations.

The technical language for examining this problem includes terms such as validity, reliability and generalizability. But as we have indicated above, these mean different things within different research traditions. In Table 5.5 we therefore summarize how these terms are discussed from the philosophical viewpoints of positivism, relativism and constructionism.

Research design template

We have argued throughout this chapter that research designs should take account of epistemology, and hence formal research designs need to focus on different issues. In Table 5.6 we list some of the main headings that need to be covered within each epistemology.

TABLE 5.5 Perspectives on validity, reliability and generalizability

Viewpoint	Positivist	Relativist	Constructionist
Validity	Do the measures correspond closely to reality?	Have a sufficient number of perspectives been included?	Does the study clearly gain access to the experiences of those in the research setting?
Reliability	Will the measures yield the same results on other occasions?	Will similar observations be reached by other observers?	Is there transparency about how sense was made from the raw data?
Generalizability	To what extent does the study confirm or contradict existing findings in the same field?	What is the probability that patterns observed in the sample will be repeated in the general population?	Do the concepts and constructs derived from this study have any relevance to other settings?

TABLE 5.6 Research design template

Epistemology	Positivist	Relativist	Constructionist
Background	What is the topic (problem) and what are the main studies that have been conducted to date.	What is the topic (problem) and what are the main studies that have been conducted to date.	What is the academic field and what are the ongoing discussions among researchers.
Rationale	What are the key unresolved questions and why are they important?	What are regarded as the main variables, and how are they related to one another?	What are the conceptual limitations in what has been said or written so far.
Research Aims	Specify testable hypotheses.	List main propositions or questions.	Identify what is the focal issue or question.
Data	Define variables and determine measures.	Define dependent and independent variables and determine measures. How will reliability and validity be assured?	Identify main sources of data. How will interviews be recorded/transcribed, etc?
Sampling (see Chapter 9)	Explain how comparison between groups will enable hypotheses to be verified or falsified.	Justify sample size and explain how it is representative of the wider populations from which it is drawn.	Explain sampling strategy. Will it be opportunistic, emergent, comparative, etc?
Access (see Chapter 6)	Not relevant unless 'natural' experiments are intended.	How can responses to questionnaires etc be assured?	What is the strategy for gaining access to individuals, organizations?

Continued

TABLE 5.6 Research design template—cont'd

Epistemology	Positivist	Relativist	Constructionist
Ethics (see Chapter 6)	Is participation voluntary, and is there any danger that anyone will be harmed by the research?		
Unit of Analysis	Groups that are to be compared to each other.	Specify. Most likely to be individuals or organizations, but might be groups or events.	May not be necessary.
Analysis (Chapters 7–11)	Probable statistical procedures for examining differences between groups.	Probable statistical procedures for examining relationships between variables.	Explain arrangements for coding, interpreting and making sense of data.
Process	Explain stages in the research process	Explain stages in the research process	Provide realistic timing including adequate provision for contingencies
Practicalities (see Chapters 7 and 9)	How will groups be recruited; where will experiments take place?	Who will gather data; how will it be recorded/stored; who will analyse it?	How will researchers share interpretations; who pays for transcriptions, etc?
Theory	Testing hypotheses through verification or falsification	In what ways will the results add to existing theories?	Is the research intended to build on existing theory or develop new ideas and concepts.
Outputs (see Chapter 12)	Where will the research results be published?	What is the dissemination strategy?	How will insights be shared with academic colleagues and research collaborators?

CONCLUSION

In this chapter we have discussed some of the key philosophical debates underlying research methods in the social sciences, and we have looked at the implications these have for the design of management research. The key points of this chapter are:

- There is a clear dichotomy between the positivist and social constructionist world views, but the practice of research involves a lot of compromises.

- Each position has its own language and criteria for evaluating research designs.

- **There is considerable diversity of methods and designs, especially within the constructionist research tradition.**
- **Differences in opinion about research methods are often underpinned by ontological differences.**

The worldview held by an individual researcher or institute is clearly an important factor which affects the choice of research methods. But there are other factors, too. Within academic organizations senior members can exert pressure on junior people to adopt methods that they do not believe in. Governments, companies and funding organizations can exert pressure on institutions to ensure that the aims and forms of research meet with their interests. The politics of research are complex, and researchers neglect them at their peril. That is why we have chosen to devote the next chapter to a discussion of these issues.

**EXERCISE
5.5**

Discussion questions (for small groups in class)

Classify the following according to whether you consider them to be ontologies, epistemologies, methodologies or methods. Explain your reasoning. (Note: many of them could be more than one thing).

	Ontology	Epistemology	Methodology	Method
Grounded theory				
Unobtrusive measures				
Narrative				
Case method				
Ethnography				
Critical realism				
Participant observation				
Experimental design				
Falsification				
Theoretical saturation				

FURTHER READING

Alvesson, M. and Deetz, S. (2000) *Doing Critical Management Research*. London: Sage.

One of the few books that articulate what 'critical' management research looks like, and how it can be conducted, for example, through increasing sensitivity to the aspects of organization life that normally lie hidden. Also provides a much deeper review of critical theory and why it is important.

Boje, D. (2001) *Narrative Methods for Organizational and Communication Research*. London: Sage.

An authoritative book on the use of stories as a source of understanding of organizational life. It provides eight different ways of making sense of stories using the idea of 'anti-narrative' which recognizes that organizational stories are not necessarily complete, that they can be fragmented and can vary with the times and purposes of the story-teller.

Charmaz, K. (2006) *Constructing Grounded Theory: A Practical Guide Through Qualitative Analysis*. London: Sage.

A good textbook which introduces grounded theory, and then leads through the steps in conducting grounded theory analysis. Charmaz argues for adopting a constructionist approach, and starts to distance herself from the more positivist leanings of the founders of grounded theory.

Locke, K. (2001) *Grounded Theory in Management*. London: Sage.

This is an excellent overview of the origins of grounded theory including the differences of opinion between Glaser and Strauss, the key methods and approaches as currently practised, and the specific adaptations that may be required when conducting organizational or management research.

Shadish, W.R., Cook, T.D. and Campbell, D.T. (2002) *Experimental and Quasi-Experimental Designs for Generalised Causal Inference*. Houghton-Mifflin.

An updated version of the classic book on experimental forms of social research.

THE POLITICS AND ETHICS OF MANAGEMENT RESEARCH

6

LEARNING OBJECTIVES

- To be able to identify stakeholders and evaluate the interests of beneficiaries and recognize those potentially at risk.

- To develop awareness of different strategies and methods for gaining access in different contexts.

- To develop awareness of personal and organizational ethics.

- To develop judgement in dealing with 'grey' ethical issues, and the ability to argue pros and cons.

Introduction

Political influences on the research question

Politics of access

Ethics

Utilization of research

Conclusion

Further reading

INTRODUCTION

One of the myths about research is that it is an 'ivory tower' activity. According to this view, research is carried out by independent scholars dedicated to the pursuit of knowledge. Questions and issues are defined as being interesting according to the current state of knowledge and the curiosity of the researcher's intellect. It is doubtful whether there was ever much truth behind this myth. Scholars have regularly got themselves into trouble for following beliefs that were politically unpopular. Socrates was condemned to drink a cup of hemlock because he did not seem sufficiently respectful of current Athenian divinities; and Galileo was forced to recant his belief, which was based on careful observation of sunspots and planetary orbits, that the Earth moved around the Sun. In China, the first Qin emperor is reputed to have buried alive some 400 scholars because he did not like their opinions.

Although many academics have tried in the past to maintain their independence it has never been altogether possible to separate scholarship from politics. But what do we mean by 'politics'? Our basic premise is that it concerns the power relationships between the individuals and institutions involved in the research enterprise, plus the strategies adopted by different actors and the consequences of their actions on others. Crucial relationships may be between student and supervisor, funder and grant holder, authors and journal editors, companies and research institutes, project leaders and research assistants, researchers and managers, or between managers and their bosses. Influence within these relationships may be exerted over questions of: what is to be researched, when, by whom; how information is to be gathered and used; and how the products of research are to be evaluated.

In this context it is important to extend the differences between management research and other forms of social and psychological research, which were identified in Chapter 1. First, 'management' is essentially about controlling, influencing and structuring the awareness of others. It is the central process whereby organizations achieve the semblance of coherence and direction. This process has, for some time, been recognized as political (Pettigrew, 1985b; Hardy, 1996; Buchanan and Badham, 2008). Although 'management' is not the only arena in which politics is important, it does mean that political issues will rarely be absent from the research process.

The second difference is linked to the first, and it starts with the observation that empirical research in the social sciences is usually carried out on members of society who are less powerful than the researchers. That is why psychologists conduct their experiments on students rather than on professors, and sociologists tend to focus on people who are relatively powerless due to their low social or economic status. It is 'the mad, the bad, and the ill' who have received most attention from social researchers in the past (Slater, 1989). This is no accident, for the more powerful members of society generally have both the awareness and the means to protect themselves from the prying eyes and tape recorders of researchers. It is rare to find researchers who have succeeded in studying powerful members of society without adopting methods of deceit, concealment or subterfuge.

When conducting research into managers and management the subjects of research are very likely to be more powerful than the researchers themselves. Furthermore, most organizations are both tightly structured and controlled, so that gaining access to the corporate boardroom, for example, is exceedingly difficult. Managers are usually in a position where they can easily decline to provide information for researchers; they are also adept at handling face-to-face interviews and at managing interactions with strangers. In such circumstances they are fully aware of the significance of information and the importance of determining to what use it might be put, and by whom. So, in the case of managerial research the boot is firmly on the other foot.

We therefore begin this chapter with a discussion of the political factors that can influence the nature and direction of research. The second part focuses on some of the problems of gaining access to organizations and managers, and offers suggestions about how this can be handled. The third part considers some of the ethical dilemmas encountered in fieldwork, particularly those resulting from strategies to gain access, and the utilization of data.

POLITICAL INFLUENCES ON THE RESEARCH QUESTION

Most positivist researchers are not keen on self-disclosure, because the admission of personal motives and aspirations might be seen to damage the image of independence and objectivity that they are at pains to cultivate. Hence they rarely explain precisely where their ideas and questions have come from.

Fortunately things are beginning to change, for two reasons. First, because social studies of the development of scientific knowledge (Latour and Woolgar, 1979) have started to show that the formal view of scientific progress is at variance with what most scientists do in practice. Second, because there is a growing acceptance among social scientists of the need to be reflexive about their own work, and this has led to more autobiographical accounts of research in practice (Czarniawska, 1998). Consequently there is less reliance on traditional 'linear' models of scientific progress.

Although it is recognized that a thorough knowledge of prior research is very important, it is very rare for good research ideas to be derived directly from the literature. Indeed, qualitative researchers often develop *post hoc* theoretical rationales for their work, which are explained when the thesis, or learned paper, is submitted (Golden-Biddle and Locke, 2007). Our argument in this chapter is that there are many other factors that can influence the kind of questions that are seen as worthy of research, and that these include the personal experiences of the researcher, the attitudes and influence of external stakeholders with whom he or she comes into contact, and the broader context within which he or she works and studies. These factors are summarized in Figure 6.1. We do not regard this as a mechanistic model; we see research ideas evolving in an incremental way through a continual process of negotiation with these factors.

Before tackling each of these factors in Figure 6.1 in turn we would like to offer a simple model which we have found useful in making sense of the politics of research. This is based on the classic study by Boissevain (1974) of social networks, especially in the Sicilian Mafia, where he identified two distinct roles played by participants: brokers and patrons. *Brokers* are social 'fixers' who use their secondary resources, such as information and a wide range of contacts, in order to achieve their ambitions.

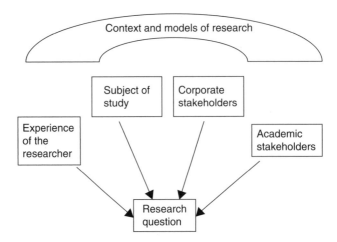

FIGURE 6.1 Influences on the research question

Patrons are people with direct control over primary resources such as people and money. But when they need information or the resolution of a problem they turn to brokers who have the contacts and a past record of solving problems. A skilful broker will also specify a tariff that is only part of the real cost – so that when the transaction is made he will have built up further goodwill with the patron. This will in turn increase the broker's overall credit for future problem-solving.

While we would not wish to suggest a direct correspondence between the worlds of Mafiosi and management researchers, there are a number of parallels. In the research world, senior academics and tutors can act as brokers because they know the way round the system, and are known by others. They may be able to advise on considerations such as: which people are able to grant access to a particular organization; assessment criteria; how to obtain funds from research councils; which external examiners would be most appropriate for a thesis; or which journal editor is most likely to be interested in a particular paper. Within companies, training and human resource managers can often act as brokers because, although they have little formal power, they usually have a wide range of contacts at all levels of the organization. Successful researchers can also develop brokerage skills. Thus a personnel manager is more likely to help provide access to his or her company if he or she thinks the researcher may be able to provide him or her with something in return – whether it be expertise, credibility or other contacts.

The experience of the researcher

We have argued in previous chapters that direct contact with the subject of one's research is most important if one is to develop new insights. This can be illustrated from the work of researchers such as Melville Dalton (1959) whose insights were based on personal experience as a manager at Milo, or Frederick Taylor who based his views of scientific management on his experiences first as a labourer, and then as a foreman, at the Midvale Steel Company in the 1880s.

The point we wish to make here is slightly different. It is that personal background affects what the researcher can see: experience acts both as a sensitizer and as a filter for the researcher. The motivations of individual researchers may be quite varied. As Platt (1976) has shown, many researchers in the early stages of projects are unclear about their aims and goals; others may have more precisely defined career goals, political aims or agendas to create change in their own institutions and environments. When it comes to fieldwork, personal background, including social class, will affect the ease with which the researcher can gain access to different settings, and this may also pre-determine responses from different groups. Those who conduct research on workers rarely get round to investigating managers, and vice versa. This may be for ideological reasons, or merely for personal and social ease. Most organizations are highly sensitive to the possibility of researchers having any kind of political agenda, particularly if it differs from theirs. Amusingly, Beynon (1988) recounts problems that he and his colleagues have encountered in gaining access both to what he regarded as a 'right-wing' manufacturing organization, *and* to a 'left-wing' trade union organization.

Although the traditional model of management research involved lone scholars, increasingly research is being conducted by teams, both as student project groups and as teams of funded researchers. These arrangements can provide added advantages through combining people with different backgrounds and interests, and the flexibility and synergy that this can create. A team that balances perspectives, backgrounds and skills may be much more effective than individuals at conducting research. Teams can also be established to take advantage of the insider/outsider perspective. This, as explained in the previous chapter, follows the ethnographic principle that insiders will be able to see and understand things that will make no sense to outsiders, while outsiders will notice things that may have become quite invisible to insiders. Sometimes a student project group will gain access to a company because, say, the mother of one of the students is a senior manager there. Similarly the growth of executive MBAs and part-time postgraduate programmes has also resulted in many students carrying out research into aspects of their own organizations. Not only does this help with access, but they may also have direct experience of the issues they are investigating. So up to a point, their insights are likely to be deeper than those of researchers who arrive from outside the organization.

However, it is within teams that political and other problems can arise. In our own research we have found that the internal dynamics of a team can be affected by external pressures. In Mark Easterby-Smith's UK–China decision-making project the research team contained both Chinese and UK nationals, but the researchers sometimes found that UK companies to which they were seeking access would only talk to the UK staff and would not respond to any communications from Chinese staff. This may seem surprising nowadays in view of the enormous economic power of China, but back in 1990 many companies were locked into racial stereotypes. Even though we resisted these external pressures they still affected internal relationships, and decisions about who was most appropriate to carry out interviews in the companies (Easterby-Smith and Malina, 1999).

In a classic paper Hyder and Sims (1979) analyse the tensions between 'grant holders' who are awarded the funds and 'research officers' who are hired to carry out the work. They suggest that the relationship can become difficult for three main reasons. First, there are different timescales: grant holders are generally tenured academics; research staff on fixed-term contracts are chronically insecure. Second, in terms of commitment, research staff are likely to be doing little else than working on the project; grant holders will have many other responsibilities and commitments. Third, most grant holders develop conflicting expectations of their research officers, expecting them on the one hand to be general factotums and dogsbodies and on the other to be creative contributors to the research enterprise.

Barwise et al. (1989) also encountered the latter issue in the context of a multidisciplinary investigation of strategic investment decisions. Although the project was conceived and 'sold' to the funders by three senior staff, it was carried out by a part-time researcher who was recruited specifically for the project. The senior academics initially treated the researcher as their 'eyes and ears', but about half way through the project they were forced to recognize that she had developed a greater understanding of the project than they, and that she now had a major contribution to make both in the interpretation of data and in the overall direction of the project. This recognition meant that they just managed to avoid the researcher becoming an alienated worker.

There is much potential for conflict here. The power of grant holders lies in their control of funds and their potential influence on the future career of the researcher. The researcher's power, conversely, lies in intimate knowledge of the research process and the potential to withhold co-operation. Thus both parties are in a position to exert influence throughout the project, although the relative balance might vary as the project evolves. Things often come to a head when arrangements are made to start publishing the results, unless clear rules can be agreed in advance which are seen as fair to all parties. This is also a growing problem for research students where there is an expectation of one or two papers emerging from the thesis possibly with joint authorship from the supervisor. It is worth clarifying expectations early in the research period – a good principle is that author order is determined by who does most of the work, and no-one should expect a 'free ride'!

Academic stakeholders

The relationship between supervisors and research staff or students is a key power dynamic. But there are many other dynamics within the academic world. Research councils exert influence on the direction of research through control of funds. Disciplinary associations, in turn, determine quality criteria in their own fields, while journal editors, referees and conference organizers act as final arbiters of academic quality. Senior academics may act as mentors, but they also control career rewards. In almost all circumstances, members of the academic community operate with a high degree of probity and professionalism; nevertheless, given the amount of competition for relatively few prizes, there are bound to be criteria and processes which are not totally transparent. Our aim in this section of the chapter is to make these criteria and processes more visible.

Funding bodies Academic funding bodies cannot entirely ignore the agendas of their political masters. These often require some explicit links to be made between research funding and national well-being. Consequently, in a number of countries, research councils have adopted policies of targeting resources towards specific initiatives which may generate sufficient critical mass to provide rapid development of theories and practical applications. Research proposals therefore stand greater chance of funding if they can demonstrate how they are meeting the priorities of their respective councils. At the present time, political pressures in the UK are demanding that government-funded research should demonstrate usefulness, which means that dissemination and 'user engagement' are now essential elements of research proposals. Even in the case of charities, which should not be affected by national political pressures, funding needs to be consistent with the objectives of the charity, as laid down by boards of trustees, and hence it is important to check out policy statements (and perhaps scrutinize the range of projects already funded by the agency) while crafting any proposals for funding. Like it or not, the days of 'blue skies research' are over.

But there is also a danger if funding becomes *too* responsive to political priorities and pressures, because research results may be used by one group directly to harm another group, and it is very easy for researchers to become compromised in the process. An extreme example of this is the work carried out by scientists in Nazi Germany on concentration camp inmates. The majority of those involved appeared to be highly principled, as scientists, and strongly denied any anti-Semitism. Yet in a review of a careful study of surviving evidence, Billig comments:

In Murderous Science, *we see academics continually writing grant applications, guessing what projects the controllers of the funding agencies will be considering socially useful: is it the Gypsies, or the degenerates; or the ability to withstand cold, which will bring the grants this year? (1988: 476)*

He who pays the piper not only calls the tune, but can also define what a good tune is. One hopes that exercises such as these would never take place in or around modern organizations. But the personal and social consequences of losing a power struggle, or a job, can be very profound indeed. Researchers should therefore be very wary of the ends that they may be serving, whether wittingly or unwittingly, and this is why increasing attention must be given to ethical issues, as we will see later in this chapter.

Funding bodies always receive more proposals than they can accommodate. Proposals in the UK are given an *alpha* rating if the independent referees consider them to be technically worthy of funding, but the Economic and Social Research Council (ESRC) only has funds for 30 per cent of the alpha-rated proposals. Thus decisions about the awards often have to take other information into account. Chief among these are whether the researcher has a good 'track record' of prior funded research, whether he or she is known to those involved in making the decision, and whether the research appears to be aligned with current funding council priorities. For those with international reputations and many years successful research experience, this is an advantage; but for the newcomer it is a major obstacle to getting started on funded research. Hence we offer below some advice to newcomers wishing to get their feet on the ladder.

- Start with modest-sized proposals[1].
- Make the best use of your own experience through highlighting any related work or publications you may have.

[1]Most research councils have schemes which fund relatively small grants (say, up to £50,000) which are available exclusively to younger researchers who have never received grants before.

- Get known by key people in the field by going to conferences and submitting papers for publication.

- Take the opportunity to attend workshops which provide guidance on crafting proposals[2].

- Make use of networks, possibly by submitting proposals jointly with people who are already established, and by sending drafts to potential referees. In both of these cases, senior colleagues may be able to act as brokers by establishing initial contacts, or they may be willing to collaborate directly.

Supervisors and institutions For those working on projects or research degrees, the main pressures come from supervisors, colleagues and gatekeepers. At the undergraduate level, the supervisor will normally use his or her personal contacts in local firms to identify viable projects. He or she will be concerned to ensure that the project meets the requirements of the company and will be hoping to source projects in future years from the same company. Research degree supervisors may have different concerns: they will be keen to ensure that the research stays fairly close both in terms of content and methodology to their own research interests (and competence). If the research is being conducted for a doctoral degree, the supervisor will increasingly be anxious about whether the work will be completed successfully within a given time; this is because both academic departments and whole institutions are now being judged upon completion rates for research students and will have funding withdrawn if the four-year completion rate falls below a given percentage (usually 60–70 per cent). The consequence of this is that both institutions and supervisors are tending to tighten up on guidelines and procedures – by reducing the maximum length of a thesis to 80,000 words, and by introducing regular review mechanisms.

The rise of professional doctorates in subjects such as education, psychology, social administration and business has added another dimension to the system. In our view they offer a distinct opportunity for working on the relationship of theory to practice. In the early days they were largely ignored by the traditional academic community, and universities were able to invent their own criteria and practices. So entry qualifications, research training requirements, assessment criteria and overall standards were left up to individual institutions, which left an impression that some universities might be abusing the qualification.

Consequently the ESRC has recently developed guidelines for institutions wishing to gain national recognition for their programmes. These start with the assumption that the research should contribute to the development of the student's practice in a professional context and institutions are expected to explain how, for example, professional bodies or senior practitioners contribute to the design and assessment of the programme. In addition they need to explain how the teaching/learning process considers the links between theory and practice, including the induction process, research training, the type of research design and the nature of the thesis. Students should also be encouraged to produce their results for both academic and practitioner audiences; both conference presentations and journal articles. Bridging the

---

[2]The British Academy of Management runs excellent workshops on grant applications every year.

gap between theory and practice also means that different arrangements for the supervision of students may need to be considered. Given that the majority of students on professional doctorates study part time, supervisory support systems have to be appropriate to their needs recognizing that most students study at a distance. In general it is expected that professional doctorates should be 'equivalent' to PhDs, although they need contributions both to theory and practice.

House styles Most academic departments have their own house styles which support and encourage particular kinds of work, whether quantitative or qualitative and there is also much pressure on departments to prioritize their research interests. This can make it hard to find the right supervisors and examiners. The ideal external examiner not only needs to share the same research philosophy as the candidate, but also needs to know a lot about the subject of investigation. It is advisable in most cases to start looking for potential external examiners at a fairly early stage in a research degree. This helps to focus the research project, because it requires the candidate to be clear about the boundaries of the field in which he or she is operating, and also to know who are the key movers and shakers in the field. Although the supervisor will need to approach the external examiner, it is important that the candidate is able to provide a list of potential examiners. If the candidate does not have such a list that is a worrying sign because it suggests that they may not be sufficiently on top of the field.

Conferences As we have mentioned above, conferences provide a valuable form of contact within the academic community, and it is essential for anyone doing a doctorate to get onto the right conference circuits. Most conferences are not too competitive, and will accept papers on the basis of one- or two-page abstracts; those that are more competitive, such as the US or British Academy of Management, will usually give preferential treatment to doctoral students. The benefits of conference participation should be obvious, but here is a list of points: they provide visibility for you and your ideas; they enable you to get feedback on papers that you will subsequently submit to journals; they enable you to identify others working in your own field; you will get early copies of publications that may not appear in journals until two or three years later; and you may be able to spot potential external examiners. In addition, conferences act as recruitment fairs, explicitly in the USA and implicitly in the UK. Gibson Burrell provides an entertaining account of how the system works at the Academy of Management Conference:

Doctoral candidates, looking for university positions, are glaringly obvious in the hotel lobbies. The males dress in blazers and grey trousers, the women in blue suits. Prestigious professors dress in Bermuda shorts and sandals. One's position in the hierarchy therefore is marked by dress, so the 'smarter' the attire, the lower is one's standing. (1993: 75)

We offer this quote partly for those who agonize over what to wear at conferences – the message being to dress down rather than up – but also to highlight aspects of power within the academic game, which is often expressed through (not so subtle) symbols. And if you are tempted to wear Bermuda shorts and Hawaiian T-shirts, remember that they should be well ironed.

Material presented at conferences is often published on CD-ROMs as proceedings or as edited books, normally on more of a selective basis than the conference itself and conference organizers often take on the editorial roles for these publications. Although peer review is normally used to support decisions, one of the easiest ways of getting included in such publications is to offer to co-edit the proceedings. But this is by no means the end of the road, because conference proceedings and book chapters only achieve modest ratings in the increasingly hierarchical world of academic publishing. The gold standard is the academic journal, and this is where some of the strictest hierarchies operate.

Academic journals There are two simple ways of judging in advance the standing of an academic journal. First, rejection rates indicate how much demand there is to get into the journal. Top journals will have rejection rates of over 95 per cent, lesser journals may be around 50 per cent. Journals that take almost everything will not be considered as serious journals (but then they are unlikely to publish their rejection rates). Second, the citation index *ISI Web of Knowledge* produces annual rankings of journals based on the frequency with which papers from a given journal are cited by papers published in other respectable journals (see http://wok.mimas.ac.uk/). These rankings use 'impact factor' as the key criterion. This is calculated as the number of citations appearing in *ISI* journals during the target year which refer to papers published in the focal journal during the two previous years, divided by the total number of papers published in the focal journal during the two previous years (see Example 6.1).

Although this varies somewhat between disciplines, journals with impact factors over 2.0 are generally considered 'world class'; those between 1.0 and 2.0 are seen as very good international journals; those between 0.5 and 1.0 are respectable international journals, and those below 0.5 are in danger of relegation. Of course, interpretation of these ratings depend greatly on where your favourite journals fall,

EXAMPLE 6.1

Calculating the 2006 impact factor for *Journal of Management Studies*

Number of citations			Number of articles		
to articles published in:	2005	92	published in:	2005	66
	2004	156		2004	58
	Sum:	248		Sum:	124
Calculation: Divide citations to recent articles by number of recent articles:					
		248÷124=2.0.			

and it is also important to look at trends over several years since these ratings can be quite volatile.

Beyond that, one must make up one's own mind, by reading past papers in the journal, or by submitting something to it. If you want to get something published quickly or easily then start with one of the more lowly journals. Top journals have much greater lead time, often running into several years. This is not because they are slow or inefficient, more that they will be dealing with a very large volume of material and they will be very exacting in their standards. For example, a paper published in the *Academy of Management Journal* (Easterby-Smith and Malina, 1999) was initially submitted in March 1996 (and that was based on earlier conference papers given in 1993 and 1995). The initial rewrite offer from *AMJ* arrived 11 weeks after submission and contained eight single-spaced pages of comments and advice from the editor and referees. Over the next two years the paper went though four rewrites, and on each occasion the guidance from the editorial office ran to four or five pages. Thus by the time the paper was accepted in July 1998 the length of comments from the editorial office was greater than the eventual length of the paper. On occasions such as this, as Golden-Biddle and Locke (2007) comment, one starts to wonder whether the referees should be included as co-authors of the paper.

As we said at the outset of this section, it is important for people carrying out academic management research to understand some of the hidden rules and procedures, because these may determine whether they are eventually successful. Despite efforts to be fair and transparent, these hidden rules and procedures are inevitable. In general it is easier for North Americans to get accepted in North American journals, and for Europeans to get accepted in European journals, because of the institutional and human networks that support these journals. US journals tend to prefer quantitative papers based on survey data, whereas many European journals prefer qualitative papers based on in-depth case studies. But there are always exceptions to these rules, and therefore it is important to be alert and not to accept stereotypes too easily.

Corporate stakeholders

We use the term 'corporate' loosely here, to include companies, public organizations and others generally within the user community. These are becoming very significant because they are both sponsors and users of management research. Many companies invest heavily in executive education, sponsoring managers to attend MBAs and other programmes, and most of these involve projects conducted within the sponsoring organization. There is also growing interaction between companies and universities through enterprise development networks, knowledge transfer partnerships, and the sponsorship of consulting/research projects for both undergraduates and postgraduates.

In the case of postgraduate projects, there are several potential sets of expectations. A production manager attending a part-time MBA might, for example, want to set up a three-month project in the marketing department. This means that the main stakeholders will include: the project sponsor in the marketing department, the academic supervisor, the training department that has organized sponsorship in the first place and the manager. Again, there is often tension between the sponsor who

EXAMPLE 6.2

Undergraduate projects

At Lancaster University, undergraduates on the Bachelor of Business Administration carry out consulting projects with local companies, which involve tackling live problems to do with human resources, marketing or internationalization. These run for about 10 weeks and require both practical presentations for the companies and academic reports for the university. In the course of these projects, students have to appreciate and deal with many issues. They have to manage their own time and make effective use of their own resources; they have to take responsibility for managing the relationship with the company, gaining the support both of the initial sponsor and key actors; they have to help the company work out what it actually wants from them, and then deliver it. Thus they have to balance the competing pressures of conducting practical consulting projects while producing respectable academic work.

wants a solution to a problem, and the academic supervisor who will be looking for a well-argued case which takes account of existing literature supported by tangible evidence obtained with a well-explained methodology. The student-manager and the training representative will have the task of reconciling the two. Sometimes it is necessary to write two separate reports. Occasionally the two sets of expectations can be met with one seamless report, which blends academic theory with practical action. Alternatively there is the 'sandwich' model where the client report is prefaced by an academic introduction and literature review, and then followed by a methodological and substantive critique.

One residual consideration is whether research which is conducted for corporate clients will become 'contaminated' because of the funding relationship. There are two ways in which this might happen. As we have already noted, funders are likely to exert some influence on the direction of research and the kinds of questions that are considered to be significant. But this is likely to be the case with all forms of funded research, whether following a positivist or constructionist approach, and we think that the differences due to corporate or non-corporate funding are merely a matter of degree. The other form of contamination may come from people within the organization deliberately feeding information into the project that is likely to support their political agenda.

Again, the same thing can happen with any kind of organization, for example a school or a hospital, whether or not there is also a funding relationship. Given that contamination inevitably arises from political factors, the question is how best to deal with it? Our view is that these political factors and their consequences should not be kept hidden. Instead, they should be incorporated explicitly into the reports of the research process. The researcher's own interests, the process of gaining access or funds from organizations, or discussions about dissemination of results: these may all be relevant. Thus we would advise researchers to keep regular records not only of formal research data, but also to chronicle their own views and moods, and the processes of organizing and conducting the research. Further, we think it important that researchers are prepared to reflect critically on all of these influences on their research, and to make these thoughts available to others. As we mentioned in Chapter 4, this requires an element of reflexivity – which should increase rather than decrease the credibility of the results.

The subject of study

The subject or topic of study may exert considerable influence on the nature and direction of the research enterprise. By the 'subject' we mean the problems or issues to be considered – rather than the people and data that will be looked at within the study. Each academic discipline, whether it be mathematics, engineering, sociology or organizational theory, tends to have a number of key debates and issues at any one time. There is also a tendency among researchers to follow fads and fashions with regard to both method and focus. As Scarbrough and Swan (1999) point out, fads often become popular because they appear to provide the solution to some contemporary problem, but they are also based on simple and ambiguous ideas. Thus both their nature and foundations are often quite shaky, and this can also account for their rapid disappearance.

For example, in the early 1990s when the first edition of this book was published some of the fashionable debates among academic management researchers in Europe were: postmodernism, business process re-engineering and critiques of the enterprise culture. A decade later some of the hottest areas were: knowledge economy, globalization and e-commerce. Now, another five years later, there is particular interest in the rise of the Asian economies, the evolution of product-service systems and innovation. There are clear advantages to situating one's work close to the mainstream: others will be interested in the subject, debates will be lively, and there will be conferences and special issues of journals being commissioned on the topic. In contract, there will be a lot of competition for space and to establish ownership of new ideas. And the fashion may also turn, so that unless the research topic is defined in a flexible way there is a danger of being stranded with good ideas and materials that excite no further interest.

A 'strategic' approach may be to try to spot issues that are currently regarded as mundane, in the hope that they will suddenly pick up interest. This is another reason for working the conference circuit to find out what the 'industry leaders' think will be important issues for the future. At a wider level, though, the focus on fashion may result in other important or 'ordinary' issues being overlooked. Very often it is the ordinary and commonplace that can be most revealing. Ryave and Schenkein (1974), for example, describe a study of the relatively trivial topic of how people walk. Their results show how a number of social rules can be identified with regard to space, control and propriety – which are by no means mundane, and have direct relevance to architecture and the design of public spaces.

If the research is to be carried out in a corporate setting it is worth talking to managers and other employees to find out what they consider to be current problems. Often practitioners are ahead of mainstream academics in identifying key problems and relevant solutions. Sometimes this can lead to tension between corporate sponsors and academic supervisors around the questions they consider to be important. But there are plenty of examples of the appropriate combination being achieved. One of our research students was asked by her sponsoring company to investigate how appraisal systems were working in practice in different parts of the company. The researcher was able to answer this practical question to the satisfaction of the company. At the same time she was able to use data from her interviews to show how organizational systems, such as appraisals, are a product of wider cultural value systems in those parts of the organizations; and conversely she could show how such systems are a channel for the transmission and articulation of value systems, particularly as defined by senior members of the organization.

There is no particular reason why academic and practical goals should not be achieved simultaneously. Indeed, as in Example 6.3, we have found that many practitioners will become enthusiastically involved in theoretical debates created from the academic perspective. Managers are not only likely to be familiar with academic debates about culture and values, they may also wish to contribute substantially to these debates. This increasingly leads to the possibility of managers, sponsors and gatekeepers being seen as collaborators in the research process itself.

Context and models of research

We now come to the effect of the broad context within which the research is taking place. By 'context' we include both the national setting and the extent to which resources and attitudes are likely to be supportive of research. We will then look at four different models of the role of the researcher. These are not derived theoretically from philosophical positions, as in the last two chapters, but based on observations of different forms of research in practice.

EXAMPLE 6.3

Collaborative research project with engineering companies

The Knowledge and Information (KIM) project is funded by two UK research councils, the Engineering and Physical Science Research Council (EPSRC) and the Economic and Social Research Council (ESRC) with teams in 11 universities looking at the social and technical problems of information management as engineering firms add a significant service element to the products that they sell. The project has a steering committee comprising representatives of 18 companies, which meets bi-annually and provides general guidance on the direction and potential outputs of the project. There are many forms of collaboration here, between two research councils, between universities, between engineers and social scientists, and between companies and academic institutions. The degree of corporate involvement and commitment is very important. Not only do the sponsoring companies allow research access to sensitive business and technological decisions, they also contribute actively to the academic debates by making presentations at the universities, and organising workshops and seminars on their own sites (see http://www-edc.eng.cam.ac.uk/kim/).

The national setting is important both because of the way resource availability affects what is possible, and because different countries and cultures may have different views regarding what constitutes 'good' research. David Hickson (1988) provides a nice description of the contrasting resources that he found when conducting research in oil-rich Alberta, compared to his subsequent experiences of research at the University of Bradford, which was at that time reeling from severe government cutbacks. Also, Pugh's (1988) account of the early period of the Aston research programme (see Chapter 4) sounds almost unrecognizable today. Thus he and his team were able to spend a whole year reading books and discussing what the focus of their research would be, with no expectation during the first year that they should collect any data or produce preliminary reports.

The case for the localization of management research is argued by Davila (1989) on the grounds that North American models of research, which require large samples and substantial data analysis, are largely irrelevant both methodologically and substantively in the context of Latin America. He advocates paying far more attention to case studies, which can draw more extensively upon local culture and problems – many of these problems being quite different from those considered significant in more highly developed countries. Teagarden et al. (1995) in turn found that US research methods could not be applied uniformly in their major cross-national study of HRM practices. The potential for co-operation from companies and managers varied greatly between countries, and it was simply not possible to adhere to the rigorous criteria for sampling and data collection that they had assumed from the USA. Thus we believe that it is important for the researcher to be at least aware of the constraints and opportunities posed by the context within which he or she is currently working.

This leads us to propose four archetypical research models, which although they are not comprehensive, offer different ways of tackling contextual variations. The first is what we call the *military* model which involves: teams of people, substantial preparation and planning and some differentiation of roles between those who design the research, those who gather data and those who make sense of the data. This is most appropriate in a resource-rich environment as in the case of the work of Pugh and his colleagues at Aston, or Hickson and his colleagues in Alberta. It does mean that substantial resources can be focused on solving major problems, as with the KIM project described in Example 6.3, but there are also downsides to the military model because large hierarchical teams can find it hard to operate within the unpredictability of the research environment – and these need to be managed carefully.

Whereas the workers in the military model are generally hired for the job, in the second model, the *private agent*, one is more likely to find research students and lone academics. This involves individuals operating independently, developing their own ideas using their own resources, and making the best of whatever opportunities are available. Occasionally there may be an element of co-ordination, or networking, among the lone researchers through the Internet and conference links. Institutions that run doctoral programmes may also establish arrangements whereby students, although conducting their research quite independently, are also members of action learning sets that provide support and guidance to each other. Indeed the existence of academic communities of sufficient size is one of the necessary conditions for government funding of research studentships in the UK.

A third possibility is the *team* model, which lies between the two previous models. It involves teams of three to seven people, either students or funded researchers, working together on the particular project or problem. In these cases there is considerable interdependence between the team members, and there needs to be both flexibility and specialization in the roles that members adopt. For example, one person may specialize in maintaining relationships with companies or research settings, another may specialize in handling and analysing data, another may specialize in logistics and group ordination, etc. The team approach is probably most appropriate for dealing with conflicting expectations and tight deadlines.

A final, and somewhat controversial, possibility is the *investigative* model. This starts from the assumption that powerful organizations and individuals will always try to control and repress research conducted on themselves, and hence some deception is both legitimate and necessary. This implies that researchers should be opportunistic, they should use any means necessary to gain access and gather data, and they should publish their findings quickly regardless of consequences. One of the main proponents of this model, sometimes known as conflict methodology, is Douglas (1976). Beynon's classic study of life on and around the assembly line at the Ford plant in Liverpool also had elements of investigative journalism in it (Beynon, 1973). But this subsequently attracted the comment from the company that: 'It's extreme left-wing propaganda . . . we don't think it merits serious discussion as it's not a serious attempt at sociology or education.' There is much sympathy for the investigative model because it can expose fraud, injustice, the misuse of power and organizational myths. But there are also concerns because of the potential backlash and the effect it may have on the opportunities for future researchers who might wish to gain access for non-investigative reasons.

All four of these models to some extent pre-determine the kind of research questions that can, and should, be investigated in their respective cases. Thus one might expect grand theoretical issues to emerge from the military model, the private agent to be focusing on detailed and small-scale processes and issues, the team to be working collaboratively with companies, and the investigator to concentrate on exposing wrongdoings.

TABLE 6.1 Summary of archetypical research models

Model	Characteristics
Military	Large, complex projects conducted by funded researchers, with considerable planning and internal structure
Private agent	Research students or lone academics pursuing a single project.
Team	Groups of students or funded researchers working on a common project.
Investigative	Investigations into potential wrong-doing or exploitation which is semi (or totally) covert.

POLITICS OF ACCESS

In this section we consider the politics that are involved in gaining access to research sites. There is also a difference between gaining *formal* access, or permission from senior management, to gather data from within the organization (generally within specific constraints), and the *informal* process of gaining access to people and documents. Similar to Buchanan et al. (1988), we would argue for an opportunistic approach. Most researchers seriously underestimate the amount of time and patience that can be required to gain this initial access. In the following paragraphs we provide some 'war stories' of how hard it can be, and offer some advice on how access may be eased. The good news is that there seems to be a growing acceptance of the value of in-company projects – possibly because a growing number of middle managers have now been through business schools themselves. Consequently, they are not so likely to feel threatened, and they may be genuinely interested in what is being investigated.

It is extremely difficult to gain access through contacting companies out of the blue (sometimes called 'cold calling'). In our experience it is essential to start with some kind of personal contacts, however tenuous. If one's supervisor or institution does not have the right links then it is often worth trying the relevant trade or professional associations, or using contacts in related organizations. We have found associations to be very helpful here, and they rarely object to being mentioned as the source of the contact – because, of course, brokerage is the lifeblood of most trade and professional associations. In a recent project conducted by Lancaster and Warwick Business School there was a need to gain access to foreign multinationals operating in China and the researchers found that the China–British Business Council, based in London, was enormously helpful both in providing lists of companies and in helping with introductions (http://www.aimresearch.org/intransfer_desc.html).

Once the initial contact has been made by phone, letter or email, the gatekeeper is likely to consider two questions: (1) is this individual worth supporting; and (2) will it be possible to 'sell' to others whose cooperation is being requested. The latter question hangs on a consideration of whether the potential benefits will outweigh the likely costs, or potential risks, of the project. Given that information about costs and benefits will be very imprecise it usually helps at this stage if:

- the project has potential relevance and benefit to the organization;
- the time and resources requested are minimal;
- the project appears not to be politically sensitive; and
- the individuals concerned, and their institution have a good reputation.

Even still, projects can still go wrong. In a recent ESRC funded project on the evolution of business knowledge led by Easterby-Smith and Antonacopoulou (http://www.ebkresearch.org/people.html) the research design required access to four distinct companies. Within the first six months of the project we managed to gain access, and to commence fieldwork, in the first three companies – and these all yielded valuable data and stories. We also gained an official letter of invitation from the fourth company, IBM, but before we were able to arrange the first meeting our sponsor, who had written the letter, abruptly left the company. Three months later at a dinner one of the researchers happened to sit next to a senior manager from IBM, and she agreed to provide another introduction. We attended a meeting and presented pro-posals to a new group of managers, but were informed a few weeks later that IBM had taken a policy decision not to initiate any new university research links at all.

A few months later the researchers discovered that a Lancaster alumnus was work-ing as PA to the UK Managing Director of IBM. She offered to organize a meeting with the top man, which meant that we might be able to outflank the earlier policy decision. Unfortunately, a week before the meeting IBM announced an international structural reorganization which threatened the role of the UK managing director, and hence the meeting was cancelled. By this time the end of the project was close, and it was too late to replace IBM with another company. The moral of this story is that it is always important to plan for contingencies: don't count your chickens, and keep something in reserve.

The principle of reciprocity is important: the more the company gives, in time or money, the more it expects in exchange; hence it is important to plan for some early 'wins' for the company. Another feature that is common to the above examples is that the initiative usually comes from the researcher, and organizational brokers may then be used to reach the patrons. However there are occasions when patrons themselves may wish to initiate some research. At least six reasons for sponsoring research are common, and these are summarized in Table 6.2.

As we have suggested above, access, whether formally or informally acquired, is only the start of the story: the next problem is to maintain access through obtaining co-operation and trust inside. This depends mainly on the researcher's skills in deal-ing with what are sometimes very complex interpersonal relationships. In our experi-ence these complex relationships derive largely from the political issues within the organization, and we divide these into micro-issues, which are about relationships with individual managers and macro-issues which are to do with the wider political conflicts within the organization.

At a *micro political* level it is important to be able to develop a co-operative rela-tionship with each informant. With most managers the relationship begins when you try to negotiate an appointment either directly or through a secretary. Most managers

TABLE 6.2 Common reasons for sponsoring organizational research

Characteristics
To tackle a known problem
To gain support for a new idea
To demonstrate the success of a recent project
To help the individual or unit defend against attack
To act as a sounding board
To support research for its own sake

EXAMPLE 6.4

Internal blockages to access

Barbara Czarniawska (1998) provides a fascinating account of her experiences in Warsaw, where she had obtained agreement to conduct a 10-day observational study of the director of finance of the City Council. Most of this period seemed to be taken up with the director finding excuses not to talk to her, or to exclude her from meetings. Even when the director, in a moment of helpfulness, tried to arrange for Barbara to meet the deputy mayor she only managed a passing contact and never managed to schedule an actual interview.

---

will be protective over their time and will also be making assessments of the personal costs and benefits of co-operating. Some managers will get interested in the topic during the interview and will want to keep talking, others will give very short replies, and you will wonder how you are going to get through the allotted hour. We will discuss the dynamics of interview situations in more detail in Chapter 7. For the time being, however, we note some of the typical problems for researchers.

Czarniawska (see Example 6.4) is a senior professor with an international reputation, so perhaps it was hard for the director to resist her openly. With younger researchers more direct 'put downs' may be used. One technique is for the interviewee to cross-examine the interviewer at the outset to demonstrate that he or she has little relevant experience of the organization under study and is naive about anything outside the academic environment. Having established who is really in control of the interaction, the senior manager may then be prepared to sit back for 40 or 50 minutes and respond honestly to questions. Even experienced researchers occasionally get caught out by this tactic. Beynon (1988) provides a nice example of a senior NCB manager attacking the credibility of an expert academic witness involved in a colliery enquiry by asking such direct questions as 'Are you qualified to manage a coalfield?', 'What practical management experience have you had in operating?', 'Have you any personal knowledge of selling to commercial buyers?' This form of discrediting the external expert provides a very effective form of corporate defence, and perhaps the minor 'put downs' given to researchers by senior managers may be an anticipatory form of defence just in case the 'wrong' results are produced by the study.

Where there is a *macro political* problem, the researcher often becomes trapped between two major groups or factions. When Mark Easterby-Smith was researching for his PhD he had been asked by the works manager of a major chemical plant to conduct a study into the consequences of a large plant closure exercise. This exercise had apparently been handled very successfully and had led to the voluntary redundancy of over 1000 workers, without any overt industrial relations strife occurring. About a week after starting the study he noticed that people were starting to become less available for interview, and people with access to personnel records were suddenly too busy to deal with requests. He was however very much reassured to be invited to lunch one day with a general manager from that site: discussion ranged over the research project which had recently started, and the manager showed much interest in some initial observations. It was later the same day that he met one of the personnel managers from the site who informed him regretfully that a meeting had been held that same morning to discuss the research project, and that one person had been very insistent that the project be stopped – this was the general manager with whom he had just had lunch.

This was unexpected, since nothing had been mentioned at lunchtime. It was even more surprising that the personnel manager thought there was nothing exceptional about this behaviour. It later emerged that the decision to ban the project was the focal point in a major battle between the works manager and the general manager with regard to the appropriate management style on the site. The former was backing a rather paternalistic line of management, and the results of the study would no doubt have helped him in his argument. His protagonist was arguing for a much harder form of managerialism; unfortunately for the research project it was an argument that the latter won. Like many organizational researchers faced with similar problems Easterby-Smith was forced to complete the study by interviewing people in their homes about the closure, and by using networks of internal contacts provided for another project who would accept some surreptitious questioning about the closure themselves.

The lesson from these political examples is that the researcher needs to be aware of conflicts that may be far deeper and more complex than will be evident to a relative newcomer in the organization. We can offer three pieces of advice on how to deal with such politics. First, try to identify one or two 'key informants' who may be prepared to help in a disinterested way. They need to be generally well-informed but not directly concerned with the issues under investigation. Informants may be able to advise on whom to talk to, and they should be able to explain why things are, or are not, happening. Second, deliberately look for people who have different perspectives on key issues. Talk further to them and others in order to understand *why* they hold different views. Third, always assume that there is more than meets the eye. People may withhold information because they think it is important, or irrelevant, or they may genuinely have forgotten things. In organizations that have a policy of moving people around every two years, the collective memory may be very short. The departmental officer may be the only person who knows that your topic has already been researched and written up twice in the last five years.

ETHICS

There are ethical issues bubbling under the surface of many of the examples we have given above. In this section we provide an analytic structure for thinking about ethical issues in the management field, and review the ongoing debate for and against the provision of ethical codes and procedures.

Management researchers, and their professional associations such as the British Academy of Management, and the (American) Academy of Management, have been relatively relaxed about the provision of ethical codes. But there is growing pressure from other academic disciplines, such as medicine and psychology for all universities to adopt definite ethical codes and practices, and there is growing coherence, especially in the social sciences, around a common set of principles. Bell and Bryman (2007) conducted a content analysis of the ethical principles of nine professional

Role-play about access

Your group has the possibility of being given access to a local Internet company, which sells broadband and associated services to small and medium-sized businesses across the country. The task is to conduct fieldwork into 'leadership' and you need to complete a number of interviews in a real organization in order to complete your assignment. The initial contact with the company is through the training manager, and she has arranged for a meeting with the chief executive to discuss the possible research. The meeting will take place on-site, and the chief executive's busy schedule only has 20 minutes available. He has also indicated that he would like to see just two members of the team on this first instance.

ROLES

Student 1, student 2 –Their aim is to gain access on behalf of their colleagues for a project which both fits their academic needs and is also ethically acceptable.

Chief executive – He is prepared to provide access providing the project uses minimal resources/time, offers some potential benefit to the company, and carries absolutely no risks for the company or individuals within it.

Training manager – She is a former employee of the University at which the students are studying, but her own position in the company is slightly insecure.

Other group members – Should act as observers during the role play and as facilitators of the debrief afterwards.

ROLE-PLAYING PROCESS

The chief executive is in control of the meeting throughout. He has given himself 20 minutes in which to make a decision about whether or not to let the students in.

TIMESCALE

10 minutes: preparation. Student reps; CEO and training manager; observers to discuss in separate groups their agendas and how they will handle/monitor the role play.

20 minutes: role-play.

30 minutes: debrief. To be chaired/facilitated by the observers. Try to cover: pre-meeting strategies of different parties; degree of satisfaction with the outcome; what was unexpected; general lessons learnt about the process of access.

associations in the social sciences. They identified 10 principles of ethical practice which were defined by at least half of the associations. These principles are summarized in Figure 6.2.

Essentially, the first seven of these principles in Figure 6.2 are about protecting the interests of the research subjects or informants; the last three concern ensuring accuracy, and lack of bias, in research results. These are of particular concern in the medical sciences because of the danger that experiments might be conducted which would bring genuine harm to participants, and also because of the enormous

1	Ensuring that *no harm* comes to participants
2	Respecting the *dignity* of research participants
3	Ensuring a fully *informed consent* of research participants
4	Protecting the *privacy* of research subjects
5	Ensuring the *confidentiality* of research data
6	Protecting the *anonymity* of individuals or organizations
7	*Avoiding deception* about the nature or aims of the research
8	Declaration of affiliations, funding sources, and *conflicts of interest*
9	*Honesty and transparency* in communicating about the research
10	Avoidance of any *misleading*, or false reporting of research findings

FIGURE 6.2 Key principles in research ethics

financial muscle of commercial funding bodies such as drug companies which might well seek to influence results in directions which would give an advantage to their products.

The circumstances of management research are largely similar, but are distinct in one important respect: although the interests of informants still need to be protected, it can no longer be assumed that the researcher is in the all-powerful position held by clinical and social researchers. Indeed, as we have said eairler when research is conducted into managers and organizations, it is the researcher who is often the least powerful party to the transaction. Although researchers should normally protect the interests of the organizations they are investigating, there may be times when they come across illegal or unethical behaviour within the organizations themselves – and some people would argue that they should publish in a way that will expose the organization. This means that in the area of management research, it becomes difficult to establish hard-and-fast ethical principles, and good practice requires considerable judgment from the researcher.

The most likely ethical dilemma may therefore be to betray the confidences given by junior managers, when one is cross-examined by more senior managers. Informants who are politically adept, often read a great deal into the question that the interviewer is asking. An example is provided by an interview with the director of a national investigatory organization about the longer term effects of a particular management development programme. The researcher happened to ask a carefully focused question about how the reward system was working, to which the director immediately came back with, 'I take it you have been talking to John Dawson about that . . . Well in that case. . .'. Even though they may not be professionally trained as investigators, managers will often be able to work out the nature and sources of information already collected by researchers who are sufficiently unfamiliar with the detailed political context of the organization to be aware of the significance of the questions that they are asking.

Two particular ethical issues frequently concern organizational researchers. The first arises from the use of participant observation research methods which, as Ditton (1977) says, are very likely to be deceitful. That is, if you are participating, and at the same time observing and recording (perhaps later) what has taken place, it is hard to avoid some deception about your real purposes. Our view on this dilemma is that one should only deceive people as far as it is necessary to 'get by'. A compromise position is provided by Taylor and Bogdan (1984: 25) when they suggest that the researcher, on being asked about the nature and purposes of his or her work, should, 'Be truthful, but vague and imprecise'. This seems to have been the approach adopted by Dalton in his pioneering study of the processes of management. He comments that he was prepared to explain to most of his informants about the nature and purposes of his study, and that this, in the long run, did not inhibit them (Dalton, 1964).

The second ethical issue is around the control and use of data obtained by the researcher. In most cases the researcher has control and ownership of the data, and therefore he or she must exercise due ethical responsibility by not publicizing or circulating any information that is likely to harm the interests of individual informants, particularly the less powerful ones. Occasionally informants will request that the recorder is switched off when discussing information that is personally or commercially sensitive. There is an interesting story however where this particular assumption was neatly turned upon its head. A senior academic happened to be interviewing a member of the British Royal Family, and at the end of the interview he offered to have the tape transcribed and to send a transcript to the interviewee who would then be asked to strike out any passages to which he objected. Whereupon the Royal Person stretched out a hand saying 'No. I shall retain the tape and will let you have the portions that I am prepared to have published'.

Finally, there is an on-going debate about the value of ethical codes in relation to research. It is argued that at least some codes need to be made explicit in order to ensure that people are alerted to some of the likely ethical dilemmas that they may face. Such codes should also provide some kind of sanction in cases of blatant abuse and exploitation. But there is a problem here. As Snell (1993) points out, ethical issues are extremely complex. They involve not only the dynamics of power but also the competing claims of different ideologies. The danger is that ethical guidelines will not only be too rigid and simplistic to deal with real cases; they will also contain the biases that are inherent in one or another ideological position.

Both Mason (1996) and Bell and Bryman (2007) make a similar point about ethical codes being generally written in abstract terms, aimed at preventing serious and unambiguous cases of abuse. The problem is that most of the ethical issues faced by the researcher are small-scale, incremental and ambiguous. Mason argues that researchers should operate as thinking, reflective practitioners who are prepared to ask difficult questions about the ethics and politics of their own research practice on a regular basis. And we will offer Melville Dalton the final word: 'The social investigator must sort his values and obligations and weigh them repeatedly throughout the research process. In a democratic society, he cannot impose one fixed code on multiple conflicting codes' (1964: 61).

UTILIZATION OF RESEARCH

The link between research and action is often very weak, and many people find this extremely disappointing. Researchers themselves are only too aware of this feeling when they find that the fruits of several years' labour are gratefully accepted by the sponsoring organization, and are simply filed away in a dust-proof cabinet. A fine example of this comes from the USA where a major AACSB-sponsored survey on management education commented on the widespread dissatisfaction of American companies with the usability of research produced by business schools (Porter and McKibbin, 1988).

To some extent this disappointment could simply be a result of different people having different expectations from research. Within the academic world, the expectations are fairly specific. Good research should lead to contented corporate sponsors, to successful PhDs (completed within target dates), to the publication of articles in refereed journals and to the timely production of end-of-grant research reports. Getting published in the appropriate academic journals is even more important for the career advancement of academics, and the main political problems are related to debates, cliques and paradigms within the academic world (as we have discussed earlier in this chapter). But since most academic journals have a very limited circulation outside academia commercial sponsors are rarely concerned about what is likely to be published in these outlets. The same cannot be said for publication of books, as Punch (1986) found out to his cost (see Example 6.5).

The advice of Punch, then, is that the researcher should *never* sign away his or her rights of publication, and this view is also strongly supported by traditional researchers such as Bulmer (1988). On the other hand, Buchanan et al. (1988) take the more pragmatic line that organizational clients have a right to receive reports from those who research them, and that they should be allowed to comment upon the reports before they are published. This collaborative approach should enable both the quality of final reports to be improved, and may also contribute to the maintenance of positive relationships between researchers and clients. It is also common practice to anonymize the company unless specific permission is granted for identification. Our advice is to ensure explicit agreement at the outset with regard to publication rights, including anonymity, the right to read and comment on publications, and the right of veto.

One way of resolving this dilemma is to consider the research 'models' involved. Those adopting the *military* model will wish to have clear agreements about issues such as access, confidentiality and publication rights agreed well in advance. At the other end of the scale it is important that the *investigative journalism* researcher does not sign anything that could be used in evidence against him or her. The two other

---

EXAMPLE 6.5

Dangers of signing away publication rights

Maurice Punch conducted some research into the Dartington Hall Trust, an educational charity. At the outset of his research he was persuaded to sign a piece of paper in which he committed himself only to publish with prior permission of the Trust. Initially he regarded this as a mere formality, and therefore he was greatly surprised when the document was used to prevent publication of a book about Dartington Hall School. Given the importance of publications to academic careers, Punch realized that his own career was effectively being blocked by what he regarded as the intransigent position of the organization he had studied. Conversely, Dartington Hall felt that publication of Punch's findings would undoubtedly do harm to the School, and therefore that he should be stopped in his tracks.

models, *private agent* and *team research*, would represent intermediate cases between these two extremes. If agreements are to be reached in these cases they should ideally specify both the rights that the researcher has to publish, as well as the right of the client to monitor and control certain kinds of output.

Issues of implementation and utilization become more serious with practical and applied forms of research. When working directly for clients or patrons, as in evaluation research, we have found it very important to tie the research closely to the question that the sponsors or clients want to have answered. This is not a one-off process, but depends on a considerable amount of discussion and negotiation between the needs of the client and the capabilities of the researcher (Easterby-Smith, 1994). Many clients already have a fairly good idea of the likely results from a research study *before* they commission it, and therefore the researcher should pay particular attention to the possibility of disproving what the client thinks to be the case. Success in this respect will lead to the clients learning something new; failure will provide the client with much more confidence in his or her existing beliefs.

The problem of utilization is not confined only to academic research. Innovatory projects conducted within organizations can have just as much difficulty being accepted and implemented. One of the ways that the fast-moving company 3M deals with this problem is to formalize the role of sponsor – usually a senior manager who is prepared to champion a particular idea or project. As Nonaka comments: 'Before a daring and promising idea can stand on its own, it must be defined and supported by a sponsor willing to risk his or her reputation in order to advance or support changes in intra-company values' (1988: 14). Similarly, when in-company research projects have been incorporated into management development programmes it has been found that the close involvement of senior managers as clients is essential if results are to be acted upon (Ashton and Easterby-Smith, 1979).

What remains crucial is the nature and relationship between the researcher and the clients: this needs to be open and honest rather than sycophantic, and above all there should be a reasonable degree of mutual trust. Where the degree of mutual trust is limited we have noticed a marked tendency for clients and sponsors to try to push researchers into more of a 'technician' role where the researcher is expected to gather data, often quantitative, within a framework defined by the clients. Interpretation of the data is then under the control of the clients rather than the researchers.

To some extent we have assumed above that the utilization and consequent action is the responsibility, and in the capacity, of these clients or patrons. In the case of policy-orientated research it is by no means as simple because one may be dealing with rather complex bureaucracies or political systems. In the case of research geared towards national (social) policy, Finch (1986) points to two distinct traditions, and assumptions, about the appropriate way of using such research.

On the one hand, there is the **social engineering** model which sees research as a rational process where research studies are commissioned so that their results feed into specific decisions and supply the missing facts to enable decision-makers to take the right course of action. On the other hand, there is the **enlightenment** model which sees implementation as an incremental process with lots of diffuse viewpoints being introduced from different levels of the social system, hence providing an *indirect* link between the research and policy implications. The former model makes full use of quantitative methods, and the latter tends to adopt qualitative methods. As one might expect, most governments and sponsoring agencies prefer to use the social engineering kind of research because it gives them more control over what will take place. But the problem with the largely quantitative studies implied by this model is that they can only describe the situation as it is now, or as it was in the past; they can give very little guidance on what should take place in the future, and this is a limitation when research is supposed to be aiding policy formulation. This is where the more democratic enlightenment model can help to some extent by providing a much wider range of options and ideas in order to guide future action.

The enlightenment model, however, still remains unpopular among sponsors, and attracts criticism from some academic quarters. Gubrium and Silverman (1989) for example, argue that even when the enlightenment model is used to provide knowledge of alternative possibilities and problems to administrators, it is still acting largely in the interests of 'the establishment'. The simple idea that the fruits of the social sciences will lead to improvements of the human condition, serves as a justification for the distinction between those who make, and those who are affected by, the rules of society. This disguises the reality of power by suggesting that it is the property of one or other group in society – rather than it being implicit in all relationships, like capillaries in the social body.

CONCLUSION

At this point we can identify a number of general implications for the researcher.

- It is important to recognize that power and political issues will be significant, even when they are not obviously present.

- There are no easy answers, nor solutions, to the political web. It exists in the form of ideologies, of personal interests (including those of the researchers), of power differences and of ethical dilemmas.

- The researcher needs both clarity of purpose, and much flexibility in tackling problems.

- Clarity of purpose can come from self-awareness of one's own interests and assumptions about the world, and these can be incorporated into reflexive accounts.

We have discussed the issues of ontology, epistemology, research design, politics and ethics in the last three chapters. In the next part of the book we turn to consider the range of methods and techniques that are at the disposal of the researcher. We stress consistently that these should not be seen as entirely free-standing; but they should be subordinated to the considerations of purpose and philosophy which have been outlined above.

Political dilemmas in conducting a student project (group discussion)

You have to do an in-company project as part of the assessment for your degree. Your tutor has arranged access to a local supermarket to investigate the quality of customer relations, and the contact, who is the deputy manager, has suggested that you talk to members of two departments, of which one appears to be very successful, and the other is regarded as problematic. Here are some possible scenarios. What would you do?

A When you arrive for the initial meeting with the deputy manager you are informed that she has been called on urgent business to the regional head office and cannot see you.

B When you meet the deputy manager she asks you to sign a non-disclosure agreement.

C During a one-to-one interview with a checkout assistant she comments that there have been incidents of sexual harassment in her department. What do you do with this information, if anything?

D After conducting a number of interviews in both departments the deputy manager asks you for your opinion of the qualities of both supervisors.

E During the project, one team member persistently fails to pull his weight. How do you deal with this?

FURTHER READING

Buchanan, D. and Badham, R. (2008) *Power, Politics and Organizational Change: Winning the Turf Game*. London: Sage.
This new edition, which focuses on how managers can act as internal change agents, emphasizes the contexts in which they initiate and achieve change. It provides an accessible overview of organizational politics which is useful for the researcher both in conducting and implementing research.

Bell, E. and Bryman, A. (2007) 'The ethics of management research: an exploratory content analysis', *British Journal of Management*, 18(1), 63–77.
The authors suggest that management researchers face ethical issues which are distinct from those encountered by other social science researchers. They provide a review of ethics codes formulated by nine social scientific associations, and argue that reciprocity is a central principle for management research.

CREATING QUALITATIVE DATA
7

Main methods of qualitative data collection

Collecting natural language data

Ethnographic approaches

Understanding through interaction

General issues in relation to qualitative methods

Conclusion

Further reading

LEARNING OBJECTIVES

- To understand a range of different methods of data collection that belong to the qualitative research tradition

- To understand how these approaches of data collection offer different perspectives according to the focus of the research

- To appreciate the advantages and disadvantages of the various qualitative data collection methods

MAIN METHODS OF QUALITATIVE DATA COLLECTION

In this chapter we examine a number of approaches and tools for collecting qualitative data. Many of them are quite loosely specified which offers the researcher considerable opportunity to use their creative abilities. We have attempted to move away from presenting a simple list of methods and instead we have grouped them into headings that depict to us the basic approaches that are available. First, we discuss approaches that set out to collect information (data) from organizational members whether they be managers or employees, which we call *natural language data*. This approach aims to discover the views, perceptions and opinions from both individuals and groups through language, and the main method to achieve this is the in-depth interview. Valuable information can also be gained, however, from diaries and the examination of a range of textual data such as company reports or video recordings. Our second grouping is *ethnographic approaches*. Here the kind of data that is collected is rather different from that in the first group and includes the examination and understanding of symbols, settings and observations in a context. There are various methods that fall into this category, including participant observation, non-participant observation and, increasingly, visual methods. Third, we examine how understandings might be gained through interactive methods. Examples of *interactive methods* are photographs or other visual metaphors. Often this approach involves research through close and direct interaction and cooperation of the researcher with individuals or groups. We also address approaches to the co-production of knowledge using action research type methods and we discuss the practicalities of Mode 2 methods of knowledge production. Fourth, this chapter contains a section that looks at some general issues affecting qualitative methods of data collection, which will include a brief discussion of the use of case studies, a reminder of ethical issues involved and the necessity of reflexivity about the researcher's own involvement.

COLLECTING NATURAL LANGUAGE DATA

Interviews: how much structure?

Before adopting any method of data collection, it always helps to be clear about the overall objectives of the research. This applies to the choice of the in-depth interview as a method, as well as to the wide range of ways in which interviews may be conducted. Jones (1985) highlights a number of issues that researchers need to consider in order for interviews to be successful. The first is the problem that all researchers must resolve – how much structure to put into the interview. Jones argues that no research exists without presupposition, by which she means all researchers have some level understanding prior to the interview of the research surrounding the interview topic. She further outlines that researchers often enter the interview situation with some key questions; however, these questions are likely to change as new and interesting areas are uncovered and researchers may want to tailor their questions depending on the participant's position or response.

Interviews can be highly formalized and structured, for example, as in market research, or they can be quite unstructured, akin to free-ranging conversations (see Table 7.1). Although interviewing is often claimed to be 'the best' method of gathering information, its complexity can sometimes be underestimated. It is time consuming to undertake interviews properly, and they are sometimes used when other methods might be more appropriate. If researchers wish to obtain answers to a number of fairly simple questions then a questionnaire might well be more appropriate. Highly structured interviews are based on carefully prepared sets of questions piloted and refined until the researcher is convinced of their 'validity'. The assumption is made that the interviewer will ask each interviewee the same question in the same tone of voice. The simplest form of such interviews is where there are short answers to questions and the interviewer simply ticks boxes and no deep thought is required by either party. These are the type of interviews that take place in the shopping areas of towns and cities every Saturday morning and their primary aim is to gain a quantitative result from a carefully targeted sample (see Chapter 9). Within certain limits of accuracy (dependent on such things as the choice of location and the time of day that respondents are asked) we can then infer that, for example, 20 per cent of a population thinks one thing, and 10 per cent think another. Large numbers (hundreds or thousands) will be required in order to have confidence that the responses obtained can be generalized to the population at large and this for example is very much the territory of the professional political pollster.

Particularly in the case of using less-structured interviews, we would encourage researchers as they collect their data to make choices as to which line of questioning they should explore further, and which lines of inquiry to discard. Certainly, researchers need frameworks from which to plot out the developing themes, but as Jones reminds us, although they are to some extent tied to their frameworks researchers should not be 'tied up by them'. One way in which this can be achieved is to prepare a checklist, sometimes referred to as a topic guide, which can be used as a loose structure for the questions. Although there may be some deviation from the sequence in order to follow interesting lines of inquiry and to facilitate an unbroken discussion, the interviewer should attempt to cover all the issues mentioned.

Finally, on the subject of structure, the researcher should be warned against assuming that a 'non-directive' interview, where the interviewee talks freely without interruption or intervention, is the way to achieve a clear picture of the interviewee's perspective. This is far from true. It is more likely to produce no clear picture in the mind of the interviewee of what questions or issues the interviewer is interested in,

TABLE 7.1 Types of interview

Level of structure	Type of interview
Highly structured	Market research interview
Semi-structured	Guided open interview
Unstructured	Ethnography

and in the mind of the interviewer, of what questions the interviewee is answering. Too many assumptions of this kind lead to poor data, which is difficult to interpret. Researchers are therefore likely to be more successful if they are clear at the outset about the exact areas of their interest. In the section on avoiding bias this issue is dealt with in more detail.

It is important to be aware of the advantages and disadvantages of the different ways of conducting interviews. Whereas the structured interviews allow for a high degree of standardization of questions and answers, more open, or semi-structured and unstructured interview questions often give a higher degree of confidentiality as the replies of the interviewees tend to be more personal in nature. In addition, the interviewer does have the opportunity to identify non-verbal clues, which are present, for example, in the inflection of the voice, facial expressions or the clothes that the interviewee is wearing and these can be used to develop secondary questions. Sometimes these verbal clues may offer important reasons for misinformation (Sims, 1993).

The present chapter deals primarily with in-depth interviews where the main purpose is to understand the meanings that interviewees attach to issues and situations in contexts that are not structured in advance by the researcher. For a more detailed use and application of highly structured questionnaires readers should refer to Chapters 9 and 10.

In-depth interviews

The importance of in-depth interviews is summarized by Burgess: '(the interview) is . . . the opportunity for the researcher to probe deeply to uncover new clues, open up new dimensions of a problem and to secure vivid, accurate inclusive accounts that are based on personal experience'(1982: 107). Most interviews are conducted on a one-to-one basis, between the interviewer and the interviewee. The label 'qualitative interview' has been used to describe a broad range of types of interview, from those that are supposedly totally non-directive, or open, to those where the interviewer has prepared a list of questions which he or she is determined to ask, come what may. While as Jones (1985) outlines there are a range of practices and therefore theory between these two extremes of interviewing technique, the main aim of qualitative interviewing is generally seen as attempting to gain an understanding from the respondent's perspective which includes not only what their viewpoint is but also why they have this particular viewpoint (King, 2004). As Kvale (1996) notes the aim of qualitative interviews should be to collect information, which captures the meaning and interpretation of phenomenon in relation to the interviewee's worldview. Researchers must therefore be able to conduct interviews so that the opportunity is present for these insights to be gained. Failure to achieve this might well result in a superficial exchange of information, which might as well have been better achieved via a semi-structured questionnaire.

In order to be able to achieve these insights the researcher will need to be sensitive enough and skilled enough, to ensure that he or she not only understands the other person's views, but also at times, assists individuals to explore their own beliefs. Later in this chapter, we will discuss a number of techniques that might help the researcher do this to advantage. Interviews, both semi-structured and unstructured, are therefore appropriate methods when:

1 it is necessary to understand the constructs that the respondent uses as a basis for his or her opinions and beliefs about a particular matter or situation;

2 the aim of the interview is to develop an understanding of the respondent's 'world' so that the researcher might influence it, either independently, or collaboratively as in the case with action research; and

3 the step by step logic of a situation is not clear; the subject matter is highly confidential or commercially sensitive; and there are issues about which the interviewee may be reluctant to be truthful other than confidentially in a one-to-one situation.

It is important to note that managers can sometimes prefer telephone interviews. They are easily rescheduled and as such offer more flexibility, and managers feel less committed, because they do not have an obligation to host the researcher at the setting. However, exactly because of these reasons, telephone interviews are not always of benefit for a qualitative researcher. However, there are some occasions when telephone interviews may be very useful. They may, for example, prove very effective in the context of real-time and process-based research. In such research projects researchers are interested in understanding the detail of a situation and an exact 'real-time' chronology of events. In order to establish chronologies it is perfectly reasonable for the researcher to have frequent telephone conversations centred on current activities and decisions rather than on retrospective developments. These kinds of telephone interviews are even more effective, as in such situations both the interviewer and interviewee have most likely already had face-to-face interviews and the additional telephone interviews simply increase the thickness of the data collected. Researchers though would be well advised to avoid telephone interviews if they have never met the interviewee before, but if they have already established a good relationship of trust then even fairly unstructured interviews over the phone can be successful.

Interviewing skills

Understanding issues from an interviewee's point of view can be extremely difficult, especially when the respondent him- or herself may not have a clearly articulated view of the answers to the questions posed, or may not wish to divulge sensitive information. It is here that the skills of the interviewer come to the fore.

McClelland (1965) conducted careful studies about commonsense notions of 'motivation'. He concluded that people cannot be trusted to say exactly what their motives are, as they often get ideas about their own motives from commonly accepted half-truths. For example, a person may say that he is interested in achievement because he has made money. But a careful check using different probing methods may reveal quite a different picture. Often people simply are not aware of their own motives. Mangham (1986) in his studies of managerial competence met this problem. From his survey work conducted quantitatively he found that many managers sought subordinates who could better motivate staff and act in leadership roles within their organizations. In follow up interviews he was able to ask managers exactly what they meant by leadership. He found immense variation in the answers and some became confused, offering examples of leadership that ranged from the highly autocratic styles to highly democratic forms.

From a positivistic standpoint, the fact that there is ambiguity about the meaning of 'leadership' invalidates the research, but for the in-depth interviewer who probes, questions and checks, this is important data. The fact that people are confused and cannot agree on what they mean by leadership or the way they construct particular situations is the essence of the research. The skills of an interviewer then, centre on the ability to recognize what is relevant and remember it, or tape it, so that afterwards detailed notes can be made. This requires one to be perceptive and sensitive to events, so that lines of inquiry can be changed and adapted as one progresses. Above all, interviewers need to be able to listen, and to refrain from projecting their own opinions or feelings into the situation. This is more difficult than it sounds, since one of the ways of obtaining trust is to empathize with the respondent. The interviewer needs to listen to what the person wants to say, and what he or she does not want to say, without helping (Mayo, 1949). In recognizing these situations, non-verbal data might be crucial in providing clues, for example the loss of eye contact, or a changed facial expression.

From time to time during the interview, as patterns or uncertainties arise from the interview, it is useful to check one understands by summarizing what has been said. This should be presented as a way of seeking clarification. The process of 'testing out' is a way of safeguarding against assuming too quickly that understanding has been achieved.

Laddering

As questions are asked the researcher might like to think about how to 'get more' from one question. Employing the technique of laddering will help the respondent move from statements of *fact* or descriptive accounts about the question posed *upwards* in such a way that they gradually begin to reveal the individual's value base. The way to achieve this is to ask *why* type questions. An example of this process can be seen in Example 7.1, and a hierarchical value map to which it relates is shown in

---

EXAMPLE 7.1

Laddering

Question: Anything else about the design?
Answer: I think the weight of the shoe is important. The shoe shouldn't be too heavy.
Question: Why is this?
Answer: Because a lighter shoe is more comfortable.
Question: Why is this important to you?
Answer: It means I can move around quickly at tennis . . .
Question: Tennis is important to you?
Answer: Yes . . . I like it . . . it means I get some fresh air . . . it's good for the heart, the nerves and your cholesterol . . . it makes me feel better. I feel good when I play tennis. (Baker and Knox, 1995: 89)

Figure 8.6. The technique is a very valuable one for qualitative researchers however sensitivity and common sense does needs to be applied as a persistent use of *why* questions can spoil an interview as the respondent will eventually run out of things to say. Varying the way in which the question *why* is asked as Susan Baker does in Example 7.1 will make the exchange more varied and interesting. Laddering down is where the researcher seeks to obtain illustrations and examples or occurrences of events.

For example the researcher might say, 'Could you give me an example of that?' or 'When was the last time that happened to you?' Through such a process it is possible to explore a person's understanding of a particular construct and laddering up and down using five or six questions (the number of themes contained in a topic guide) will quite easily fill out the whole of an interview, whilst in the process gaining significant insights into the topic under investigation.

Avoiding bias

Readers will see in Chapter 9, on quantitative research methods that interview bias – where the process of conducting an interview might influence the responses given – is regarded as crucial. With in-depth interviewing the issue is a slightly different one. Since the aim of in-depth interviews is to uncover the meanings and interpretations that people attach to events, it follows that there is no one 'objective' view to be discovered which the process of interviewing may bias. However, there is a very real concern about interviewers imposing their own reference frame on the interviewees, both when the questions are asked and when the answers are interpreted. The researcher is in something of a dilemma for, as has been suggested in an earlier section, open questions may avoid bias, but they are not always the best way of obtaining the information one may wish to know nor are they always the best way of putting an interviewee at ease. But the issue of bias gives a pull in the other direction. In order to avoid bias, there is often the tendency for researchers to leave questions open. There will be some occasions when researchers will want to focus on discovering responses to specific alternatives, and in this case 'probes' can be useful as a intervention technique to improve, or sharpen-up, the interviewee's response. A number of probes are listed in Example 7.2.

General interview issues

Using in-depth interviewing as your main method of obtaining qualitative data in a successful way, however, does not only depend on a researcher's personal interview skills, it also involves his or her capacity to organize and structure his or her interviews. There are six important practical issues involved in conducting interviews that may affect the outcome of an interview of which the researcher should be aware. These six issues are: obtaining trust, being aware of social interaction, using the appropriate language, getting access, choosing the location for the interviews, and recording interviews.

Obtaining trust is an important element in ensuring that interviews will render researchers with the information they are looking for. Obtaining trust can be a difficult issue, especially in one-off interviews where the people involved have not met before. Failure to develop trust may well result in interviewees simply resorting to telling the

EXAMPLE 7.2

Probes in interviewing

- The *basic probe* simply involves repeating the initial question and is useful when the interviewee seems to be wandering off the point.
- *Explanatory probes* involve building onto incomplete or vague statements made by the respondent. Ask questions such as: 'What did you mean by that?', 'What makes you say that?'
- *Focused probes* are used to obtain specific information. Typically one would ask the respondent,' What sort of …?'
- The *silent probe* is one of the most effective techniques to use when the respondent is either reluctant or very slow to answer the question posed. Simply pause and let the interviewee break the silence.
- The technique of *drawing out* can be used when the interviewee has halted, or dried up. Repeat the last few words the interviewee said, and then look expectantly or say, 'tell me more about that', 'what happened then'.
- *Giving ideas or suggestions* involves offering the interviewee an idea to think about – 'Have you thought about . . .?', 'Have you tried . . .?', 'Did you know that . . .?', 'Perhaps you should ask Y . . .'.
- *Mirroring* or *reflecting* involves expressing in your own words what the respondent has just said. This is very effective because it may force the respondent to rethink the answer and reconstruct another reply which will amplify the previous answer – 'What you seem to be saying/feeling is...'. To avoid bias, probes should never lead. An example of a leading probe might be: So you would say that you were really satisfied?' Instead of which the interviewer should say: 'Can you explain a little more?' or 'How do you mean?'

researcher what they think he or she wants to know. But an open and trusting relationship may not be possible or sufficient when dealing with particular elites or individuals in positions of power as we have discussed in Chapter 6. One way of ensuring trust is obtained is to make sure that one is well clued up about the company. A scan through the company's web site will give a quick impression of the issues that are currently considered significant. Another way to obtain the trust of the company one wishes to research, is to present the research in a professional and enthusiastic way so that the company sees a benefit, as managers will be weighing up the likely costs (and benefits) of the potential intrusion.

Social interaction between the interviewer and the interviewee is another important factor that may influence the interview process. Jones (1985) suggests people will attribute meaning and significance to the particular research situations they are in. The questions an interviewer may ask and the answers an interviewee gives will often depend on the way in which their situations are defined. Similarly Jones (1985) points out that, interviewees will 'suss out' what researchers are like, and make judgments from their first impressions about whether they can be trusted and be told everything or whether they might be damaged in some way by data that could be misused. Such suspicions do not necessarily mean that interviewees will refuse to be interviewed, but it might mean, as Jones indicates, that they just: '. . . seek to get the interview over as quickly as possible, with enough detail and enough feigned interest to satisfy the researcher that he or she is getting something of value but without saying anything that touches the core of what is actually believed and cared about in the research' (1985: 50). Furthermore an important aspect of the interview process is to be able to recognize when an interviewer is being misinformed (Sims 1993). Individuals will often select answers between complex truths, rather than providing the 'whole truth', simply because it would take too long to give all the nuances.

Using the appropriate language is another practical issue that should be kept in mind when preparing for and conducting one's research. It is not a good strategy to baffle a potential gatekeeper by using too many theoretical concepts, but clarity also needs to be ascertained with respect to the interviewee's use of language as what is said may not always be what is meant and the sky might indeed be blue like an orange. In Table 7.2 we provide a few examples of the way words may be interpreted.

Getting access is a fourth issue that may have an effect on the research. Once a gatekeeper has shown some interest, then preliminary contacts are best followed up by letter. This can fulfil three distinct purposes. The first is credibility, especially if the approach can be made using the headed note paper of an independent body – a university, institute or college. Second, it may assist co-operation in the future; and third, it provides the opportunity to send further details about the research. This last purpose is the researcher's opportunity to set out in detail what is required. The phenomenal growth in business and management courses over the last two decades has had both negative and positive effects on the likelihood of gaining access. On the one hand, there are now a lot of other students and institutions competing for access to a limited number of organizations; on the other hand, there are now large numbers of managers who have taken management degrees themselves (and some may still be studying on part-time schemes), and they are likely both to understand, and be sympathetic towards, the researcher's objectives.

TABLE 7.2 Use of words and the different impressions they can give

Words	Impression given
Student	Implies an unskilled 'amateurish' inquiry, which may be a waste of time, although unthreatening.
Researcher	Implies a more professional relationship, although questions of access might need to be managed more carefully.
Interview	Gives the impression of a formal structured interrogation, which is under the control of the researcher
Discussion	May make managers feel more relaxed and less threatened, with the potential for genuine exchange.

The location of the interview and the setting in which the interview takes place is a fifth element that can be important. Using a manager's office for example might not be perceived as a neutral space by other employees as was experienced first hand in a study by Thorpe (Bowey and Thorpe, 1986). One strategy used by a PhD student was conducted well away from the work place. When researching into aspects of management development, he undertook this fieldwork by sitting in the first class compartments of trains. He would sit next to executive-looking individuals armed only with a folder marked management development in the hope that managers would talk to him. This they usually did, and without prompts he was able to elicit their views on a range of management development issues. What struck the researcher was the extent to which the views and opinions expressed by managers, off-guard and to a person they were unlikely ever to meet again, contradicted the 'reality' contained in much contemporary management literature. Had the interview taken place in the manager's office, the results might well have been quite different. This example not only illustrates how a researcher managed to obtain data, which the manager may have found hard to articulate in his office, it also shows how a method can be undertaken in a 'natural setting' where each views the other as having equal status. This kind of research would normally be extremely costly, yet it does illustrate the lengths that might be required to obtain particular kinds of data.

Recording interviews is a sixth aspect that may affect the outcome of an interview. The decision of whether or not to use a tape recorder depends on an interviewee's anxiety about confidentiality and the use to which any information divulged can be put. Anxiety can be minimized, for example, by handing over the responsibility for switching the tape on and off to the interviewee, so that when he or she does not wish certain parts to be recorded, they can just switch off the machine. The main reasons in favour of using a tape recorder are that it aids the listening process and gives the opportunity of an unbiased record of the conversation. Good audio recordings are essential for accurate transcripts and also enable the researcher to re-listen to the interview and so hear things that were missed at the time. A PhD student was even able to gain the trust of three managers of medium-sized companies, and these were examined in depth to such an extent that she was allowed to video them over a three-month period. This included company meetings and also meetings with clients (see further reading at the end of the chapter). In cases where interviewees are opposed to the use of recording devices of the researcher will need to depend on his or her own ability to take accurate notes and write down everything he or she is able to remember as soon as possible after the interview has ended.

Critical incident technique

One method of teasing out information which is often used alongside interviews is the critical incident technique. Proposed by Flanagan (1954) the technique offers an opportunity to go straight to the heart of an issue and collect information about what is really being sought, rather than collecting large quantities of data that may or may not be directly relevant to what is wanted to be understood. Flanagan saw the approach as a 'set of procedures for collecting direct observations of human behaviour in such a way as to facilitate their potential usefulness in solving practical problems and developing broad psychological principles'. By 'incident', Flanagan meant any observable human activity that is sufficiently complete in itself to permit inference or prediction to be made about the person performing the act. To be 'critical' the incident must occur in a situation where the purpose or intent of the act seems fairly clear to the observer and where its consequences are sufficiently definite to leave little doubt concerning its effect.

The technique has been used by qualitative researchers to great effect, particularly in conjunction with in-depth interviews as we have indicated above. Respondents might, for example, be asked to track back to particular instances in their work lives and to explain their actions and motives with specific regard to those instances. In Thorpe's PhD research he used the technique to ask owner/managers of small companies what had been their particular barriers to growth. At a given point in the interview he would ask if there had been any particular problems in the development of the company. He would then encourage the manager to explain that problem in some detail and illustrate how the problem was eventually surmounted. From this example he would begin to develop ideas about how individuals managed particular problems and about the information they used in doing this. It is important to use material that can be substantiated since there are criticisms of the technique relating to recall, and the natural tendency of individuals to use hindsight in rationalizing the past.

Group and focus interviews

Interviews need not necessarily take place on a one-to-one basis, and for some types of investigation group interviews can be very useful. These take the form of loosely structured 'steered conversations'. They are used extensively in market research and increasingly in politics.

In any interview, the skill of the interviewer both as initiator and facilitator is of vital importance. In focus group interviews this role is called a moderator, and the added complexity of the situation means that the skills of initiating and facilitating are of particular relevance in a group interview. As Walker (1985) outlines a group interviewer should not attempt to conduct numerous interviews simultaneously but rather to create a situation where all participants feel comfortable expressing their views and responding to the ideas of those around them. Although the focus interview is loosely structured, it should never be entirely without structure (Stokes and Bergin, 2006). The format of the interview should be organized by using what is called a 'topic guide'. This is a résumé of the main areas of interest that are to be explored. It is designed so that while still covering the general areas of interest it also allows unforeseen areas to emerge. In addition, the discussion venue needs to be chosen with care. Ideally, in common with in-depth interviews, it should take place in surroundings within which the participants feel relaxed and unthreatened. This can often be on their home ground, for example in a meeting or conference room close to the office. Alternatively, it might be in neutral territory such as a business school, a club or a hotel. However the problems of group interviews can sometimes outweigh the advantages. Social pressures can condition the responses gained, and it may well be that people are not willing to air their views publicly. Our own view is that criticisms such as this illustrate the mistake of applying the wrong criteria for assessing the technique. Focus group interviews can be extremely useful in applied market research studies and are used to great effect as an exploratory tool in other types of qualitative research. Curran and Downing (1989), for example, used the technique to good effect as a means of validating the questionnaire responses made by owner managers in a largely quantitative study which sought to understand the utility of the UK government's consultation strategies with small- and medium-sized firms. Further reading is given at the end of the chapter for those who wish to study this method in more detail.

Diary methods

There is quite a long history of using diaries as a basis for social research in the UK. One of the most interesting examples is the mass-observation studies during World War II. Here a substantial number of ordinary people were recruited to keep diaries of everything they did for one day each month, and they were also asked to report on specific days, such as bank holidays. Analysis of these diaries was intended to show how the British population in general was reacting to different aspects of the war (Calder and Sheridan, 1984). Diaries can be either quantitative or qualitative depending on the kind of information that is recorded. They can be useful in management and organizational research on a number of levels. At one level, diary keeping by organizational members can be a simple journal or record of events. A quantitative analysis might take the form of activity sampling from which patterns may be identified statistically. This approach is sometimes used by management services practitioners who wish to measure the frequency of certain activities so that they can reorganize or 'improve' the work, whereas at other times it is used by managers to reflect on aspects of their own work, like in time management analysis (see, for example, Stewart, 1967, 1982). At another level, diaries might take the form of a personal journal of the research process and include emergent ideas and results, reflections on personal learning, and an examination of personal attitudes and values which may be important at the data analysis and writing up stages. At yet another level they can provide a rich qualitative picture of motives and perspectives, which allows the researcher to gain considerable insight into situations being examined. It is this latter use of a diary that we wish to explore in a little more detail here.

There are a number of advantages to using diaries. First, they provide a useful method for collecting data from the perspective of the employee. Whereas in participant observation the researcher cannot help imposing to some extent his or her own reference frame as the data is collected, in the diary study the data is collected and presented largely within the reference frame of the diary writer. Second, a diary approach allows the perspectives of several different writers to be compared and contrasted simultaneously, and it allows the researcher greater freedom to move from one situation or organization to another. Some detachment also prevents the researcher becoming too personally involved.

Third, they allow the researcher to collect other relevant data while the study is in progress and enable him or her to carry out much more analysis than the participant observer would be able to carry out in the course of their fieldwork. This is the opportunity to collect information not only from the perspectives of different individuals, but also through using different data sources. Finally, although diary studies do not allow for the same interaction and questioning they can sometimes be an alternative to participant observation when, for example, it is impractical for a researcher to invest the time in an extended longitudinal study as observer.

A number of important lessons were learnt from a multiple diary study conducted by Bowey and Thorpe (1986) in an English coal mine during a national study into incentive schemes. These lessons are described in Example 7.3.

All diarists in the study described in Example 7.3 (including those who stopped writing before the end of the three-month period) maintained that they had welcomed the opportunity to express their feelings, observations and opinions about their life and work to somebody who was interested. All maintained that they enjoyed writing them, and some confided that they were flattered that outsiders were taking an interest in them as individuals. No payment or other inducements were made, although pens and folders were regularly provided. This was sufficient reward for many and it reinforces the point, made in the section on interviewing, about how important it is to find out what individuals wish to gain from participating in the research. As with participant observation, the setting up of a research study such as this involves considerable time and effort. There were numerous meetings required to gain access and our purpose had to be explained to management and union officials separately. The practicalities of undertaking diary research are fully discussed in Bowey and Thorpe (1986).

Video recording

Despite the pervasive nature of the 'visual' in our everyday lives, management research has continued to privilege verbal forms of communication over visual forms. Historically, visual methods of data collection have been viewed as being highly subjective, difficult to interpret and prone to researcher bias, consequently most qualitative management research has been limited to textual data gathering techniques. Yet, as Secrist et al. (2002) note, despite all the eloquent verbal descriptions of their research experiences that writers provide, it is often suggested that words alone cannot communicate the complex and intricate situations they encounter. Consequently, there has been an increasing interest in what visual methods can offer management researchers. Despite the potential insights afforded by visual data, there remain very few examples in the field of management where visual methods of data collection have been applied. One attempt at applying a visually based methodology is Cunliffe's (2001) postmodern perspective on management practice, in which she video-taped interviews she conducted with a number of managers. She subsequently played these video-taped interviews back to the managers to explore with the manager how they had co-created meaning together through the course of the interview. In this way the meaning of the interviews was discussed and deciphered in collaboration with the participant, as a form of co-inquiry. In another vein, a body of research known collectively as 'workplace studies' (Luff et al., 2000; Heath and Hindmarsh, 2002) has made use of videotape to examine the effects of the material environment on action and interaction. Such studies focus on interaction and technology in a variety of organizational settings. Although interesting neither of these approaches aim to understand what the visual means in relation to wider understandings but rather focus on in-depth, context reliant and micro-level understandings.

EXAMPLE 7.3

Diary study of incentive schemes

First, it was found to be important to select participants who were able to express themselves well in writing. In cases where there was doubt a judgement had to be made as to the likely consequences of the individual taking offence if he or she was excluded. Second, some structure was found necessary to give the diarist focus. To assist this, a list of general headings developed from earlier pilot studies was provided.

Please write about the following:

- Your relationships with other people, including your supervisor, your workmates, anyone you supervise and other people you come into contact with.
- Any particular difficulties you encountered during the day with: machinery, raw materials or other people.
- If the incentive bonus scheme affected you at work, and if so in what way.
- Anything you were especially pleased about or made you feel angry.
- Anything else you feel is important, especially if it is anything to do with the incentive bonus scheme.

A third lesson highlighted was the need for continued encouragement and reassurance during the study. An earlier pilot study had left diarists very much to their own devices, and they had continued to write for only four to six weeks. In the main study, where regular contact was maintained and feedback given in the form of additional questions or classification, almost two thirds of the sample kept writing into the third month, and more than one-quarter completed the full three-month period. An improvement we might have made would have been to supplement the diaries with interviews. This would have enhanced the effect of maintaining interest as well as providing the opportunity to probe areas of interest further.

Fourth, the importance of the need for confidentiality was confirmed. In a pilot study, jotters had been issued to record instances that occurred during the day and this had led to problems. One particularly uncomplimentary entry in a respondent's jotter had been left in an accessible place and was read by the person described. This caused the relationships between the two people to be soured even though thoughts entered 'in the heat of the moment' did not generally reflect the opinions of the individual. It was therefore decided that even at the cost of a loss of spontaneity it was preferable for diaries to be written up away from the workplace.

Finally, the study confirmed individuals' willingness and enthusiasm for cooperating at every level. There was no evidence to justify the view that individuals might be nervous of participating in this kind of research. The experience showed that there was more nervousness among the researchers themselves who felt that they 'dare not ask' or that asking people to maintain a diary for up to three months would be unacceptable to those under study.

EXAMPLE 7.4

Visual tools in a PhD study

The PhD student attempted to examine how entrepreneurs use both linguistic and visual means to create meaning and convince others of the legitimacy of their venture. This involved three visual ethnographies which included videotaped interviews and also images of entrepreneurs, employees and customers performing their everyday jobs. The findings suggested that in addition to linguistic meaning-making entrepreneurs use a range of visual tools to 'make' and 'give' meaning to others in their contexts and engage others in their venture, including their dress, appearance of physical settings, and physical artefacts such as high-status vehicles which represent wider meanings in the social and cultural domain. These artefacts do not have a fixed meaning in the entrepreneurial context; rather they can be used to create a variety of meanings depending on the 'audience' with whom the meanings are being developed. In addition, she found that verbal and material meanings must align in order to be most effective in persuading others of the legitimacy of the business venture. This study shows that without attempting to use a method of visual data collection, an understanding of how entrepreneurs use their visual environments to create meaning would not have been developed.

There have been a very limited number of studies which use visual methods to understand aspects of the wider context (e.g. Buchanan, 1999), and Example 7.4 used here to illustrate the utility of visual methods is from a recent PhD study (Clarke, 2007).

Images however, do not need to be the main focus of attention or topic in order to warrant a researcher using visual data in their research. Indeed, as Pink (2001) highlights the relation of images to other sensory, material and linguistic details of the study will result in the images being of interest to most researchers. Pink goes on to argue this is not a suggestion that video and other visual data collection strategies should replace text-based approaches in research, but rather they should be used as a complimentary and additional source of data.

ETHNOGRAPHIC APPROACHES

Watson (1994) understands an ethnographic approach as implying some kind of close involvement in an organization. The object is to gain an insider perspective so that detailed understandings can be gained of *other people's realities*. Bryman and Bell (2007) also reflect on the differences between ethnography and participant observation and conclude that they may not be entirely synonymous in people's minds as many see ethnographic approaches as being more than simply observation alone and involving perhaps the collection of information in a variety of different ways. One of the interesting developments in recent times has been the way, through the growth of digital media that researchers can get access to contemporary records made by individuals, which blurs the distinction between researcher and the researched. Les Back, for example, has been illustrating how the use of mobile phone cameras and photographs shot at the time, can be used by researchers to better understand events. The picture in Figure 7.1 illustrates passengers walking down one of the London underground tunnels following the bombings in 2005.

In our view participant observation offers a broad framework for understanding ethnographic approaches. There is a very extensive literature on participant observation and ethnography, particularly in sociology and anthropology. Since organizations can easily be viewed as 'tribes' with their own strange customs and practices, it is by no means surprising that observation has also been used in organizational and management research. Donald Roy (1952) used the method to great effect when working as a company employee in the machine shop of a large company. He was able both to show how workers manipulated the piecework incentive scheme, and to understand the motives behind this. For anyone wishing to learn about the craft of participant observation and how the method might be written up could do no better than to read one or two of the original articles Roy produced from his research *'Quota Restriction and Goldbricking in a Machine Shop'* (1952) *or Efficiency and the Fix'* (1954).

The role of the participant observer is by no means simple. There are many different ways of handling it. In the last edition, we proposed a different scheme, based more explicitly on the possibilities available in management or organizational research. These were: researcher as employee; research as explicit role; interrupted involvement; and observation alone. These we still feel are useful to researchers, however we now propose a fifth, what Collinson (1992) refers to as semi-concealed research

Complete participation

One role a researcher can take is that of employee. Here he or she works within the organization, alongside others, to all intents and purposes as one of them. The role

SOURCE: PA Photos/AP.

FIGURE 7.1 Reinventing the observer.

of researcher may or may not be explicit and this will have implications for the extent to which he or she will be able to move around and gather information and perspectives from other sources.

This role is appropriate when the researcher needs to become totally immersed and experience the work or situation at first hand. Sometimes it is the only way to gain the kind of insights sought. For example, in a study conducted by Thorpe (1980), which used this approach, the researcher was able to gain an understanding of how management's failure to address the motivational needs of the workforce led to disillusionment and apathy (Thorpe, 1980).

Naturally, in the Example 7.5 his questioning did not stop at just what was observed, for it then became of interest to know *why* the extra pay was required, why was this strategy used in preference to others, and so on.

In the above mentioned example, not all individuals involved were aware of the research taking place. However, the company chairman and the works convener had agreed to the research being conducted as they saw the merits of the research. It is important to remember then, that it is perfectly possible to negotiate access with the consent of everyone at the location where the study is to take place as long as no harm comes to any of the respondents. In a recent example, a PhD student was able to gain access to conduct a three company case comparison of the effect of performance related pay on the behaviour of school teachers by taking a job as a 'dinner lady' in one school, a playground supervisor in another and a classroom assistant in another. Although the 'dinner lady' role was not ideal it served its purpose in getting close and helped the early formulation of ideas. In such studies gaining access can be extremely difficult and in cannot pretend that getting agreement is a simple

---

EXAMPLE 7.5

Researcher as employee

Poor planning of work meant that men were often bored: by experiencing this boredom himself he was better able to understand its causes and the ways in which the employees attempted to alleviate it. His team developed a pattern of activity where they worked for the first hour or so, and then they took a break, had a wash and a walk outside. On certain days they changed their overalls in the laundry which involved a walk of about 600 yards and a break of about half an hour. After mid-morning the pace became much slower, and after lunchtime very little work was done at all.

On one occasion, (a Wednesday afternoon) the researcher saw that the conveyor belt was beginning to back-up for no apparent reason. On questioning his colleagues about it, he learnt that they saw this as a good strategy to put pressure on management and guarantee themselves overtime at the weekend at time and a half. Since overtime working had to be notified to the employees three days in advance it was important to slow things down on Wednesday. By Friday the backlog had all but been cleared but the promise of the overtime remained, making for a fairly easy Saturday morning's work!

matter; the point is that it should not deter. Of course those who study part time have a ready access for this kind of study although, the problems of 'insider research' raises its own issues. But for students who require part-time work to undertake their studies to make ends meet, they can be sitting on a very rich research material without really realizing it. As we have indicated in Chapter 6, participant observation invariably raises *ethical* dilemmas, particularly when conducted in a covert way. These dilemmas need to be considered carefully by researchers, preferably before they embark on fieldwork. People may be resentful when they learn of the presence of a covert researcher, but as more and more people study for management qualifications on a part-time basis there is a growing acceptance that employees may be researchers. The final section of this chapter will briefly return to the question of ethics.

This latter point raises another issue related to complete participation: the problem of a crisis of identity. Getting to know people quite well, even being invited into their homes and then reporting on them in a covert way is, for most researchers, regardless of ethics, a difficult task. The researcher in the Example 7.4 remembers his own experience vividly. He was some 300 miles from his academic base and unable to obtain help or support from colleagues and found it difficult not to experience a confusion of roles. For complete participation is not just a matter of being an employee for three months or so, keeping a diary and analysing the results at a distance at a later date. It involves observing, participating, talking, checking, and understanding and making interpretations, all of which are required if complete participant observers are to share and understand the employee's experience.

Linked to this is the time period over which this kind of activity has to be sustained. It is not unusual for studies to take several months with results taking a long time to produce. It must also be noted that the method is one of high risk. As we have discussed, studies are often extremely difficult to set up, anonymity is a problem, and considerable resources may be consumed in their execution with no guarantees that the method will yield the insights sought. Finally, and this also applies somewhat to other qualitative methodologies, the complete observer role can be both a physical as well as an intellectual challenge. In the case of Thorpe's research, for example, the researcher was required to complete a day of manual work and then in the evening continue the process of interpretation so that new lines of enquiry could be continued the following day.

Research as the explicit role

A second way of managing the role is for the researcher to be present every day over a period of time; but this time entry is negotiated in advance with management and preferably with employees as well. In this case, the individual is quite clearly in the role of a researcher who can move around, observe, interview and participate in the work as appropriate.

This type of observer role is the most often favoured, as it provides many of the insights that the complete observer would gain, while offering much greater flexibility without the ethical problems that deception entails. Roy describes the advantages of the approach as, 'the participant as observer not only makes no secret of his investigation: he makes it known that research is his overriding interest. He is there to observe. The participant observer is not tied down; he is free to run around as research interest beckons'(1970: 217). Eileen Fairhurst (1983), used this type of approach in a study of employee's attitudes to organizational rules. She chose for her research a geriatric nursing ward, and this is where she met her first problem. It took a considerable amount of time to obtain agreement to conduct her research in a particular unit, for two reasons which illustrate a number of problems involved in this type of research. The first was that different consultants in the hospital viewed 'research' in two distinct ways. Some saw it as something in which they must become personally involved and 'vet'; others saw it as a self-indulgent activity of which they wanted no part.

Even after she had gained agreement for the location of the research, there were additional problems associated with the sensitive focus of the study. Old people are especially vulnerable, and there was real concern that researching them might be viewed as a form of exploitation. To experience delay in the setting up of this kind of study is not in any way unusual. Thorpe's researcher-as-employee study, and the diary study that will be discussed later, took a number of months. Researchers, as we have discussed with interviewing, must find strategies that will allay people's fears, and offer the organization or the managers and employees who control access either reassurance, or something in return. This might involve many meetings and even presentations to the employees about the aims and potential value of the research. Once accepted, Fairhurst explained how a principal task was to move from a position of stranger to that of friend – someone who could be trusted. When she had achieved this she found individuals were very willing to tell her about the organization, whether they were nurses, cleaners or ward clerks. While on the wards, she felt it appropriate to help make beds and assist generally, for example, with the distribution of food and drink at meal times, and to collect bed linen or clothes for patients. At such times she was not only participating but strengthening relationships. She also recalls that there were times when she simply had to observe, for example, when patients were spending time with occupational therapists or physiotherapists, or on the occasions when she did not possess the technical qualifications to take any role in the work. People understood this and accepted it.

The key skill is to be sensitive enough to know just what role is required in each situation. This is influenced almost entirely by the circumstances at that particular time. For example, Fairhurst explains that it would have been conspicuous if she had stood or sat apart, rather than offering help when the wards were short staffed. On the other hand, night staff were always short of work, and as a consequence she spent much of the time during this period observing, listening and talking with nurses.

Interrupted involvement

A third kind of role involves the observer being present sporadically over a period of time, moving, for example, in and out of the organization to deal with other work or to conduct interviews with, or observations of, different people across a number of different organizations.

The essential characteristic of the researcher taking this role is that the process is not one of continuous longitudinal involvement as we have described in the previous examples. In addition, the role is unlikely to contain much actual participation in work. Instead, it provides a model for what is often seen as the participant observation method: spending a period of time in a particular setting, and combining observation with interviews.

Observation alone

In many ways, the role of complete observer is hardly a 'qualitative' method, since the researcher avoids sustained interaction with those under study. This type of observation is used in the field of management services where, for job design and specification purposes, requests are made for 'objective' accounts of the content of work; it can also be used in conjunction with other methods when lists of managerial competencies are being developed.

As a technique it is of very little use to those interested in a social constructionist view. Even when used in the discipline of management services, practitioners often fail to obtain people for accounts of their own actions because of the requirement for detachment. The observer role is often disliked by employees since it seems like snooping, and it prevents the degree of trust and friendship forming between researchers and respondents which, as we have noted, is an important component of the other methods. However, for trained practitioners, such techniques do give extremely accurate pictures of what takes place and how long they take, even if they fall short of giving a full account of why things are happening.

Semi-concealed research

This kind of research is not entirely the same as the categories we have discussed above. Rather, it relates to an increasingly popular 'critical management studies' tradition and involves researchers negotiating access into organizations with research agendas that they do not always want to reveal to all of the respondents they meet, for fear of being presented with an image of the company from a particular perspective. Semi-concealed research is not the same as covert research in that the researchers are open about their rationale for studying in the company. The aspect of concealment relates to the way the focus of the research is defined and the view the researcher takes on the practices under observation. An example of this would be the research of Collinson (1992) who conducted his research into the recruitment and selection practices in large companies. His particular focus was on how the mainly white, male, middle-aged managers controlled entry into the companies in ways that had the effect of excluding women.

Finally, it could be argued that much management research conducted for postgraduate qualifications is a form of auto-ethnography (Hayano, 1979), or self-ethnography (Alvesson, 1998). Defined in this way, it is possible for a student to study their own work context or observe their own colleagues using the opportunity as an insider. According to Hayano (1979) for this kind of process to be completely self-ethnographic, the researcher needs to be able to identify completely with the group under study and to be accepted as a full cultural member of the group that they seek to study. This approach to the research though, does have its drawbacks as although it appears to avoid many of the practical difficulties associated with participant observation (distance, time and so on associated with conducting research in someone else's organization), it doesn't enable an outsider to see differences and ask difficult questions. To study those 'not like us' is one of the main features of traditional ethnography; as telling someone else's story, it is argued, comes better from an outsider, and in doing so we come to know ourselves better. Conducting auto-ethnography also raises complex questions as to the role of the researcher at both the data collection stage and the writing stage. These issues we touch on in more detail later in the chapter.

Choice of roles

Clearly the choice the researcher makes of which role he or she will assume in his or her project is important. Some factors that may be kept in consideration when making this choice are addressed in this section.

- The purpose of the research may provide a researcher with an indication of which role is most appropriate. Does the research require continued longitudinal involvement, or will in-depth interviews conducted over time give the kind of insights required?

- The cost of the research is another factor that needs to be kept in mind. To what extent can the researcher afford to be committed for extended periods of time, and are there any additional costs involved such as training or housing costs?

- The extent to which access can be gained may seem a simple issue, but is also important to be aware of when choosing a researcher's role. Gaining access where the role of the researcher is either explicit or covert, can be difficult, and may take time.

- The extent to which the researcher is comfortable in the role is of course another important print. If the researcher intends to keep their identity concealed, will they also feel able to develop the kind of trusting relationships that are important?

- The amount of time available can also be influential. Some methods involve a considerable commitment of time.

Whichever method is chosen, they all provide the means to obtain a detailed understanding of values, motives and practices. As Fairhurst comments 'the crucial personal skill is to be seen as someone who can be trusted no matter what role is adopted – this will enable much to become possible'.

Advice for those going 'into the field' is not hard to come by. Legend has it that Evans-Pritchard, a very eminent anthropologist would advise all his research assistants before they set off to distant lands to go and get themselves a decent hamper from Fortnum and Masons, and to keep away from the native women (Barley, 1986: 17). Evans-Pritchard also advised students to 'get a large notebook and *start in the middle, because you never know which way things will develop*'.

UNDERSTANDING THROUGH INTERACTION

In this section our aim is to illustrate the ways in which researchers can work with respondents to make joint sense of what is taking place. Many of these methods also illustrate a distinction between the use of the method as a way of collecting 'data' or information, and the way that tools can be used to stimulate respondents into reflecting on their practice (as well as their views and ideas) with the distinct purpose of bringing about change. Used in this way they become 'tools for thinking' that can be extremely helpful for both individuals and for groups.

The use of tools in this way to stimulate discussion and debate, although varying in their richness, act also to simplify and reduce the uncertainties and ambiguities that so often surround many management situations. So for example we suggest here that if there are likely to be differences between the researcher and the researched that stand in the way of arriving at common understandings, then 'richer media' such as face to face interviews and visual tools (as opposed to questionnaires or reports) should be introduced.

To develop this notion we point to Daft and Lengel's (1986) study, which suggested that most organizational situations are characterized by uncertainty and that this uncertainty is very often caused by an absence of information or ambiguity, caused by equivocality. What researchers need to do therefore is find ways of reducing the uncertainty and the equivocality, both in obtaining data and in the way that the information is exchanged. In this section we point to just some of the tools and approaches that can be used to do this, many of which will be seen to employ some kind of visual media component (e.g. cognitive mapping, visual metaphors, photographs and repertory grids). Of course an additional feature of this approach is that both parties learn and as a consequence the approach can lead to development for those being researched. The following section offers some suggestions as to the approaches that might be considered.

Photographs and visual metaphors

The use of photographs and visual metaphors can be a useful way of gathering information when there is only a small amount of data on an issue to begin with or when information is proving difficult to get hold of or the matter under discussion is seen as contentious or problematic.

Assessing the role that photography has played in organizational research, Buchanan (1999) found that while photography has enjoyed a rich tradition in disciplines such as sociology and anthropology (Banks, 1995; Collier and Collier, 1986: Harper, 1994), it has been used far less within the field of management. As a consequence he deliberately planned his research so as to use photographs to stimulate discussion and debate between members of staff at a hospital as part of a programme to reengineer the patient's experience. He argued that if something of relevance can be seen, it can be discussed and possibly altered. Buchanan's purpose was to collect photographs in order to record complex scenes and processes that could provide 'non reactive' records and observations. He found that the photographs really helped the study. The use of photographs clearly triggered informants to talk much more about the ideas they had around the images and this helped to develop a more complex understanding of the chains of activity that occurred. Photographs of the process also contributed to a more accurate sequencing of the process as well as to a more detailed written analysis of the process. Once accomplished, the sequence was shown to a number of groups within the hospital and again additional complex details were added in the discussions and debates that they engendered. Drawing on the notion of social poetics, it can be suggested that the pictures offered the opportunity for a situation to be held captive (Wittgenstein, 1953) such that it allowed the possibility for new connections and relationships to emerge that would otherwise remain hidden from view, and that, once recognized, the new connections can help set a course for managerial action.

In the postindustrial age this is perhaps not so conceptually different from the way work study engineers used photographs including cyclographs and chronocyclographs to determine the paths of movements but unlike the industrial engineers from the past there isn't the same belief that all members of the organization will interpret this information in a similar way from the common standpoint of shared interests and values. The use of images it appears does enable great complexity to be represented and better understood.

Using visual metaphors is another approach that aims to elicit the views of individuals or groups. Individuals for example might be asked to represent the issues that concern them in the form of a picture or drawings. This use of pictures, this time created by the individuals or groups themselves, can be a powerful way of developing understanding and for groups to move forward with a vision for the future. An example of a group of managers being asked to draw a picture of the organization as if it were a person is shown in Example 7.6.

EXAMPLE 7.6

Example of a visual metaphor

In research conducted in a large multi-national the approach was used to explore how the senior staff viewed their organization (Simpson, 1997). The research was conducted using a series of focus group interviews. At each session the groups were asked the following questions:

A If the organization was a parent, how do you think it would relate to its children?

B If you were asked to write an honest character reference for the organization, what would it say? Some guidance here included, how well it performed in its most recent job, it's most recent job, its achievements, anything else that individuals thought was important.

C Try to imagine the company as an old friend whom you have not seen over the last 10 years. How would you judge if their personality had changed?

D Finally, individuals were asked to draw a picture of the company as the 'person' is today.

The questions produced very rich data indeed, which was taped and analysed, but perhaps the most interesting aspects of this metaphor approach was the drawings the individuals produced and their interpretation. An example of one is show below.

EXAMPLE 7.6—cont'd

Example of a visual metaphor

'Picture of the man'

The way the group discussed the drawings were as follows:

Jean: He's a man again is he?

Mirjam: Yes …

David: Yes I think he is a man.

Mohamed: It's impossible to get away from that I think.

Jean: Tell us about your picture, what does your picture show for us?

Mohamed: Shall I defend this? Since I drew it I got the shorter straw! Well, I was thinking of the bumbling uncle type person, perhaps not the sharpest person in the world, but at least you might get you pocket money off him. Next time you meet him he's got 30 years young, he'd got a flat top, a nice suit and a BMW. What was I trying to show (indicating hand on the drawing) I'm not much of an artist as you can see, was basically just no! It looks like on yer bike, which is just as appropriate.

Lisa: What's this in his other hand?

Mohamed: It's a mobile phone, it's trying to show he's a yuppie, flat top hair, double breasted suit, trendy glasses, small chin.

Lisa: It's interesting about the other hand because we thought there would be a lot of gesticulation rather than the sort of verbal interaction it's sort of hi and over there …

Liam: We were going to put him with a bag of money in one hand …

Lisa: But the portable phone gets that across …

Jean: So he's gone from being a friendly uncle to a yuppie?

EXAMPLE 7.6—cont'd

Example of a visual metaphor

Mohamed: Yes

Clare:… And younger instead of older?

Mohamed: Yes. Yes

Jean:… Perhaps we should all find out what he is on then!

Lisa: Didn't that also happen to the bloke who sold his soul to the devil …

Jean: I don't know.

Mohamed:….What's the film called, it's a baseball film, basically this about an old guy who sold his soul to the devil, it's the Faust legend – and became a young baseball player – I don't know what happened to Faust, whether he got younger.

The interpretations in Example 7.6 of the changes that had occurred revolved around the symbolism of a more business like future, the more conservative style of dress – double breasted suit and a more frantic (even harassed) appearance – and symbolized the increasing pace of organizational change and activity. An overall theme of the pictures from all the groups was the recognition of the change there had been from a friendly, caring calm demeanour to an aggressive impersonal characterization of the organizations. This example illustrates how, by making comparisons, in this case with something invented, a metaphor picture can help people to articulate their hopes and fears in a relatively non-threatening, non-confrontational and even humorous manner. Drawing pictures and drawing metaphors in groups may also enable employees to work to create a shared landscape, to which they all have contributed and to which they all can see their contribution and role.

Action research

As we have discussed in Chapter 5 action research is a particular method that is about change and intervention and within which researchers and practitioners work with practitioners on matters of concern (Eden and Huxham 1996, Saunders et al. 2006). Eden and Huxham (1996) suggest that as the interventions will naturally be 'one offs' they can be criticised for their lack of repeatability and lay themselves open to a claim of lack of rigour. Those contemplating their use do need to be clear on their endeavour which is through a process of change and improvement, bringing theory and practice together. Action research transcends descriptive and explanatory accounts of organizations. According to Gummesson (1991) a researcher comes with a theoretical trajectory or a 'pre-understanding' of a research topic and setting. While it is common for other research approaches to be explicit about researcher biases at the outset of a research project, it is important for action research to resist making assumptions before the project, because alternative interpretations are likely to emerge if pre-understanding is suppressed (Eden and Huxham 2002). Although they recognize that this might be difficult to achieve in practice at least it should be pushed into the background as far as possible. As a result, the analysis of the research may be enriched which in turn may facilitate finding new insights and concepts.

Researchers who want to use the method of action research should be aware that the skills that are required to conduct action research are not entirely the same as the skills needed for other research methods. Eden and Huxham (2007) identify 15 characteristics of action research which they recognize might be hard to achieve but nevertheless need in their view to be considered. Of course, the researcher needs to be skilled in techniques for probing and eliciting information from respondents. But the researcher is also required to have good facilitation skills and have the ability and flexibility to alternate between the roles of co-interventionist with practitioners and the academic researcher who steps back and derives abstractions about the immediate experience. Example 7.7 offers an understanding of what action research may entail. For a more detailed literature on the use of action research see the recommended reading list at the end of the chapter.

GENERAL ISSUES IN RELATION TO QUALITATIVE METHODS

A major issue to be kept in mind while doing qualitative research is the *relevance that the research has to the respondents*. If respondents do not see any benefit or value in the study they might produce fake or exaggerated information. As such, the issue of relevance to the respondents can be linked in with the above issues of obtaining trust and balancing the right social interaction. However, many individuals find benefit in talking to an independent outsider about themselves or learning something about future changes in the organization as in action research. In any event researchers should be able to recognize and capitalize on these situations and offer them as benefits or advantages to interviewees in exchange for participation. This is the strategy which underlies much work in the tradition of participative action research (Reason and Bradley, 2006). The more they are willing to be open the more that both parties are likely to gain. In addition, interest and commitment shown by the interviewer often produces far better results than clinical detachment.

Another important issue to be aware of at all times when conducting research, whether it be qualitative or quantitative in nature, is *ethics*. Although we have, in Chapter 6, reviewed some of the main ethical issues that may be encountered in any form of management research, we feel it is necessary to stress the importance of the issue. The most important thing to keep in mind is that under no circumstances should the researcher bring harm to the people he or she is researching. This refers to issues such as being sensitive to difficult issues and handling them in a discreet fashion, but also to not disclose confidential information. It also includes issues of being honest with the people the researcher works with, for example in the case of semi-covered participation. What is important is that researchers understand the ethical issues involved when dealing with qualitative methods. By understanding the implications of the choices they make they will be better placed to recognize any effect they may have on the nature of the relationship formed, and therefore on the data that is collected.

Lastly, some attention needs to be given to the issue of *reflexivity*. When collecting data, researchers need to think about their roles and the way they affect the research process. As discussed earlier on in this chapter, qualitative research attempts to

EXAMPLE 7.7

An example of an action research study into leadership

Huxham (2003) relates a retrospective account of how a particular research team set about analysing data on leadership in a health promotion partnership with which the research team worked. In the first instance, each of the researchers individually studied the data and identified what occurred over the course of the interventions, either through verbatim quotations or general and interpretive descriptions. Then, the team convened meetings and started negotiating on meanings of those interpretations and why these are considered of relevance to leadership within the particular setting. The researchers proceeded with forming categories of related issues and interpretations. Huxham explains: 'Gradually clusters of data and interpretations began to emerge. We also added in concepts deriving from the literature. On this occasion we used the mapping software, Decision Explorer. (…) Decision Explorer is a convenient tool because it allows large volumes of data to be handled flexibly' (2003: 244).

In the example given, Decision Explorer was not the only means of data analysis; Post-it® notes were also employed at times. A third stage involved sifting through and dissecting the contents of each cluster with a view to identifying linkages from which a conceptual framework was created. Here, again, the researchers first attempted to identify the linkages individually and then came together to discuss and agree how the various clusters might be linked. The outcome was a combination of the acceptance of some of the clusters and an abandonment of others for lack of adequate data. At the end of this third step a core number of clusters were formulated all linked with leadership.

The subsequent step incorporated reflection on what had been achieved up to that point, but it also encompassed testing the emerging framework in contexts other than the setting in which it was generated.

The fifth, and final stage, focused on refining the different clusters into a framework, enriching with theoretical justifications and disseminating in academic circles through conferences while at the same time ensuring their was a practice link by engaging with other practitioners.

capture subjective understandings of the external world from the perspective of participants and abandons the task of representing an 'objective' unchanging external reality. Rather qualitative research aims to develop knowledge on how participants' understandings are created through patterns of social interaction. In this way communication is seen as a 'formative' process in which individuals and worldviews are created through interaction with the social world around them. In relation to this, qualitative researchers suggest that meanings are continuously negotiated and renegotiated.

However, failing to take account of the place of the researcher in the construction of these understandings enables researchers to remove themselves from the processes that are occurring and allows them to make pronouncements on the role of others. This unfortunately brings a static understanding to meanings that are inherently fluid in nature (Alvesson and Skoldberg, 2000).

For this reason, the notion of reflexivity has become central to any discussion of the collection and representation of qualitative data. While reflexivity may be seen to involve the questioning of 'the threads of philosophical and methodological certainty implicit in the goal of mainstream social science to provide an absolute view of the world' (Cunliffe, 2003: 984), it is difficult to find a commonly agreed definition of reflexivity. In effect, a range of diverse definitions from all corners of the social sciences have been put forward. However, what they all share is a deep underlying scepticism for the truth claims forwarded in any form of social science research. One definition commonly used which may be helpful to students in attempting to understand what is meant by reflexivity is that outlined by Alvesson and Skoldberg who define reflexivity as continuous awareness and attention to 'the way different kinds of linguistic, social, political and theoretical elements are woven together in the process of knowledge development, during which empirical material is constructed, interpreted and written' (2000: 5).

Aiming to incorporate reflexivity into their research practice, many qualitative researchers aim to be aware throughout the research process of how the various elements of their identities become significant during the research process and write this into the research presentations (e.g. Brewer 2000; Pink 2001). This often involves paying tribute to social categories such as race, gender, class and writing these attributes into the research process. This strategy, it is proposed, allows the researcher to understand how their personal characteristics may have in some way influenced the research process and affected their understanding of the results. However, there has been increasing criticism of such approaches to reflexivity. As Cunliffe outlines 'critics of reflexivity argue it has little to offer ... questioning what is real, what is knowledge, and who (or what) is self, leads only to intellectual chaos, self indulgent navel gazing aporia...and politically motivated subjectivism' (2003: 990). Therefore some qualitative researchers argue that reflexivity involves too much introspection on the part of the researcher, which may both problematize the research process and paralyse the researcher. While reflexivity has been discussed in a chapter dealing with the collection of qualitative data, these issues are no less relevant in the representation of this data; therefore, students should keep these ideas in mind when reading the chapter on qualitative data analysis.

CONCLUSION

In this chapter we have aimed to provide an overview of some of the main methods for collecting qualitative data. We can emphasize three key points:

- Qualitative research is a creative process which aims to understand the sense that respondents make of their world.

- There are many techniques for doing this and although we can give guidelines each piece of research is unique and the decision must be taken as to which of these alternative and often competing approaches is most appropriate.
- Since the research process is close and emergent the relationship of the researcher to the researched must be taken into account.

Thus far, Chapter 7 has focused on the collection of qualitative data, and has discussed issues that may be of importance while collecting data. The analysis of qualitative data, however, is a whole different story with different issues that need careful consideration. Chapter 8, therefore, will elaborate further on this.

Interviewing

EXERCISE 7.1

The qualitative researcher needs to have good personal engagement to gain trust so that 'good' data can be obtained. Think about a time when you have been interviewed, either as a research respondent or at a recruitment interview. Did the interviewer appear to do anything to gain or lose your trust?

Keeping a research diary

EXERCISE 7.2

It is a good idea to keep a research diary in which you record the current stage of your research, your ideas about what is emerging that might represent findings and your contribution, as well as how you feel about the research at the time of writing. If there are difficult issues in relation to the research process these should also be recorded.

In pairs, discuss whether you think keeping a research diary could help you, particularly in relation to your research approach.

Experiment in laddering

EXERCISE 7.3

In pairs, ask one another a simple question that relates to a personal view or preference the person might have. Then try to ladder up from this question to see if you can learn something about the person's values (normally this can be done by asking 'why' type questions). Then ladder down to see if you can learn something about the detail that surrounds these preferences (this is normally done by asking about specific instances).

FURTHER READING

Alvesson, M. (2003) 'Beyond neopositivists, romantics, and localists: a reflexive approach to interviews in organisation research', *Academy of Management Review*, 28 (1): 13–33.

This paper provides a useful critique of dominating views on the research interview. In addition Alvesson attempts to develop a reflexive theoretical framework which may provide more useful qualitative insights.

Lupton, T. (1963) *On the Shop Floor: Two Studies of Workshop Organization and Output*. New York: Macmillan.

A seminal ethnographic study which outlines an in-depth, contextualized and culturally based understanding of the positions shop-floor workers adopted in relation to those in management positions.

Reason, P. and Bradbury, H. (2006) *Handbook of Action Research: Participative Inquiry and Practice*. London: Sage.

This work provides a useful insight into the relationship between theory and practice, a question which remains at the forefront of management inquiry. The authors aim to address the issue of how to turn 'messy' field research into usable data.

MAKING SENSE OF QUALITATIVE DATA

8

LEARNING OBJECTIVES

- To understand the different approaches to the analysis of qualitative data and what this means for the practice of data analysis.

- To understand how information technology has enabled analysis through the use of computer packages.

- To understand how interaction can inform understanding.

Introduction

Analysing transcripts

Discourse analysis

Using computers and software to analyse qualitative data

An example of using Atlas.ti

Conclusion

Further reading

INTRODUCTION

There are many ways in which data can be analysed. What researchers need to bear in mind is that most methods of analysis can be used for a wide variety of data. It is important, however, that the researcher chooses methods of analysis that are consistent with the philosophical and methodological assumptions made in the research designs that underpin the study.

One of the most common issues that qualitative researchers face is how to condense highly complex and context-bound information into a format that tells a story in a way that is fully convincing to others. In the case of management research, this goes beyond the requirements of 'good journalism' where sources are well referenced and interpretations are 'balanced'. It requires both a clear explanation of how the analysis was undertaken and how the conclusions were reached, as well as a demonstration of how the raw data was transformed into meaningful conclusions. Chapter 7 has given the reader some ideas of how qualitative data might be collected and Chapter 12 discusses just how findings might be written up in the project or thesis. Chapter 8, then, indicates a number of ways in which we might make sense of qualitative data and how systems can be developed that will make the links between the data collected, the analysis undertaken and the inferences drawn explicit. Most of the time this does not mean that all the data collected has to be displayed, but at least a sample of the data is needed for illustration so that the same logic path can be followed and an independent view drawn.

In many ways the issues about the analysis of qualitative data are closely linked to the different research philosophies discussed in Chapter 4. If the researcher is working from a social constructionist perspective, then he or she will attempt as much as possible not to draw a distinction between the collection of data and its analysis and interpretation. Researchers who prefer a more positivist approach will see a sharper distinction between data and the process of analysis, to the extent that the data collection and analysis may well be performed by different people. They will also be more concerned with examining frequencies within qualitative data which will enable them to turn it into numeric form, although as we will see later in this chapter this is not always the case. We present for instance a number of hybrid examples which have become more popular and appealing with the advent of computer data analysis software. After all, numbers are both seductive and persuasive, and for many managers, or funders, the political need for numbers wins through against attempts to provide rich descriptions.

ANALYSING TRANSCRIPTS

The next sections will examine the different ways in which a researcher can analyse natural language data. As Chapter 7 has demonstrated, there is more than one way to collect natural language data, such as in-depth interviews, diary studies or video records. Similarly, there is more than one way in which the collected language data can be analysed, and the following section will cover six different methods that allow for an analysis of natural language data which are: content analysis, grounded analysis, discourse analysis, narrative analysis, conversation analysis and argument analysis. As with collecting qualitative data, the choice that the researcher makes for a particular method of analysis depends largely on what the researcher wants to find out.

Building on the differences in research approach and thus analysis, the first two methods of natural language analysis will be discussed together: *content analysis* and *grounded analysis*. In the first approach, content analysis, the researcher interrogates the data for constructs and ideas that have been decided in advance. In the second, he or she tends to let the data speak for itself and although the researcher is still employing a process the researcher allows for more intuition to guide him or her in the development of understanding of the data. This latter approach is more holistic than content analysis and often takes on a cultural and historical dimension, which may even suggest the need for a longitudinal approach. With grounded analysis, the researcher stays closer to the data and any observations made need to be carefully placed in context. As with any research it is important that the data that forms the basis of the research conclusions remain available for scrutiny, which practically might extend to taking transcripts in a separate folder or ring binder in with you to the oral defence.

Although we characterize these two positions as competing alternatives, between them lies a raft of practice and in many ways the choices that researchers face lie on a continuum (see Table 8.1) between **content analysis**, where as King (2004:118) suggests, codes are all predetermined and where their distribution is analysed statistically, and **grounded analysis** where there are no *a priori* definitional codes.

Content analysis

Content analysis methods have been used successfully in the examination of historical artefacts. In one such study, analysis was made of Caesar's accounts of his wars in Gaul. Researchers identified certain key phrases or words which they counted, and the frequencies were then analysed. The selection of these would depend on the hypothesis the researcher wished to prove or disprove. In the case of Caesar's accounts of his campaigns, the hypothesis that was tested related to the forms of money that were used. A similar kind of content analysis has been used to try to determine the authorship of anonymous plays by analysing the use of words and the

TABLE 8.1 Qualitative data analysis: content versus grounded methods

Content analysis	Grounded analysis
Searching for content (prior hypotheses)	Understanding of context and time
Causally linked variables	Holistic associations
Objective Subjective	Faithful to views of respondents
More deductive	More inductive
Aims for clarity and unity	Preserves ambiguity and contradiction

EXAMPLE 8.1

Research into payment systems – content analysis

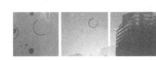

In the study of payment systems see Chapter 7 (Bowey and Thorpe, 1986) content analysis was used to analyse data. A number of problems immediately became apparent: control over the data collection process had been poor due to the number of people who had been involved – not all the core questions had been asked of each respondent and in addition, due to a shortage of tape recorders, field notes had been taken but transcripts were not available for all the interviews, which made comparability difficult. This was far from satisfactory! However, to solve this difficulty, all the material was read by each member of the research team.

Subsequently, three substantial interviews were chosen and read in detail and coded by three researchers. Issues that appeared to require further elaboration in further interviews were identified. Then, the coding frame that had been developed was discussed with all the researchers and modified in the light of inconsistencies. At the same time definitions were agreed in relation to the three pilot interviews and detailed notes were made of how answers might be interpreted. Finally, all the interviews were distributed to all the researchers and the same analysis framework used to interpret them.

Regular checks were done to reduce the number of inconsistencies between coders. Once all interviews had been coded they were transferred into SPSS to sit alongside data derived from a large scale survey of over 1000 employees.

In this example all the information had derived from interviews although many of the themes identified had been identified as relevant in advance. However, new unexpected themes were able to be accommodated and added into the framework. At a later date, using this method, it was possible to compare answers derived from interviews with those derived from questionnaires; moreover it was possible to separate these into definite responses and probable responses.

recurrent patterns of certain words or phases, and even more recently to determine whether criminals' statements have been added to, or amended, by others at some later date!

We have seen in Example 8.1 that more than one hypothesis was tested and multiple interviewers and coders were used. Moreover, the separation between the collection and the analysis stages is clear. There are also issues raised about how common understandings were arrived at between those involved. The study offers an example of the way in which qualitative data was coded and then imported in to a quantitative data set and analysed together. One of the most influential sourcebooks on content analysis is by Miles and Huberman (1994). They offer a range of ways whereby information might be analysed in order to capture the complexity of all sorts of qualitative data in a whole variety of circumstances. At the heart of the process is a matrix format which captures the constructs (extant or emergent) usually on one axis and the respondents or occurrences on the other. Although this method of data analysis is quite definitely still qualitative, it is possible to introduce some element of quantification into the process. An example from Miles and Huberman is shown in Table 8.2. The aim of the research in the example was to predict the level of assistance provided by an organization at 12 field sites shown in the left hand column (column 1). The most likely predictors 'expected' were arranged across the top of the matrix. Note that the first three columns in this analysis matrix, although they have been scored in a qualitative way (columns 2–4) have been bundled together to give some numerical value (column 5) presumably so as to signify the strength of these variables. What follows (columns 6–8) are three more antecedents (scale of finding, central office commitment and administrative latitude). Note again that in this matrix all the variables are summarized qualitatively this time (column 9).

Miles and Huberman (1994) argue that displays of this type can help with another objective of the analysis, which is that of looking ahead to the consequences (column 10) for early implementation and then to column 11 for a summary of later implementation.

Miles and Huberman furthermore explain what is happening in the matrix using very 'quantitatively derived' terminology. For example, they suggest that although the degree of assistance was the dependent variable for the earlier analysis, it is, in turn, the main predictor of the later consequences.

In this analysis the researchers are going beyond a simple calculation to attempt to identify whether the predictors that accounted for the degree of assistance make sense when they are combined with the level of assistance, to lead to different levels of later outcomes. So in this matrix, there is the beginning of a causal chain – going beyond a simple configuration to sort and order data, and onto an understanding of the causal linkages – very much in the same way that linkages are gained from manually analysed **repertory grids**.

Of course, this is only one type of matrix design that is constructed for one particular purpose and what we want to draw attention to is the degree of flexibility that is possible. As such, matrix designs can range from simply counting the occurrence of various phenomena, to matrices that order variables against the dimension of time (for an example of this, see Miles and Huberman, 1994: 201), to those that simply display qualitative data.

Grounded analysis

Grounded analysis offers the more 'open' approach to data analysis and is closely linked to the concept of grounded theory. Again, the source of data can be texts produced from empirical research, (for example interview data) or extant texts which might take the form of company reports or diaries. At this end of the qualitative data analysis spectrum the structure is derived from the data rather than imposed on the data externally, as often is the case with the positivist approach. This means that the data is systematically analysed so as to tease out themes, patterns and categories that will be declared in the findings. As we pointed out in Chapter 5, we are in difficult territory here as there is no one clear agreed approach, and even the methodology that

TABLE 8.2 Predictor-outcome consequences matrix: antecedents and consequences of assistance

ANTECEDENT CONDITIONS CONSEQUENCES							ASSISTANCE			
Sites/scale of assistance	Actual size/scope of innov.	Required practice change	Actual classroom/organiza-tional fit	Implemen-tation require-ments	Scale of funding	Central office commitment to change	Admin latitude	Overall presence	Smoothness/roughness of early implemen-tation	Practice stabilization (later implemen-tation)
(1)	(2)	(3)	(4)	(5)	(6)	(7)	(8)	(9)	(10)	(11)
					Substantial assistance					
Masepa(E)	Large	Major	Mod/good	12	$30–50K	High	Low	High	Very rough	Mod
Plummet(L)	Large	Mod/major	Good/poor*	12	$300K	High	High	High	Very rough	Mod
Carson(L)	Large	Major	Mod/good	12	$969K	High	Mod	Mod/high	Rough	Mod
Tindale(L)	Large/mod	Major	Mod	12	$87K	High	Low	Mod/high	Rough	High

Site									
Perry-Parkdale(E)	Mod	Mod/major	Mod	10	$300K	Mod	High	Mod/high	Mixed	Mod/high
Banestown(E)	Small/mod	Major	Mod	10	$5.6K	High	High	Mod	Very rough	Mod
				Initial assistance, then minimal						
Lido(E)	Small	Mod	Mod	7	$6.1K	Low	High	Low/mod	Mostly smooth	Mod/high
Astoria(E)	Small	Minor	Good	3	None	High	High	Low/mod	Smooth	High
Carlston(E)	Small	Mod	Poor	9	None	Mod/high	Mod/high	Low/mod	Mixed	Mod/high
				Nearly none						
Dun Hollow(L)	Small	Minor	Poor	7	None	Low	Mod	Low	Rough	Low
Proville(L)	Mod	Minor	Good	7	$180K	High/low	High	Low	Very rough	Low
Burton(E)	Small	Minor	Poor	3	$3.1K	Mod/high	High	Low	Smooth	Mod

was proposed by Glaser and Strauss originally to give some structure to the process, has undergone many changes and developments and has been the subject of acrimonious debate. Locke reminds us that the original methodological monograph was written 'as a polemic against hypothetical-deductive; speculative theory-building and its associated research practices that characterised the sociological context of the time' (2001: 33). Glaser and Strauss's work not only encouraged researchers to be more courageous in using their imagination and creativity when developing theory but their work also showed researchers a rigorous method by which this could be done.

Below we suggest a practical approach to sifting through volumes of non-standard data. In order to make the procedure more understandable we explained it in the way we and our colleagues have used it. We introduce some coding terminology into the process so links can be made to texts on grounded analysis. The method assumes that one is working with transcripts of in-depth interviews – one of the more intractable analysis problems. We consider that there are seven main stages to such analysis:

Familiarization First, re-read the data transcripts. When reading, draw on unrecorded information as well as recorded. This is where any additional field notes and your personal research diary can be important to the process of analysis. Glaser (1978) suggests that at this initial stage researchers should remind themselves just what the focus of the study is, what the data suggests and whose point of view is being expressed. The relationship between the research and the people interviewed should also be accounted for.

Reflection At this stage desperation may begin to set in. There is usually so much rich data that trying to make sense of it seems an impossible task. Evaluation and critique become more evident as the data is evaluated in the light of previous research, academic texts, and commonsense explanations. The kind of questions researchers might ask themselves are:

- Does it support existing knowledge?
- Does it challenge it?
- Does it answer previously unanswered questions?
- What is different?
- Is it different?

Conceptualization At this stage there is usually a set of concepts which seem to be important for understanding what is going on. For example in an examination of performance these might include: management style, technology, absence rates, demographic qualities of the labour force, locus of power, and so on. These concepts which respondents mentioned are now articulated as explanatory variables, and now need to be coded. Charmaz, (2006) suggests codes should be simple and precise and actions preserved with the process remaining open and the researcher staying close to the data.

Cataloguing concepts Having established that these concepts do seem to occur in people's explanations, they then can be transferred into a database. *Focused codes* are more directed and more conceptual and analytical and *axial codes* specify categories or sub-categories and specify the dimensions of a category. There is an issue of labelling that needs to be resolved which relates to whether the language used is that of the people concerned or do you use your own terms? Our view is that it is probably helpful at this stage to use your own terms providing a trace is kept of how they were derived. Although there may be pressure to use computer packages for your analysis there is a debate about the way the software structures the data and where there are modest amounts of data it may still be worth considering manual methods.

Re-coding Whether computers are used or not the process is usually highly iterative and there will need to be an element of going back and checking against the original data and comparing incidents in order to identify particular properties. It may well be individuals in the same organization were interpreting what appears to be similar concepts in very different ways. In these cases re-coding will be necessary.

Linking At this stage the analytical framework and explanations should be becoming clearer with patterns emerging between concepts. This is the stage of developing **theoretical codes**. This is achieved by conceptualizing 'how substantive codes may relate to each other as hypotheses to be integrated into a theory' (Charmaz, 2006). One can now begin to link the key variables into a more holistic theory. At this stage it is often worth producing a first draft which can be tried out on others, both colleagues and respondents so that the argument and supporting data can be exposed to wider scrutiny and some degree of verification.

Re-evaluation In the light of the comments of others, the researcher may feel that more work is needed in some areas. For example, the analysis may have omitted some factors or have over-emphasized others. This stage takes some period of time, and as with the other stages it may have to be undertaken more than once. The researcher may well feel that for much of the time the analysis of qualitative data is chaotic and extremely messy.

Since the early development of grounded theory there has been considerable development of the method, not least by Glaser (1978, 1992, 1998), by Strauss (1987), and by students of both authors, notably Corbin (Strauss and Corbin, 1990, 1998). What is more, over the years their published views have diverged considerably. Glaser has persistently advocated a more open, flexible approach in which the theory emerges from the data, almost without human intervention. He is hostile to the elaboration of analysis procedures and wrote a critical book where he claimed that the fractured, technical approach being adopted by Strauss's approach was tantamount to a 'whole new method' which forced data into categories. This made the process too rigid and uncompromising (Glaser, 1992). Strauss and Corbin (1990, 1998) on the other hand moved in the direction of increased prescription and elaboration. Their strategy for sampling data operates at three levels open, axial and selective which are defined in Table 8.3.

Example 8.2 is taken from a research project conducted by Thorpe and Danielli on the use of a local park. It follows some, but not all of the advice from the protagonists discussed above. First, the researchers used a pre-determined sample framework (and hence did not use theoretical sampling). Second, they did not use the

TABLE 8.3 Data sampling process recommended by Strauss and Corbin (1998)

Coding practice	Theoretical sampling strategy
Open	Open sampling – relatively indiscriminate sampling of people, places and situations that will provide the best opportunities for collecting relevant data.
Axial	Variational and relational sampling – focused sampling of people, places and situations that will provide opportunities to gather data about the properties and dimensions of the categories as well as how the categories are related to each other. Data gathering in terms of coding paradigm is also clearly implicated here.
Selective	Discriminate sampling – very focused and deliberate sampling of people, places and situations that will fill in and refine the story line of the core categories and the proposed relationships between categories.

system of open, axial and selective coding in a systematic way; and third, they focused on identifying a clear story line using information from outside their own study (which goes against the advice of Glaser).

Whatever approach is adopted, the content analysis of qualitative data is time consuming, often costly and requires either good (written-up) field notes or verbatim transcripts to be available. Often in applied research where the focus of the investigation is relatively clear and a large number of interviews may have been conducted by different people, some standardization of the process may well be necessary. However tackled, the method should allow the researcher to draw key features out of the data, whilst at the same time allowing the richness of some of the material to remain so it can be used to evidence the conclusions drawn and help to 'let the data speak' for itself.

EXAMPLE 8.2

A study of a northern park

Their study was into the use of a local park, and information was collected from 10 different groups of park users. These included: a women and toddler group, representatives from two schools who used the park as a consequence of changes in the requirements of the national curriculum, an Asian women's group (the area was predominantly built up with a high ethnic population), a disabled group (who used the uncongested pathways to exercise and use their wheel chairs), a young Asian youth team (who used the bowling green to play football!) as well as others. Interviews were transcribed and analysed using the grounded theory approach described. What was striking as a category from the data collected from each group, was the way *fear* emerged as one of the main constructs for each. This is what Strauss and Corbin would describe as an *axial code*.

EXAMPLE 8.2—cont'd

A study of a northern park

But further sampling of the data in the transcripts showed the manifestation of fear was quite different in each group. For the women and toddler groups, it was fear of large groups of Asian boys playing football on the bowling green. For the Asian boys, it was fear of being intimidated by white youths if they went to the sports hall in the town centre. For the Asian women's groups, it was a fear of spirits which they thought inhabited parts of the park, particularly those parts which were poorly lit, where the trees hung over the walkways. Through further discriminant sampling it was possible to connect this category to other categories such as *absence*. Over the years for a variety of reasons there had been a gradual withdrawal of park staff, the community charge had put pressure on the level of service the council was able to provide, which curtailed the time park staff could spend in the park, and into this space left in the park, anti-social elements and behaviour had begun to develop. Understanding the context and interrelationships between variables in this way is extremely important for qualitative researchers and hence the researchers decided to go beyond the specific case under examination to show the context within which it was located. So, for example, when explaining and presenting the results of the above park study and the experiences of individuals in relation to the park, Thorpe and Danielli placed the concept of a northern town park in the context of its role in civic society in late 19th-and early 20th-century Britain.

The story is one of a six-day working week for many manual workers when religion still played a significant part in people's lives and, when going to church on Sunday was a time when the family could be together and when 'Sunday best' clothes were worn. One of the places where individuals could promenade was in the park. Cars were few and far between and other forms of transport limited and expensive, so parks were local places where people could meet and enjoy themselves and congregate. The increase in affluence and the decline of religion, the changing hours of work and now Sunday shopping have all been contextual factors to the traditional uses of town parks and a reason for their decline and the problem needs to be understood in this context.

One final lesson from this particular study is perhaps apocryphal and relates to what happened when the findings were presented to the Council. The leader of the Council sub-committee thanked Richard for his presentation but questioned him as to the validity of the study as there were no large samples or statistics. Later during coffee, park warden staff approached him to say that the report revealed something very close to their experiences on a day-to-day basis.

DISCOURSE ANALYSIS

A third approach to the analysis of natural language data is **discourse analysis**. This particular approach takes into account the broader social context in which the conversation takes place, and is therefore is less concerned with simply a detailed analysis of transcripts. It also does not restrict itself to conversations alone, but may for example use other textual sources such as newspaper articles, computer conferences or advertisements as the basis for analysis. In addition, discourse analysis might consider data such as signed language – such as body movements, hand signals and so on – to make a point about meanings where there is a response. **Critical discourse analysis** is a slightly different form of analysis, which further emphasizes the power relations and ideologies that are created by and represented in language (Fairclough and Hardy, 1997).

Marshall (2000) points to the use of discourse analysis as an alternative perspective to the examination of psychological issues. She indicates the way the approach has been developed from fields such as literary theory, linguistics and activity theory and as a consequence it has been represented by many different approaches. With reference to interpretation Potter and Wetherell (1988) identify three interconnected concepts, namely function, variation and construction, which are explained below.

- *Function* refers to the practical ways discourse might be used for example, to explain, justify or excuse and as well as to legitimise the power of particular management groups.
- *Variability* refers to the fact that the same event, the same social group or the same personality may be used to describe the same thing in many different ways as *function* changes.
- *Construction* relates to the notion that discourses are manufactured out of pre-existing linguistic resources and in this manufacturing process an active selection process takes place whereby some formulations will be chosen and others will not. (Potter and Wetherell, 1987)

In summary, two important issues need to be noted. One relates to the concept of contradictions, dilemmas and arguments that exist within discourse (Billig, 1988, 1991). A second relates to the notion of identity. Shotter (1993) and Wertsch (1991) both build on different theoretical traditions that highlight the dialogic nature of human thought and action, a concept which sees language as a mediator of social means, whereby its active use serves to unify the internal and external world, the subject with the object, and thought with action.

Narrative analysis

Narrative analysis, a fourth approach to analysing natural language data, is based on the analysis of how people describe or account for events, real or imagined, often referred to as the telling of stories. As a research tool this approach has become increasingly useful in organizational studies, where much research involves the interpretation of stories in some form or another. The method is useful in the analysis of interview data but can also be used with other text based media. Tsoukas and Hatch

(1997) suggest that stories give '... us access to and appreciation for context', which is a vital requirement for the making of meaning and our understanding if a constructionist analysis is to be adopted. Narratives:

- are concerned with the temporal ordering of ideas;
- usually tend to focus on the sequential patterning of events and the role of various actors within them;
- enable a researcher to build a complex picture of social situations in order to examine the actions of the various actors in a story, and explore their own values, ideas and beliefs.

Narrative analysis, then, can be applied to data (e.g. interview, corporate texts, but also videos or web sites) in which there is a description of a sequence of events in which a self and others are involved. The self could be related to an individual, as in an autobiographical account, or could be related to a corporate entity. For example, there may be a founding myth about how a company came to embody certain values (see Boje 1995, 2001).

Conversation analysis

A fifth method of analysis for natural language data, is **conversation analysis**, and can be used when the data is in the form of transcripts of naturally occurring conversations between two or more people. Conversation analysis has been used extensively by Silverman (1993, 2000) to examine, for example, the way judgements are formed in selection interviews and how teachers converse with classes of schoolchildren. There are three fundamental assumptions to conversation analysis: (1) that all conversations exhibit stable, organized patterns irrespective of who is talking; (2) that conversations are organized sequentially, and that it is only possible to make sense of a statement in relation to an on-going sequence of comments; and (3) that analysis should be grounded in a detailed empirical examination of the data.

This emphasis on detailed empirical analysis has resulted in very precise conventions for transcribing tapes. We give some examples in Table 8.4.

Argument analysis

Yet another way in which discourse can be used and analysed, this time in an active way, is through **argument analysis** which is particularly relevant when there is an explicit management development agenda. In argument analysis the respondent is directly involved and the approach has been used both to interpret an individual's view of their role or their understanding of the management process and in a developmental way. The approach involves getting managers to write stories of events at work and then asking them to critically reflect on what they have produced so that they can reflect on what they have written and can become more conscious of the ideas they have, how they were formed and how they might be changed. Such a process can lead to a change in their behaviour. In this section, we present two approaches to argument analysis. The first employs the ideas of Toulmin (2001), and the second, based on the work of the philosopher Gadamer, (1989) aims to develop critical thinking in managers.

TABLE 8.4 Simplified transcription symbols

Symbol	Example	Explanation
[	A: for quite a [while talk B: [yes, but	Left bracket indicates the point at which the current speaker's is overlapped by another's talk
=	A: that I'm aware of = B: = Yes.Would you confirm that?	Equal sign, one at the end of a line and one at the beginning, indicate no gap between the two lines.
.hhhh	I feel that.hh	A row of h's prefixed by a dot indicates an inbreath; without a dot, an outbreath. The number indicates the length of breath.
( )	Future risks and ( ) and life ( )	Empty parentheses indicate an undecipherable word.
_____	What's up?	Underscoring indicates some stress through pitch of amplitude.

SOURCE: SILVERMAN, (1993: 118)

EXAMPLE 8.3

Helping managers become more reflective

In their study of Barclays Bank managers, Gold et al. (2002) asked managers to write accounts to help to reflect and change. The aim was to develop the quality of critical thinking which was defined as the ability to reflect on actions taken or views held in a group of the bank's middle managers.

The research process was part of their programme for development, and a number of managers (eight in total) were asked to reflect on their practice with a view to develop their skills of critical reflection and through the process to strengthen their practice. There were many stages:

A Develop a 'story log' and write about significant incidents (note the use of critical incidents here as discussed in Chapter 7). Where possible the managers were encouraged to choose stories that involved themselves and others.

B State why they cared about the particular issues described and what they believed was the explanation for events as they emerged in the story – this part of the task was completed in small groups.

C Identify the claims that they had made in the stories and provide an explanation for these claims.

EXAMPLE 8.3—cont'd

Helping managers become more reflective

D Go back into their organizations and substantiate the data on which these claims were based. That is search out the data that supported the claims made.

What became apparent immediately, and is important to note, was that some managers quickly became aware that they lacked sufficient evidence to support the claims they made, while others found that the evidence that they had offered was at best spurious at worse wrong. For example, one manager had misread someone else's opinion as a fact.

For many, the process described above was profound. Not only because they had gained an insight into how to understand and analyse arguments, a skill that is considered useful, but rather because many took so much for granted without checking. Accordingly, the insights that they had gained offered a new approach to a key managerial task.

USING COMPUTERS AND SOFTWARE TO ANALYSE QUALITATIVE DATA

Computer Aided Qualitative Data Analysis Software (CAQDAS) is the general term for the computer software packages that can be used to analyse qualitative data. CAQDAS, then, are database packages that can be used to store transcripts and data, and even to conduct simple searches for specified concepts. Depending on the software program chosen, the researcher may simply be aided in the thematic analysis of his or her data, but many qualitative analysis software packages (**QASPs**) have the ability to manage large volumes of data.

In this section we consider a number of these packages, from the most routine, to the more sophisticated. The code and retrieve routines are the ones that are the most useful, but the better programs are capable of far more sophisticated analytical operations. Some programs, for example, are capable of providing graphical output for idea mapping, others use numbers and statistical techniques in order to plot the relationships between variables (as in the analysis of **repertory grids**). There are even programs that handle quantitative as well as qualitative data and audio visual data as well as performing hypothesis testing.

Qualitative research involves the researcher attempting to make sense of a mass of data, and CAQDAS may be used to facilitate the analysis process and to make this mountain of seemingly shapeless data more manageable. Seale (2000) outlines several advantages of CAQDAS, including their contribution to speed, rigour and team research. The *speed* of these packages when sorting or searching data is most obvious, since it is now possible to search through hundreds of pages of transcripts in a moment, and a particular advantage is in identifying patterns within, or between, data sets. *Rigour* is important because qualitative researchers are easily accused of selecting data and quotes which support their case and neglecting all counter-indicators. CAQDAS can enable rapid counting of the occurrences of items as well as being able to search for negative instances by examining the whole corpus of data. When put under pressure the qualitative researcher can provide precise figures to substantiate their qualitative research.

When people are conducting different interviews in the same study it can be very hard to share and compare data. The ability to transmit transcripts and memos electronically makes it much easier to share data, but CAQDAS can also enable those not involved with data collection to become fully involved in the analytic phases. This facility would have greatly helped the team that worked on the China/UK decision making project (Easterby-Smith and Malina, 1999) where the full-time research staff controlled the primary data and principal investigators found it increasingly difficult to contribute to analysis and interpretation.

Currently there are two packages which dominate the market: **NVivo** and **Atlas-ti**. **NVivo** (http:// www.qsrinternational.com/) is said to take the best of NVivo 2 and NUD*IST (another software package) and is furthermore said to have added new features and tools. The original package NUD*IST was developed initially for the Apple Macintosh, and then adapted for use on PCs. The program quickly overtook another earlier program, *Ethnograph*, in popularity partly because it has been promoted energetically, but also because it contains some additional analytic features which earlier programs did not have. One of those features is the facility to store analytic memos produced by the researcher while interacting with the data, and for these memos to be searched along with the rest of the data in the file (a process known as 'system closure'). Another feature is the ability to provide a visual display of the coding system in the form of a hierarchical tree structure. In many ways NVivo is the program that has captured the attention of those teaching qualitative methods in universities and for this reason it is a program that is often subscribed to by the university's information systems departments.

Atlas-ti (http://www.atlasti.de), the second software package that we discuss in this section, adds further sophistication, and is especially oriented to the development of grounded theory. In particular it has the capacity to create conceptual diagrams which show the relationship between emergent concepts, and which can also be linked to the original instances in the data, thus facilitating the selection of appropriate quotes that support the theoretical argument. Once again there is a complexity which means that researchers will have to decide whether the sophistication of their required analysis justifies the additional effort needed to master the package.

Choosing the particular software package that will suit the needs of each research project is difficult especially as most are commercial products, and liable to have their benefits oversold. CAQDAS packages offer researchers the facility to get to grips with very large data sets (whether interviews or ethnographic field notes), as well as offering the rigour of the analysis process. But if the data set is relatively small (say, fewer than 20 interviews) then it may be that the investment of time, money and energy will not be justified. These relatively small data sets may still be best understood and analysed through the older methods of multi-coloured highlighting pens and close reading on screen or paper.

In conclusion, we feel it is important to emphasize four general points about the use of computers for analysing qualitative data. First, the success and the strength of the analysis always depend on the judgement of the researcher, and computers cannot substitute for this. Second, packages and programs need to be chosen for, and be appropriate to, the tasks required. Third, it may sometimes be easier to analyse qualitative data by hand. Finally, it is important to beware of the possibility that the availability of computer analysis may lead to an emphasis on counting the frequency of categories, at the expense of understanding the *quality* of ideas and experiences.

NVivo in use: evolution of business knowledge in SMEs

This study was conducted by a PhD student at Manchester (MacPherson, 2006) and involved interview data collected from 23 owner-managed firms in addition to four case studies conducted in-depth. The aim was to understand the ways these organizations gained knowledge, to overcome significant difficulties faced at work. The interviews conducted incorporated the use of critical incidents that related to difficulties that the managers had faced at work in order to give some focus to the managers' answers and enable them to answer in respect to a particular event. Initially, Nvivo was used to identify and analyse themes in the data developed guided by a theoretical framework, in this case, activity theory. This served as a lens through which the data could be 'viewed' and helped to guide the analysis of interview and observational data collected. The activity theory framework, together with the coding nodes is shown in Table 8.5.

What proved important in this example was the way in which the framework allowed for a thorough review of the cultural and historical dimensions that were thought to have an influence on the way knowledge was understood and enacted. As a consequence the categories in this example did not so much 'emerge' from the data as were realized through the application of this theoretical framework. However, even though the activity system framework provided the researcher with a template, it was still possible to create a range of sub-categories that identify themes from the data in *vivo*. *Nvivo* (the software package) allows the development of 'trees' of subnodes that are related to categories or branches of higher level '**nodes**'. As indicated, the initial nodes in this research were adapted from Engeström's (2000) activity triangle, the initial sub nodes identified being shown in the right hand column of Table 8.5.

While the main categories of tree nodes were developed *a priori*, in the manner described above, the identification of the sub nodes for the coding framework came about in an emergent manner. The new categories were produced through the process of close reading of the transcripts and texts. The relevance of these was then discussed with others and views were taken as to how they might be interpreted. This process of producing a refined coding framework by coding and recoding and by reading the transcripts is a highly iterative one. In the parlance of NVivo the objective of that particular process of coding and recoding is to create *a codebook*.

One of the advantages of using software tools such as Nvivo is that it handles the creative messiness of this process extremely well, allowing the researcher to merge, delete or rename nodes as the analysis progresses. Where nodes are merged or renamed, the data that is coded is automatically updated without having to re-code texts and all the nodes in the new codebook are stored electronically. A useful tool, then, is the inclusion of a description or definition for each node which can all be handled by the software. This acts as an effective 'aide memoir' since it allows for cross-checking of code applications and assures consistency by referring to the defined code parameters. So for example, it is possible to revisit some of the texts that have been coded in an earlier period (when a view of the data may have been less sophisticated)

TABLE 8.5 Initial codes identified

Activity system concept	Initial identification of nodes
Agent	Aspirations Motivation Abilities Experience and background Criteria of success Style and outlook Qualifications Rule of thumb
Object	Planning Knowledge tools Knowledge claims Metaphor or analogy Future strategy Existing activities Significant learning episode
Community	Creating and using networks Tension in network Investors Peers Employees and unions Traditional professions Business advisors Suppliers Customers Friends and family Competitors
Norms and principles	Demographic and social influences Regulations Working atmosphere Vision Conflict Training Ethics
Tools and signs	Technology Aesthetics (non personal appearance) Aesthetics (personal appearance) Writing and imagery Signs and symbols Certification Business image and ambience Objects of symbolic value Socializing Promotion Verbal and meetings

and it is possible to check the consistency of interpretation across all the coded data as knowledge develops. The codes or 'nodes' established can then be used to 'mark up' all of the interviews and observations in the study. The advantage of using a meta-level theoretical framework, such as activity theory, to code the data initially is that all relevant categories of data can be retrieved and re-coded as further insights develop, or as alternative research questions emerge. While coding allows the researcher to get into the data and to develop some kind of feeling for the issues this is really only the first stage of the data analysis process.

The next stage involves making sense of the codes and creating conceptual models from the data as we have discussed earlier in this chapter. Building conceptual models means in effect attempting to understand the ways particular concepts and themes are linked together. This second stage of analysis involved interrogating the data using the themes that were developed through the activity theory framework in order to retrieve texts that might show for example, how knowledge comes about, where it comes from and how it might be improved, reconfigured and applied. What NVivo is able to do is to use its code-and-retrieve capabilities so as to allow rapid searches of transcripts and suggests the ways in which coded texts might be linked. So for example, if a section of text has been coded under two different themes, then the computer program displays a matrix that shows the amount of text that is co-coded, and this can be reproduced for comparison purposes between any set of codes. Comparisons can also be made by doing a search based on 'attributes' that might have been applied to the individual text files. So for example it is possible to make comparisons between sectors, companies and size, sex of owner, product market and so on, provided these had been identified in the file. In addition, the search facility also allows retrieval across all texts coded within the documents under a specific theme. By exploring the data in this way, it is argued that data analysis has a system-atic quality that in the same way as quantitative data analysis methods opens up the potential for the identification of new links to be seen between themes that may have been ignored, overlooked or simply hidden. Finally, one facility that is often found very useful is the way in which the software helps to develop a high level understand-ing of the data which enables cross-case comparisons.

When examining concepts such as the extent of the managers' intellectual capital, searches may be conducted using those themes from an initial coding framework that would highlight just how the manager acquired and used knowledge. Relevant pas-sages containing this concept from all of the interviews may then be analysed and re-coded. In this second stage of analysis the objective is primarily to gain an over-view of the learning processes taking place in the firms and to develop concepts that can point to where a more detailed analysis could be found.

In presenting and analysing the data in the above mentioned PhD study, a number of the more important themes that had been identified from a systematic review of the literature were used to inform the development of a conceptual framework. Then, using the codes developed through the first level of analysis, the data were searched under codes that were likely to contain data related to the themes that had emerged in the literature review. As a consequence this second level of analysis was conducted to provide a general overview of the manager's learning processes in the sample and the data were re-coded. On this occasion this second codebook constructed nodes that represented activities that influenced learning. As before these were organized and grouped into tree nodes as Table 8.6 shows.

TABLE 8.6 Second level node structures

Literature review theme	NVivo tree node	Nvivo sub-node
Development and application of agent's intellectual capital	Experience and acquired knowledge	Formal education Functional competence Technical competence
	Agent's knowledge in action	Sensemaking Critical reflection Trial and experimentation
	Approach to control	Centralized to decentralized Formal to informal
	Business outlook	Progressive Reactive Conservative
Available human capital	Endogenous human capital	Management team Staff involvement Staff capability Developing human capital
	Exogenous human capital	Social networks Business networks Technical networks Professional advisors
Organizational processes, routines or systems	Routines of knowledge exploitation	Co-ordination and control Quality management Continuous improvement Rigidities
	Routines of knowledge exploration	Capacity building Innovation management Scanning and benchmarking Developing networks Collaboration
Guiding principles and structures of knowledge and knowing	Structural influence	Coercive Normative Mimetic
	Agent's influences	Learning leadership Personal principles Socialization Ad Hoc and unstructured

Literature review theme	NVivo tree node	Nvivo sub-node
Boundary and discursive activities	Negotiating knowledge claims Knowledge transfer and transformation	Character and credibility Emotional investment Utility and logic Information exchange Negotiating meaning Transforming activity Politics and conflict

By doing this, the number of coding instances and the percentage of cases coded at each node were able to be included when the data was finally presented for publication. This was not done in order to offer any kind of quantifiable justification of the identified themes, but rather because the number of coding references and percentage of cases coded under a particular node could provide insight into the issues that might be important. And, as such, could offer a strong sense of how influential these 'issues' might be both across and between cases. The coding statistics returned during searches were used as indicators of potentially important issues that might require closer analysis. This could include consideration of why a particular issue was being discussed frequently, or even why a particular issue was relatively silent in the data.

Finally, once all the analysis had been concluded, cross-case comparisons were conducted on four detailed case studies. Here the code-retrieve search functions were also useful to explore the centrality of particular concepts within each case. As the software does not attach meaning to the link or the concepts in a particular setting this remains the researcher's responsibility through sensemaking, which involves the application of prior knowledge, insights and the construction of new ideas. Using the coding links allowed access to the relevant sections of data and to develop a narrative description of the situated activity, and the changing nature of that activity within each case. It is possible that by accessing the data in this way relevant parts of coded (or un-coded) text may be missed but through re-reading and developing the narrative, it is possible to go back to the 'raw data' in order to put the coded text back into context if sense requires to be made of it. NVivo allows this to be done automatically by retrieving text that surrounds the coded section, which makes contextualization of the narrative a relatively simple process. In this way the concepts were used to provide structure to the data analysis in order to present a coherent narrative out of a mass of data. Finally, we do want to restate that NVivo only really enables the construction of a database of information, it is a powerful tool that can help arrange and access information systematically, but it is no substitute for the academic challenge of the researcher to try and make sense out of complexity.

AN EXAMPLE OF USING ATLAS.TI

A second PhD study on schools also used a grounded approach to the data analysis. In this case the PhD student (Norman, 2006) used Atlas.ti and she tried to develop her codes from the data (rather than them being prescribed from a previous framework or theoretical model as was the case in the example of the use of NVivo above). She also tried as far as possible to use Strauss and Corbin's more formulaic process of analysis which, as we have discussed introduces axial codes, which serve to specify the properties and dimensions of the categories as an interim step before weaving the categories together at the theoretical coding stage. The process she adopted involved three stages discussed earlier – an open coding stage (substantive), an axial coding stage (core) and selective coding (theoretical) following (Punch 1998). As we have already discussed above, substantive codes are attributed to identified pieces of texts, axial codes are attributed to subcategories that are formed from substantive codes and core codes are where larger categories come together from a number of smaller *collapsed* subcategories, which are woven together to build into the theoretical contribution the research is to eventually make. Axial and selective coding then is the point where subcategories and categories are formed. In this description of the process used in the PhD study, the open, axial and selective coding levels are referred to as Levels 1, 2 and 3 respectively.

As with NVivo there are a number of technical terms that are used in connection with Atlas.ti; which are shown together with their meanings in Table 8.7 below.

In this case Atlas.ti was chosen as the PhD student considered it to have the following qualities;

- large quantities of data needed to be analysed;
- multiple codes could be attached to quotations;
- a record of the number of quotations attached to a specific code could be maintained to produce quantitative output if required;

TABLE 8.7 Glossary of Atlas.ti terms

Technical term	Meaning
Quotation	Piece of verbatim text
Code	The identifying name given by the researcher for one or more quotations
In vivo	Codes are directly taken from the data
Network diagram	A diagram illustrating codes and the relationships between codes
Open coding	The process of coding quotations
Nodes	The boxes on the network diagrams in which the codes are presented
Primary documents	Text documents entered into Atlas.ti for analysis
Hermeneutic unit	A collection of primary documents and associated analysis

SOURCE: ATLAS.TI (2005)

- the codings given to all quotations could be tracked;
- visual network diagrams could be constructed by importing, placing and linking codes together in order to show the relationships between or among codes; and
- it appeared to offer a logical and creative approach to analysing the data.

One of the important attractions of using the package was the ability to produce network diagrams. Network diagrams are used to indicate relationships and again there is a notational convention to be followed with the symbol that disrupts the arrow indicating the type of relationship. The example below shows a number of these relationships and the symbols that are defined by the Atlas.ti software. All were used in the final presentation of Norman's findings.

$—\square→$ *is part of* (indicates that the code at the back of the arrow is a part of the code at the head of the arrow);

$—\Rightarrow→$ *is a cause of* (indicates that the code at the back of the arrow is a cause of the code at the head of the arrow);

$—=→$ *is associated with* (indicates that the code at the back of the arrow is associated with the code at the head of the arrow);

$—\diamond→$ *contradicts* (indicates that the code at the back of the arrow contradicts the code at the head of the arrow).

As with all computer assisted analysis packages the software is only a tool that serves to aid the process of analysis. The student thus had complete control over the way the analysis was shaped and evolved at all times, and her decisions both about what text was coded and how it should be coded that determined her understandings.

Again, as with NVivo her first step was;

1 to create Word documents of all her narrative accounts, e.g. questionnaires and interview notes. In this case there were 122 such documents in total.

2 Her next step was to convert the documents to text files and assign them to hermeneutic units in Atlas.ti as primary documents; in this particular study there were four of these hermeneutic units.

3 She then gave each primary document an identifying name in order to identify a number of characteristics, for example, the source of the data (in her case, whether the data was from interviews, questionnaires, her research log or a report); the respondent number; the respondent's gender. Naming primary documents in this way ensures that all documents that relate to a particular research activity can be identified and by so doing ensures that documents aren't overlooked when the data is analysed. This also allows filters to be applied, for example, selecting out all female subjects and comparing this population with males.

4 Her next step was to code the text and develop network diagrams that illustrated the findings diagrammatically. The process as we have discussed involves several levels of coding, as described below.

Coding

The primary documents were analysed in a line-by-line analysis following the approach outlined by Strauss and Corbin (1998). This involved rereading the interviews and highlighting and coding relevant text. Level 1, 2 and 3 codes comprise two parts – a prefix and a label for the quotation. The prefix identifies the source of data and the theme. The symbol _ separates the source of the data and the theme. The label used for the quotation identified is usually short and indicates the respondent's response. This structure is illustrated in Figure 8.1.

Where coding was in vivo, that is codes directly taken from the data, the quotation itself becomes the label for the quotation and all the student added was a prefix so that the source of the data and the theme to which it referred could be identified.

Finally, a fourth level of coding was used so as to represent the theme of the network as a whole. This fourth level simply consisted of the name of the theme, for example, BEING A TEACHER, and the protocol that specifies the properties and dimensions of the category demands it is presented in upper case.

Network diagrams

Figure 8.2 illustrates the structure of a network diagram. What this network diagram explores (and what the codes above relate to) was the nature of the concept of confidence within schools. Confidence was shown to be a complex construct and, while it has received a great deal of anecdotal attention, is not one which has been subject to systematic analysis that indicates the conditions that promote confidence building and how confidence might be developed. It is the areas and factors that hinder the development of confidence in a teacher, to which this sub part of the network diagram is only a part of a much more complex set of factors and relationships.

Again as in other kinds of qualitative data analysis of this type, the process is an iterative one. As quotations are coded they are imported into the relevant network diagram and so the picture slowly begins to emerge. In network diagrams the convention states that codes should be displayed in boxes, known as nodes; these nodes can be moved around on the network and arranged in groups to form subcategories and categories. This visual representation is similar to the working of cognitive mapping software such as Decision Explorer. As several codes can be attached to one quotation the network diagrams show clearly which Level 1 codes form the particular

FIGURE 8.1

Structure of Level 1, 2, and 3 codes

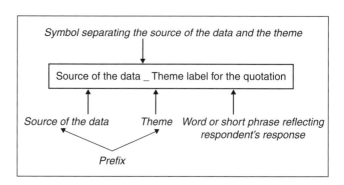

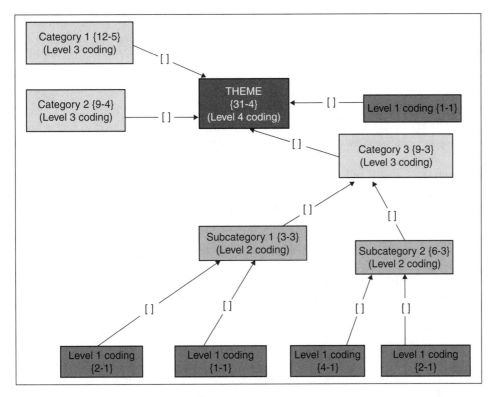

FIGURE 8.2 Structure of a network diagram

subcategories, and which subcategories form categories; this means that a very detailed visual display of results can be produced. Atlas.ti keeps track of the number of quotations attached to a code and the number of codes each code has a relationship with. This is illustrated by the two numbers assigned automatically by the software to each code, for example, {6-3}. This shows that there are six quotations attached to the code i.e., the *code frequency* or *code groundedness* (Atlas.ti, 2005) and that this code is linked to three other codes i.e., the *code density* (Atlas.ti, 2005). The number of quotations attached to a code also serves to indicate the importance of the code. Care however needs to be taken when interpreting the numerical data, first, because several quotations could be from the same primary document (i.e. from a single participant), and second, there may well be codes with a single or very few quotations which may be highly significant. Atlas.ti keeps track of the primary document from which each quotation emanates and the specific quotations attached to each code. It is possible therefore to easily tell from where the primary documents came and hence which participant, each quotation is from. The network diagram shown in Figure 8.2 illustrates the following in relation to the network diagram:

- There are 31 quotations attached to the theme and there are three categories – category one has 12 quotations and categories two and three each have nine quotations.

- Category three has two subcategories – subcategory two has six quotations (four of the quotations share a code and two quotations share a code) and subcategory one has three quotations (two of which share a code and one of which has a separate code).

- There is one miscellaneous quotation that is not attached to any subcategory or category.

- The theme is related to four other codes, category one is related to five other codes, category two to four other codes, and category three to three other codes.

- All the relationships are illustrate that, for example, the three quotations in subcategory one and the six in subcategory two are each part of the nine quotations that form category three, and that the nine quotations in category three are part of the 31 that make up the theme.

Due to limitations of space, only category three is fully displayed in the diagram below, but as most of the network diagrams the student constructed as part of this research were fairly large (as well as extremely detailed) it is often only the cores (contained in the diagrams) that are usually included in presentations of the analysis. Themes, categories and miscellaneous codes that do not fit into any of the subcategories or categories are usually always displayed in the core. In a number of cases, codes are part of more than one category and they are simply shown as such by using the arrow notation — [] —> which means, is part of. Where codes are part of more than one category they are also usually displayed in the core as in the example shown in Figure 8.3.

Figure 8.3, illustrates that the codes I_H experiences and Q_H culture shock are both part of the categories QI_H Self and QI_H External factors. Atlas.ti automatically colours the nodes using two colours – red and blue. According to the descriptions of the auto-colour facility provided by Atlas.ti (2005), nodes are coloured according to their groundedness (i.e. number of quotations) and their density (i.e. links with other codes). Groundedness increases the red component and density increases the blue component of the node colour (Atlas.ti, 2005). As will be seen from Figure 8.3, the

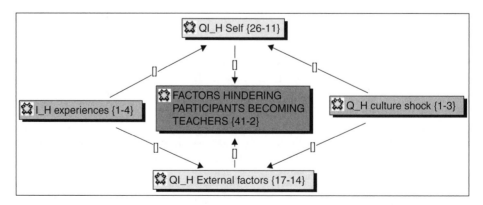

FIGURE 8.3 Codes forming more than one category

codes QI_H Self and QI_H External factors are coloured light blue, illustrating their density, whereas the codes I_H experiences and Q_H culture shock appear in mid blue, indicating they are not as dense or grounded.

Repertory grids

Repertory grids and cognitive maps are tools for uncovering individuals' or a group's view of the world and enable the simple and relatively immediate presentation of complex information.

Based on personal construct theory (Kelly 1955), a repertory grid is a representation of a manager's perception of their world. The technique is useful for investigating areas that the respondent might not have thought much about, or where they find hard to articulate and has been used extensively in areas such as career guidance and for the development of job descriptions.

Repertory grids then help individuals to look, not just at the words people use but also at the wider constructs they use when making decisions and taking action. Often these may not even be known to the individuals themselves, so representation in the visual form of a grid can be the beginning of a process whereby individuals learn more about the ideas they have, how they might have been formed and how they might be changed.

Grids can also be used in group situations as a basis for discussion about how different people view the world and they enable complex relationships to be represented with the objective of building up shared understandings (Easterby-Smith et al., 1996). The technique is used to understand an individual's perceptions and the constructs they use to understand and manage their world. A repertory grid is a mathematical representation of how an individual differentiates between objects or experiences in his or her world. Repertory grids can also be used with people who have low verbal ability, making them particularly useful for children and people with language difficulties. Mackinlay piloted his study by attempting to deduce what his young children would appreciate for their Christmas presents that year.

EXAMPLE 8.4

For example, a masters student (Mackinlay, 1986) used the repertory grid technique to elicit the values and perceptions that householders in a particular housing district had of different types of bathroom and kitchen colour schemes and layouts as elements, he showed these to householders, and asked them to compare and contrast the different photographs and in so doing eliciting the 'constructs' they used to differentiate between the photographs and to reveal their likes and dislikes. The method proved extremely useful, with the photographs helping to resolve differences and deal with the complex issues involved in the notion of what people valued and preferred. This demonstrates that grids can elucidate what might not be immediately observable, so that new insights or perspectives can be gained.

The standard procedure for generating a repertory grid is as follows:

1 Decide on the *focus* of the grid. This should be quite specific and the interviewee should be reminded of this focus at regular intervals. These might be qualities required of a manager in a particular function, the particular work content of a given job, or the features of products currently competing with one's own.

2 Select with the interviewee a group of *elements* (between 5 and 10) which are relevant to the chosen focus, and which are also likely to provide a good range. If, for example, the focus of the grid was on the skills required of a manager it would be appropriate to choose individuals who were familiar to the interviewee, some of whom he regarded as particularly able, some of average ability and some of below average ability.

3 *Constructs* are elicited, usually by asking the respondent to compare and contrast elements in groups of three, known as triads. Each element is written onto a card and then three cards are selected at random. The interviewee is asked to decide which pair of cards are similar in a way which also makes them distinct from the third. They are asked to provide a word or phrase which describes the pair, and a contrasting word or phrase to describe the remaining card. For example, in the case of a grid with the focus on the competencies required of a manager, someone might choose two cards of named people as similar because they see them both as *dynamic*, and the third as *staid*. In this case the construct elicited is a continuum on which *dynamic* is at one end and *staid* is at the other. This process is repeated with different triads of elements until a reasonable number of constructs (perhaps 6 to 10) have been produced.

4 Each of the elements needs to be *linked* to, or rated against, each of the constructs. This can be done in several different ways: by deciding which of the two 'poles' of the construct provides the best description of the element; by determining the position of the element on a rating scale (often 7 points) constructed between the poles of each construct; or by rank-ordering each of the elements along the dimension indicated by each of the constructs. The results of these ratings or rankings are recorded as ticks and crosses, or as numbers in a matrix. Table 8.8 shows a grid completed by a PhD student who (Easterby – Smith et al., 1996) was interviewing a group of first line managers in food manufacturing with the purpose of developing a recruitment and appraisal system that valued the qualities that managers *really* required in their subordinates. It was intended to explore the qualities required of tmembers and lead directly to the redesign of a system for their perform appraisal. The linking process in this case involves simply indicating wlthe two poles is most appropriate.

Small grids can be analysed manually, or by eye, by looking for patterns of relationships and differences between constructs and elements. This can form the basis of an interesting collaborative discussion between interviewer and interviewee. With larger grids (say, 5 × 5, or upwards) it is more common to use computer analysis packages. There are two main families of these, based either on **principal components analysis,** or on **cluster analysis.** The former produces a map which plots the elements within dimensions, and axes, defined by the constructs.

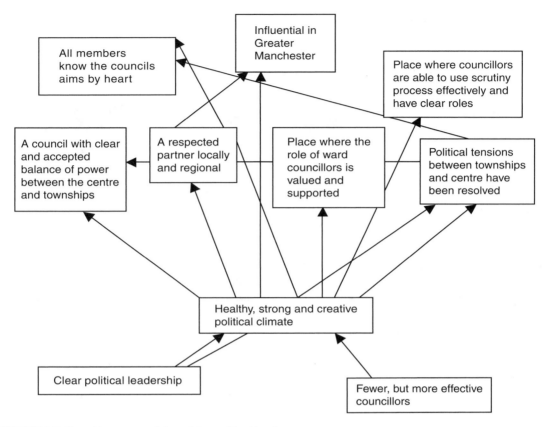

FIGURE 8.7 Cognitive map – vision of the political landscape

An initial review of the map, a part of which is shown in Figure 8.7 indicated the complexity of the problem. There were a multiplicity and diversity of social, economic and governmental issues facing the council as well as conflicting views about the current state of the organization and the likely challenges it faced. Despite these differences we observed that during the cognitive mapping process we faced few difficulties achieving interaction between team members as they negotiated their way through the dynamics of reaching consensus on the key strategic issues presented which can be seen to indicate a collective form of organizational learning, (Churchill, 1990). The main issues broken down by cluster were political, performance related, staff development, communications and reputational. What we found using this technique with the chief officers' team, enabled them to experience the difficulties of other departments and with this insight begin to understand how the council organization functioned as a whole.

The map produced reduced the messiness and ambiguity that characterized the situation and provided the different groups with the ability to: (1) manage the resultant complexity by identifying emergent themes; and (2) prioritize these themes so that they could be subsequently developed.

As a consequence, discussion of the cognitive map as a group not only enabled the transmission of information, the implications that the issues raised might have for the management of the local authority, but it also helped to overcome disagreement about goals, the interpretation of issues, or subsequent courses of action.

CONCLUSION

In this chapter we have attempted to provide an overview of some of the main ways of capturing qualitative data and making sense of it. The main points which we raise are that:

- A commitment to qualitative research is likely to derive from the researcher's view about which features of the world are significant and relevant to his or her enterprise.
- A key question will be whether the quality of experience is more important than the frequency of opinions and events.
- The best method for the analysis of the data and whether computers can be employed to aid

the analysis process and the presentation of the results

Along the road of qualitative research there are also many dilemmas. There is the problem of gaining public access to private experiences, and the difficulty of deciding how and when to impose any interpretive frameworks on this. There is the question of how accurate is one's information, and how accurate it needs to be, or can be. And there is the continual tension underneath the research process between creating meanings and counting frequencies. It is in the next chapter that we consider some of the methods and issues associated with the latter problem.

EXERCISE
8.1

Piloting your approach to analysis

In pairs, discuss the focus of any pilot study that you intend to carry out before your main study. Discuss how extensive this should be and how it can be carried out to best effect including how much analysis will be carried out and the method(s) that will be used.

EXERCISE
8.2

Dominoes

Ask a colleague to identify five people in their life. These should be a mixture of people they both like and dislike. Get them to write them down on cards and place them on the desk in front of you. Now ask them to find a feature that differentiates some of these individuals from the others and ask them to place the names of those with similar features adjacent to each other. Now ask them to supply a word or phase that best describes the common attributes held – this is one construct. Now repeat the process and see how many different constructs can be found.

FURTHER READING

Bazeley, P. (2007) *Qualitative Data Analysis with NVivo*. London: Sage.

This book is written by a very experienced researcher well versed in the use and application of the NVivo computer-assisted analysis software package. There are many examples given from her own work as well as the work of others, and reference is made also to the wider methodological literature. Readers are guided in very practical ways on how to make best use of the capability the program offers at each stage in the analysis of a research project. And the material is presented through each stage of their research projects. Resources provided by Pat Bazeley to support her book (see www.researchsupport.com.au). .

Boje, D. (2001) *Narrative Methods for Organisational and Communication Research*. London: Sage.

This book in the Sage series of Management Research offers researchers a guide to alternative discourse analysis strategies. The book sets out eight options that researchers might consider – all related to organizational and communications research.

Charmaz, K. (2006) *Constructing Grounded Theory: A Practical Guide Through Qualitative Analysis*. London: Sage.

This book uses worked examples of grounded theory in order to provide an alternative approach, one that moves the method on from its positivist origins and incorporates many of the ideas that qualitative researchers have raised over the years as this approach to analysis has developed.

Lewis, R.B. (2004) 'A comparative review of the qualitative data analysis programs', *Field Methods*, 16. 439–63.

A comparison of NVivo and Atlas.ti.

Miles, M.B. and Huberman, A.M. (1994) *An Expanded Sourcebook Qualitative Data Analysis*, second edition. London: Sage.

Very much at the content end of the spectrum this book, as the title implies, offers a comprehensive handbook of approaches to qualitative data analysis. As such it provides a very wide range of techniques (together with examples) that will assist in making inferences from qualitative data. The methods of analysis presented are practical, credible and reliable.

Wright, R.P. (2006) 'Rigor and relevance using repertory grid technique in strategy research', *Research Methodology in Strategy and Management*, 3: 295–348.

This chapter illustrates how repertory grids can be used as a tool to understand the strategic thinking of senior managers. It gives an overview of the past applications of repertory grid applications within the management field before taking the reader through the ways in which grids can be created and applied to a group of senior managers as an aid to understanding aspects of their strategic thinking.

CREATING QUANTITATIVE DATA

9

LEARNING OBJECTIVES

- To select an appropriate form of sampling design for the objectives of the research.

- To select among alternative sources of quantitative data according to the purpose of the research, taking into account the benefits and drawbacks of each.

- To design structured questions and select appropriate forms of measurement scale.

Introduction

Sampling design

Sources of quantitative data

The process of measurement

Conclusion

Further reading

INTRODUCTION

This chapter is divided into three main parts. The first section examines the importance of sampling design, starting with an analysis of why sampling matters and an introduction to different forms of sampling design. The second part covers three sources of quantitative data: collecting data through surveys, collecting data through observation, and using secondary data sources. Each has benefits and drawbacks, and we consider how to make choices between them. The last section looks at the process of measurement in two parts: how to design structured questions for surveys and interviews, and alternative forms of measurement scale for recording responses.

SAMPLING DESIGN

When decisions are made that can have important consequences for people it is important that those decisions are based on evidence. The trustworthiness of the evidence base for decisions depends on many factors, and in this chapter we focus on how to collect evidence in the form of quantitative data. We begin with the difference between a **population** and a **sample** drawn from that population. The term population refers to the whole set of entities that decisions relate to; while the term sample refers to a subset of those entities from which evidence is gathered. The **inference** task then is to use evidence from a sample to draw conclusions about the population.

Samples are very commonly used, both for research and for policy making. Companies estimate morale among employees from surveys of samples of employees (either by deliberately picking names from the payroll, or by letting employees choose whether or not to respond). The University of Manchester conducted a **stress survey** of its staff in 2005, and the company that undertook the work achieved a 46 per cent response rate across the staff as a whole. While this is quite a high response rate for staff surveys it is far from perfect, and indeed the detailed report shows how there were large variations across different sections of staff. Nevertheless, the senior management team were happy to use the report (http://www.campus.manchester.ac.uk/medialibrary/human-resources/wellbeing-stress-survey-2006.pdf) as the basis for conclusions about its HR priorities for all university staff (including those who had not responded). The UK government uses sample surveys of companies on their annual pay negotiations in order to get an estimate of wage inflation in the economy. In most countries, estimates of activity in the labour market (whether people are unemployed, self-employed, economically inactive and so on) are derived from samples and not from complete counts.

Principles in designing a sample

Sometimes, a research project involves collecting data from every member of an organization, but more often this is not the case and the researcher needs to decide on a sampling strategy. A sample might be: a proportion of employees in an organization, a selection of companies operating in a specific market, a number of specific periods of time for assessing the quality of customer responses in a call centre, or a selection of transactions for audit purposes. For each of these examples, the researcher has to make a decision about what the sampling unit is (the person, the company, the transaction and so on), how many sampling units to take, and on what basis sampling is to be undertaken.

Generally speaking, the purpose of collecting data from a sample is to enable the researcher to make statements about the population that the sample is drawn from. The claims that are made from sample data depend absolutely on the relationship between the sample and the population. Get the sampling wrong, and accuracy in calculating the results is of no consequence. The opposite is also true: get the sampling right, and even rough-and-ready calculations or 'eyeballing' of the data can be immensely valuable. There are two basic principles that underlie decisions about sampling design: **representativeness** and **precision**.

Representativeness in sampling The accuracy of conclusions drawn from a sample depends on whether it has the same characteristics as the population from which it is drawn. If the sample is systematically different in some way, then the sample is biased. A simple definition of bias in sampling is that it occurs when some members of the population have a higher chance of being included in the sample than others. There are two steps involved in defining a sampling design. The first step is to draw up a **sampling frame**, a list of all who are eligible to be included in the study. The second step is to achieve a valid response from all those included in the sampling frame. **Bias** can be introduced into a sampling strategy in many ways, through choices made in the design of the study itself and also through features of the process of collecting data.

1 *Exclude groups of people:* leave out home-workers, casual staff, new recruits, part-timers.

2 *Distribution method:* send out your survey using an out-of-date list of mailing addresses to exclude those who have recently moved; distribute by email to exclude those without a PC on their desks.

3 *Language used:* use English to exclude those who don't speak English, and introduce biasing factors for those who do because of differences in how well people can use the language.

One of the key ways of judging the representativeness of a sample is to compare the characteristics of the sample to those of the population; and this kind of information is commonly reported in published papers that are based on surveys. Even if the sampling frame accurately represents the population, non-response is a major source of problems in getting outsiders to believe the results. In itself though, non-response is not a problem, as long as those who do respond have the same characteristics as those who do not. Of course, there is usually a big problem in assessing whether this is true, because (obviously) non-respondents did not respond. It is sometimes possible to get some idea about potential bias due to systematic non-response by comparing those who respond quickly with slow responders on demographic variables and also on the central variables in the research. The idea is that the slow responders will be more similar to non-responders than are those who reply quickly. If the slow responders have similar characteristics to rapid responders, then the researcher can have greater confidence that non-responders would also have been similar; and this helps to build credibility in a survey.

Improving response rates in surveys A high response rate in a survey is clearly important: it gives a larger body of data which the researcher can use to address research questions and it makes it much more likely that the sample is representative of the population of interest. We list below a number of steps that the researcher can take to increase response rates:

- make the task easy and short;
- explain the purpose clearly, so that respondents can see its value;
- give incentives to take part;
- give assurances of confidentiality and anonymity; and
- send out reminders.

Underlying them is a simple principle: because providing data is a cost to each respondent then the principle is to reduce the effort involved as much as possible and increase the perceived benefit as much as possible.

The shorter the questionnaire, and the simpler the questions, the more likely it is that people will reply; so thinking carefully through the objectives of the study and making sure that every question contributes to those objectives will have a payoff. The researcher should also try to convince people that the effort they put into replying will be of benefit, either to the respondents themselves or to something that the respondents will find worthwhile. Incentives to participate can sometimes make a difference, though this can be expensive if respondents are paid. Rewarding those who reply may also be difficult if the survey is anonymous (since the researcher will not be able to identify individual respondents). Offering guarantees of confidentiality and anonymity is important for ethical reasons (see Chapter 6), but will help to build trust and therefore response rates. Finally, most people lead busy lives and the researcher's survey may not arrive at a convenient time. Sending out reminders is an important factor in increasing the likelihood of response.

Precision in sampling – sampling proportion and sample size Precision is about how credible a sample is. For example, opinion polls conducted before elections, in the UK as well as in many other countries, use samples that are very much smaller than the population of registered voters. How confident is it possible to be about predicting election outcomes from opinion poll samples? Does the precision of the estimate depend on how big the sample is? It seems plausible that it should. Does it also depend what proportion of the population the pollsters talk to? If the number of electors is 10,000 then a sample of 1000 (i.e. 10 per cent) might be OK. However, many people would be less happy with a sample of 1000 if the number of electors was one million instead (0.1 per cent). Intuitively, this proportion seems too small. However, the first intuition is correct, but the second is not.

Nguyen (2005) provides a clear and graphic example of cooking chicken soup to show why the size of a sample matters but how big a proportion the sample is of the population (the **sampling proportion**) does not. Consider three scenarios: cooking at home for four people using a small pot, cooking for a dinner party with 12 guests using a medium pot, and cooking a banquet for 200 wedding guests using a huge pot. Regardless of the number of guests, the only way to tell if there is enough salt in the soup is to taste it. The way to find this out is: first stir the soup so it is well mixed and is the same all the way through, and second use a tablespoon to draw off some soup. A tablespoon will do because there is no point taking more than that. Taste it all and there is no soup left for the guests; taste more spoonfuls and each will taste just the same, so nothing is learned. It is not necessary to use a large ladle to sample from the large pot simply because the pot is bigger, or a tiny spoon to sample from the small pot because the pot is smaller. There is no need, because the same sized tablespoon is enough to judge the adequacy of the seasoning regardless of how big the batch of soup is, as long as the pot is stirred first.

The soup in the pot is the *population*; the spoonful to taste is the *sample*. The size of the spoon is the *sample size*, and that is what matters. The cook needs enough soup to be able to make a judgement about the pot as a whole. Now apply these principles to the task of making judgements about attitudes in a society towards an issue of concern. Consider the question of whether organizations should aim to maximize their profit or should consider their social responsibilities. The precision of the answer to this question has nothing to do with the size of the population but rather depends on the size of the sample. Small samples will always be less precise than large samples.

Combining precision and representativeness to achieve a credible sample We have looked at the two design principles of bias and precision, and clearly both are important in achieving a credible sampling design for a quantitative research project. Low bias means that conclusions from a sample can safely be applied to the population, and high precision means that the margin of error in the claims that are made will be low – the researcher can expect to be precisely right (see Table 9.1). However, high precision is no way of saving a study where the sample is biased. Giving very precise answers to the wrong question will not endear a researcher to his or her supervisor, just as it does not help in getting high marks in an examination! Most projects carried out by students (at whatever level) are a compromise in some way, simply because resources are limited. As a result, there will always be trade-offs when it comes to decisions about design. Is it better to have a large sample (giving higher precision) if the cost of achieving it is to introduce bias into the sample achieved? Put more simply, which is better: to be imprecisely right or to be precisely wrong? In our opinion, the answer is straightforward. Imprecisely right is better: it is preferable to have a sample that properly represents the population even if the precision is lower because of a small sample.

TABLE 9.1 Principles in designing a sample

		Bias	
		High	**Low**
Precision	High	Precisely wrong	Precisely right
	Low	Imprecisely wrong	Imprecisely right

Probability sampling designs

This section describes forms of sampling design where the probability of each entity being part of the sample is known. Some sampling methods have the same probability for every entity in the sample, while others have that within segments of the design but differing probabilities across segments.

Simple random sampling   Every sample entity (company, employee, customer, etc.) has an equal chance of being part of the sample. In the olden days, this was done using printed random number tables. Now computers are used for this, and it is easy to draw up a list of random numbers as a basis for selecting a sample.

Stratified random sampling   One drawback of simple random sampling is that it can mean that small but important parts of the population are missed altogether or sampled so little that the researcher cannot make confident statements about them. For instance, customer surveys of a healthcare facility would be badly served by a simple random sample. Most users of a healthcare facility have relatively minor ailments and perhaps visit only once or twice in a year. There will however, be a small number of patients with major health problems whose treatment is perhaps extensive. It is quite reasonable to expect that a sample should be informative about the very ill minority as well as the mildly ill majority. The way to achieve this is to divide the population up into homogeneous groups called **strata**, and then take a simple random sample within each stratum. **Proportional stratified random sampling** has the same sampling proportion within all strata; but this has the disadvantage that rare groups within the population would be badly represented. The way to deal with this problem is to take a larger proportion of sample units in small strata, and a smaller proportion in the larger strata. This is called **non-proportional stratified random sampling.**

Systematic random sampling   This method of sampling relies on there being a list in some form or other of the units in the population that the researcher is interested in. This might be a customer database, or a list of employees of a company or students registered in a university. Suppose that a researcher wants to achieve a sample of 500 students in order to assess their satisfaction with the virtual learning environment (VLE) system that a university has just introduced. If there are 20,000 students then 500 represents a 2.5 per cent sample, corresponding to selecting 1 in 40 students from the population. This proportion could be achieved by choosing a number at random between 1 and 40. If that number were 27, then the researcher would go down the list taking every 27th student in order to derive a sample list of 500 names. What this process relies on is that the population list is essentially organized randomly, so that picking in this systematic way does not introduce bias. There could be a problem if the list is ordered alphabetically by individuals' last name, since all those students with the same name will be listed together and individuals with the same name will have less chance of being selected than if the list were randomly ordered.

Cluster sampling   Any method that involves random sampling will lead to practical problems where the population units are spread very widely such that the cost of approaching them is very high. **Cluster sampling** deals with this by first dividing up the population into what are called clusters, and then by sampling all the units within the selected clusters. A study of company success in emerging economies might first identify all the countries where the company operates, select randomly a number of those countries to study in detail, and then approach all the relevant contacts in those countries. This would allow the study to use local research staff who are familiar with the language and culture of each country.

Multi-stage sampling Multi-stage sampling combines together the methods described above in order to achieve higher operational and technical efficiency. For example, stratified random sampling divides the population into strata and then samples from within all of them. Instead, a study might use a sampling approach at each level, and this is very common in large-scale social research. Suppose there was a national change in the organization of schools to give greater management autonomy to head teachers, and researchers wanted to know whether this change had any effect on the performance of students in schools. It would be very inefficient to select students at random, even if the research team actually had a national database of all school students. It makes more sense to divide the country up into regions, select some regions for detailed attention, identify all the schools in the targeted regions, and then select a sample of schools. Having defined a sample of schools within selected regions, the same process could be used to sample classes within the selected schools, or perhaps take a sample of students from all of the classes in a selected school. In this example, the criterion of randomness applies at each of several stages in the design of the study; hence the name **multi-stage sampling**. The aim is to balance the need for representativeness of the sample with the highest possible cost effectiveness.

Why are probability sampling designs valuable? It is only with probability sampling that it is possible to be precise about the relationship between a sample and the population from which the sample is drawn. Knowing what this relationship is allows the researcher to make a firm judgement about the relationship between characteristics of a sample and characteristics of the population from which the sample was drawn. All forms of probability sampling design have this feature in common – it is always possible to state the probability of each individual respondent being selected for inclusion in the research study. The statistical theory behind the inference process (often called significance testing) relies fundamentally on sampling based on probabilities.

Non-probability sampling

By contrast, **non-probability sampling** methods all share the same characteristic, that it is not possible to state the probability of any member of the population being sampled. As a result, they can never give the researcher the same level of confidence as probability-based sampling does when drawing inferences about the population of interest from a specific sample.

Convenience sampling This method of sampling involves selecting sample units on the basis of how easily accessible they are, hence the term **convenience sampling**. A student who uses an MSN Messenger contact list for his or her dissertation is taking a convenience sample. Such a sample may well be representative of the individual's own social network, but is clearly not representative of students as whole or of the population of the UK. Convenience samples are very common in research, because they are – well – convenient! They clearly are not proper probability samples, and it is impossible to guarantee that any sample achieved in this way represents a specific population that may be of interest. However, they can have a value. It rather depends on what the purpose is for collecting data. For a very long time, people thought that all swans were white because no one had ever seen one of any other colour. As explained in Chapter 5, it only takes an Australian researcher with a convenience sample of one black swan to prove the old generalization to be wrong.

Quota sampling Quota sampling divides the relevant population up into categories (perhaps male/female, or country of origin for students) and then selection continues until a sample of a specific size is achieved within each category. The aim is to make sure that each of the categories is represented according to the quota proportions. For example, in doctoral research on whether the Internet empowers consumers, quota sampling enabled the researcher to ensure she had users of a variety of ages; while a convenience sample would be more likely to result in a preponderance of people similar to the researcher and her friends.

Purposive sampling In this method, the researcher has a clear idea of what sample units are needed, and then approaches potential sample members to check whether they meet eligibility criteria. Those that do are used, while those that do not are rejected. Market researchers (the people in shopping centres with clipboards) often use this approach, when they target, for example, women in a particular age range who are also mobile phone users. The first questions would establish the respondent's age and mobile phone use – presumably it is not necessary to ask the person's gender!

Snowball sampling Snowball sampling starts with someone who meets the criteria for inclusion in a study who is then asked to name others who would also be eligible. This method works well for samples where individuals are very rare and it is hard to identify who belongs to the population. Dissertation students often do this by starting out with people they or their supervisor know personally, and then ask those people to pass them on to others who would also be suitable. It works well too for individuals, groups or companies which are part of networks whose membership is confidential.

Why are non-probability sampling designs valuable? The sampling approaches described in this section are answers to a variety of practical problems that researchers have encountered in carrying out their work. But how do these sampling methods stack up against the key quality criteria of bias and precision that we started this section with? *Precision* is most straightforward, since its main focus is the size of the sample achieved. A convenience sample can meet the first requirement of a big-enough sample most easily; quota sampling and purposive sampling both aim to ensure that every sector in a sampling design is filled; while snowball sampling addresses the problem of ensuring an adequate sample of hard-to-find people. However, the principle of *bias* is where non-probability sampling methods can most easily fall down, especially for convenience sampling. Many management researchers have been seduced by the lure of large samples (perhaps at the insistence of journal editors) and achieved them simply through collecting respondents by any means (MBA classes, postal surveys and so on). There is no guarantee that samples achieved like this are representative and that the findings reported are credible. It is not surprising then, that reviews of research often highlight contradictions in findings between different studies, given that researchers often take little care in defining their sampling design.

SOURCES OF QUANTITATIVE DATA

In thinking about where to get data that could be analysed using quantitative methods, there are broadly two ways of going about it: researchers can collect their own primary data or they can use secondary data already collected and stored within archival databases. Each approach has advantages and disadvantages. Broadly, collecting one's own research data gives control over both the structure of the sample and the data obtained from each respondent. This gives greater confidence that the data will match the study objectives. Conversely, that benefit comes at a price since it can be much more expensive (in time and effort) to collect one's own data, in comparison with using secondary data from an existing archive. The downside of using secondary data sources is that the quality of the data may be more uncertain, and the researcher does not have control over either the sample or the specific data collected.

Collecting data through surveys

Surveys can be good ways of collecting data about the opinions and behaviour of large numbers of people, as long as they are done well. The choice between them will depend on many factors, so that there is no single best way. Traditional texts such as that by Moser and Kalton (1971) cover only two ways of collecting data from surveys: **postal questionnaires** which are mailed to potential respondents and **structured interviews** conducted face-to-face. Although these two methods still have an important place, advances in communications technology have brought a variety of new options within the scope of the researcher in business and management.

Postal questionnaire surveys have the advantage that the cost per respondent is low for large samples compared with any method that requires face-to-face contact with individuals, especially when the sample members are widely dispersed. In contrast, response rates can be very low (for many researchers, a 20 per cent response rate would be regarded as good) because there is no personal contact with the respondent which can encourage cooperation. Financial or other inducements are sometimes effective, but the normal guarantee of anonymity makes it difficult to reward people for responding because the researcher has no way of knowing who has replied and who has not. The researcher has little control over whether the person targeted is the one who answers the questions (CEOs are reputed to hand survey questionnaires over to their PAs to fill in on their behalf), and also over how they answer them. As a result, checking the quality of data from postal surveys, both completeness and accuracy, is particularly important.

Structured interview surveys are much more expensive per head because an interviewer has to be present while each respondent's answers are recorded. The cost of interviews includes the time of the interviewer, which has to cover initial training, time spent in setting up each interview, travel to where respondents are located and an allowance for broken appointments. They are most often used when accurate data are the main priority, and where there are complicated instructions for how to answer survey questions or where different questions need to be asked depending on individual circumstances. It is almost always better to have a smaller dataset of accurate answers than a larger dataset riddled with errors. Many people are understandably reluctant to divulge confidential or personal sensitive information in a postal questionnaire, and a skilled interviewer can build a relationship of trust with respondents that can reassure them about why the data are needed and how it will be kept secure. An interview method may be the most effective way to collect survey data for groups such as customers in a shop or a service facility, where postal addresses or other contact details are not available.

Telephone interview surveys are now commonplace in many research projects, since they combine the low cost of the postal survey with the interactivity of the face-to-face interview. So much of day-to-day business is conducted now by phone that most people are very familiar with the technology. Collecting data by telephone is of most value where the design of the research project requires contact with respondents who are widely dispersed (so that travelling to them would be time-consuming and expensive) or where the researcher is located in a different part of the world (for example, many Asian students studying in the UK want to conduct their research in their own country, but cannot afford to travel there to collect data). This task has been made much cheaper in the last few years by the rapid development of voice over Internet protocol (VOIP) technologies such as Skype (http:www.skype.com) which use the Internet to transmit voice, so that the cost of a call does not depend on distance.

Another application of modern communications technology is the *web-based survey*. As the Internet becomes a taken-for-granted part of business and domestic life, carrying out web-based surveys (Gunn, 2002; further sources are: Couper et al., 2001; Crawford et al., 2001; Dillman, 2000) is rapidly becoming commonplace. Instead of mailing a questionnaire to each potential respondent and asking them to mail it back, the questionnaire is located on a web site, and each respondent is sent the web address in order to access it. The survey is then completed online, and responses are stored directly in an online database for statistical processing later. Tools such as WebSurveyor (now called VoVici - http://www.vovici.com) have dramatically reduced the cost of web surveys by making each step in the process easy for those without technical training. The Internet offers a number of attractions for web surveys. Internet-based surveys can be customized for individual respondents much more easily than can postal surveys. Moreover, the interactivity of web technologies gives a number of advantages: pop-up instructions and drop-down boxes can explain parts of the web survey which are more difficult to understand; questions at different points in a survey can be personalized using responses to earlier questions; and through skip-logic and conditional branching it is easy to skip over topics that are not relevant based on answers to earlier questions. It is also possible to build in dynamic error checking of answers to ensure that people respond consistently throughout. Finally, data can be downloaded directly into analysis programs such as Excel or SPSS, avoiding cost of data entry and transcription errors. Berghman et al. (2006) is a good example of a web survey.

EXERCISE
9.1

Selecting a survey strategy

Below are three different research projects where a survey methodology might be appropriate.

A A project in a small company with 25 staff to assess views of employees on introducing charges for car parking.

B A worldwide survey in a multinational company of staff attitudes to human resources management practices.

C An investigation to understand the nature of bullying within the social services department of a local authority.

You need to decide what type of survey administration method would be most appropriate: postal, web-based, face-to-face interview or a telephone interview.

In pairs or small groups, draw up the advantages and disadvantages of the four methods of administering the survey for each project. Taking into account the topic and the target group, which method will you use for each project and why?

Collecting data through observational methods

Observational methods are used in order to code and analyse behaviour. Behaviour may either be coded live or be recorded (for example using audio or video or by capturing key presses and screen displays on a computer) for later coding. The commonest way in which observational methods are used is with the observer as a non-participant, although participant observation can also be used, as was discussed in Chapters 7 and 8.

Types of observational data There is no single way of classifying observational data, because behaviour is very complicated and the purposes of studies vary enormously. The most obvious distinction is between verbal and nonverbal aspects of behaviour. The researcher may be interested in *verbal* behaviour – the words that people use to express meanings through the content of messages, complexity of syntax, formal versus informal language – in order to explore different ways of explaining how to perform a task. *Non-verbal* behaviour is divided into vocal aspects to do with tone of voice (angry, apologetic, loving, calm and so on), pitch (high or low) and the pacing of speech (talking quickly or slowly), and also visual aspects to do with facial expressions, gestures, body posture and so on. A detailed analysis of the success or failure of a negotiation exercise would need to include an analysis of these aspects of *non-verbal* behaviour since they carry a substantial proportion of information. For example, Mehrabian's (1981) experimental studies of communications of feelings and attitudes led him to the following formula (http://www.kaaj.com/psych/smorder.html):

Total liking = 7% verbal liking + 38% vocal liking + 55% facial liking. In other words, most of the information about whether one person likes who they are talkir to comes not from what is said (only 7 per cent) but on how it is said and on th facial expressions (93 per cent). We can conclude that relying for data only ou written transcript of what was said during a conversation or a meeting will miss most of the most important information about what is going on, particularly regarding relationships between people.

Factors affecting observational data There is a number of things that need to be kept in mind when designing studies that will use observational data. First, **observer effects** are common, which refers to the fact that most of us behave differently when we know (or think) that we are being observed. Often, initiatives within local communities rely on exactly these effects to influence the behaviour of members of the public: those boxes on poles at the side of the road often do not contain speed cameras (but they might, so we slow down). From the perspective of research, observer effects are bad news since they alter the very thing that the researcher is interested in learning about. Consider how difficult it is for many people to pose naturally for a photograph: it is easy to tell the difference between a natural smile and a posed smile since the muscle groups used are different. In practice though, people whose behaviour is being recorded quickly get used to being observed and forget about the cameras. One way to avoid observer effects is to act covertly so that no one knows that they are being watched, but this violates one of th basic principles of ethical research, that research participants give their infor consent to take part in a study (see Chapter 6). Indeed, recording of teleph calls without consent is illegal in the UK, and that is why calls to companies of start with a message saying that calls may be recorded or monitored for security and quality control purposes.

The second factor to bear in mind when using observational data relates to how decisions are made about *what behaviour is sampled*. Some kind of selectivity is inevitable, simply because human behaviour is so rich and complex. One approach is to try to obtain a complete record, and then sample from within it later. A popular television programme in many countries is Big Brother (first developed in the Netherlands), where individuals live in the 'Big Brother House' and a large number of cameras record what they do. Each person also wears a microphone at all times so that what they say is recorded. Even if the output from every camera and every microphone is available for analysis, some kind of selectivity is essential. The programme editors broadcast a tiny proportion of all that material; and their editing judgements can be a source of complaint and comment. For example, inmates of the House often complain that the programme did not show the 'real me' when features of their behaviour that show them in particular way are selected and others neglected. A second approach is to record only a sample of behaviour: either by *time* sampling (for example, take a photo every two seconds, or record for five minutes every hour through the day) or by *activity* sampling (for example, record every phone call which is a customer complaint, or select company orders for a specific range of products).

that company managers had made several changes during the study period to how they recorded productivity. Line managers had designed productivity indices that helped them to achieve the objectives set for them by the company's senior management; but there were frequent changes to corporate priorities during the study period and managers responded to shifting priorities by adjusting what they measured and how they measured it.

The task of the researcher is to interpret the data recorded in a secondary data archive in terms of particular study objectives. This might mean forming *derived* measures by aggregating variables together to form an index or by creating rates rather than absolute amounts. For example, comparing absolute change rarely makes sense, while percentage change relative to a starting point is generally more informative. Other examples are: measures of earnings per share which take into account differences in company capitalization; productivity indicators (such as those used in Wall et al. [1992]) which relate outputs to the resources needed to deliver them; sickness rates for companies which adjust number of days of recorded sickness absence according to the number of employees.

THE PROCESS OF MEASUREMENT

In the last section of this chapter, we look at structured forms of asking questions and recording the answers that people give to them. Research on how politicians respond to questions asked by probing journalists showed apparently that there are 46 ways of avoiding answering a straight question. If that really is true, then how much more difficult is it to interpret answers when the questions themselves are not well structured?

Principles in designing structured questions for surveys and interviews

There are five principles of good design when thinking about how to word questions. The first principle is that *each item should express only one idea*. If a question asks more than one thing at the same time, then how is it possible to know which one people are thinking of when they give an answer? The second principle is to *avoid jargon and colloquialisms*. Jargon is insider knowledge in the form of expressions that some people (but not others) know. So, using it only makes sense where it is possible to be confident that respondents are all 'in the know'. Colloquialisms are informal expressions in a language that may not be familiar to people who are not native to that country, or do not belong to a specific group. Mobile phone text-speak is becoming that, where **cu l8r** is simple for some (see you later) but impenetrable to others. The message is clear: play safe and use plain language. The third principle is to *use simple expressions*. Using the active rather than the passive tense is generally better ('I did it' is better than 'It was done by me'). Dividing up complicated arguments into a series of simple steps is better than expressing it all in one long sentence.

The fourth principle is to *avoid the use of negatives*. In English, this is often done by adding 'no' or 'not' to a verb in order to give the opposite meaning; but two problems can arise. The first is that a quick read of a sentence may miss the negative, so that the respondent answers a question the wrong way around. There is research by Schmitt and Stults (1985) that suggests that around 10 per cent of respondents in large-scale studies may make this kind of mistake; and it obviously disturbs the clarity of data analysis. The second problem is that scales such as the **Likert scale** are bipolar – they go from negative (*disagree*) through neutral (*not sure*) to positive (*agree*). People who feel good about something would have to show it by disagreeing with a statement worded negatively. This means it can get tricky to work out how to report what they feel.

The final principle is to *avoid leading questions*. The concept of a **leading question** comes from legal settings, where the way that a question is phrased gives a strong lead on what answer is expected. All research has an element of 'leading' about it – the researcher chooses what to ask about, and this focuses attention on some areas and not on others. However, leading questions do more than this: they make it easier for the respondent to give the answer that the researcher wants, instead of the answer that the respondent thinks is right.

Exercise 9.3 gives some examples of poorly worded questions that might be asked in a questionnaire survey or an interview. Some have been taken from real research, while others have been invented to make a point. Exercise 9.3 invites the reader to think through the design principles, work out what is wrong with each example question and then devise a better form of words. Like many things in life, asking clear questions seems remarkably easy until we set out to do it ourselves.

Measurement scales for recording responses

There are two kinds of measurement scales which researchers commonly use, and they differ according to the number of distinctions between alternative points on the measurement scale. *Category* scales consist of few distinctions, while *continuous* scales consist of many distinctions.

Category scales These may be either unordered (these are called nominal scales) or ordered (these are called ordinal scales). The difference between nominal and ordinal category scales lies in whether shuffling the assignment of numbers to categories makes any difference to the meaning of the variable. **Nominal scales** have no natural ordering. A study by Goldacre et al. (2004) considered the ethnic origin of UK medical consultants, recorded as White, Black, Asian, Chinese and Other. It makes no sense to treat a concept like ethnic origin as anything other than a nominal scale since the five ethnic groups could equally well be written in any order. Similarly, studies of branded consumer products coding countries of origin could list them in any order. By contrast, **ordinal scales** have a natural ordering. An example of an ordinal scale is socio-economic status, such as the classification scheme used by the UK government (the Registrar General's classification: I professional, II Intermediate, IIIa Skilled non-manual, IIIb Skilled manual, IV Partly skilled, V Unskilled) which is based on such criteria as educational qualifications and occupation. Similarly, honours degrees awarded to UK undergraduates are graded as first class, upper second class (2:1), lower second class (2:2) and third class. The higher the aggregate mark in assessed work, the higher the degree classification.

Sometimes, however, the status of a variable in a research study is less clear. For the purpose of recording trade flows, country of origin would be recorded on a

Framing questions

For each question below:

1) What is the problem with the way that the question is worded?

2) Which of the five principles is violated?

3) Re-write the question, and explain why your version works better than the original.

If you are on the voting register, how good is your voting record in local elections?
  A ☐ Poor   ☐ Quite good   ☐ Very good

How strongly do you agree that smoking is harmful to health?
  B ☐ Not at all ☐ Slightly   ☐ Quite strongly ☐ Very strongly

If you wanted to express your opinion about genetically modified foods, would you consider taking part in a boycott of your local supermarket?
  C ☐ Not at all ☐ Probably not ☐ Not sure   ☐ Probably   ☐ Definitely

How much do you agree with the following: Politicians never keep the promises they make before an election, once they are in office.
  D ☐ Not sure ☐ Agree a little   ☐ Strongly agree

How much do you agree with the following: My supervisor is dynamic and well organized.
  E ☐ Strongly   ☐ Disagree   ☐ Not sure   ☐ Agree   ☐ Strongly agree
     disagree

How much do you agree with the following: I am not satisfied with the progress of my research.
  F ☐ Strongly   ☐ Disagree   ☐ Not sure   ☐ Agree   ☐ Strongly agree
     disagree

How much do you agree with the following: The presence of humorous literary allusions is conducive to an accessible presentation mode in academic pedagogy.
  G ☐ Strongly   ☐ Disagree   ☐ Not sure   ☐ Agree   ☐ Strongly agree
     disagree

nominal scale. However, a project on boycotts within Arab countries of consumer products might well rank countries according to how closely they are associated with the USA, thus giving an ordinal scale. This illustrates an important point: that concepts or variables do not carry around with them a measurement scale which is intrinsic to them. Rather, the properties of scales are just that, properties which apply when we measure something, and those properties can vary depending on the purpose of the study.

Measurement of attitudes and opinions Psychologists are not alone in being interested in what people think about things: the effect of the proposed EU constitution on political relationships within Europe, the reputation of the company that supplies their electricity, and so on. Everyone has opinions, and there is a lot of money to be made out of knowing what those opinions are. It is no surprise then that a lot of attention has gone into understanding effective ways of measuring attitudes and opinions.

EXAMPLE 9.4

Alternative attitude response scales

My organization is a friendly place to work. How much do you agree or disagree with this statement?

☐ Agree   ☐ Disagree (agree/disagree scale)

☐ Strongly   ☐ Disagree   ☐ Not sure   ☐ Agree   ☐ Strongly
   disagree   agree
                                                              (Likert scale)

Consider the statement 'My organization is a friendly place to work' (see Example 9.4). The simple-minded approach would be to ask people whether or not they agreed with the statement. However, this approach misses out on a lot of useful information because strength of opinion varies. There is a world of difference between someone who likes to listen to rock music from time to time and the fanatic who has every Guns N' Roses CD plus bootleg copies of their live concerts. To capture some of this subtlety, Rensis Likert developed a five-point response scale, which still bears his name, the **Likert scale**. The scale, has a neutral mid-point to allow for the possibility that an individual may have no opinion on an issue. Then, on each side of the mid-point there are two alternative response options to record moderate and extreme views for or against. Both types of attitude response scale are ordinal scales in that *agreeing* reflects a more positive attitude towards the issue raised than does *disagreeing*.

Continuous scales Continuous scales are types of ordered scale so that it is possible to speak of more or less of whatever is being measured according to the value on the scale. The difference between the two types of continuous scale, interval and ratio, lies in whether there is a true zero point. If there is a true zero point on a scale, then that gives a **ratio scale**; and it is possible to speak meaningfully of a data point of 20 being twice as high as another data point with a value of 10 (for example). Height is measured on a true ratio scale, and we can meaningfully speak of an adult being twice as tall as a child. Time is also measured on a ratio scale, for example how long it takes for MBA graduates to get a job after their programme finishes. A graduate's income compared to what it was before joining the MBA programme is also measured on a ratio scale.

If there is no true zero point (for example temperature, where we have Celsius and Fahrenheit scales), then we have an **interval scale**. On an interval scale, differences between alternative values can be described meaningfully, but ratios cannot. Suppose we have four data points with values of 1, 2, 9 and 10 measured on an interval scale. We may say that the difference between the first two data points is the same as the difference between the last two; but not that the last data point is 10 times bigger than the first. Travelling from England with a temperature of 15° to

Hong Kong with a temperature of 30° is a doubling of temperature when we measure in degrees Celsius but not in degrees Fahrenheit (15° Celsius is 59° Fahrenheit, while 30° Celsius is 86° Fahrenheit). Many continuous measurement scales in social science are truly interval scales rather than ratio scales. The difference is captured succinctly by asking the question: is the data still meaningful if a fixed value (say 50) were subtracted from each score? For much data on attitudes or preferences, scales are arbitrary and such an adjustment would not matter.

CONCLUSION

The assumption that underlies the methods described in this chapter is that the researcher uses data from a sample in order to make generalizations about a defined population. The points we want to emphasize are:

- **Good sampling design can make it easier to draw sound conclusions about data from a sample.**
- **There are many sources of data in management research, and each has good and bad points.**
- **Framing questions appropriately as well as designing scales to record responses are both vital to the process of creating quantitative data.**

The next two chapters describe methods for analysing quantitative data. In Chapter 10, we first consider ways of summarizing key features of data and then examine the principles and practice of hypothesis testing which allow the researcher to make inferences about populations based on evidence from samples. Chapter 10 considers univariate tests, taking one variable at a time; and Chapter 11 extends this treatment to cover the multivariate case where many variables are dealt with simultaneously.

FURTHER READING

Gunn, H. (2002) 'Web-based surveys: changing the survey process; *First Monday,* 7(12).
    Is a good and very readable article on web-based surveys. Groups (SYMLOG – Bales, 1988; Bales et al. 1979).
Sapsford (2006) *Survey Research*, 2nd edn. London: Sage.
    Gives a comprehensive introduction to different kinds of sampling design for social science research and the principles that inform how a researcher might choose between them.

MAKING SENSE OF QUANTITATIVE DATA

10

LEARNING OBJECTIVES

- To choose effective ways of summarizing key features of data.

- To know which summary measures to use for location and spread of data.

- To understand which statistical tests to use when comparing groups and testing association between variables.

Introduction

Summarizing and describing data

Going beyond a sample

Conclusion

Further reading

INTRODUCTION

Business and management is maturing as a discipline, and this maturity is shown in many ways. Its conceptual thinking is becoming more sophisticated, and there is increasing evidence that scholars are not just developing clever ways of thinking about the business of business but are also putting their ideas to the test. The gathering of quantitative data has been dealt with in the previous chapter. Here, we will look at the tools that management scholars use when their empirical evidence is in the form of numbers – quantitative data.

The most obvious feature of quantitative data – evidence expressed in the form of numbers – is their sheer quantity. It is generally expensive in time and money to accumulate good quality data, and so researchers make the most of each study participant by collecting as much data as possible from each person, and quantitative research designs also often involve large samples. The big challenge then is seeing the wood for the trees – identifying patterns in numerical data and making sense of those patterns. In this chapter, we address this in two parts. First, we consider the key features of numerical data and the common indices that are used to assess those features. The second part of the chapter introduces the logic of statistical inference as a tool for 'going beyond the data' and introduces a variety of statistical tests for looking at data one variable at a time.

Quantitative methods are an important part of the research process in business and management, something which, as we discussed in Chapter 6, is especially true of American journals. The Table 10.1 below gives some examples from two of the leading journals in strategy and marketing of research questions that have been addressed using quantitative data. Behind the most sophisticated research question and the most complex datasets, however, is a simple basic principle. All quantitative researchers do the same two things: they identify what features tell the best story about the data (we call this **summarizing** the data) and then they look for patterns in the data that can be used to draw conclusions about the study's research questions (we call this making **inferences** about populations based on sample data).

The idea behind summarizing and making inferences is a simple one which can be illustrated quite easily. The company iSoft is one of the suppliers of software to the major NHS Connecting for Health initiative the aim of which is to put all UK patient records online, so that patients can book appointments online and doctors (whether in general practice or in a hospital) can access a patient's record regardless of where treatment has taken place. Delays in iSoft delivering workable software have threatened the future viability of the company. One of the ways in which this threat has shown itself is in a 90 per cent drop in the company's share price during 2006. The 90 per cent figure summarizes the data on share prices (expressed as the amount of the drop relative to its starting price at start of year). The aim of this kind of summary is to capture relevant features of data in a form that makes sense. Behind the bald figures of share price movements is also an inference process – one might say a kind of guesswork or betting – that predicts what the future profits of the company will be based on its past performance. The sell judgements of analysts in the newspapers of August 2006 are based on an inference process (not formal statistical inference, but rather informed guesswork) about future data on the performance of the company.

TABLE 10.1 Examples of studies using quantitative methods from recent issues of *Strategic Management Journal* and the *Journal of Marketing*

State-owned enterprises (SOEs) in China (Ralston et al., 2006). They compared the organizational cultures of state-owned enterprises with private-owned enterprises and foreign-owned businesses in order to decide whether SOEs are dinosaurs or dynamos for China's economic future

Should multinational enterprises (MNEs) adapt their marketing strategy to each market or standardise across markets? (Katsikeas et al., 2006). They looked at the international marketing strategies of US, Japanese and German MNEs operating in the UK. They found that standardisation only makes sense when there is a good fit to the market environment

Knowledge transfer in business-to-business relationships (Dyer and Hatch, 2006). They found that Toyota were much better than US car companies (GM, Ford and Chrysler) in getting better quality out of their suppliers. They concluded that there can be specific capabilities within relationships between customers and suppliers that are not easily transferable to other relationships

How to influence a company on environmental issues (Eesley and Lenox, 2006). They used a database of secondary stakeholder actions to check out what it takes to get positive responses out of companies

Home or away? - where to put your HQ (Birkinshaw et al., 2006). They found that MNEs put their business unit headquarters overseas when it made sense for ***internal*** reasons; while the location of their corporate HQ was influenced most strongly by the demands of ***external*** stakeholders – global financial markets and shareholders

Is corporate social responsibility (CSR) smart as well as good? (Luo and Bhattacharya, 2006). They used secondary data archives to test the link between CSR activities such as cash donations and employee volunteerism, customer satisfaction and the market value of the firm. They found that CSR can be smart – good for the company – but there is a dark side too

What do web site visitors value on a manufacturer's site? (Steenkamp and Geyskens, 2006). The authors found that the answer depends on the country where the consumers live. They looked at over 8000 consumers from 23 countries, visiting the sites of 16 consumer packaged goods companies.

Example dataset for the chapter

The chapter will use example data from a survey of consumer reputation. Walsh and Beatty developed a measure of the reputation of an organization in the eyes of its customers: 'the customer's overall evaluation of a firm based on his or her reactions to the firm's goods, services, communication activities, interactions with the firm and/or its representatives or constituencies (such as employees, management, or other customers) and/or known corporate activities' (2007: 8). The scale covers five facets of reputation – customer orientation, good employer, reliable and financially strong company, product and service quality, and social and environmental responsibility – and is formed by averaging together responses to 23 items, each measured on a five-point scale (from strongly disagree coded 1 through to strongly agree, coded 5). A 15-item sub-set of this reputation scale was used in a follow-up study by Walsh et al. (in press) with samples of German customers of two utility companies.

Frequencies The **frequency distribution** for a sample of 676 people is shown first in Table 10.2, and a number of features can be seen relatively easily. The first column

TABLE 10.2 Frequency distribution of reputation scores from two samples of customers of German utility companies

	Frequency	Percent	Valid percent	Cumulative percent
Valid 2.12	1	.1	.1	.1
2.41	3	.4	.4	.6
2.47	6	.9	.9	1.5
2.53	6	.9	.9	2.4
2.59	4	.6	.6	3.0
2.65	5	.7	.7	3.7
2.71	3	.4	.4	4.1
2.76	6	.9	.9	5.0
2.82	7	1.0	1.0	6.1
2.88	13	1.9	1.9	8.0
2.94	9	1.3	1.3	9.3
3.00	14	2.1	2.1	11.4
3.06	7	1.0	1.0	12.4
3.12	22	3.2	3.3	15.7
3.18	16	2.4	2.4	18.0
3.24	14	2.1	2.1	20.1
3.29	13	1.9	1.9	22.0
3.31	1	.1	.1	22.2
3.35	17	2.5	2.5	24.7
3.41	27	4.0	4.0	28.7
3.47	15	2.2	2.2	30.9
3.53	20	3.0	3.0	33.9
3.56	3	.4	.4	34.3

TABLE 10.2 Frequency distribution of reputation scores from two samples of customers of German utility companies—cont'd

	Frequency	Percent	Valid percent	Cumulative percent
3.59	13	1.9	1.9	36.2
3.65	38	5.6	5.6	41.9
3.69	1	.1	.1	42.0
3.71	38	5.6	5.6	47.6
3.76	34	5.0	5.0	52.7
3.80	1	.1	.1	52.8
3.81	4	.6	.6	53.4
3.82	28	4.1	4.1	57.5
3.88	30	4.4	4.4	62.0
3.94	24	3.5	3.6	65.5
4.00	22	3.2	3.3	68.8
4.06	14	2.1	2.1	70.9
4.06	1	.1	.1	71.0
4.12	15	2.2	2.2	73.2
4.18	14	2.1	2.1	75.3
4.24	18	2.7	2.7	78.0
4.25	2	.3	.3	78.3
4.29	19	2.8	2.8	81.1
4.33	1	.1	.1	81.2
4.35	13	1.9	1.9	83.1
4.41	13	1.9	1.9	85.1
4.47	11	1.6	1.6	86.7
4.53	13	1.9	1.9	88.6

Continued

TABLE 10.2 Frequency distribution of reputation scores from two samples of customers of German utility companies—cont'd

	Frequency	Percent	Valid percent	Cumulative percent
4.59	9	1.3	1.3	89.9
4.63	1	.1	.1	90.1
4.65	16	2.4	2.4	92.5
4.71	3	.4	.4	92.9
4.76	12	1.8	1.8	94.7
4.82	4	.6	.6	95.3
4.88	1	.1	.1	95.4
4.88	14	2.1	2.1	97.5
4.94	1	.1	.1	97.6
4.94	4	.6	.6	98.2
5.00	12	1.8	1.8	100.0
Total	676	99.9	100.0	
Missing	1	.1		
Total	677	100.0		

SOURCE: WALSH ET AL. (IN PRESS)

records each alternative value that occurs in this data and we can see that the data values vary between 2.12 and 5.00. The next column in the display shows the frequency of occurrence of each alternative data value. The smallest value, 2.12, occurs only once in this sample; while the largest value, 5.00, occurs 12 times. The most frequently occurring values occur 38 times.

Percentages The third column of Table 10.2 records the occurrence of each alternative response in the form of a percentage, worked out simply by dividing the frequency by the total sample size: it records what percentage of the sample reported each alternative. One person in the sample does not give a valid reputation score, probably as a result of missing out at least one of the component items. Thus, the percentage figures are based on the sample of 677 minus the one person who missed out at least one response (the base therefore is 676). Finally, the last column shows the cumulative percentages, showing for any particular value the percentage of people with scores at least as high as that value.

EXERCISE
10.1

How to interpret a frequency distribution table

Look at the frequency distribution Table 10.2, and answer the following questions:

A Why do the values in this dataset all fall in the range of 1 to 5?

B How many people strongly agreed with every item in the scale?

C Without doing any calculations, where roughly is the average in this sample? Do people broadly think that their utility company has a good reputation?

D What is the commonest score in this sample? Is this close to the average for the whole sample?

Cumulative percentages It is relatively easy to pick out some features of the Table from these numbers. For example, we can see that a quarter of the sample (25 per cent) scored 3.35 or less; while three quarters (75 per cent) scored at least 4.18. Another feature of this data is the way in which there are runs of uncommon frequencies among commonly occurring values (for example, there are these runs of adjacent values: 13-1-17; 20-3-13; 38-1-38; 18-2-19-1). The reason why these happen derives from the way in which the aggregate reputation score for each respondent was calculated from the answers that respondents gave to a set of questions in the original survey.

Having introduced the dataset, we now turn to describe different ways of summarizing key features of the data.

SUMMARIZING AND DESCRIBING DATA

There are three sections to this part of the chapter. The first looks at ways of showing the shape of data distributions, capitalizing on the highly developed capabilities that humans have for seeing visual patterns. The second section considers a variety of measures that summarize data in terms of different attributes. The third section draws out two formal characteristics of summary measures that we can use to help us understand why alternative measures work the way that they do. These formal characteristics give the criteria for making smart choices about which summary measures to use in practical situations.

Showing the shape of data distributions

Although Table 10.2 reports the reputation scores in summary form, the general shape of this set of data is really hard to visualise from a table of numbers. Many of the characteristics of data distributions that have important consequences for analysis and interpretation can be seen very easily provided that data can be displayed informatively. Two obvious forms of data display are provided by most statistical packages: bar charts and histograms. A **bar chart** summarizes the distribution of a category variable: bars are drawn to represent each category and the length of the bar reflects the number of cases in the category – the more people, the longer the bar. If variables are measured on an ordinal scale, then it would be strange to do other than order the bars in the chart accordingly. For variables on a nominal scale, where the categories are not ordered, it makes sense to apply some thought to how to order the bars on the chart. A **histogram** is a bar chart drawn for a continuous variable, after grouping adjacent scale points together.

Bar charts Figure 10.1 shows a bar chart for the reputation data from Table 10.2. The scale along the bottom of the chart is the measurement scale for the variable, in this case the reputation of the utility company. The bar on the left is labelled 2.12, which is the lowest value recorded in this dataset; while the bar on the right of the figure is labelled 5.00, the largest value recorded for these data. Essentially, the bar chart is a visual representation of the frequency table: there are 57 different values for reputation scores listed in Table 10.2, and there are 57 bars on the chart in Figure 10.1. Each figure in the frequency distribution shown in Table 10.2 is translated into the height of a bar in Figure 10.1. The height of each bar is marked by the vertical axis of the figure, labelled frequency; and this shows how many respondents gave each alternative response. The higher the bar, the more respondents recorded this answer.

The shape of the data is much easier to see in this picture than it was in the table which reported only the numbers. There are peaks in the middle, where the commonest responses are; while the distribution tails off towards the low end of the scale (to the left, showing poor reputation) and towards the high end of the scale (to the right, showing good reputation). Another obvious feature is the fact that there are lots of 'holes' in the distribution. In among the common values are also some very uncommon ones.

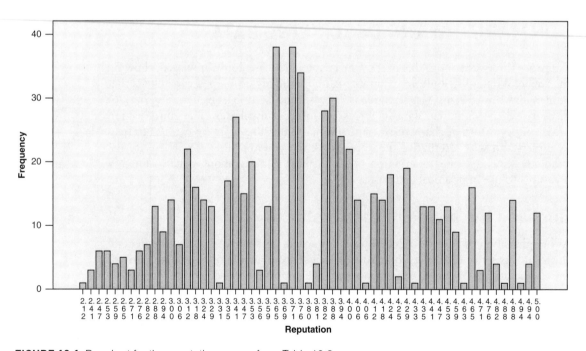

FIGURE 10.1 Bar chart for the reputation scores from Table 10.2

Histograms A histogram is special form of bar chart, with the points on the scale grouped into a manageable number of categories. The histogram in Figure 10.2 shows the reputation data with the 57 different scores grouped together into a smaller number of categories. The labels on the x-axis are the mid-points of the categories shown by each bar. Histograms have immediate visual appeal, and show gross features of data very easily. The peak in the data between 3.5 and 4 is now obvious, and the 'holes' in the data have been hidden by combining categories together. The shape is thus smoother to the eye. We can also see that there are more values at the top end of the scale than there are at the bottom. These data thus are not completely symmetrical.

Thinking about the most extreme score possible at the top and bottom of the scale – values of 1 (strongly disagree) and 5 (strongly agree) – there are a number of people (Table 10.2 shows that there are 12 in all) who strongly agree with every item giving them an average score of 5 – shown by the peak at the far right of the chart above. By contrast, no one strongly disagreed with every item (this would give them an average score of 1). Perhaps that isn't surprising, since the survey was done on existing customers of German utility companies. Customers who were so disenchanted with a company that they strongly disagreed with every positive statement about it would presumably have already taken their business elsewhere.

This chapter started with a table showing (in slightly abbreviated form) 677 data points; but it is obviously impossible to carry all that information around in one's head. Instead, it is much more efficient to capture some key features of the data in convenient summary form. This section covers three features of data that are most informative and most useful: **location**, **spread** and **symmetry**. We will describe summary measures of some of these key features of data. In the next section, we will examine a number of formal properties of summary measures that will allow us to make informative choices between them.

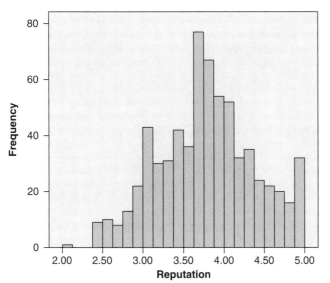

Mean = 3.7774
Std. Dev. = 0.5934
N = 676

FIGURE 10.2

Histogram for the reputation scores from Table 10.2

Summary measures of location

The obvious starting point for summarizing a large set of data is with an index that locates the data as a whole on its measurement scale: in general *high*, *middling* or *low*. For example, if there is a risk to consumers caused by contamination of a batch of chocolate during manufacture, as was the case with some Cadbury's chocolate early in 2006, then how big is the risk? Is it so minute that any impact on community health would be hard to detect, as the company argued when challenged by the UK Health and Safety Executive? As a second example, how big will the market be for television on mobile phones? Will it catch on, or will it go the way of the tiny market for us sending our pictures to others with our mobiles? Whatever the researcher is interested in measuring, and however large or small the dataset, most people would be interested in where on its measurement scale the data as a whole are located. Four summary measures of location are commonly used: the mode, the median, the mean and the mid-mean; and we now consider each one in turn.

Mode The **mode** is a simple form of summary measure of location: it is the commonest value among a set of scores. For some purposes, the mode as a measure of location can be informative (for instance the music charts focus on who sells the most copies of their work), however, the mode has some quite severe drawbacks. It ignores the rest of the data and conveys nothing at all about what other values there might be in the data. Although George W. Bush was elected President of the USA in 2000 because he polled most votes, Al Gore would have been President if it were not for a few thousand disputed voting papers in Florida. A supreme example of the winner-take-all principle enshrined in the mode as a summary measure of votes cast. Second, there may be more than one mode so that this measure of location need not have a unique value. Thus, Table 10.2 records that both 3.65 and 3.71 occur more often than any other value: both are modal values for the reputation dataset. The third problem with the mode as a summary of location for data on a continuous scale is that it depends upon how scores are grouped.

Table 10.3 shows a 3 per cent random sample drawn from the data in Figure 10.2. In this data, there is no unique mode because there are two sets of tied scores. Grouping the scores together in different ways would create a different modal value depending on how the grouping is done. Since the value of the mode depends upon fairly arbitrary decisions about grouping scores, the mode is not of much use for serious research.

Median The **median** is the middle value once scores have been placed in rank order, either from largest to smallest or from smallest to largest. It is the value that divides a set of data in half. The 16 scores in Table 10.3 listed in rank order are:

> 2.41, 2.47, 2.94, 3.47, 3.65, 3.65, 3.71, **3.82**, **3.94**, 3.94, 4.00, 4.24, 4.29, 4.65, 4.71, 4.76

Here, there are an even number of data points, and the median is halfway between the middle two (shown in bold above), in this case 3.88. For an odd number of data points, the median is simply the middle one, counting in from either end.

TABLE 10.3 Frequency distribution of reputation scores for a random 3 per cent sub-group of the sample shown in table 10.2

	Frequency	Percent	Valid percent	Cumulative percent
Valid 2.41	1	6.3	6.3	6.3
2.47	1	6.3	6.3	12.5
2.94	1	6.3	6.3	18.8
3.47	1	6.3	6.3	25.0
3.65	2	12.5	12.5	37.5
3.71	1	6.3	6.3	43.8
3.82	1	6.3	6.3	50.0
3.94	2	12.5	12.5	62.5
4.00	1	6.3	6.3	68.8
4.24	1	6.3	6.3	75.0
4.29	1	6.3	6.3	81.3
4.65	1	6.3	6.3	87.5
4.71	1	6.3	6.3	93.8
4.76	1	6.3	6.3	100.0
Total	16	100.0	100.0	

The median has some important properties which are easy to grasp intuitively:

1 Every observation in the data contributes something to determining the value of the median, unlike the mode. That makes the median more meaningful as a summary measure of location because it uses more of the information in the data in estimating location.

2 Most of the data points do not contribute much – it is the rank position of a data point that matters rather than its precise value. That makes the median less efficient than it might be (it throws away the values of each observation and replaces them with rank-order information) but it has the great advantage that the median is insensitive to odd things happening to extreme scores: adding a million to the largest data point (perhaps by forgetting to put in the decimal point when entering the data) does nothing to the median because it

does not change the fact that this is still the largest data point. It also makes the median useful where the measurement scale is not particularly precise, and the researcher cannot be certain of the accuracy of the numbers.

3 It sometimes happens that the category at the top of a grouped continuous scale is open-ended: for example, all we may know is that the highest paid employee in an organization earned *at least* £100,000. This gives no trouble at all for calculating the median, because there is no doubt that this is the highest score.

Mean The **mean** is the average value formed by adding all the scores and dividing by how many data points there are. The formula for the mean is:

$M = \Sigma(X)/n$

where M stands for the mean, X represents each data value, n indicates how many data points there are, and the Σ symbol is a summation sign.

Adding up the 16 data values in Table 10.3 gives a total of 60.65, and the mean is 60.65 / 16 = 3.79. Just like the median, every score contributes to forming the mean; but the mean differs because it takes into account how big each score is. This can be both a benefit and a disadvantage. By using the mean as a summary measure of location, the researcher can be confident of making the most of the information in the data about where the data are centred. Conversely, using the mean assumes that each data point is accurately recorded. In the example in the previous paragraph, we may only know that salary is not less than a particular value. This level of uncertainty is not helpful when it comes to calculating the mean.

Mid-mean The **mid-mean** is an average formed by first removing scores equally from both extremes of a dataset and then working out the mean of the remainder. It is part of a family of summary measures called **trimmed means**, which differ in how much is trimmed from each end of the distribution of data points. The mean is a 0 per cent trimmed mean (with nothing trimmed); while the median is a 50 per cent trimmed mean. The mid-mean is a 25 per cent trimmed mean, the mean of the middle half of the data. It uses rank order information (like the median) to select data points to ignore; but then uses the data values themselves (like the mean) to calculate the summary index. Using the data in Table 10.3, trimming off the four lowest values (the bottom quarter) and the four largest values (the top quarter) gives:

2.41, 2.47, 2.94, 3.47, 3.65, 3.65, 3.71, 3.82, 3.94, 3.94, 4.00, 4.24, 4.29, 4.65, 4.71, 4.76.

Adding up the remaining eight values gives a total of 30.95, and the mid-mean is 30.95 / 8 = 3.87.

Comparing summary measures of location Of course, not all datasets give conclusions that look like this small subset of the reputation data; but the results show what can happen with real data:

mode – cannot calculate;
median – 3.88;

mean – 3.79;
mid-mean – 3.87.

Which of these summary measures is most useful? The answer is all of them, and none of them. Each summary measure uses different aspects of the data which contain information about the feature of locatedness. When researchers calculate one of these summary measures to report where a dataset as a whole is located on its measurement scale, they are implicitly making a judgement about what matters in the data. If they want to emphasize what is typical, they might prefer the mode. However, attention on inequalities in income in an organization, for instance, might lead someone to choose the median, which will show that half of the organization earn less than £x, while another group might prefer the mean because it takes into account the much higher pay of the most senior officials in the organization which makes the pay levels look generally higher.

The most widely used summaries of location are the mean and the median. Less common, but useful, are the mid-mean and other forms of the trimmed mean. An important point to note is that even something so simple as working out an average is a choice. The consequences of making different choices about summary measures of location depend very much on the characteristics of a specific dataset, and which features of the data the researcher wishes to emphasize.

Summary measures of spread

Of course, most samples of data will contain some variability around a central value with some people scoring higher than others. How much spread there is around a measure of location is a valuable way of capturing something extra about a dataset as a whole. Three common measures of spread are the range, the mid-range and the standard deviation. Like the measures of location considered in the previous section, each one captures different aspects of data.

Range The **range** is the distance between the largest and the smallest scores. The smallest data value in Table 10.3 is 2.41 and the largest is 4.76, so the range is 4.76 – 2.41 = 2.35. This measure of spread is the easiest to calculate, but also potentially the most misleading. Most people have seen the banner headlines in shop windows – up to 50 per cent off? This means that at least one item is discounted by this much, but says nothing about how many other items are treated in the same way. The same goes for the cheap holidays – two weeks in the sun 'from £15' – but can you find any specific holiday in the brochure for that price? Any summary index based on an extreme statistic (largest or smallest) can be dangerously misleading.

Mid-range (interquartile range) The **mid-range** is the range of the middle half of the data, calculated by dividing the data into four quarters. Calculating the mid-range starts in the same way as calculating the mid-mean: trim off the top and bottom quarter of the data values. Then, the mid-range is the difference between the largest and the smallest values in the middle half of the data. For the data in Table 10.3, the mid-range is 4.24 – 3.65 = 0.59. The values in the data that mark the boundaries between four equal-sized segments are called quartiles, and the mid-range is the difference between the first quartile and the third quartile. It is often given the name **interquartile range**. The second quartile is the median, with two quarters below and two quarters above. The mid-range gives an indication of how diverse the data are, without being unduly affected by a few extreme scores at either end.

Standard deviation The **standard deviation** measures average spread around the mean; it is the most typical distance (or deviation) of scores from the mean. The formula for the standard deviation is:

$$SD = \sqrt{(\Sigma(X\text{-}M)^2 / n\text{-}1)}$$

where SD stands for the standard deviation, $\sqrt{}$ is the square root symbol, and the other symbols are the same as in the formula for the mean.

The SD is calculated by working out the average squared deviation around the mean (this is called the **variance**) and then taking the square root. For each data point in turn, first work out how far it is above or below the mean (these are called deviations). The mean of the scores in Table 10.3 is 3.79, so the deviations around the mean are calculated like this:

$2.41 - 3.79 = -1.38$
$2.47 - 3.79 = -1.32$
....
$4.71 - 3.79 = +0.92$
$4.76 - 3.79 = +0.97.$

Next, each of the deviations is squared to remove the $\pm$ sign, and the average squared deviation is calculated by dividing by the number of items minus one. This gives the variance. The reasoning behind subtracting one before calculating the mean deviation is technical – dividing by n-1 rather than n makes the sample SD an unbiased estimate of the population SD. Finally, take the square root of the variance to give the standard deviation. For these data, the variance (based on using $16 - 1 = 15$ as the sample size) is 0.505, and the standard deviation is 0.71.

Comparing summary measures of spread

Just as we argued for summary measures of location, there is no single answer to the question of which measures of spread is most useful. The range is a measure of how much of the measurement scale is covered by sample data, from largest to smallest. This is sometimes useful to know, but is heavily influenced by a few extreme scores; while the mid-range is more informative especially for data which are distributed symmetrically and follow roughly a bell-shaped curve.

The most widely used summaries of spread are the standard deviation and the mid-range; and measures of location and spread tend to be paired together. Thus, the mean and the standard deviation are the basis for many parametric significance tests; while the median and the mid-range are the basis for many non-parametric significance tests. Both types of test are described in the next section of this chapter.

Importance of symmetry

A third characteristic of the shape of a set of data is the extent to which scores are distributed evenly around a central value: that is, whether the data are symmetrical. *Positively* skewed data have many small values and few large values. By contrast, *negatively* skewed data have many large values and few small ones. Why pay attention to symmetry in data? This feature is important for two reasons. Extreme values at either end of a distribution (but most likely at the high end of the range) may indicate gross errors, for which reason they should be sought out (perhaps by looking to a completed questionnaire in order to correct transcription errors, or by returning to the source of derived data) and correct values inserted instead. Data which are strongly asymmetrical are less naturally described in terms of summary measures of location. When data are symmetrical the mean and median will tend to coincide, while a symmetrical and unimodal distribution will tend to have the modal value (the most frequently occurring one) at the same point as the mean and median. When data are skewed, the different summary measures will not coincide. The mean will be influenced by the relatively small number of extreme scores, while the median will not be because it simply records the value below which 50 per cent of the scores lie.

Formal features of summary measures

This section looks at two characteristics of summary measures, robustness and efficiency, which give a stronger conceptual basis for the choices which a researcher makes between alternative summary measures of location or spread.

Robustness The extent to which a summary measure is sensitive to disturbances in data quality is known as **robustness**. There has been a lot of work by statisticians examining the consequences of robustness (or the lack of it) for commonly used summary indices and analyses which are based on them (see Jackson, 1986). Disturbances in data quality can arise either from small changes to many data values (for example by grouping of values on a measurement scale into a few categories) or by large errors in a few data values (for example by transcription errors). A summary measure is robust if disturbances like these do not greatly alter its value; while summary measures which are very sensitive to such disturbances are not robust.

We now examine three of the summary measures of location: the mean, the median and the mid-mean. Since the *mean* is the total of all the data points divided by the sample size, changing even a single data point through a transcription error would alter the mean. The more extreme the value introduced in error, the bigger would be the influence on the value of the mean. Similarly, small changes to all of the data values through, for example, grouping adjacent scores together on the measurement scale, would also alter the mean. It is obvious, therefore, that the mean is not very robust.

Since the *median* is based on the ranked scores, the effect of a single transcription error would be small, and if the error were made with either the largest or the smallest data value the media would not change at all. Changes such as coarse grouping of adjacent scores on the measurement scale would also have little effect on the value of the median. The *mid-mean* uses rank-order information to define the middle half of the data, and so extreme scores introduced in error will not have a major impact on its value, and in this respect it is robust like the median. Both the mid-mean and the median are thus more robust than the mean, and using either of them in preference to the mean would protect the researcher against disturbances in measurement quality.

Efficiency Think of getting the juice out of a lemon. First, you have to cut the lemon in half. After that there are options. However, the way that Jamie Oliver (a UK celebrity chef) uses is to squeeze each half in his hand; and this has high screen appeal but does not give all the juice that is there – its efficiency is quite low. Another way is to use a juicer to macerate the flesh of the lemon and then filter out the juice. The juicer does not look so appealing on the television, but it is more efficient because it yields more juice. Applying this principle to statistical analysis, **efficiency** refers to how much a summary measure captures all the information within the data that is relevant to what is summarized. For summary measures of location, the mean is the most efficient index we know because it uses everything about the data which is relevant to summarizing where the data are located on their measurement scale. Of course, that is the very reason why we sometimes do not use it, because some scores are suspiciously large or because we do not trust the fine detail. The median is much less efficient than the mean, since it replaces scores with their ranks; while the mid-mean (as well as other varieties of trimmed mean) is almost as efficient as the mean.

Summary of formal features of summary measures The two characteristics of summary measures tend to work in opposite directions: the mean is generally preferable to the median because it is more efficient, conversely, the median is more robust. A lot then depends on the quality of data that the researcher has available and on how well variables are measured. Researchers who have confidence in the quality of their data will tend to prefer using summary measures which are high in efficiency, such as the mean for location and the standard deviation for spread. These will work particularly well for data which are broadly symmetrical and do not have rogue values which are more extreme than the bulk of the data. In contrast, where data are more rough and ready, making the researcher uncertain about measurement quality, summary measures based on ranks (the median for location and the mid-range for spread) may be used with more confidence.

EXERCISE

10.2

Review questions for summarizing data

A A positively skewed distribution has a tail on the left hand side of the graph.

  (a) true

  (b) false

B A distribution has a mean of 65 and a median of 100. This distribution is:

  (a) symmetrical

  (b) negatively skewed

  (c) positively skewed

C A distribution can have more than one:

(a) mean

(b) median

(c) mode

D What is the median of the following set of scores: 1, 6, 17, 4?

(a) 4

(b) 5

(c) 6

(d) 7

E The value of one score in a distribution is changed from 20 to 30. Which measure(s) of location is/are bound to be changed?

(a) mean

(b) median

(c) mode

F The measure of spread that is least likely to be influenced by extreme scores is the:

(a) range

(b) mid-range

(c) standard deviation

GOING BEYOND A SAMPLE

Rationale of hypothesis testing

The greatest part of the craft of quantitative data analysis is defining the limits of generalization about study variables beyond a specific sample. The studies listed in Table 10.1 at the start of this chapter each used quantitative data to address important research questions. The authors of those studies presented their data, but their conclusions relate not just to the specific sample but to claims about theory based on the data. In general, scholars never theorize on the basis of specific data sets alone; instead, theories are statements about relationships between concepts, about boundary conditions for when those relationships occur, and about causes and consequences. **Hypothesis testing** is about making inferences about populations based upon data drawn from samples. Because we want to go beyond a sample, there is always an element of judgement or guesswork involved, and mistakes can be made. Hypothesis testing allows the researcher to define how safe it is to go beyond a specific sample of data.

To illustrate this point, we go back to the reputation data summarized in Table 10.2, where the whole dataset of 677 respondents is summarized. However, there were actually two surveys, using different methods for collecting the data.

Before drawing firm conclusions for the whole sample, it would be prudent to review the wisdom of combining data from the two sources. The first section of the data consists of 509 respondents who were customers of one utility company while the remaining 168 respondents were customers of a different utility company. For reasons of practicality, data from the two groups were collected differently. For the first sample, 2000 questionnaires were mailed to customers, and those who replied were used in the published study. For the second sample, the data were collected through a structured interview with customers entering the company's customer services department. There are a number of reasons why recorded opinions might be different between the samples:

1 The samples are made up of customers of different companies, and so responses would reflect whatever difference there might be in the reputation of the companies.

2 The same questions were asked in both surveys, but by different methods: by structured interview and by self-completion questionnaire sent in the post. It is quite possible that the method of posing the questions makes a difference to the answers that people give.

3 Respondents were approached in different ways – in the interview sample only people going to visit a company office were sampled, while the postal sample included not just that type of customer but also included people who might never visit a company office. It is difficult to be sure what difference this makes, but it is plausible to expect that it might.

The authors of the study initially hoped to be able to combine the two samples. However, they quickly hit a number of problems that led them to leave out the smaller dataset and consign it to the desk draw. Look at the histograms in Figure 10.3,

FIGURE 10.3

Histogram of reputation scores for data collected by postal survey ($n = 508$)

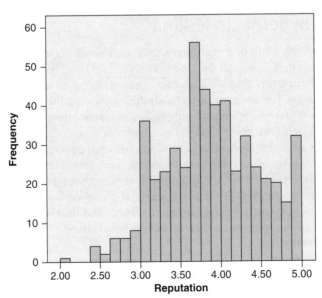

Mean = 3.8735
Std. Dev. = 0.58952
$N = 508$

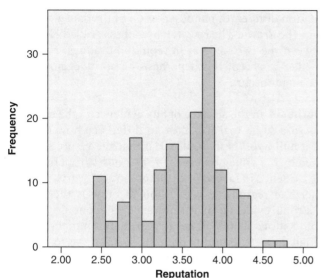

FIGURE 10.4
Histogram of reputation scores for data collected by structured interview ($n = 168$)

Mean = 3.487
Std. Dev. = 0.50528
$N = 168$

which shows the pattern of reputation scores for the sample where data were collected by postal survey, while Figure 10.4 shows the equivalent for the data collected by structured interview. The shape of the data is broadly the same for the two samples, but there are more scores at the top end of the scale for the postal survey than for the interview survey. The mean scores are also shown beside the histogram, and they reflect what we can see in the pictures: the average reputation score for the postal survey respondents is 3.87, compared with 3.49 for those respondents who were interviewed. So, it would appear that the two groups might have given different answers to the questions put to them – people who completed the postal survey seemed to be more positive about their utility supplier than those who responded to the questions in a face-to-face interview. But how confident can we be about that? The purpose of hypothesis testing is to enable the researcher to draw conclusions such as this.

Formal steps in hypothesis testing

Whatever the statistical procedure that is applied, the underlying logic is the same. This chapter concentrates on the **univariate** case (taking one dependent variable at a time) while the next chapter looks at the **multivariate** case (where many variables are considered at once). However complex the dataset, the steps are the same. We spell out the five steps using the reputation data problem as an example, and then set out in more general form what choices the researcher has in setting out to test hypotheses with data.

Step 1 – defining a research hypothesis to be tested The initial research question reflects the purpose of the study – to explore sample differences in reputation as reported by customers. The researchers had reason to believe that the two samples of customers might report reputation differently, but observation of the data alone does not allow any firm conclusion to be drawn. The research hypothesis, called H_1, is that there is a real difference between the two samples in reputation ratings. Note that making a decision about whether to accept this hypothesis or not does nothing to explain *why* such a difference might occur.

Step 2 – defining a null hypothesis In the absence of any evidence to the contrary, the simplest starting point is to assume that it makes no difference how the data were collected. This defines a **null hypothesis** (called H_0) that the responses from the postal survey are generated by the same process as the responses from the structured interview survey. If the evidence in favour of the alternative research hypothesis (H_1) is inconclusive, then the reasonable conclusion to draw is the starting position (H_0). In contrast, strong evidence of a difference in reputation scores between the two samples would allow the researcher to modify this initial position. It is important to note the logic here. The null hypothesis has nothing to do with what the researcher *wants* to be true, and neither is it anything to do with a specific theory. Instead, it reflects a simple agnostic position that the data from the two samples were generated by the same process unless there is strong evidence otherwise.

Step 3 – deriving a summary measure of a characteristic of interest Having defined a null hypothesis, the third step is to calculate a summary index based on the characteristic of interest. In this case, the natural way to express the hypotheses is in terms of summary measures of the location of the data on the reputation measurement scale. Section 2 of the chapter described three summary measures of location which could be used to test the research hypothesis: the median, the mean and the mid-mean. Whichever summary measure is chosen, the null hypothesis is that the difference between the location measures for the two samples is zero, while the alternative research hypothesis is that the difference is not zero. Thus the hypothesis test is expressed in terms of the group difference in a measure of location. The previous section showed the mean reputation scores for the two groups and the group difference is 0.39. Of course, it is unrealistic to expect a difference of precisely zero in a specific study even if it can be guaranteed that the method of collecting data makes no difference. Repeated studies with the same structure would be expected to show differences in means (or medians or mid-means) between samples; but the differences would be expected to be small most of the time and very different only infrequently. The problem that the researcher faces is: what does similar mean? How different is very different? For these data, is a mean difference of 0.39 a large or a small difference? Addressing this problem is the job of the **reference distribution** in the next step.

Step 4 – choosing a reference distribution and calculating a test statistic The logic of hypothesis testing is that convincing evidence is needed from the study data before the researcher is prepared to move away from the null hypothesis in favour of an alternative. If the null hypothesis were true, how likely is the outcome observed in the study data? Quantifying the answer to this question require the use of a **reference distribution**, which summarizes the alternatives available if the null hypothesis were true. Text books often refer to this as a **sampling distribution**, but we prefer the more general term to reflect the process of calibrating a result from one study against a reference standard. The reference distribution is not the distribution of the observations in a dataset, but rather it is the distribution of the hypothesis summary index for all possible outcomes, of which the one from a specific study is just one.

Sources of reference distributions Selecting a reference distribution involves either using extra data (over and above that from a sample) or making assumptions about the data and the process that generated it. There are four different sources of reference distributions:

1 *Standard reference distributions* are drawn from statistical theory, and choosing them is the commonest way of testing hypotheses. There are many families of reference distributions derived from theorizing about different kinds of idealised situations. For example, the **normal distribution** is the distribution of the sum of independent measures where the standard deviation of the reference distribution is known. The ***t*-distribution** is the same as the normal distribution, but differs only in that the standard deviation of the reference distribution is estimated from sample data. The **binomial distribution** is the distribution of entities which are binary (present/absent, success/failure). These distributions are used for testing hypotheses about differences in location. The **chi-square distribution** is the distribution not of means but of variances, and is used for testing hypotheses about spread. The ***F*-distribution** is the distribution of ratios of variances, and is used for testing hypotheses about group differences in the spread of mean scores. All standard reference distributions share a number of characteristics:

   a They are mathematically well-defined – their shape reflects a few features called parameters (this is the reason why tests using standard reference distributions are called **parametric tests**). For example the precise form of the normal distribution depends only upon just two quantities, the mean and standard deviation.

   b Their theoretical properties are well worked out – for example, the normal distribution is symmetrical and bell-shaped. For a normal distribution with a mean of zero and a standard deviation of one, two thirds (68 per cent) of the area under the curve lies in the range between -1 and +1 on the measurement scale: 34 per cent on either side of the mean. A further 13 per cent of the area under the curve lies either side of the mean in the range between -1 and -2 and between +1 and +2 on the measurement scale.

   c They are theoretical entities that do not exist in the real world, but researchers can use them as approximations to their own data. Thus, many of the tests to be described below (see Table 10.5) are said to assume normally distributed data. Since real data never follow precisely any of the standard reference distributions, this assumption is almost never valid. However, the practical issue is whether the approximation to normality is close enough to allow reliable inference. Statisticians agree that most statistical tests that use standard reference distributions are robust in the face of departures from the ideal assumptions provided that sample sizes are more than about 50 and that the distribution of sample data is approximately symmetrical.

2   *Permutation distributions* are reference distributions formed by finding all possible **permutations** of ranked data. For example, consider tossing two dice. Overall, there are six different outcomes for each die, making 36 outcomes in all; and the distribution of all of these 36 alternatives is the permutation distribution. There is only one way of achieving a total score of 12, by throwing two sixes; similarly there is only one way of achieving a score of 2, by throwing two ones. However, there are six ways of achieving a score of 7 (1&6, 2&5, 3&4, 4&3, 5&2, 6&1), and this is the commonest total score from throwing two dice.

As the dice example shows, permutation distributions are derived by taking all possible alternative outcomes for a specific setting, and they do not rely on assuming anything about an underlying theoretical parametric distribution for data. As a result, tests using them are called **non-parametric tests**. Examples include the Mann–Whitney U test and the Kruskal–Wallis test for differences between groups, and Kendall's rank order correlation test of association (see Table 10.5).

3   *Bootstrap distributions* are reference distributions formed by treating the available data as all there is, and drawing repeated samples from it. The **bootstrap** procedure requires heavy use of computational resources, and is only used when there is no real alternative. We will not go into details here, though an example of how it works is given by Jackson, (1986).

4   *Using archive data to form reference distributions* treats archive data as all there is, and derive the reference distribution from it. If there is a lot of information available about how data are distributed, it is sometimes appropriate to make use of that information. Again we do not go into detail, but Box, et al. (2005: ch. 2) show how it is done.

The next step in the hypothesis testing process is to calculate the difference between the two summary measures – either medians or means – for the two samples.

Step 5 – drawing a conclusion What is the probability of getting a difference as big as this if the null hypothesis were true? If the probability is small enough (the conventional criterion that is used is 1 in 20, equivalent to 5 in 100 or 5 per cent), then the researcher can conclude that the observed outcome is too surprising for the null hypothesis to be true, or stated another way, that the evidence from the data are convincing enough to modify the starting position. This is usually stated as: reject the null hypothesis at the 5 per cent level, or the difference between the groups is significant at the 0.05 level.

When someone makes a claim about how the world is on the basis of data, there are two kinds of mistakes that can be made, and these are shown in Table 10.4. In the case of the example of the two sets of data collected by structured interview and questionnaire survey, there are two conclusions that could be drawn: either that there is a difference between the two groups in how people see the reputation of the utility company, or that there is no difference. If there really is no difference between the

TABLE 10.4 Options in drawing conclusions from data

Conclusion from data	True state of affairs	
	There is no difference	**There is a difference**
Data shows no difference	Correct conclusion	Type II error
Data shows a difference	Type I error	Correct conclusion

groups but the researcher uses sample data to make the false claim that there is a difference, this is called a type I error. A **type I error** is made when someone claims a difference where none exists. On the other hand, if there really is a difference between the groups but the researcher falsely concludes that there is none then this is called a **type II error**.

The convention is that type I errors are more serious than type II errors, since the type II error is the same as retaining the initial starting point before the data were collected. The type I error amounts to changing the initial state of affairs in falsely claiming something new about the world based on data. After all, it is possible to correct an error of omission by gathering more data, while making false claims on the basis of a sample is altogether different. From time to time, there are dramatic examples of such type I errors reported in the press. These include claims of finding so-called 'cold fusion' (offering potential for unlimited free energy for the world), emissions from computer screens being harmful to unborn babies, the triple MMR vaccine as a cause of autism. All of these claims were subsequently found to be false, but each one was a source of confusion for researchers and sometimes alarm for members of the public.

Selecting the right kind of statistical test So far, we have set out the general principles of hypothesis testing, using as an example the case of comparing the means of two samples of data. We next turn our attention to deciding how to choose the right significance test for a given situation. Broadly, statistical tests can be divided into two types: those that involve testing for group differences and those that involve testing association between variables. Table 10.5 presents in summary form the key features of a number of common statistical tests in each of these two categories.

For each type of test, two versions are listed: a parametric test, which assumes that the variables are measured on continuous scales, and also that the data are at least approximately bell-shaped, like the normal distribution; and a non-parametric test, which makes the simpler assumption that the variables are measured on ordinal category scales. Thus, the choice between tests depends on what the researcher is prepared to assume about the measurement scale for the variables involved (see Chapter 9). Sometimes the answer is very straightforward. When a study asks whether there are more men than women employed at top level in a company, gender cannot be anything but measured on a *category* scale: male versus female. At other times, the issue is more a matter of judgement about the quality of measurement. When measurement quality is high, the researcher will probably be confident to think of the

TABLE 10.5 Selecting the right kind of test

Purpose	Measurement scale	Characteristic of data	Test	Null hypothesis	Test statistic	Reference distribution
(a) Testing for group differences – comparing groups						
Compare 2 groups	Continuous	Location: means	t-test	Groups are from a single population	t-value	t
	Ordered category	Location: medians	Mann–Whitney U test	Groups are from a single population	U statistic	All combinations of ranks
Compare 3 or more groups	Continuous	Location: means	Analysis of variance (ANOVA)	Groups are from a single population	F ratio	F
	Ordered category	Location: medians	Kruskal–Wallace test	Groups are from a single population	W statistic	All combinations of ranks
(b) Testing association						
Association in a contingency table	Nominal category	Co-location of scores on two variables	Chi square test	Overall distribution applies to all groups	χ^2 (chi square)	χ^2
	Category – two binary scales (0 / 1)	Co-location of scores on two variables	Phi coefficient	Overall distribution applies to all groups	Φ (phi)	R distribution
Correlation between variables	Continuous	Co-location of scores on two variables	Pearson product-moment correlation	Independence	r	R distribution
	Ordered category	Consistency of ranking on two variables	Rank-order correlation (Kendall)	Independence	τ (tau)	τ distribution

measurement scale as *continuous* and use the mean as a measure of location (choosing the mean because it is very efficient). This leads to choosing a parametric test such as the t-test or ANOVA (**analysis of variance**) for testing group differences. When there is more uncertainty about measurement quality, it is probably wiser to treat the scores as no more than ranked (an *ordinal* scale) and then rely on the median as a measure of location. This then leads to choosing non-parametric tests, which are more robust (because the summary measures they use are less influenced by extreme scores) but less efficient (because they throw away information that is in the data).

Testing for group differences – comparing groups

Table 10.5(a) lists procedures which can be used to test hypotheses about group differences in location. We distinguish between tests for comparing two groups, and more general alternatives for datasets involving three or more groups. Table 10.6 picks out research questions that involve comparing groups from some of the studies listed in Table 10.1. Table 10.6 shows the kinds of questions from each study that might involve comparing groups. Where there are only two groups to compare, the choice is between the *t*-test for comparing means and the **Mann–Whitney U test** for ranked data. For each, the table sets out how the groups were defined and what variable was involved in the group comparison. The second two examples concern hypotheses for differences between three groups, and the appropriate choice here is between the ANOVA for comparing means and the **Kruskal–Wallace test** based on ranked data. We illustrate the process of using the *t*-test for testing for differences between two groups; though the general principles apply to analysis of variance too.

TABLE 10.6 Examples of research questions which involve comparing groups

Study	Groups to compare	Dependent variable
(a) Testing for group differences – comparing two groups		
B2B relationships (Dyer and Hatch, 2006)	Two car companies - Toyota versus US	Quality of supplier products
Locating your HQ (Birkinshaw et al., 2006).	Two types of HQ – business unit versus corporate	Satisfaction of stakeholders
(b) Testing for group differences – comparing three or more groups		
SOEs in China (Ralston et al., 2006)	Three categories - privately-owned versus foreign-owned versus state-owned	Culture
MNEs' marketing strategies (Katsikeas et al., 2006)	Three groups of MNEs - US versus German versus Japanese	Marketing strategies

Worked example of the *t*-test for the reputation data The *t*-test is used to compare the mean scores of two groups of independent observations. The research hypothesis is that the two groups differ in their view of the reputation of their energy supplier, and the null hypothesis is that there is no difference such that two groups could have been defined by splitting the sample randomly into two groups. The null hypothesis is accepted unless there is sufficient evidence from the data to discard it in favour of the alternative that the two sets of observations are drawn from different populations.

The appropriate summary index that captures the relevant feature of the data is the difference between the group means. Table 10.7 shows that the mean (M_1) for the postal survey group is 2.873 ($n = 508$) and the mean (M_2) for the structured interview group is %3.487 ($n = 168$). The difference in group means is 0.386 (this is reported in Table 10.8 in the column headed 'mean difference'), and the null hypothesis is that this group difference is zero. The formula for the *t*-test is a ratio:

$$t = M_1 - M_2 / SE \text{ (diff)}$$

The top line is the difference between the group means (0.38642), and the bottom line (which makes it possible to judge how big a difference this is) is the standard error of the difference (0.05071, called *Std Error Difference* in Table 10.8 drawn from the output of SPSS). The standard error is calculated from the standard deviation and the sample size in each group. The smaller the spread of scores around the group mean and the larger the sample size, the smaller is the standard error. Applying this formula gives a *t*-value of $0.38642 / 0.05071 = 7.620$, and this is labelled as *t* on the output.

If the null hypothesis (H_0) is true, the difference in means will be close to zero most of the time, and far from zero seldom. If the alternative hypothesis (H_1) is true, the difference in means will be far from zero most of the time and close to zero seldom. Where there is prior expectation about the direction of difference between the groups, the test is called a **2-tailed test**; and where one group is expected to have a higher mean than the other, the test is called a **1-tailed test**.

In order to get an idea of how big the observed difference actually is, it is necessary to locate it on the *t*-distribution. The shape of the *t*-distribution is defined by two parameters: the mean as an estimate of location and the standard deviation as an estimate of spread. The mean of the reference distribution is estimated from the difference between the group means under the null hypothesis. The standard deviation of the reference distribution, also called the **standard error** (SE) of the difference in group means, forms the bottom line of the *t*-test formula. It is a scaling factor that allows us to say whether a given difference is large or small. The size of the standard error depends on the sample sizes in the groups and on the spread of scores around

TABLE 10.7 Summary statistics of reputation scores for two samples

Sample	N	Reputation	Std Dev.	Std. error mean
Postal survey	508	3.8735	0.58952	0.02616
Structured interview survey	168	3.4870	0.50528	0.03898

TABLE 10.8 Results of independent groups *t*-test for comparing reputation scores from two samples

| | Levene's test for equality of variances | | *t*-test for Equality of Means | | | | | 95% Confidence Interval of the Difference | |
	F	Sig	t	df	Sig. (2-tailed)	Mean Difference	Std error difference	Lower	Upper
Reputation Equal variances assumed	4.653	0.031	7.620	674	0.000	0.38642	0.05071	0.28684	0.48599
Equal variances not assumed			8.231	329.225	0.000	0.38642	0.04694	0.29407	0.47876

the mean in each of the groups. The standard error is inversely related to the total number of observations in the study, and this makes sense because most people would have more confidence in means based on large samples. It also depends on the spread around the group means in the observed data (as measured by the standard deviations of the two groups); and this too makes sense. If data points are widely dispersed around their respective group means, then the mean is a less precise indicator of where the data in each group lie on the measurement scale. Overall then, the size of the t-value obtained depends upon three things:

1 the difference in group means;

2 the spread around group means; and

3 the sample size in each group.

In general, convincing evidence about whether groups differ comes from big differences between means, small spread around those means (thus increasing their precision) and large sample sizes.

The bigger the t-value obtained, the more convincing is the evidence from the data that the initial starting position of two samples from a single population is incorrect, and needs to be modified in the light of evidence from the data. The final step is to select a significance level (conventionally $p < 0.05$), and find in the test tables the value of t which would be necessary to achieve the desired significance level. If the researcher finds that the actual t-value is greater than the tabulated value, then he or she will reject the null hypothesis that the groups are random samples from a single population at that level of significance, in favour of the alternative hypothesis that they are sampled from different populations.

The shape of the reference distribution depends on a quantity called **degrees of freedom** (or *df* on the output). For the two-sample t-test, this is calculated as the total sample size (676) minus the number of groups (2), giving the value of 674 shown in the output table. So, what is the probability of achieving a t-value as big as 7.620 if the null hypothesis were really true? This probability is shown in the column headed *Sig. (2-tailed)* as 0.000. It isn't really zero (nothing ever has a truly zero probability) but this is where SPSS has rounded to three decimal places – we would refer to this probability as less than 0.00049 (because that is the largest number that we would round down to give 0.000). Whatever it is called, this value is a small probability, and the conclusion is that the null hypothesis is very unlikely to be true, and is rejected in favour of the alternative that the groups really do differ. Expressed in the language of the study, the group surveyed by postal survey have a more positive view of their energy supplier's reputation than the second group surveyed by structured interview. Most people would be very confident about this conclusion from these data, because the test statistic is so large. However, it is possible that the conclusion is wrong and the null hypothesis may actually be true. In that case, the claim that the two groups differ would be a type I error.

Testing association between variables

If there is an **association** between two variables, then knowing how someone responds on one variable carries information that can be used to predict their response

TABLE 10.9 Examples of research questions which involve testing association between variables

Study	Association between	
Influencing companies on environmental issues (Eesley and Lenox, 2006)	Different stakeholder actions	Positive corporate responses
MNEs' marketing strategies (Katsikeas et al., 2006)	Standardisation of marketing strategy	Market environment
Locating your HQ (Birkinshaw et al., 2006).	HQ – business unit/corporate	Satisfying stakeholders
Is CSR smart as well as good? (Luo and Bhattacharya, 2006)	CSR activities of companies – cash donations/employee volunteering	Market value of company/ customer satisfaction

on the other. There is a *positive* association between two variables when high scores on one tend to occur with high scores on the other, and similarly for low scores. A *negative* association is shown by people responding with high scores on one variable but low scores on the other. A *zero* association indicates that knowing about one variable does not help in telling us anything about the other. Table 10.9 shows examples of association between variables from the studies in Table 10.1.

Different kinds of association between variables can be illustrated using artificial data for 10 people. Figure 10.5 shows a strong *positive association* between two variables, labelled as Var1 and Var3. Along the bottom of the plot is the scale for Var1, with high scores to the right and low scores to the left. Along the side of the plot is the scale for Var3, with high scores to the top and low scores to the bottom. The data points tend to congregate along the diagonal of the plot – top right and bottom left. This is what would be expected of a strong positive association, and knowing an individual's score on one of the variables would allow a reasonable guess about that person's score on the other. Figure 10.6 shows a strong *negative association* between two variables, labelled as Var1 and Var2. Once again, the scale at the bottom shows Var1, with high scores to the right and low scores to the left. Along the side of the plot is the scale for Var2, and high scores are to the top and low scores to the bottom. This time, the data points tend to congregate along the opposite diagonal of the plot – top left and bottom right. This is what would be expected of a strong negative association. Finally, Figure 10.7 shows two variables with no obvious pattern of association to suggest a relationship between the two, and the correlation coefficient is zero.

The specific test for association between two variables depends on the measurement scale. For variables measured on nominal category scales the *Chi-square test* (χ^2) is appropriate. Where the measurement scale is either ordinal or continuous association between variables is assessed by a *correlation coefficient*. The correlation coefficient for continuous scales is the Pearson product-moment correlation. For data measured in the form of ranks, the Kendall rank-order correlation is used.

FIGURE 10.5

An artificial dataset showing a positive association between two variables (Pearson product-moment correlation = 0.954; Kendall rank-order correlation = 0.867)

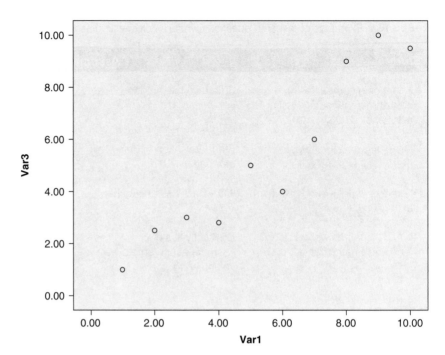

FIGURE 10.6

An artificial dataset showing a negative association between two variables (Pearson product-moment correlation = -0.954; Kendall rank-order correlation = -0.867)

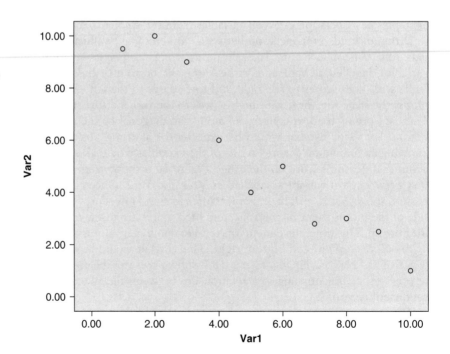

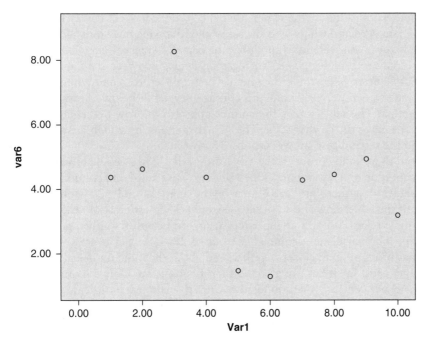

FIGURE 10.7
An artificial dataset showing no association between two variables (Pearson product-moment correlation = –0.264; Kendall rank-order correlation = –0.156)

Testing association for category measurement scales: the Chi-square test While it is possible to draw a scatterplot looking for association between variables measured on category scales, it is generally more convenient and informative to use a contingency table to show how a sample is divided up according to each person's score on the two variables under consideration. Contingency tables do not have to be two-way, but they get much harder to read when we use more than two variables to divide up the sample. The Chi-square test is used to test association between two category variables measured on nominal scales.

An example of a contingency table is shown in Table 10.10, and this is taken from a study by Anya Johnson, a doctoral student. She carried out a worldwide survey (18 countries) of over 3000 professional managers (both men and women) who had been made redundant by their company and then enrolled in a career transition programme to help

EXERCISE

10.3

Performing a significance test

Use the applications in Table 10.6 for comparing groups and in Table 10.9 for testing association between variables. Select one of the following examples from each table, and describe in narrative form the five steps of performing a significance test, and write a short description of your conclusion if the significance test were:

(1) statistically significant;

(2) statistically not significant.

them get another job. One of the things that the student looked at was the effect of job loss on family relationships, and she asked the following question: 'What is the effect of job loss on your relationship with your partner/spouse?' They could select from three responses: *bringing you closer together, having no effect at all* and *causing relationship difficulties*. She wondered whether unemployed men and women would answer this question differently, and the contingency table below shows the two variables together. The table shows the counts, and also the row percentages: each count as a percentage of the row total. The first row shows how men answered the question, and the second row shows responses for women.

The bottom right-hand corner of the table shows that 2861 people answered the relationship question and also reported their gender. The right-hand column with the row totals shows that there are 2232 men in the analysis, and 629 women. The bottom row of the table shows how people answered the question about the effect of job loss on their relationship, and the effect seems to be mostly either positive or neutral. About four out of ten people (1175 out of 2861, 41 per cent) say that the experience has brought them closer together, and about the same number (1150 out of 2861, 40 per cent) say it has not affected their relationship. Only a minority (536 out of 2861, 19 per cent) say that job loss has caused relationship difficulties.

One of the key questions that Johnson asked was whether the effect of the experience was different for men and women. In other words, is there an association between gender and the effect of job loss on the quality of the relationship with partner? An initial step in addressing this question is to look at the pattern of responses for men and women separately, using the row percentages. For men, 43 per cent say that job loss has brought them closer together compared to 35 per cent for women – so men tend to be more positive about how job loss has affected the relationship with their partner. Corresponding to this, 18 per cent of men say that job loss has caused relationship difficulties, compared to 21 per cent of women – men are again more positive, or less negative than women. Overall then, there does seem to be an association between gender and impact of job loss on partner relationship.

Interpretation of this result is quite complicated. It could be that losing a job is really more damaging to the family relationships of women than it is for men; but it could also be that that harm is equally strong for both sexes, but that women are more aware of it than men are. From the semi-structured interviews that Johnson carried out she suspected that the second interpretation was more likely. These tended

TABLE 10.10 Contingency table showing frequencies of men and women according to the reported effect of job loss on the relationship with their partner

	Brings closer	No difference	Causes difficulties	Total
Men	952 (43%)	874 (39%)	406 (18%)	2232
Women	223 (35%)	276 (44%)	130 (21%)	629
Total	1175 (41%)	1150 (40%)	536 (19%)	2861

to show that men are less aware of their own feelings and those of their partner than are women, and so do not notice when relationship problems exist.

Having looked at the data, it would appear that there is an association between gender and the effect of job loss on the relationship, but this can be tested formally using the χ^2 test of association. The null hypothesis for the χ^2 test of association is that there is no relationship between the two variables. For a contingency table this means that the distribution of responses for the total sample (shown by the percentages in the bottom row of the table) applies equally to both men and women. The alternative hypothesis is that the distribution of responses is different for men and women; and that seems to be the case for these data.

Just as with any significance test, the purpose is to estimate how likely would be the pattern observed in the data if the null hypothesis were true; and the test statistic, χ^2, for this table is 10.522 (see Table 10.11, where it is referred to as Pearson χ^2). The degrees of freedom for the test with these data are 2 (for χ^2 this is calculated as (number of rows – 1) times (number of columns – 1) = 2). The probability of getting a distribution of data like this if there really is no association between gender and the effect on relationship is shown as 0.005, or five in a thousand. This is a small number, so the odds of the null hypothesis being true are small; and the null hypothesis is rejected at the 0.005 level. Johnson concluded that there is a gender difference in how people see the effect of job loss on the relationship with their partner.

Testing association for continuous and ordered category scales: correlation between variables For variables measured on scales which are at least ordered, association can be tested using a correlation coefficient. For continuous scales (whether interval or ratio), the test of choice is the Pearson product-moment correlation (r); while the test of choice for ordinal category scales is a rank-order correlation coefficient developed by Kendall (Kendall's *tau*) though there is another one developed by Spearman (Spearman's *rho*) which is less commonly used. We have already seen (Figures 10.6–8) examples where the two forms of correlation lead to the same conclusion. Here, we look at more complex circumstances.

Figure 10.8 shows the scatterplot for two artificial variables and the Pearson product-moment correlation coefficient is 0.516, suggesting a positive relationship. But this is nonsense for the dataset as a whole as the scatterplot clearly shows: all the data points bump along at the bottom of the plot, apart from a single extreme score in the

TABLE 10.11 Chi-square test of association between gender and effect of job loss on relationship quality

	Value	df	Significance (2-sided)
Pearson chi-square	10.522 8.380	2	0.005
N of valid cases	2861		

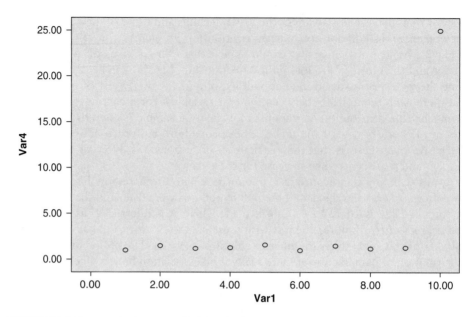

FIGURE 10.8 Scatterplot for two artificial variables showing a spurious positive correlation (Pearson product-moment correlation = 0.516; Kendall rank-order correlation = 0.116)

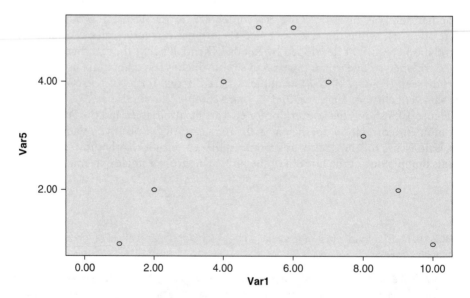

FIGURE 10.9 Scatterplot for two artificial variables showing a systematic but not linear association (Pearson product-moment correlation = 0.000; Kendall rank-order correlation = 0.000)

top right-hand corner. The Kendall rank-order correlation coefficient uses information only about the ranked scores for each variable and its value is much lower (0.116).

Figure 10.9 shows the scatterplot for two more artificial variables, this time with a perfect positive association between the variables on the left hand side and a perfect negative association on the right hand side. The value of both correlation coefficients is zero, and the researcher would conclude that there is no relationship between the two variables. However, this conclusion is misleading because there clearly is a relationship – as Var1 increases, the other variable first goes up and then goes down, but it is not a straight-line relationship. This form of relationship is called **curvilinear**; and it is not easy to summarize such complex relationships with a single measure of association. Instead, it often makes sense to divide the data into segments and calculate correlation coefficients for each segment separately. Here the correlation coefficient is +1 for the first five cases of Var1 and -1 for the second five cases.

There are two lessons to learn from this simple example. First, correlation coefficients summarize only **linear** forms of association between variables. Second, while it is tempting to rush straight into hypothesis testing there is real value in looking at graphical displays first.

CONCLUSION

In this chapter we have described methods of looking at data and the key features that the researcher should pay attention to before summarizing those features using summary statistics. Our key points here are:

- **Choosing one form of summary measure of location and spread over another has the effect of emphasizing some features of data and neglecting others.**

- **There is a common logic for all forms of hypothesis test regardless of complexity.**

- **Choosing a specific test depends on what is the form of the hypothesis and the measurement scale of the variables involved.**

The next chapter builds on the principles of hypothesis testing, applying them to the multivariate case where variables are considered together.

FURTHER READING

Howell, D. (2001) *Statistical Methods for Psychology*, 5th edn. Wadsworth.

Howell, D. (2007) *Fundamental Statistics for the Behavioral Sciences*, 6th edn. Wadsworth.

Both books go into more detail on the logic of hypothesis testing and describe a much more extensive set of statistical tests for comparing groups or testing association between variables. The strengths of the author's approach are that he emphasizes the importance of looking at data intelligently before making decisions about forms of analysis, and he also explains clearly the conceptual underpinnings of the methods that are covered.

MULTIVARIATE ANALYSIS

11

Introduction

Multivariate analysis of measurement models

Multivariate analysis of causal models

Conclusion

Further reading

LEARNING OBJECTIVES

- To identify the variables in a narrative statement of a research question.

- To frame research questions according to alternative forms of multivariate statistical models.

- To turn a research question into a form that can be analysed statistically.

- To identify the appropriate form of multivariate method for a specific research question.

INTRODUCTION

Domain of multivariate analysis

The social world that we all live in is a complex system, and can't really be understood by looking at one thing at a time: causes interact with each other in complex ways; effects are not always simple to measure. Table 11.1 lists studies from the management literature that use **multivariate methods** to test theoretical propositions.

The complication arises because most of the interesting things researchers want to look at are correlated with each other. The tools and methods that we considered in the previous chapter are basic ones for working with quantitative data, but they are not enough to deal with the complexities of the world of work. This chapter on multivariate analysis builds on the previous two, but it is more advanced because it deals with analytical methods for looking at complex data, and these are intrinsically more difficult than the univariate methods that were considered in the previous chapter.

The purpose of multivariate analysis is to find a way of summarizing the relationship between variables that is simpler than the original data but also captures the essence of that relationship. In that respect, working with quantitative data is no different from working with research evidence in any other form (see Chapter 8): research seeks out a conceptual model which is both simpler and richer. Simplicity is desirable so that the model is understandable; richness is desirable so that the model can stimulate new ways of thinking about the world. The models that are used in multivariate analysis are mathematical models, and a full understanding of multivariate statistics requires a fair amount of facility with matrix algebra. However, in this chapter we give a conceptual introduction to some of the methods which can then be built on in a more advanced way.

TABLE 11.1. Examples of studies using multivariate statistical methods

Authors and date	Dependent variable (DV)	Predictor variables (PV)
Coyle-Shapiro and Kessler (2000)	Commitment of employees to the organization	Fulfilment of the psychological contract
Brouthers and Brouthers (2003)	Mode of entry into foreign markets	Service and manufacturing organizations
Thompson (2004)	Decline in national competitiveness	Cost factors or institutional arrangements
Filatotchev (2006)	The entry of firms into public ownership	Characteristics of executives and involvement of venture capital

Forms of interdependence in management research

There are many kinds of interdependency among concepts within the domain of management research. The first kind of interdependence is *interaction effects* where variables have different effects depending on the context, and these have been examined in the form of **contingency theories**. Examples of contingency theories can be found in cross-cultural management (for example, what works well in a US business negotiation would cause deep offence among Arabs), in organizational design (different forms of organizing are needed to deal with rapidly changing markets compared to the stable bureaucracies that most people work in (Brown and Eisenhardt, 1998), and in guidance on how organizations can effectively manage worker stress (Jackson and Parker, 2001).

The second kind of interdependency is that of **synergy;** one of the favourite buzz words of the management change consultant. The idea is a simple one: plant a seed, give it both warmth and water and it will grow. Water alone will make it rot, warmth alone may lead the seed to become dormant; but both together can achieve the miracle of making a new plant. This is the logic behind many organizational mergers where the capabilities of different partners are brought together with the intent of making a step change in performance.

The third kind of interdependency is that *influences on performance tend to occur together*, either because they affect each other or because they have common causes. Several of the studies in Table 11.1 share the same feature, that they control for organizational size in their analysis (for example, Brouthers et al., 2003; Filatotchev, 2006). Looking at the Brouthers et al. study first, their logic was simple – they were not directly interested in differences between large and small firms but they know that size makes a difference to lots of things, so ignoring it would probably bias answers to questions they were interested in. They wanted to study how service and manufacturing firms went about internationalization by entering new foreign markets. If the service firms in their sample were smaller (or larger) on average than the manufacturing ones then conclusions based on a comparison between the two sectors would be confounded by differences in size. As a result, including the size of the firm in statistical analysis makes sense. Filatotchev used the same logic in his efforts in explaining what happens when entrepreneurial firms first go into public ownership through initial public openings (IPOs).

Ways of dealing with interdependence within quantitative analysis

In this section, we consider four ways of dealing with interrelated influences (see Table 11.2). Three of them involve simplification: through design, through selecting sub-samples and through statistical control. The final method is multivariate analysis, and this forms the main focus of this chapter. While all four methods are useful, most people develop a preference to suit their own style or the options open to them in their research area.

Simplification through design The first way of dealing with interrelated influences is to design the study so that relevant causal factors are made independent of each

TABLE 11.2 How to deal with interrelated factors

Method	Action
1. Simplification through design	When sampling select equal numbers within sub-groups
2. Simplification through selecting sub-samples	Restrict sample to one level of a key variable
3. Simplification through statistical control	Take variables two at a time, and use partial correlations to achieve statistical control
4. Multivariate analysis	Use multiple predictors and consider their joint influence

other through the design itself. Consider the case of age and salary level: as people get older their experience grows and their salary level tends to go up. Thus there is an association between age and salary that can be summarized by a positive correlation (see Chapter 10). If a researcher picks employees at random then the sample will be likely to reflect this association. However, another approach would be to divide the potential sample into groups based on age, and then select equal numbers of people at a number of salary levels within each age range. Even though age and salary may be correlated within the organization as a whole, the effect of this sampling strategy would be to create a sample of respondents where the two are independent of each other. The linkage between the two variables would not then be present in the sample.

The craft of research design (Shadish et al., 2002) is about developing imaginative ways of achieving simplicity of inference through creating a study design within which factors are orthogonal where they are not independent of each other in the world at large. Such study designs are linked to statistical methods called **analysis of variance (ANOVA)**, and designs with multiple factors are called factorial designs. Because they make analysis and inference simple even in research areas with many inter-related complicating factors, they have developed a strong appeal for some kinds of people. Experimental approaches based on structured research designs are widely used particularly in work psychology, marketing and information systems research.

Simplification through selecting a sub-sample The second way of dealing with interrelated influences is through selecting samples to be equal on potentially confounding factors. It is common to find that women are paid less than men, and one of the reasons is that women and men tend to do different jobs, which in turn command different pay levels. In random samples of men and women at work then, there will be different mixes of jobs for the two groups as well as differences in pay levels; and it is difficult to disentangle the relative influence of gender and job type. However, restricting a study sample to people doing the same job would mean that any gender difference cannot be attributed to job type but must be due to something else. The same logic was used by Hofstede (1991) in his research on national culture, where he gathered data only from IBM employees working in many countries across the world rather than by drawing random samples in each country. The differences he found led him to conclude that there were four basic dimensions of national culture: power distance, masculine–feminine, individual–collective, and uncertainty avoidance (he later added long-term orientation). Relying on samples drawn from only one company means that he is controlling for differences in labour markets across the world (though critics have argued that he has reduced the generalizability of his findings by doing this).

Simplification through statistical control The third way to deal with interrelated influences is through a form of statistical control called **partial correlation**. We have already seen in Chapter 10 that a correlation is a way of summarizing the extent to which people respond to two variables in consistent ways. A partial correlation is a correlation between two variables (we call them A and B) where the value of a third variable (we call this S) is adjusted statistically as if it were equal to the sample mean for everybody (this is usually referred to as *holding constant* a third variable). The correlation between A and B is written as r_{AB}. The symbol for the partial correlation is $r_{AB|S}$. The method of partial correlation allows the researcher to see how much of an observed correlation, say between A and B, can be accounted for by the relationship that both variables have with a third variable, S.

Table 11.3 presents three possible patterns for r_{AB} and $r_{AB|S}$. We will use an example to explain the three patterns. Social media technologies such as blogs (Scoble and Israel, 2006) are rapidly becoming popular, and it would not be surprising to find correlations between willingness to use blogs for external marketing, B, and both age, A, and salary level, S. A correlation between age and blogging, r_{AB}, could be interpreted in terms of conservatism of older people when it comes to embracing change. A correlation between blogging and salary, r_{BS}, could be interpreted in terms of more senior people in the organization having fewer direct links with customers. We have already suggested that a correlation between age and salary is plausible, r_{AS}; and so all three variables are likely to be correlated. The partial correlation of age and blogging with salary held constant identifies that part of the total correlation which is independent of salary. Pattern 1 shows a high AB correlation and also a high AB|S partial correlation, and here the S variable has not altered the correlation between A and B. Pattern 2 shows a high AB correlation but a zero AB|S partial correlation, and in this case the researcher would conclude that A and B are not really correlated at all. The relationship suggested by the AB correlation is spurious. Finally, pattern 3 shows an unusual but interesting case, where the AB correlation is zero suggesting that A and B

TABLE 11.3 Example of possible relationships between correlation and partial correlation

Pattern	Interpretation
1. r_{AB} is high; $r_{AB|S}$ is high	A and B are related; and S is irrelevant to both
2. r_{AB} is high; $r_{AB|S}$ is zero	A and B are not really related at all; but S has contributed to the appearance of a relationship between A and B
3. r_{AB} is zero; $r_{AB|S}$ is high	S is masking the 'real' relationship between A and B

are not related at all. However, a high partial correlation implies that there really is a relationship between the two, but one that has been masked by the third variable, S.

Multivariate analysis The final way of dealing with many interrelated factors builds on this logic of statistical control but extends it to many variables and also to predictive relationships rather than simple associations as measured by correlations. Multivariate statistical methods are designed to allow researchers to include many variables in a single analysis and to assess the separate contribution of each variable within an overall model. These methods are the focus of the rest of this chapter. Their main feature is the specification of a conceptual model that expresses the researcher's hypotheses about the relationships among variables. The variables to be included in a model will be defined by the focus of the research. Business and management researchers get excited by very different things. For example, in some of the studies considered already in this chapter, the size of the firm is treated as a 'nuisance' factor, which gets in the way of finding clear answers to interesting questions. However, there are other scholars for whom understanding the factors that make firms grow is the very focus of their work, and the size of the firm is not a nuisance factor at all.

Once a decision is made about which variables to include in a model, the next step is to specify what role each variable has in the model, usually as a cause (a predictor variable) or as an effect (a dependent variable). Making a decision about whether something is a dependent variable or a predictor variable is really a decision about how a variable is treated in the researcher's thinking. It is not an intrinsic characteristic of a variable, but instead a function of how it is used in a particular circumstance. This will depend to a large extent on the focus of a specific research project. Note that the role that a variable plays in statistical analysis reflects its position in the researcher's thinking, not something about the variable itself. The role that a variable plays in a researcher's model may even change within a study. Thus the paper by Coyle-Shapiro and Kessler (2000) reports one analysis where perceived organizational support is treated as a dependent variable; and later in the paper the authors use the same variable as a predictor of organizational commitment. So, its role changes from dependent variable to predictor variable.

Multivariate models can be specified using matrix algebra for those with a strong mathematical training, and also represented graphically for those without such a background. We will use the graphical representation in this chapter for the sake of simplicity (see Figure 11.1). Variables are shown by boxes, which may be either rectangular or elliptical; and relationships among variables are shown by either single-headed or double-headed arrows. The variables used in multivariate models may be of two kinds: those which are measured directly by the researcher, called **observed variables**, and **latent variables** which are not measured directly but are inferred from observed variables. Observed variables are shown by rectangular boxes, and latent variables are shown by elliptical boxes.

Figure 11.1(A) shows a model for observed variables, with a single dependent variable to the right (DV) and two predictor variables (PV1 and PV2). The assumed causal relationship between the PVs and the DV is indicated by the single-headed arrows. The double-headed arrow connecting the two PVs indicates an association between them which may or may not reflect a causal relationship (this relationship is

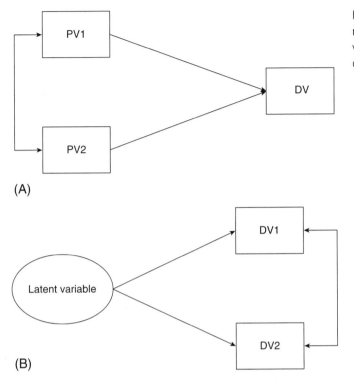

FIGURE 11.1 Graphical representation of multivariate models: (A) three observed variables (one DV and two PVs); (B) two observed DVs and one latent PV

(A)

(B)

called **exogenous**, because the specified model does not concern itself with its origins: it is taken as a given). Figure 11.1(B) shows a model with two observed variables (DV1 and DV2) and one latent predictor variable (LV). The LV is assumed to be a cause of both DV1 and DV2.

The next sections provide introductions to two kinds of multivariate analysis methods: methods for analysing measurement models and methods for analysing **causal models**. Measurement models explore the relationship between observed variables and latent variables. Causal models are of two kinds: those that involve only observed variables and those that involve both observed and latent variables.

MULTIVARIATE ANALYSIS OF MEASUREMENT MODELS

Rationale for measurement models

It is often not possible to measure directly the characteristic that a researcher is interested in, and it may be necessary to rely on indirect indicators of it. This is very common in studies using secondary data sources (see Chapter 9) where variables that are present in a dataset are often used as *proxies* for constructs that are the main focus of interest but are not themselves available directly. For example, the success of a company entering into a new market could be shown using a number of different ways of defining success (e.g. market share, speed of growth, cost of capital to fund the expansion, satisfaction of new customers, profitability, share price), and looking at just one of them would probably be misleading.

Where a construct cannot be observed directly, it is common practice to select a set of items that are assumed to reflect the construct. A **measurement model** is then the relationship between a set of observed variables and the construct that they are intended to measure. Then answers are combined together to form a composite variable to represent the construct (Spector, 1992). The rationale behind this approach is that many of the characteristics that management researchers are interested in are complex (particularly in marketing and work psychology), being made up of different elements. A simple-minded approach to measurement would take the following view: If we want to measure how people see the reputation of an organization, then just ask them 'does company X have a good reputation?'. While this approach has some appeal on grounds of simplicity, it scarcely does justice to the complexity of the concept of corporate reputation (Davies et al., 2002). Individuals' attitudes, motivation and commitment are all impossible to observe directly, but understanding them is key to explaining why consumers buy what they do, and why workers either stay in a job or leave it. In such circumstances, the researcher is faced with the choice of whether to select a single variable for analysis or to combine several variables together into a single index. The latter approach has many advantages: it allows greater richness in measurement, capturing nuances of a construct, and it also allows the researcher to assess how reliably the construct has been measured.

Structure of measurement models

The basic logic here is that items which reflect features of an underlying construct will show common patterns of answering. For example, a manager who feels good about his or her job will tend to respond in a consistently favourable way to questions about different aspects of that job. Consistency in responses from study participants will produce correlations among items, and these correlations are the starting point for identifying patterns that reflect underlying constructs. In a measurement model (Figure 11.2), the observed variables are those which are measured directly by the researcher, and the latent variables are the constructs which the researcher assumes are causal factors in how sample members respond to the observed variables.

Figure 11.2 shows a measurement model for six measured variables and two unmeasured latent variables. The model distinguishes between two influences on how respondents answer for each observed variable:

1 Those that reflect common features of the constructs being assessed, indicated by the two **common factors**. The first common factor is what respondents are assumed to have in mind when they respond to variables 1–3, while the second common factor is assumed to influence answers for variables 4–6. The stronger the influence of the common factors (this is the value attached to each of the paths in Figure 11.2, and is called a **factor loading**), the higher will be the correlations among the observed variables.

2 Those that are idiosyncratic to the wording of each variable, indicated by the **specific factors**, one for each observed variable. These are unique to that question and will not influence answers to other questions.

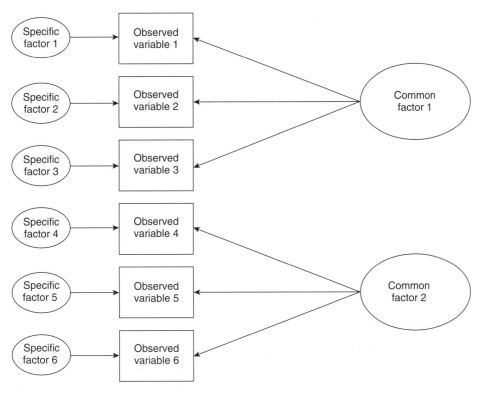

FIGURE 11.2 A measurement model for six observed variables and two latent variables

The **reliability** of a composite scale depends on the average correlation among the observed variables and is measured by the **Cronbach's alpha coefficient** (a value greater than 0.80 indicates an acceptable level of reliability).

Table 11.4 shows what the pattern of correlations would look like if the factor loadings for all observed variables were set at 0.60. Taking the correlation between observed variable 1 and observed variable 2 as an example, the value of 0.36 for the correlation between them is calculated by tracing the paths linking the two variables in the figure and multiplying the loadings for each path. Thus, $0.6 \times 0.6 = 0.36$. The first group of three observed variables are all correlated with each other, reflecting the fact that they share loadings on the first common factor; and the second group of three observed variables are also correlated reflecting the influence of the second common factor. Furthermore, the bottom left area of the correlation matrix contains only zero correlations because the two blocks of variables (1–3 and 4–6) do not share loadings on a common factor with each other.

Analysis methods for measurement models

Sometimes, the researcher has a set of questionnaire items with no clear idea of what constructs might underlie them, and here the method of choice for analysing the

TABLE 11.4 Hypothetical correlation matrix showing the pattern of correlations for six observed variables and two latent variables

	1	2	3	4	5	6
1	-					
2	0.36	-				
3	0.36	0.36	-			
4	0	0	0	-		
5	0	0	0	0.36	-	
6	0	0	0	0.36	0.36	-

measurement model is **exploratory factor analysis** (EFA). More commonly, though, researchers know what constructs they are trying to measure and design their questionnaires to do just that. In that case, the aim is not to explore what constructs there might be but rather to confirm (or otherwise) a structure that has been designed into a study. This leads to **confirmatory factor analysis** (CFA) as the method of choice. Both types of model share a distinction between common factors and specific factors. Where the methods differ is in the prior specification of a measurement model. EFA analyses can be carried out by many general purpose statistical packages, such as SPSS (Bryman and Cramer, 2004); while CFA requires one of the specialist SEM programs which we consider later.

In the *EFA* method, there may be as many common factors as there are observed variables; and all the observed variables have loadings on all the common factors. The method derives estimates for the factor loadings of each of the common factors and the specific factors, and gives summary indices (called **eigenvalues**) of the importance of each of the common factors, shown by how much of the covariation among the observed variables each one accounts for. The researcher uses these estimates to select a subset of common factors, usually retaining only the largest. The size of the loadings for the common factors determines the correlations among the observed variables. The size of the loadings for the specific factors determines the reliability of the common factors.

In the *CFA* method, the researcher defines in advance how many common factors are expected and the pattern of predicted loadings for observed variables. Observed variables are usually assumed to load on only one factor. The method derives estimates for each of the factor loadings for common factors and for specific factors, and gives an overall test statistic for how well the measurement model fits the data. Ullman (2006b) gives a readable introduction to CFA with particular reference to personality assessment, and shows how measurement models can be fitted and tested using the EQS program (http://www.mvsoft.com).

EXAMPLE 11.1

Measurement models for measures of work design characteristics: EFA and CFA results

This examples takes six variables from the dataset used by Sprigg and Jackson (2006) in their study of the impact of work design on the health of call handlers in UK call centres. The variables fall into two groups: three items measuring timing control, the extent to which call handlers had control over work timing (TC), and skill utilization (SU), how much their work enabled them to use the skills they had. The sample was large, over 1000 people drawn from a large number of call centres throughout the UK.

The matrix of correlations is shown in Table 11.5(a). It is clear that they form two groups reflecting the constructs that the items were designed to measure. The factor loadings from exploratory factor analysis are shown in Table 11.5(b). The first thing to note is that there are two factors, as would be expected, and that all six variables have loadings on both factors. The second thing to note is that the loadings of the three timing control items are very high on the first factor, but very low on the second factor; while the reverse is true for the skill utilization items. It would be reasonable to label the two factors according to the content of the times that load on them, and that is what we have done in the table. However, this is an inference on our part; the statistical analysis is agnostic about what these latent variables are called.

Table 11.5(c) gives the factor loadings for confirmatory factor analysis, and the major difference is that each item is constrained to loads only onto one factor. The values of zero are called fixed values because they were constrained as part of the input specification for CFA. The reason is that we hypothesized that the first three items would measure a timing control construct and the second three items would measure a skill utilization construct. The factor loadings from CFA are not identical to those given by the EFA analysis, because the models that were fitted to the data are different; but the conclusion is broadly the same. Finally, the measurement model from CFA is shown diagrammatically in Figure 11.3.

MULTIVARIATE ANALYSIS OF CAUSAL MODELS

Rationale for causal models

Causality cannot be proved Using multivariate statistical methods to test causal models is a very powerful technique that is widely used within management research. Its major value is that it forces the researcher to define very precisely both the variables to be included and the way in which they relate to each other. In return, the statistical methods offer specific tests of hypotheses that can allow the researcher to

TABLE 11.5 Measurement model for measures of work design characteristics: EFA and CFA results

(a) Matrix of correlations among variables

	TC1	TC2	TC3	SU1	SU2	SU3
TC1	-					
TC2	0.40	-				
TC3	0.48	0.45	-			
SU1	0.16	0.16	0.14	-		
SU2	0.16	0.18	0.15	0.52	-	
SU3	0.16	0.15	0.13	0.55	0.56	-

(b) Factor loadings from exploratory factor analysis

	Timing control	Skill utilization
TC1	0.78	0.10
TC2	0.76	0.11
TC3	0.82	0.06
SU1	0.09	0.82
SU2	0.12	0.82
SU3	0.09	0.84

(c) Factor loadings from confirmatory factor analysis

	Timing control	Skill utilization
TC1	0.61	0
TC2	0.67	0
TC3	0.63	0
SU1	0	0.78
SU2	0	0.73
SU3	0	0.71

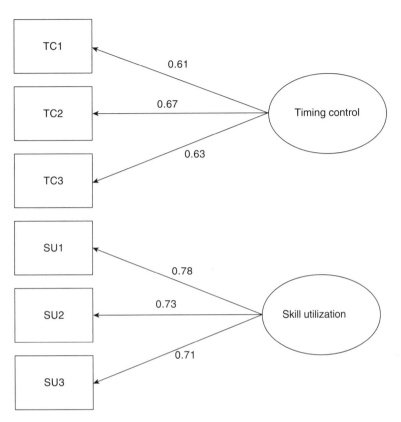

FIGURE 11.3 Measurement model for measures of work design characteristics: CFA results

judge how good those models are. However, what causal modelling methods cannot do is prove a causal relationship. Instead, they allow decisions to be made about whether a given model is consistent with observed data. The plausibility of a particular model needs first to be established conceptually from theory, and then quantitative evidence can be used to assess whether the model is consistent with data. Consider again the study by Coyle-Shapiro and Kessler (2000) from Table 11.1. In their article, they developed a theoretical rationale for treating employee commitment as a dependent variable and psychological contract fulfilment as a predictor variable. Unless they have longitudinal data, with variables measured on more than one occasion, it is impossible for them to prove that this assumption is correct. Instead, all they can do is assess whether the conceptual model that they formulated is consistent with their data.

Defining what variables to include in the model This step is important because any causal model will estimate the best values that it can for the contribution of each variable that is included. However, the estimation procedure can only take into account the information it has available to it. If the researcher leaves out (by accident or by design) a factor that is critically important, then the modelling procedure cannot find it, and the results obtained can be misleading.

Specifying causal models Research propositions should be translated into formal causal models that can be tested statistically; either as a single model or as a sequence of models of increasing complexity. Comparison of a simple model with a more complex one is a powerful way of testing research hypotheses, but it is important to remember that a more complex model, one which includes more variables or has more complex relationships among them, will always give a better fit to a given dataset. So, **goodness of fit** alone is not the most important criterion in selecting the best model. Instead, the researcher needs to take into account what the gain in the quality of the model is relative to the added complexity needed to achieve it. An example of the development of a series of causal models is shown in Example 11.2.

EXAMPLE 11.2

Stakeholder relationship management and corporate financial performance: formulating alternative causal models

This example considers different accounts of how stakeholder relationship management links to corporate strategy and to the performance of the organization (Freeman, 1984; Cornelissen, 2004). Berman et al. (1999) propose two kinds of model, the normative model and the instrumental model, and show how they can be tested empirically. The *normative* model states that looking after the interests of stakeholders is the right thing to do, and that the strategic goals set by senior management will be determined by a need to protect and promote the interests of their stakeholders. So principles of stakeholder relationship management guide how the organization formulates its corporate strategy, and strategy in turn has some influence on financial performance. Figure 11.4 expresses the normative model using blocks for the key variables and arrows to show the hypothesised causal relationships among them.

The *instrumental* model (Figure 11.5) states that organizations should pay attention to their stakeholders because they will benefit financially; and thus the model proposes that both stakeholder relationship management and corporate strategy influence corporate financial performance. Berman et al. propose two variants of the instrumental model: the direct effects model shown in Figure 11.5(A) and the moderation model shown in Figure 11.5(B). The direct effects

FIGURE 11.4 The normative model of stakeholder relationship management and corporate financial performance

SOURCE: Used with permission of Academy Management from *Does Stakeholder Orientation Matter* by Berman et al., Volume 42(5) 1999; permission conveyed through Copyright Clearance Center, Inc.

EXAMPLE 11.2

Stakeholder relationship management and corporate financial performance: formulating alternative causal models—cont'd

model differs from the normative model in that there is no path between corporate strategy and stakeholder relationship management but there is a direct path from stakeholder relationship management to financial performance. The moderation model is a more sophisticated version of the direct effects model which proposes a different mechanism for the role of stakeholder relationship management, as modifying the link between strategy and performance. The logic behind this form of the model is that companies will find it easier to put their strategic goals into practice and benefit from them if they foster good relationships with their stakeholders.

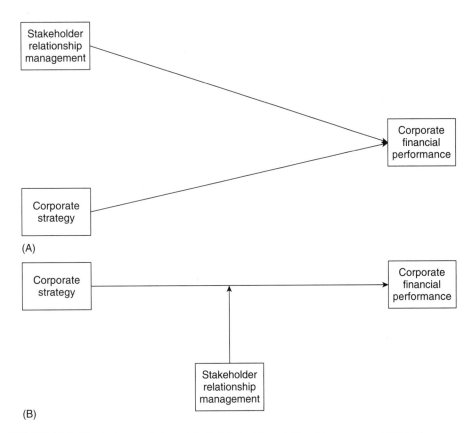

FIGURE 11.5 The instrumental model of stakeholder relationship management and corporate financial performance: (A) direct effects version; (B) moderator version

SOURCE: Used with permission of Academy Management from *Does Stakeholder Orientation Matter* by Berman et al., Volume 42(5) 1999; permission conveyed through Copyright Clearance Center, Inc.

Sample size The trustworthiness of a model depends on how stable it is, and that means the sample size needs to be large enough to give confidence that the results could be replicated in new samples. Analyses based on small samples tend to give quirky results that may not be repeatable. The adequacy of a sample depends on the complexity of the model that is fitted to the data: complex models need larger samples. As a useful rule of thumb, multiplying the number of predictor variables by 10 gives a minimum sample size (though this really is a minimum, and other factors such as the reliability of measurement would lead us to recommend larger samples than this).

Assessing the appropriate form of a causal model Once the researcher has defined the conceptual model in a form that can be tested statistically, the next step is to check that the data available are expressed in a form which is appropriate for the assumptions required by the statistical method. This involves assessing both measurement quality and that the form of the statistical model is appropriate. The input for all multivariate analysis methods is a matrix containing the variances of each variable (indicating the spread of scores: see Chapter 9) and the covariances among them (these reflect the associations among each pair of variables and are used to calculate correlations). It is important therefore that there are no extreme scores on any of the study variables (outliers) that can distort the value of the variance as a measure of spread (see Chapter 9). It is also important to check the form of the association among each pair of variables to ensure that relationships are linear. We showed in chapter 10 that correlation coefficients can be seriously misleading if relationships between variables are not linear.

Assessing the quality of fitted causal models All multivariate methods for analysing causal models share common characteristics. They give a summary measure of how good the prediction is for the model as a whole, generally expressed in terms of the proportion of variance in the dependent variable(s) accounted for by a set of predictors. They also report specific measures for components of the model, indicating the separate contribution of each predictor variable.

Generalized linear models The multivariate methods considered in the chapter, multiple regression analysis, MANCOVA, MANOVA and logistic regression, have the same formal structure and they are all referred to as **generalized linear models** (McCullagh and Nelder, 1989; Dobson, 2001). The technical details are beyond the scope of this book; but the management researcher benefits from these theoretical developments in statistics because they provide both a theoretical 'cleanness' to the models and a unified set of computational algorithms used by statistical packages such as SPSS (http://www.spss.com).

Analysis of causal models for observed variables

Three general classes of multivariate model for observed variables are described in this section in order to illustrate how researchers can approach the analysis of causal relationships. Our purpose is to demonstrate what the methods have in common rather than their differences, and to show part of the craft of multivariate modelling. The main features of class of model are summarised in Table 11.6. The table is

TABLE 11.6 Multivariate methods for analysis of causal models for observed variables

	MRA/ANCOVA	MANOVA/MANCOVA	Logistic regression analysis
(a) Variables	DV – a single continuous variable PVs– • MRA – one or more continuous variables • ANCOVA – one or more category variables and one or more continuous variables (covariates)	DVs – two or more continuous variables PVs – • MANOVA – one or more category variables (factors) • MANCOVA –one or more category variables and one or more continuous variables (covariates)	DV – a single dichotomous category variable PVs – one or continuous and/ category variables
(b) Assessing quality of the model as a whole	Multiple R shows the validity of the model as a whole; multiple R^2 shows the proportion of variance in the DV accounted for. An F-ratio tests whether the multiple R is significantly different from zero	Wilks' Lambda – multivariate test for each effect (category and continuous variable) shows the significance level for all DVs jointly An F-ratio tests the significance of Lambda	Model χ^2
(c) Contribution of individual elements of the model	Regression weights show the independent contribution of each PV; beta weights are regression weights standardized onto the same measurement scale for all variables A t-test assesses whether a regression weight is significantly different from zero	Separate tests for each dependent variable: o univariate tests (which ignore correlations among the dependent variables) o stepdown tests (which partial out the effects of dependent variables entered according to a pre-determined sequence)	Regression weights and odds ratios for each predictor variable
(d) Options available	• simultaneous entry of all predictors • hierarchical regression – entry of variables in a sequence according to their researcher • stepwise regression – sequential entry of variables determined by the predictive value	• stepdown tests require a pre-determined sequence for the dependent variables • tests could be performed with and without covariates in the model	• simultaneous entry of all predictors • hierarchical logistic regression – entry of variables in a sequence determined by the researcher • stepwise logistic regression – sequential entry of variables according to their predictive value

presented in four parts for each method in turn. Part (a) shows what kinds of variables are appropriate for the method, according to the number of dependent variables
used and the measurement scale for both DVs and PVs. Part (b) describes how the
quality of the model as a whole is assessed in that method; and part (c) lists how the
individual elements of the model are represented in the model. Finally, part (d) outlines
alternative options that are available within each method. First, we consider the
multiple regression and analysis of covariance models whose characteristics are
shown in column 1.

Multiple regression analysis (MRA) The basic multiple regression model consists of
a single dependent variable measured on a continuous scale and a set of predictor
variables which may be measured on continuous or category scales (see Table 11.6(a))
The model for two predictor variables can be expressed algebraically like this:

$$Y = a + b_1 X_1 + b_2 X_2 + e$$

where the symbol Y is used for the dependent variable; while the symbol X is used for
each predictor variable; a is called the intercept or the constant (it is the value of
Y when each X is zero); b is called a **regression weight**; e is a **residual** (or error term).
On the predictor 5 side of the model above, there are two kinds of variables. The PVs
(shown here by X_1 and X_2) are the systematic part of the model chosen by the
researcher. All other factors that influence the spread of scores on the DV are combined together into the residual term, e. The graphical form of this regression model
is shown in Figure 11.6.

The quality of the regression model as a whole (Table 11.6 (b)) is summarized by
the squared multiple correlation, R^2, whose value varies between 0 and 1 and shows
how much of the spread in DV scores can be accounted for by the predictors in the
model. In MRA, the measure of spread that is used is the variance (see Chapter 9),
and the R^2 measure is the proportion of variance in the DV accounted for by the PVs
collectively. It is often multiplied by 100 to give a percentage of variance accounted
for, from 0 to 100 per cent. R^2 indicates the relative importance of the PVs and the
residual term which is shown to the right in Figure 11.6. Thus where a set of predictors account for 20 per cent of the variance in a DV, this means that 80 per cent of the
variance is accounted for by all other causal factors combined into the residual term.

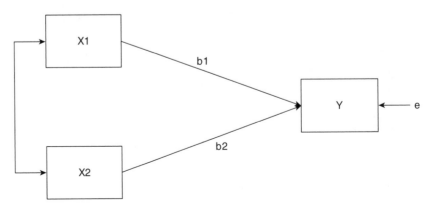

FIGURE 11.6 Graphical
representation of a
multiple regression model

An F-test (see Chapter 10, Table 10.5) is used to test the null hypothesis that the proportion of variance accounted for by the PVs is zero against the alternative hypothesis that it is greater than zero.

The individual components of the model are summarised in Table 11.6(c). The regression weights indicate the size of the independent contribution that each PV makes to predicting the spread in scores on the DV. When predictor variables are measured on different scales, the relative size of regression weights for different variables cannot be compared. So it is usual to transform each of the variables in MRA to a common measurement scale (this is called **standardizing**), and then the regression weights are referred to as either **standardized regression weights** or β (beta) weights. The significance test for regression weights gives a t-value; and the null hypothesis tested is that the regression weight is zero against the alternative that it is different from zero.

EXAMPLE 11.3

Multiple regression analysis of predictors of quality commitment

Jackson (2004) reported a study of one aspect of employees' commitment to the values of their organization, their commitment to quality. There were three stages to the research: defining the concept of quality commitment itself, formulating a way of measuring it, and developing and testing a conceptual model of how quality commitment relates to both personal and organizational variables. Here, we focus on the third stage where a sequence of regression analyses were used to test the conceptual model.

Table 11.7 shows a matrix of correlations for quality commitment, demographic variables (age, company tenure and gender) and a number of measures of work design. Row 10 of the table shows the correlation between quality commitment and each of the other variables in the study. There is a strong relationship with age (column 2, $r = 0.30$, $p < 0.001$), indicating that older workers show higher quality commitment; and the relationship with company tenure is much lower but also significant (column 4, $r = 0.14$, $p < 0.001$). Gender differences are significant but small in size (column 3, $r = 0.09$, $p < 0.05$), with women showing higher quality commitment. The table also shows, not surprisingly, that age and company tenure are correlated: those who have been employed longer with their company tend to be older. There are also consistently strong correlations between quality commitment and work design characteristics. Workers with more control over the timing and methods aspects of their jobs report higher quality commitment ($r = 0.21$, $p < 0.001$ and $r = 0.24$, $p < 0.001$ for timing and method control respectively); workers whose jobs are more mentally demanding in terms of problem-solving ($r = 0.11$, $p < 0.001$) and system monitoring ($r = 0.23$, $p < 0.001$) also report higher quality commitment; and quality commitment is correlated with production responsibility

Continued

TABLE 11.7 Correlations among study variables

	1	2	3	4	5	6	7	8	9	10
1. Organization	--									
2. Age	0.13	--								
3. Gender	-0.43	-0.09	--							
4. Company tenure	0.02	0.48	-0.11	--						
5. Individual timing control	0.28	0.26	-0.23	0.23	--					
6. Individual method control	0.29	0.19	-0.28	0.24	0.67	--				
7. Monitoring demands	-0.08	0.11	-0.03	0.17	0.16	0.28	--			
8. Problem-solving demands	0.09	0.00	-0.22	0.21	0.20	0.34	0.52	--		
9. Production responsibility	0.00	0.02	-0.11	0.05	0.02	0.15	0.42	0.34	--	
10. Quality commitment	0.02	0.30	0.09	0.14	0.21	0.24	0.23	0.11	0.16	--
Mean	0.22	30.78	0.78	5.74	2.83	3.09	3.85	3.00	3.19	3.97
Standard deviation	0.62	11.12	0.41	6.16	1.21	0.93	0.84	0.88	1.06	0.51

EXAMPLE 11.3

Multiple regression analysis of predictors of quality commitment —cont'd

($r = 0.16$, $p <.001$): workers reporting more expensive consequences if they make a mistake have higher quality commitment.

However, interpreting these relationships is not simple, because the table shows that there are strong correlations among many of the study variables. For example, people who have been employed in the company for longer tend to report higher levels of the work design variables, presumably because they have jobs with more responsibility. We have also seen that age and company tenure are correlated. Testing the conceptual model means that it is necessary to tease out these relationships, and that is the purpose of multiple regression analysis. In the analyses reported in Table 11.8, the DV is quality commitment, and the predictors are the demographic and work design variables.

TABLE 11.8 Hierarchical regression analysis for predicting quality commitment from demographic and work design variables, adapted from Jackson (2004)

	Step 1	Step 2
Organization	0.04	0.02
Demographics		
Age	0.30 **	0.27 **
Gender	0.14 **	0.19 **
Company tenure	0.01	-0.05
Work design		
Individual timing control		0.07
Individual method control		0.15 **
Monitoring demands		0.12 **
Problem-solving demands		0.00
Production responsibility		0.10 **
Multiple R^2	0.10	0.18
Change in Multiple R^2	0.10	0.08
F-ratio for test of change in R^2	36.03 **	18.47 **

Continued

EXAMPLE 11.3

Multiple regression analysis of predictors of quality commitment —cont'd

Two steps in hierarchical regression analysis are shown in the table. In the first step, column 1, the demographic variables are used as PVs and the results show that both age and gender are significant predictors of quality commitment, while company tenure is not. This suggests that the correlation between company tenure and quality commitment arises because both variables are correlated with age: it would appear that quality commitment reflects a person's age rather than their tenure with the employer. The second step (column 2) adds the work design predictors in order to test how much each one adds independently to predicting quality commitment, but also how important work design factors are relative to demographic factors. The regression weights shown here give a different picture from the correlations. Although all five work design variables were significantly correlated with quality commitment (Table 11.7), only three of the five regression weights are significant. Interpreting how important each individual work design variable is on the basis of how strongly it correlates with quality commitment is clouded by the correlations among the work design variables themselves. The difference in interpretation between pairwise correlation analysis and multiple regression analysis in this example shows how important it is to consider variables together.

An example application of multiple regression analysis is shown in Example 11.3. It illustrates the basic elements of MRA, but also shows the value of a variant of MRA called **hierarchical regression** (see Table 11.6(d)) where predictors are entered sequentially in more than block. Hierarchical regression allows the researcher to test hypotheses not just about the importance of individual predictors but also about variables entered into a model as groups. Table 11.8 (bottom row) shows that it is possible to compare the overall fit of a model to another one with one or more predictor variables added. Each model has an R^2 value and the same F-test that was used to assess each individual R^2 can be used to test the change in R^2 between models. The first F test (step 1) shows that the demographic variables together predict quality commitment; while the second F test (step 2) shows that the set of work design variables add significantly to that prediction.

Figure 11.7 shows two versions of a hypothetical regression model for three observed variables. In both models, the variable PV1 is assumed to be a cause of PV2, shown by the single-headed arrow between them and PV2 in turn is assumed to be a cause of DV. The difference between the models lies in how PV1 relates to DV: in Figure 11.7(A) there is a direct path between the two, while in Figure 11.7(B) there is no path and any causal influence of PV1 on DV would have to work through PV2. Such a causal influence would make PV2 a mediator between PV1 and DV; and the model is called a **mediational model**. Hierarchical regression analysis could be used to test the mediational model as follows. First, model (A) is tested using both PV1 and PV2 as predictors of DV. The multiple R^2 shows what proportion of the variance in DV is accounted for by both predictors. Second, model (B) is tested by dropping

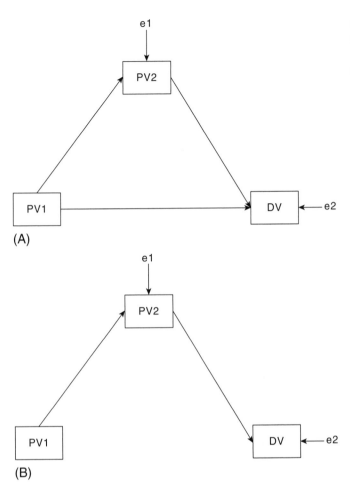

FIGURE 11.7 Hierarchical regression analysis for testing mediational effects: (A) full form of the model; (B) reduced form of the model with one path removed

PV1 from the set of predictors of DV, and again multiple R^2 is calculated. The only difference between model (A) and model (B) is the removal of PV1, so the difference between the two values of R^2 shows whether PV1 is a significant predictor of DV and therefore the path between them in Figure 11.7(A) is necessary.

There are other forms of regression analysis, called **stepwise regression**, which involve an automatic process of adding or subtracting variables according to how well they contribute to predicting the dependent variable. However, they rely on a blind search among predictors in order to identify those that make the greatest contribution to predicting the dependent variable; and such methods rarely have a useful place in management research.

Analysis of covariance (ANCOVA) is the name given to a form of multiple regression analysis where some of the predictors are continuous variables and others are category variables. It is a generalization of the methods for assessing differences between groups that were considered in Chapter 10, which allows the researcher to include predictors measured on continuous scales (these are called the covariates). Conclusions based on hypothesis tests about group differences can be seriously misleading if groups differ on variables other than the dependent variable. **Analysis of covariance** adjusts the dependent variable scores to what they would have been had the treatment groups been equal on the covariate. ANCOVA achieves a statistical matching between treatment groups, by adjusting groups means on the DV to what they would have been had the groups scored the same on the covariates.

The next class of methods that we consider are multivariate analysis of variance (MANOVA) and covariance (MANCOVA) and their characteristics are listed in column 2 of Table 11.6.

MANOVA/MANCOVA These methods bring together a number of methods that we have already considered, generalized to the situation where the researcher is interested in assessing the predictability of more than one dependent variable. MANOVA is used for comparing groups which are classified on the basis of one or more category variables. MANCOVA is the multivariate generalization of ANCOVA which includes one or more continuous variables as covariates as well as at least one category variable.

The practical problem addressed by this class of methods is that of interpreting the causal influences of predictors on dependent variables which are correlated among themselves. Taking correlated dependent variables singly can be misleading because each one carries not just information about the thing it measures but also something of what it shares with other dependent variables.

The quality of the model as a whole is shown by a multivariate test for the whole set of DVs taken together. There are several test statistics available, but the one most frequently used is called **Wilks' Lambda** (this varies between 0 and 1 and a small value is better), and an F ratio tests the significance of Lambda. Having looked at each of the effects for the set of DVs taken together, the next step is to explore individual components of the model, and there are two options here. The first option is the **univariate *F*-test** and this is the same test as if the analysis had been performed for each DV separately, but with an adjustment in significance level made to take account of the number of dependent variables in the model. The univariate *F*-test thus ignores correlations among the DVs, and so its usefulness depends on how high those correlations are. Another option is a **stepdown *F*-test**, where the DVs are tested in a sequence decided upon by the researcher. In effect it is a form of analysis of covariance which holds constant previous DVs. The first test is carried out ignoring the others DVs; the second test adjusts for the first DV; and so on. Stepdown tests are preferable to univariate tests because they take into account the correlations among the DVs, but their value is dependent on whether the researcher can give a justifiable ordering of the dependent variables. While the results from the univariate tests will be the same regardless of which order the DVs are listed; this is not true of stepdown tests. Univariate tests and stepdown tests will only give the same answers when the DVs are completely uncorrelated with each other.

The final class of multivariate methods that we consider for causal analysis of observed variables is logistic regression analysis.

Logistic regression analysis addresses the same questions as multiple regression analysis except that the DV is a dichotomous category variable rather than a continuous variable (Table 11.5, column 3). Like MRA, predictor variables may be continuous or

EXAMPLE 11.4

Worked example of MANOVA

This example uses the same data as Example 11.3 from a developmental study of employees' commitment to quality (Jackson, 2004). Earlier, we used gender and a number of work design characteristics as predictors of individuals' quality commitment; and this example tests the hypothesis that there are gender differences in work design. Table 11.7 showed that there are correlations among the work design variables, so it may be misleading to ignore these relationships by taking each variable alone. Table 11.9 gives the main results from MANOVA with gender as a category variable predictor and five work design characteristics as dependent variables.

The mean scores for males and females on each work design variable are shown in Table 11.9(a), together with the results of univariate *t*-tests (ignoring the correlations among the DVs). This shows that women report significantly lower scores on four out of the five work design characteristics: they have less control over work timing and methods, the problem-solving demands on them are lower, and the consequences of mistakes they might make (production responsibility) are lower. These results would suggest that women's jobs in this sample are more routine and undemanding than those of the men in the sample.

However, the individual tests ignore the fact that there are correlations among the work design variables, and the multivariate test of the gender effect is shown in Table 11.9(b). This shows the Wilks'

TABLE 11.9 Results of multivariate analysis of variance: gender differences in five work design characteristics (*n* = 967)

(a)Univariate tests for each variable separately	Male (n = 520)	Female (n = 316)	t-test
Individual timing control	3.37	2.69	7.24 **
Individual method control	3.60	2.96	9.25 **
Monitoring demands	3.89	3.84	0.76
Problem-solving demands	3.37	2.89	7.16 **
Production responsibility	3.41	3.12	3.51 **
(b)Multivariate test for all variables together			
Wilks' Lambda = 0.047, *F* = 3899.94 **			

Note: ** Indicates significant at 0.01 level.

EXAMPLE 11.4

Worked example of MANOVA—cont'd

Lambda coefficient and its associated significance test, an *F*-ratio. The null hypothesis being tested is that there is no gender difference in the set of DVs taken together, and this is rejected with a high level of confidence. There is clear evidence for a gender difference in work design in general, confirming what was observed for the analysis of the individual DVs.

Follow-up analyses could go in a number of directions, depending on the interests of the researcher. One direction would be to examine in more detail what jobs the men and women in this sample actually do in order to determine whether men have higher grade jobs in this sample or whether the observed effects reflect gender differences among people doing the same jobs. A different avenue to explore is whether there is a common factor underlying the work design variables (see the earlier section on measurement models) which might give a greater conceptual clarity to this analysis. Finally, we focused here on gender, but there may be other influential demographic differences between men and women, such as age or organizational tenure, that have been ignored. If so, any interpretation that focuses purely on gender would be misguided.

category variables or any mix of the two. Examples of dependent variables that might be used in **logistic regression** analysis include: the presence or absence of a risk factor for stress; the success or failure of a merger; the survival or not of a joint venture partnership. The dependent variable in logistic regression analysis is based on an **odds ratio**, which expresses the relative likelihood of the two possible outcomes. For example, if 20 per cent of mergers in a dataset of companies succeed while 80 per cent do not, then the odds of success are 4:1 against (20 / 80 per cent). It is the log of these odds that is used as the DV in logistic regression:

$$\log p / (1\text{-}p)$$

where p is the probability of succeeding and 1-*p* is the probability of failing. The model is used to assess the independent contribution of several predictor variables to the prediction of these odds.

Because the DV in logistic regression is a complex function of the probability of being in one category rather than another, the method used to fit the model is different from that used in multiple regression. This method gives a different test statistic for the quality of the model as a whole, a **likelihood ratio chi-square**. Despite this difference from multiple regression, the significance test tells the same story: whether the set of predictors as a whole account for significant variation in the DV. The individual components of the model are also evaluated by their regression weights; and each is tested by comparing its size relative to the standard error. In logistic regression, the result is called a **Wald test**; but its meaning is the same as in multiple regression. A worked example of logistic regression analysis is shown in Example 11.5.

EXAMPLE 11.5

A worked example of logistic regression analysis

This example uses data from the study by Sprigg and Jackson (2006) of stress in call centre staff. The DV is whether or not the respondent had experienced musculoskeletal disorder (MSD) caused by his or her work in the previous seven days (this includes back pain, aches in the wrist or shoulders, and so on). Logistic regression is appropriate because the DV is a category variable with two levels. The two predictors that we focus on here are: workload, a continuous variable assessing aspects of the demands of the job, and scripting, a three-point ordered category variable assessing to what degree call handlers followed a strictly worded script when they answered calls. The sample size for this analysis was 836, and of these 520 (62 per cent) reported MSD in the previous seven days. MSDs are thus relatively common in this sample of call handlers. The odds in favour of MSD are 62 per cent relative to 38 per cent, and the odds ratio is calculated as:

$$\text{Odds ratio} = p \,/\, (1 - p) = 0.622 \,/\, 0.378 = 1.65.$$

Logistic regression takes the log of this odds ratio as the DV, and the hypothesis being tested is whether the predictor variables either increase or decrease the risk of experiencing MSD while working as a call handler. Table 11.10 shows the results of logistic regression. The quality of the model as a whole is shown by a chi-square test statistic, and its value is 5.46, with 2 degrees of freedom (because there are two predictors). This is statistically significant, so we conclude that the two predictors together do account for a difference in the relative risk of MSDs.
The separate contribution of each predictor variable makes is shown by the standardized regression weights (labelled as beta weights in Table 11.10), just as in multiple regression. The hypothesis that the beta weight is zero is tested by a Wald statistic rather than a *t*-value for testing significance, but otherwise the interpretation of the coefficients is the same as for multiple regression. Both beta weights are positive in sign and statistically significant, indicating that higher workload is associated with an increased risk of MSDs and more use of a set script is also associated with an increase in risk. These influences are independent, so that someone who has high workload **and** greater use of a set script will tend to experience greater risk of MSD than someone who is high on only one predictor.

TABLE 11.10 Results of logistic regression analysis for MSD as a function of workload and following a set script

Variable	Beta weight	Wald statistic
Workload	0.50**	29.90
Script	0.28*	5.31

Note: Overall fit of the model: Chi-Square = 5.46 (df = 2), p <0.01.

The options available to the researcher within logistic regression are exactly the same as for multiple regression analysis (see Table 11.6(d)). Predictor variables may be entered in a single block, or the researcher may have theoretical reasons for defining a sequence of models to be fitted hierarchically. Finally, stepwise logistic regression can be used to enter predictor variables purely on the basis of how well they predict the dependent variable. Just as for stepwise options in multiple regression analysis, we see limited scope for this within management research.

Analysis of observed and latent variables – structural equation modelling

Introduction Structural equation modelling (SEM – Hair et al., 2005; Tabachnick and Fidell, 2006) bring together the two kinds of multivariate methods that we have considered so far in this chapter: *measurement models* for assessing hypotheses about relationships between observed and latent variables, and *structural models* of the causal relationships among both observed and latent variables. As such, they provide within the same framework a way of expressing and estimating many of the different kinds of model that are used by management researchers. There are several statistical packages available for fitting structural equation models, and the best known are: LISREL (http://www.ssicentral.com), EQS (http://www.mvsoft.com) and AMOS (http://www.spss.com). While the detailed characteristics differ among them, they all share the same underlying models and the graphical interface used to develop the model. AMOS has a reputation for being easier to use than the others, but, according to Ullman (2006a), the craft of SEM involves five steps whatever software is used (see Table 11.11).

The first step in SEM is to *define model hypotheses* specifying what variables are included within the model (both measured and latent variables), and what the relationships are among them. Any model fitting procedure will use the relationships among the variables that are included to estimate the parameter in the hypothesised model. There is no substitute for careful consideration of which variables to include in a model: leave out something important and the model obtained can be seriously biased and misleading. Furthermore, the use of latent variable models places the

TABLE 11.11 Steps in structural equation modelling

1. Define model hypotheses
2. Specify the model
3. Estimate model parameters
4. Evaluate the quality of the model
5. Consider alternative models

responsibility onto the researcher to think carefully about what indicators to use for each latent variable and to ensure that they are measured reliably. The most sophisticated of statistical treatment cannot overcome the deficiencies introduced by sloppy thinking or poor measurement practice.

The second step in SEM is to *specify the model* including either fixed or free parameters. Free parameters are those elements of the model whose values are to be estimated from data; while fixed parameters have a pre-defined value allocated to them (usually, but not always, zero). Fixed parameters are usually necessary to make a model identifiable (see next page), and they also give the basis for testing theoretical propositions by comparing different models where fixed parameters are set free. The full structural equation model has both measured variables and latent variables, and may also include causal relationships among the latent variables. The model in Figure 11.8 looks at first sight quite different from the ones considered so far in this chapter, but it is almost the same as the model in Figure 11.2. Both models have three kinds of variable: observed variables shown in rectangles, latent variables (we called these common factors earlier) and specific factors both shown in ellipses. Apart from a cosmetic change in layout, the only difference is that there is a causal arrow linking the two latent variables in the centre of the model.

The left hand side shows the measurement model for the latent variable labelled as PV (see the earlier section of this chapter). This model hypothesises that the PV is a common factor which accounts for the correlations among observed variables 1–3, while the specific factor associated with each of the observed variables captures all influences on observed variable scores which are specific to that variable. The right hand side shows the equivalent measurement model for the DV (observed variables 4–6). At the centre of the figure is the structural model showing the hypothesised causal link between the two latent variables.

Each of the arrows in the figure represents a path between two variables and also a parameter to be estimated from the data. For measurement models, these parameters are called factor loadings; while for causal models, they are called regression weights or path coefficients. Since (by definition) latent variables cannot be measured directly, the only information the researcher has about them comes from the observed variables. For a structural equation model, there are two kinds of parameter that need to be defined. The first is the covariances among the latent and observed variables.

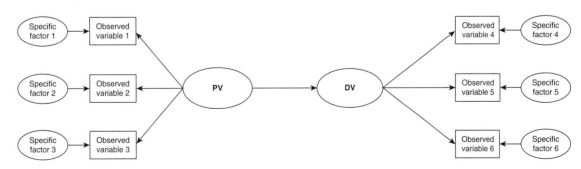

FIGURE 11.8 Full structural equation model

The second is the variance of each latent variable, so that its measurement scale is defined. The variance of an observed variable indicates the spread of scores around the mean on its measurement scale and thus defines the scale, and the same is true of the variance of a latent variable. However, the scale of a latent variable is unobservable and so it has to be defined in another way. One common option is to assume that the measurement scale of a latent variable is the same as that of one of its indicator variables (it does not matter which one), and another is to assume that the scale is a standardized one with a variance of one. For each parameter, the researcher can either define a fixed value for a parameter (as shown in the CFA example earlier in the chapter), or estimate a value from data. The commonest fixed values are zero for paths between variables, and one for variances of latent variables.

The input to a model fitting procedure consists of:

- The variances of the observed variables which define their measurement scale.
- The covariances among the observed variables.

If there are p observed variables, then the number of items of information available for model fitting is p variances and $p*(p-1)/2$ covariances. The model in Figure 11.8 contains six observed variables, so the number of items of information available is $6 + 6\times5/2 = 21$. There are three possibilities for the relationship between the number of parameters to be estimated and the information available to do it, and together they define the **identifiability** of a model:

1 Just-identified – there are the same number of parameters to estimate and information available. A just-identified model will always fit the observed data perfectly. Unique values for the parameters of the model can be estimated and their significance tested, but the model is as complex as the original data.

2 Under-identified – there are more parameters to be estimated than information available to define unique values for them, and it is then impossible to fit a model.

3 Over-identified – there are fewer parameters to be estimated than items of information. Here, the fitted model is simpler than the original data, and it is possible to calculate a significance test for the model as a whole as well as unique values for the individual parameters.

The third step in SEM is to *estimate model parameters*. All the programs work broadly in the same way. First, starting values for model parameters are formed, and these are used to calculate the initial estimate of the population covariance matrix, Σ. The difference between this and the sample covariance matrix, S, is called the *residual matrix*. The initial parameters are modified, and a new Σ matrix is formed. This procedure is repeated until no further improvements in goodness of fit can be achieved. The logic of SEM is to find estimates of the parameters in the statistical model in order to produce a population covariance matrix which is a close fit to the covariance matrix from the sample data. A close fit indicates that the hypothesised model is a plausible way of describing the relationships within the sample data. The goal of SEM therefore is to achieve a good fit between hypothesised model and the data – shown by a small and non-significant index of goodness of fit.

Evaluate the quality of the model A goodness of fit index is calculated based on the estimated Σ and the S. A common estimation method is called maximum likelihood, and the goodness of fit index that is minimized is called Chi square (χ^2). The value of χ^2 depends on a function of the S and Σ matrices and on the sample size. This means that large values of χ^2 reflect either poor model fit or a large sample size, or both. Studies with large samples (say over 1000 participants) will almost always show significant χ^2 values regardless of how good the fitted model is. As well as indices for the model as a whole, it is also important to look at the individual parameters within the model. A significance test for each parameter is reported by all of the programs, testing the null hypothesis that the population value of the parameter is zero.

The fourth step is to *assess the fit of a model*. The quality of the overall fit between a hypothesised model and the data can be assessed in a variety of ways: indeed one version of AMOS has 24 different fit indices, and most published papers report three or four different indices (Jaccard and Wan, 1996). They fall into three broad categories:

- Discrepancy-based indices. The commonest index is the chi-square value which is reported by every SEM program. It indicates the goodness of fit between the observed covariance matrix from the data and the predicted covariance matrix from the hypothesised model. A small value of chi-square indicates a close fit between the two, and suggests that the hypothesised model is a good one. However, there are problems with the chi-square index since a large value need not mean that the model is poor because chi-square varies with sample size(see above).

- Relative fit compared to a null model. As well as the hypothesised model, most of the SEM programs also fit a **null model** which assumes that all the covariances among the observed variables are zero (this is often called the independence model). A number of fit indices have been developed which adjust the chi-square value for a specific model according to how much better it is than the null model and also takes into account the complexity of the model (the number of parameters needed to achieve fit). One of these is the **non-normed fit index** (NNFI), whose values can vary between 0 and 1, and a value above 0.95 is regarded as acceptable (Bentler and Dudgeon, 1996).

- Relative fit adjusted for the complexity of the model. Complex models will fit data better than simple models, and some indices assign a cost to this extra complexity: in other words, they reward **parsimony**. On these criteria a model which achieves a reasonable fit with few parameters is better than a model which gives a marginally better fit achieved at the cost of a large increase in complexity. One of these measures is **RMSEA** (the root mean squared error of approximation) which adjusts chi-square according to the degrees of freedom of the model and the sample size.

The fifth step in SEM after examining the fit of a particular model is to *consider alternative models*, and it is most unusual to fit only a single structural equation model to a set of data. Almost all SEM work involves modifying the model in some way, either to improve the fit of an initial model or to test hypotheses derived from theory. The logic of SEM is strictly confirmatory, since the method requires that the researcher define a set of observed and latent variables together with a hypothesised model for the relationships among them. However, many tests of theoretical propositions involve comparisons between models rather than fitting a single model. We have already considered two examples in this chapter. Example 11.2 presented three models of the impact of stakeholder relationship management on corporate financial performance. Testing these alternatives involves fitting a sequence of models. Similarly, mediational models (see earlier section) can most effectively be tested by comparing a model including direct paths with a model that fixes the value of all these paths to zero. Model comparison tests like these are done by chi-square difference tests, the difference in goodness of fit between two models, in exactly the same way that we have seen already in hierarchical regression.

However, most researchers find that their *a priori* model does not fit the data to an acceptable degree and so they often undertake an exploration of alternatives using **modification indices**. The **Lagrange multiplier (LM) test** corresponds to forward stepwise regression, and test what would happen if each one of the fixed parameters in the model were to be set free. The second type of index is called the **Wald test** and this corresponds to backwards stepwise regression. It tests which parameters currently included in the model have a value so small that they could be dropped from the model. The logic behind these procedures is similar to that used in the stepwise options available in the methods for multivariate analysis of causal models among observed variables (for example, multiple regression and logistic regression). They involve a search through fixed parameters to see what the effect would be if fixed parameters were allowed to be free.

For example, the CFA model in Figure 11.9 (repeated from Figure 11.3) has six free parameters representing the loading of each observed variable on a single latent common factor. Their paths are shown by solid lines. However, there are also an additional seven fixed parameters which are implied by the model in Figure 11.3. They are shown by dotted lines in Figure 11.9: six additional arrows linking observed and latent variables, and also a double headed arrow between the two common factors indicating a correlation between them. There are even more implied fixed parameters, because the model also assumes that the specific factors to the left of the diagram are uncorrelated with each other. We have not drawn the double headed arrows for those because it would complicate the diagram considerably.

If the hypothesised CFA model does not fit the data well, the researcher might decide that at least one of the items should load on both common factors, and thus relax the constraint of a fixed zero loading for that path. If this process is guided firmly by conceptual considerations, there could be a strong justification; but blind searching through multiple alternative models in the hope of finding one which is 'best' violates both the statistical requirements that underpin the SEM method and also the principles of sound research practice that we have described in this book. Theory development should be guided both by conceptual rigour and by the weight of evidence from data. Holding to theory regardless of what the data say is not good practice; but neither is blindly following data regardless of the theoretical justification.

Advanced features The SEM area of statistics is developing rapidly, and each update of the programs adds features and options:

- New goodness of fit indices for assessing the quality of models.
- New estimation procedures for fitting the parameters in a hypothesised model.

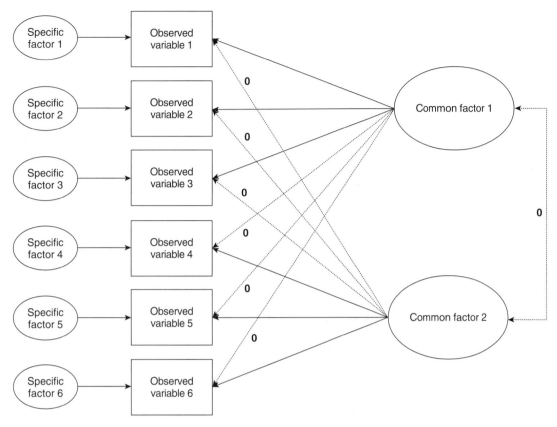

FIGURE 11.9 CFA model showing free parameters (solid lines) and fixed parameters (dotted lines) – the value of each of the fixed parameters is set to zero in this model

- Additional methods for the preliminary assessment of data characteristics before fitting SEMs.
- New models – for analysing multiple groups, for longitudinal designs, for testing differences in the means of latent variables and for complex sampling designs.

Going further Researchers interested in keeping up with developments in SEM can go to the software distributors' web sites listed at the start of this section. There is also a journal *Structural Equation Modeling* published by Taylor & Francis, but be aware that the articles here tend to be quite technical. There is also a comprehensive web site owned by Ed Rigdon (http://tinyurl.com/2ahnyc) which lists many resources for both beginners and experts. This site gives an introduction and a link to an online discussion network called SEMNET (http://tinyurl.com/yunk9e). SEMNET is invaluable for researchers at all levels, because they can ask questions without fear of intimidation and get advice from the real experts. There is also an archive of past posts that can be searched.

CONCLUSION

This chapter has introduced a number of methods for analysing the complexity of the world of business and management using quantitative data. We have described some methods for working with complex concepts, which often cannot be measured directly but have to be inferred from observed variables. We have also given a conceptual introduction to ways of modelling causal relationships among both observed and latent variables, particularly using structural equation models.

The most important points that we would like to make are:

- Following sound design principles can make the process of drawing conclusions from complex data much simpler.

- Fitting statistical models to quantitative data is not an automated process of blindly finding the 'best' model but must be guided firmly by conceptual considerations.

- Good quality models are grounded both in rigorous conceptualisation guided by existing literature and also in an evidence base of data collected according to sound design and measurement principles.

EXERCISE

11.1

Turning a research proposition into a testable causal model

This exercise follows the same format as Example 11.2, and involves practising how to turn a written statement of a research question into a causal model that could be tested statistically. Here are two studies from Table 10.6.

Home or away? Where to put your HQ

Birkinshaw et al. (2006) looked at where multinational enterprises (MNEs) put the headquarters for business units and for their corporate HQ. They located the business unit headquarters overseas when it made sense for *internal* reasons; while the location of their corporate HQ was influenced most strongly by the demands of *external* stakeholders – global financial markets and shareholders.

Take the statement above and answer the following questions:

A What are the elements in the description of this study?

B What are the dependent and predictor variables?

C What is the model being tested?

Should multinational enterprises (MNEs) adapt their marketing strategy to each market or standardize across markets?

This study by Katsikeas et al. (2006) looked at the international marketing strategies of US, Japanese and German MNEs operating in the UK. They found that standardization only makes sense when there is a good fit to the market environment.

Take the statement above, and answer the following questions:

D What are the elements in the description of this study?

E What are the dependent and predictor variables?

F What is the model being tested?

Performing a significance test

For each of the applications in Exercise 11.1, describe in narrative form the five steps of performing a significance test, and write a short description of the conclusion if the significance test were: (1) statistically significant; (2) statistically not significant.

FURTHER READING

Hair, J.F., Black, B., Babin, B., Anderson, R.E. and Tatham, R.L. (2005) *Multivariate Data Analysis*. Upper Saddle River, NJ: Prentice-Hall.

This is an excellent book on the use of multivariate methods in social science. The strength of the book is the applications it uses as illustrations of the methods covered, and the focus on preparatory work to examine the properties of the data first before embarking on complex multivariate analysis.

Tabachnick, B.G. and Fidell, L.S. (2006) *Using Multivariate Statistics*, 5th edn. Boston, MA: Allyn & Bacon.

This too is an excellent and thorough text on multivariate statistical methods for social science researchers. Its approach is practical rather than theoretical, and the authors cover all of the methods described in this chapter as well as others not covered here. For each method, they give its rationale, practical guidelines about how to use it, worked examples using a variety of statistical packages, and show how to present the results of analysis.

WRITING AND DISSEMINATING MANAGEMENT RESEARCH

12

LEARNING OBJECTIVES

- To develop personal strategies for writing.

- To recognize the needs and interests of different audiences.

- To develop awareness of the requirements of different forms of output.

- To develop skills in writing research reports and publications.

Introduction

The skills of writing

Outputs and evaluation

Dissemination strategies

Conclusion

Further reading

INTRODUCTION

This book has discussed the different aspects that are important in doing research. It has examined the various ways of designing research, it has looked at how to choose and use the particular methods that will provide the relevant data, and it has offered insights into the political and ethical sides of doing research. This last chapter, then, focuses on how to write up research findings, and how and where one can disseminate one's research.

There are many potential audiences for research results, including tutors, clients, academics, policy makers and the general public, and these audiences correspond roughly to the stakeholders that we discussed in Chapter 5. However, as there are many ways of effecting dissemination, we think it is important to consider dissemination early in the research process, preferably at the design stage. Although the written word dominates in the form of reports, articles and books, there are other important ways of getting the message across including presentations, videos and media interviews. A dissemination strategy, therefore, may include the use of different media at different points of time during the research, and after it has been completed.

We start the chapter with writing, and argue that there are generic skills, which apply to any context. We then look at different forms of output, concentrating on how evaluative criteria vary and provide guidance on the stylistic differences between, for example, qualitative and quantitative reports. Third, we consider different audiences and the media available for communication, and finally we draw the threads together by looking at dissemination strategies.

THE SKILLS OF WRITING

The main aim in writing about research is to communicate with an audience, and to persuade them that the research is serious, important and believable. This means that it is important to be clear about the potential readership at which the paper or report is aimed. One technique used by a number of successful authors is to hold two or three 'typical' readers in mind while writing something. The authors of *Exploring Corporate Strategy*, the best-selling book on corporate strategy (Johnson et al. 2008), wrote their book with two imaginary individuals in mind: a lecturer and a student, both of whom are endowed with archetypal characteristics they can refer to in the writing of the book. These imaginary people helped them to focus on the potential readership and also to communicate with each other about the appropriateness of new material in new editions.

A second point is that readers will be more interested in the document if it relates to their ongoing concerns and this is where Huff (1999) stresses the importance of trying to link in to any existing 'conversation'. Thus it is important to start a journal article with a summary of the main debate that has appeared up to that point, and upon which the current paper intends to build. Here the researcher needs to be aware of who are the main contributors in the field. Similarly, when writing a client report it is important to start with a brief statement of how the client has articulated the problem.

TABLE 12.2 Academic introductions

		Finding the new niche		
		New data	New theory	New methods
	Progressive coherence	13	18	3
Past research	Synthesised coherence	11	11	3
	Non-coherence	6	13	2

will be of similar quality; but if the initial page is unclear or confusing this bodes badly for the rest of the document.

Golden-Biddle and Locke (2007) provide a very interesting analysis of the way successful academic authors structure the introductory paragraphs. They conducted an analysis of 82 qualitative papers which had appeared in two leading journals (*AMJ* and *ASQ*) over the 20 preceding years and identified two factors that were always present. First, the authors provided a coherent overview of the previous literature using one of three strategies: they either used a *progressive coherence*, showing how concepts and literature developed cumulatively over time; or *synthesized coherence*, where they identify links between streams of research or theory which have not been spotted before; or *non-coherence*, where the field is characterized by arguments, debates and general fragmentation. Second, authors try to identify a new niche which demonstrates how they can add to previous research. Again, three methods appeared to be most commonly used, either through introducing new data, or new theory, or new research methods.

In Table 12.2, we show the frequency with which different strategies were adopted in the 82 papers. As can be seen, the most common way of developing a new niche was to claim that new theory was being introduced, and the least common way was through introducing new methods. Progressive coherence was the most common way of characterizing past research, and this was most likely to be linked to the introduction of new theory.

It is possible to summarize the four key elements that need to be in the introduction of an academic paper as follows:

1 Establish the *theoretical field* and why this particular topic is important.

2 Summarize previous research.

3 Identify the *niche*. What is the problem or question that is to be addressed.

4 State what the present study will *contribute* to this problem/question, and how it is tackled in this paper

Exercise 12.1 provides an opportunity to test out skills in writing a credible academic introduction. This can be done either individually, or as a small group exercise.

EXERCISE
12.1

Writing academic introductions

The following text was written on the back of a bottle of *pesto*. (Thanks to Nickie Hedge for drawing our attention to this example.) Try to rewrite this piece of text as if it is the introduction of an academic article. You will have to use your imagination with regard to references. Use the four key elements listed above as the basic structure, and limit the introduction to a maximum of two paragraphs. Think about how you are going to characterize the past research and establish your niche using the categories in Table 12.2. Add a title which in your view encapsulates the essence of the paper. Present the finished product on a flip chart or computer projector for critique by tutors and colleagues!

Pesto is a mainstay of Italian cooking; yet surprisingly it is little known in the UK. The inviting ease with which Sainsbury's Pesto can be used belies the difficulty with which it is made. The fresh basil that gives the sauce its distinctive colour and flavour is by far the most troublesome ingredient.

It occupies some of the most desirable real estate in Europe: the Ligurian hills that frame the Italian Riviera. Here, a unique mix of soil and sea breezes infuse the herb with an aroma and texture unmatched in any other part of Italy. Throughout June and July the farmers brave the summer sun to survey the maturing crop. They wander from bush to bush, sniffing and chewing the young leaves until the day they are deemed to be perfect. Then, to ensure the leaves are harvested at their aromatic peak, the whole crop is picked within the space of a few days.

In Exercise 12.1 we suggested writing a title that captured the essence of the paper. Good titles are short and memorable. In academic work it is very common to write a title in two parts, separated by a colon. The first part summarizes the topic of the research, and the second part indicates the argument that the paper is taking, or the question that it is addressing. Sample titles for the example in Exercise 12.1 might be: 'The marketing of exotic foods: the role of image and metaphor', or 'The globalization of food products: can local production methods survive?' Once you have a good title the rest should be easy! Conversely, lengthy and convoluted titles usually indicate that the author is unclear about the central topic and main message of his or her document. Given the importance of the title we would recommend developing a provisional title very early in the writing process. This should evolve as the work develops, but at any point in time it provides a point of reference against which to check the coherence of what has already been written.

Then we have the conclusion. We have indicated above in Table 12.1, the precise form of the conclusion may vary with different kinds of work: essentially it needs to summarize the nature of the research, the main findings or contributions, provide an indication of the limitations of the work, and make suggestions for future research directions. Once again, it needs to be clear and reasonably succinct (three or four paragraphs is enough for an academic paper, and 10 to 15 pages is enough for a doctoral thesis).

OUTPUTS AND EVALUATION

So what, then, are the different forms of output that can be generated by research, and how may they be evaluated? To some extent, the answer builds upon the discussion of political issues in Chapter 6. Here we can distinguish three main types of output: *private outputs*, such as reports and dissertations, which are generally targeted at a very small number of people, such as clients and examiners; *public outputs*, such as articles and books, which are intended to be widely disseminated; and *presentations* which will be more ephemeral, mainly verbal, but probably backed up by Powerpoint slides.

Private outputs: reports, dissertations and theses

Private outputs are generally aimed at a small number of people, and are not intended for public dissemination. Moreover, the evaluation generally takes place after the final version of the document has been presented, and this takes the form of a grade, or some kind of educational qualification. We will start with research reports, and then discuss dissertations and theses.

Research reports Client projects are increasingly being incorporated into undergraduate and postgraduate degree schemes where small groups of students tackle a real problem located in a company or other organization. Normally a senior manager will act as the client and will make arrangements or appropriate access to people and documents. Since the client project is being conducted as part of an educational qualification, those working on the project will face two different kinds of evaluation. First, they must come up with results or recommendations which satisfy the client, and, second, they must produce a written document which satisfies the academic tutors and examiners.

The written output from the project can seek to resolve the potential tension of expectations in three ways: (1) as a single report for the client which has sufficient elements of reflection and critical thought to pass academic muster; (2) as a distinct consultancy report which can be sandwiched within a more academic commentary that reflects on choices made, evaluates experiences, and develops relevant theoretical insights; or (3) as two completely separate documents tailored to the distinct needs of the client and the academic assessors. We have a preference for the first two as there is increasing integration between academic and practical discourse; also, integrated reports are more feasible nowadays since a growing proportion of 'clients' are former students of business and management courses, and therefore have a greater understanding of the mutual contribution of theory and practice.

Funded research projects These are normally carried out by small teams of established academics working with research associates employed on fixed term contracts. All of these projects require full reports at the end which describe the conduct of the research, any problems encountered in doing it, and give an overview of the theoretical and practical contributions provided by the project. Research reports are sent out to external referees with expertise in the area of the project for evaluation, and who will be expected to comment on the degree to which the project achieved its original objectives, whether any departures from the original proposal have been adequately justified, and the quality of the public academic output. In general, the academic output needs to include conference papers, journal papers (at least under submission), and perhaps an edited book.

Dissertations For business undergraduate and postgraduate courses the required dissertations are often longer than research reports (perhaps 10,000 to 20,000 words), and are the product of individual rather than group efforts. In most cases they are written solely for academic evaluation, and therefore do not have the potential competing objectives of project reports. In general it is worth following the suggested report structure in Table 12.1, although there is less of a requirement to demonstrate theoretical contribution than in the case of a doctoral thesis (see below). Evaluative criteria will depend both on the nature of the dissertation, and on the formal expectations of tutors and examiners. A general guide to criteria is given below in Table 12.3, which summarizes seven features that should normally be present in a good dissertation. The list is based on Bloom's taxonomy of educational objectives (Bloom and Krathwohl, 1956) and is organized hierarchically in terms of the increasing complexity of each feature. Thus, demonstrating knowledge of the field or comprehension of the problem to be addressed are relatively basic elements; the evaluation of literature and ideas, and clear argumentation are regarded as more complex processes which will therefore gather more brownie points when the dissertation is being evaluated.

There is some uncertainty at the moment about whether it is more important for management dissertations to demonstrate evidence of application or analysis. As we noted in Chapter 1, there is a long-standing debate in the UK about whether management education should emphasize practical or academic training (Whitley et al., 1981), and this has translated into the debate between Mode 1 and Mode 2 forms of research (Tranfield and Starkey, 1998; Huff, 2000). The rise of the MBA puts greater emphasis on practical relevance and application (see comments below on consultancy

TABLE 12.3 Hierarchy of evaluative elements

7. Quality of *argumentation*
6. *Evaluation* of concepts
5. *Synthesis* of ideas and concepts
4. *Analysis* of data and evidence
3. *Application* of theories/ideas to practice
2. *Comprehension* of the problem addressed
1. *Knowledge* of the field

projects); while academics are likely to value the analytic and evaluative elements of the dissertation. Since most degrees are awarded by academics it is prudent to include some elements of analysis and synthesis in the work submitted.

Doctoral theses These are similar to postgraduate dissertations in that they require a synthesis of ideas and data. In addition they must provide critical evaluation of relevant work, and demonstrate some kind of original *contribution* to the field. This contribution can be provided in three main forms: as new knowledge about the world of management (**substantive contribution**), as new theories and ideas (**theoretical contribution**), or as new methods of investigation (**methodological contribution**). In each case, the contribution needs to be stated explicitly in the conclusions, and there also needs to be a clear link back to the early part of the thesis where the existing theories and methods were reviewed and evaluated. The theoretical contribution is most important, although it may be supplemented by each of the others.

The final award of a doctorate depends on the judgement of independent examiners (though practice in this respect varies surprisingly widely across Europe and North America), and it is very important that the right choices are made. Not only do the examiners need to be conversant with the field of study, but they should also be sympathetic to the worldview and methodology of the researcher. In this context it is worth developing a provisional list of examiners early in the period of study, which gets refined and updated as the theoretical and empirical work develops. If the candidate has done has sufficient networking through conferences and learned societies (such as the BAM or the AoM), he or she should be clear about who the best examiners would be.

Public outputs: conferences, journals and books

Nowadays, it is essential for aspiring academics to get their research into the public domain. It is advisable to attempt publication from doctoral research while the work is being conducted, and occasionally it is possible to publish results from postgraduate dissertations (but after they have been completed). In each of these cases the evaluation takes place before the final copy of the work is produced, and this acts as a filter on the quality of work that appears in public. In general, it is easier to get a paper accepted for a conference than for a journal, although significant hierarchies exist within both categories. Hence many researchers will take an incremental approach, submitting the results of their work to a conference, and then on the basis of feedback rewriting the paper and submitting it to a journal.

With some conferences it is possible to submit extended abstracts which are evaluated by two or three referees, and the feedback from the referees can be incorporated into the paper before the conference takes place. Other conferences, such as the Academy of Management, will only accept submission of full papers, but in these cases the feedback from referees can be more focused, and this can be combined with discussion and feedback at the conference itself in helping the authors revise the paper for submission to a journal. As we have mentioned earlier, participation at conferences is very important for publishing contacts and building up research networks. However, conference papers *per se* have limited value for academics wishing to build up their careers or to gain tenure. The 'gold standard' is acceptance of papers in academic journals, and preferably the more highly rated ones.

As we noted in Chapter 6, there are very clear hierarchies in the reputation of different journals, and metrics such as the ISI Impact Factor are regarded as indicators of quality. There are a number of factors that help to sustain the position of the top journals: they get large numbers of submissions and are therefore able to be very selective; people will usually only submit their very best work to the top journals; and the reviewing process is conducted with such rigour that the finally published paper is often significantly better than the initial submission. Our general advice regarding publication strategies is to aim for good journals wherever possible, and perhaps seek to submit papers with others (supervisors, examiners, people met at conferences) who have already been successful in getting published in the target journal.

It is important to understand the decision-making process for most journals, especially the role of referees. In Figure 12.3 we summarize the decision-making process of a typical journal. In this figure the numbers indicate the percentage of the original submissions which move to each of the successive stages. A number of papers (perhaps 50 per cent) will be rejected by the editors without being sent to the referees, a further number will be rejected after receipt of referees' reports, and most of the remainder will be sent an offer to revise and resubmit (R&R). It is extremely rare for a paper to be accepted outright by a good journal. For those lucky enough to have been sent an R&R, they then move into the critical stage of responding to the criticisms/recommendations of reviewers and the editors. Frequently the reviewers will provide conflicting advice, and a good editor will notice the conflicts and provide guidance on which lines to follow.

The resubmitted paper needs to be accompanied by a letter to the editor (and referees) explaining how recommendations have been implemented and providing a rationale where the authors feel that the recommendations are not appropriate. Sometimes these letters can get very lengthy, perhaps 10 to 20 pages, but long letters can irritate editors and make it difficult for referees to see how their suggestions have been implemented – so the advice is to deal with every point the editors and reviewers have made, but only discuss the critical issues at any length.

FIGURE 12.3 Flowchart of journal decision-making

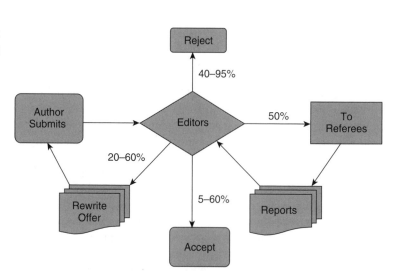

Finally there is the possibility of publishing a book. Although in some subjects, such as history, it is quite normal to turn theses into books, this is relatively rare in the management field. Publishers have a preference for textbooks and handbooks because they have more general and sustained appeal than research monographs. In order to develop a book proposal with broad appeal, it is generally necessary to collaborate with other scholars who can provide complimentary perspectives, and this may not be a sensible option until several years after the PhD is completed. In the short term there are few academic credits for publishing books in the management field. Nevertheless, in the longer term they can contribute substantially to personal reputation and visibility, and this can also be measured in terms of 'hits' in the ISI index, or Google Scholar.

Peters and Waterman (1982) are reputed to have received royalties of US$1.8 million in the first year of their book's publication, and Mintzberg (1973) did well out of his book (unusually, based on his PhD thesis). But these are the exception: for most people the direct financial rewards are not great. Fortune is most likely to follow the fame of being a published author, and academic careers depend on both the reputation of the publisher and the quality of the reviews that ensue. The nice thing about books is that it is usually possible to develop ideas over a period of time with the help of the publisher. Once again contacts with publishers are most easily established at conferences, where more of the relevant firms are represented.

DISSEMINATION STRATEGIES

In the previous section we concentrated on dissemination mainly to academic audiences, and here we focus on other audiences, especially policymakers and practitioners. We start with some general comments on making public presentations (although this applies equally to client and conference presentations), then discuss publishing in practitioner journals and making the best use of the public media.

We hesitate to provide much advice on the technicality of presentations since most of our students nowadays are very expert and professional at structuring and presenting data using Powerpoint. However, a common mistake is to provide too much material, especially in the form of slides, which puts the presenters under considerable time pressure and makes it extremely difficult for them to introduce any kind of interaction into the presentation. Our preference is to use a minimal number of slides (four or five for a 10-minute presentation) to provide a basic structure, and then provide stories and vignettes to illustrate the points that are being made. If it is a team presentation, then people can take different roles according to their strengths: providing introductions, telling stories, making jokes, encouraging interaction and dealing with questions. If the presentation is being made by an individual, it is often worth recording the session because you may be so focused on providing answers to questions that you do not listen to what people are really saying.

Publications in practitioner journals are also important because they reach much wider audiences and demonstrate that you are engaging with potential 'users'. However, it can be very difficult to get into the famous practitioner journals, such as *Harvard Business Review, Sloan Management Review* or *California Management Review*, because the majority of papers are written by established academics, who may have been invited by the editors to submit because they have recently published

EXAMPLE 12.1

Guidance on writing press releases

Press releases should be quite short, with a maximum of 600 words printed on two sides of a single sheet of paper. From the outset, you have to convince the reader that you have something interesting to say, perhaps a new fact about the world or a new way of looking at an important issue that has topical relevance. The press release should start with the conclusions, and then provide the supporting evidence – which is opposite to the normal way of writing academic papers which end with the conclusions. In summary:

- Begin with a catchy headline.
- Provide a general statement that sums up the main finding.
- Distil into three or four points the essence of the research.
- Back up these points with facts and figures.
- Finish with the main policy implications or the 'way forward'.
- Add your contact details including email address and phone numbers.
- Above all, keep the language intelligible and jargon-free.

(Pers. comm, Romesh Vaitilingam)

some interesting material in a top academic journal. So, there is a virtuous cycle operating, and it may be quite difficult to break in.

Another way to increase the exposure of one's research results is to approach the media. This can most easily be done through a press release which is circulated to relevant newspapers and radio stations. Most universities and learned societies have considerable experience in dealing with the media and should be able to provide advice on whom to contact. In Example 12.1 we provide some general guidance on writing press releases.

Naturally there is much competition about getting access to the media and those academics who excel in this respect generally build up excellent relationships over time with journalists and make themselves available 24/7. There are also wider political implications of building up reputations: credit for research should not be taken for granted; it depends very much on how much the researcher is able to exploit his or her work through contacts, publications and other forms of dissemination. In Chapter 2, we used the story of Fleming's discovery of penicillin to illustrate some of the factors that underlie scientific discoveries. There is a sequel to that story which relates to capitalizing on research (see Example 12.2).

It is important to develop a dissemination strategy at the outset of any funded research projects, and perhaps halfway through doing a doctoral thesis. This should normally include two or three conferences with a brief synopsis of the possible paper in each case, and potential target journals for the next phase of each paper. It is also worth thinking about potential media strategies, including developing press releases towards the end of the research period. As with all forms of publishing it is important to believe that one has something worth saying.

ANSWERS TO EXERCISES

CHAPTER 1

Exercise 1.1 Classical: mapping organizational structures, observing and analysing physical work. Human relations: talking to managers/employees about their likes and dislikes at work. Decision theory: combining external and internal data to predict most favourable courses of action. Work activity: observing what mangers do, under different circumstances. Competencies: comparing behaviours of supposedly good and bad managers to determine successful patterns. Critical: concentrating on maintenance of elites or the experiences of less powerful organizational members. Learning: focusing on episodes where learning takes place, or fails to take place.

Exercise 1.2 Here are some possibilities: systems view; management by walking about; delegation; participative management; management by objectives; just in time management; operations management; ...

CHAPTER 4

Exercise 4.1 (A) Positivist: 'empirically validating'; 'corresponding measures' (B) Constructionist: 'holistic model'; or Relativist: 'perspectives' (C) Constructionist: 'drawn from a longitudinal study' in one company; (D) Relativist: 'has a stronger influence on'...

CHAPTER 5

Exercise 5.1 (A) Either aiming to show that some forms of triticale have the potential to produce very high yields, or to test the effect of irrigation on triticale, or both. (B) Two main variables: seed type and irrigation. The 10 seed types provide an internal comparison group though they are not compared directly with non-triticale seed types. The plots receiving 12 mm irrigation are the main experimental group, those not receiving irrigation are the controls. (C) *Strengths*: a large-scale study with some yields that are exceptional. Multiple comparisons between seeds and treatments. *Weaknesses*: no information about rainfall/precipitation, so hard to judge the added value of irrigation; yields are almost 'too good to be true', hence raise questions about whether other (unreported) factors are involved; researchers are protagonists and are not independent of the experiment.

Exercise 5.2 (A) *History* and *maturation* threats were excluded in the design by repeated measurement, in the Greenfield site (condition A) and in the conventional site (condition C), over the period during which autonomous group working was introduced in condition B. Another potential threat to internal validity is that workers on the two sites might have competed with each other, but the researchers believed that this was unlikely due to the distance between the sites (250 miles apart), and the lack of contact between them. (B) In a design where random allocation to groups cannot be achieved, problems of *selection* may arise. The researchers checked for differences in production processes, in the ratio of men to women, and in length of service. Where differences were noted they conducted supplementary analyses with sub-samples selected to be equivalent on these dimensions. There was also a danger that labour turnover could lead to missing values over time, and therefore to threats of *mortality*. Full inclusion or exclusion of leavers and joiners could be misleading because leavers and joiners may be different from those who stay throughout the study. To address this issue, the authors performed analyses to compare leavers and joiners to the group of those ever-present through the study. No differences were found; and the threat of mortality was therefore excluded. (C) A simple effect of work design would be shown by a pattern of results corresponding to the existence of autonomous workgroups, and unaffected by other factors such as site, shift or time. If autonomous group working is associated with higher job satisfaction, we would expect employees in conditions A_1, A_2, A_3, B_2 & B_3 to report higher job satisfaction that their counterparts in conditions B_1, C_1, C_2 & D_1. (D) More specific patterns of predictions are also possible. The first three patterns relate to cross-sectional comparisons between conditions at each of the three measurement occasions; while the second set of three patterns relate to predicted change or no change over time for conditions A, B and C where longitudinal data were available: (i) *Time_1 comparisons:* $A_1 > (B_1, C_1, D_1)$. Lack of difference between C_1 and D_1 would help to discount shift differences; while lack of difference between B_1 and D_1 would help to discount site differences. Full support for this predicted pattern would strengthen the case that differences between A_1 and the other conditions is attributable to autonomous group working. (ii) *Time_2 comparisons:* $(A_2, B_2) > C_2$. An effect of autonomous group working would be shown by C_2 different from A_2 and B_2; while a lack of difference between A_2 and B_2 helps to rule out a shift effect. (iii) *Time_3 comparisons: (A_3, B_3).* Similarly no difference between A3 and B3 would be expected if the only influence on job satisfaction is the form of work design. (iv) *Change for condition A: (A_1, A_2, A_3).* No change over time in job satisfaction scores would be expected, since autonomous group working was introduced in Condition A at the outset of the study. (v) *Change for Condition B: $B_1 < (B_2, B_3)$.* Since autonomous group working

was introduced in Condition B after the first measurement occasion, an increase in scores would be predicted from B_1 to B_2 with no change subsequently. (vi) *Change for Condition C: (C_1, C_2).* Finally, autonomous group working was never introduced in Condition C, and no change in scores would be expected from C_1 to C_2.

Exercise 5.3 (A) The study involved gathering data from multiple sources over a period of time, and this was appropriate to studying the complex interrelationships and processes within the company. But also the feedback to key actors in the company added to the validity of the conclusions we drew. (B) Because this is a unique study, the findings can only be generalised theoretically. That is, that the case study needs to be able to demonstrate something about dynamic capabilities, knowledge management, or the relationship between the two of them, which supports, contradicts, challenges or adds to current theories in the literature. (C) They do make sense if you want to publish the results of the study in an academic journal. However, there are plenty of stories which came out of the study which can provide useful anecdotes to illustrate decision-making processes, group dynamics, etc. – which we had not expected in the first place, but which made good stories in their own right (an expressive outcome).

Exercise 5.4 (A) This depends on whose version of grounded theory she follows. She uses open coding, which leads to a central category (see Chapter 8), but, there is no theoretical sampling, nor saturation. The interplay between external theory/literature and data is more complex than as outlined in Glaser and Strauss. (B) We think this deviation is quite appropriate, provided she is able to articulate what and why. Reasons include the constraints of the research setting/access, the nature of the theory she is looking at, and the conscious combination of theory development and deduction.

Exercise 5.5

	Ontology	Epistemology	Methodology	Method
Grounded theory	*	***	**	*
Unobtrusive measures		*		***
Narrative	*	*	**	*
Case method		*	***	*
Ethnography	*	**	**	
Critical realism	***	**	*	
Participant observation			**	*
Experimental design		***		
Falsification		***		
Theoretical saturation		*	**	**

Exercise 6.2 Here are some possibilities (although no single response is necessarily best). (A) Persist and ask to see another manager; start 'covert' observation of the two departments; phone your tutor; say you will return the next morning. (B) Sign it; renegotiate; refuse; (C) Confidentiality vs. duty to expose? Is there any corroborating evidence from elsewhere? (D) There is a dilemma here between full, partial and zero disclosure; try to buy time; (E) Confront him/her as soon as this is noticeable; disccuss group norms in order to apply group pressure; shop to tutor.

CHAPTER 9

Exercise 9.1 (A) face-to-face interview; (B) web-based survey; (C) face-to-face or telephone interview.
Exercise 9.2 (A1) *Coding scheme*: need to code types of buying behaviour such as entering the store, browsing, trying goods, interacting with selling staff, purchasing goods. (A2) *Sampling strategy*: comparisons require different types of background music, either in a specific type of store (for example clothing, DIY, electronics, music) or could compare effects of music in different types of store. Data could be collected from in-house CCTV or by trained observers. Sampling would need to cover a long time period, and take account of days of the week and times of the year. (B1) *Coding scheme*: need to specify particular kinds of behaviour: non-verbal behaviour (e.g. eye contact, gestures, body posture, distance), verbal behaviour (focus on task versus relationship). (B2) *Sampling strategy*: first, select a sample of female and male bosses (doing as far as possible the same kind of work); second, select a sample of subordinates (probably both male and female); third, select a sample of work tasks to observe. Sampling would need to take account of the fact that many critical kinds of behaviours are very rare. Data could be collected by observation of specific interactions (for example, meetings), or by self-report (C1) *Coding scheme*: need to code the different communication media that people use, and also distinguish between task-focused and relationship-focused interactions. (C2) *Sampling strategy*: first, select a sample of virtual teams (taking account of characteristics such as their size, demographics of members, and how long they have worked together); second, decide on types of project and time points within the project (start-up, mid-point, and wind-up); third, decide on sampling of interaction exchanges. (D1) *Coding*

scheme: need a coding scheme for the style of the call handler, and for the specific queries which they deal with; also need to define effectiveness. For style: distinguish between task and social-emotional aspects of interaction. For queries: distinguish between, for example, requests for information, updating information already on a database, changes to an order, complaints about treatment of a customer. (D2) *Sampling strategy*: since telephone helplines are usually recorded (with consent), data could probably be collected from these recordings; and the critical thing would be to define whether a specific interaction was effective or not. Possibilities include: sample interactions which are known to be either effective or ineffective, and then select calls from each for analysis of style; sample call handlers who are know to have different styles, and then select calls for analysis of effectiveness.

Exercise 9.3 (A) Only relevant to those on the voting register, and so needs a screening question; the question does not define what is 'poor' or 'good'. It would be better to ask how often the person had voted in local elections in a specific period (say, two years). (B) A leading question which assumes agreement. It would be better to frame this as a statement ('smoking is harmful to health') and then record whether the respond agrees or disagrees. (C) A complex expression which asks at least two questions at once. Break it up into: what is the person's opinion about genetically modified food; would the person take part in a boycott. (D) A leading question which assumes that politicians are dishonest and break promises. Express the question in a neutral form:

a. how much do you agree or disagree with the statement .....

   or

b. how often do politicians keep the promises they make ....

(E) Asks two questions at once: your supervisor may be dynamic but disorganised. Ask them separately. (F) Worded as a negative – if you are satisfied, you have to disagree with a negative statement. Express the question in a neutral form: how satisfied are you with .... (G) Full of jargon and complication. All this asks is whether the person likes teachers who tell jokes in their lectures!

CHAPTER 10

Exercise 10.1 (A) The response scale for each item is scored from 1 to 5, and the scale is an average of a number of items. (B) 12 – the only way to achieve a score of 5 is to strongly agree with every item. (C) The media value is around 3.75; this is above the mid-point of the response scale (which is coded as 3), so people tend to think that the company's reputation is good rather than poor. (D) There are two – 3.65 and 3.71. These are close to the median.

Exercise 10.2 (A) (a) false; (B) (b) negatively skewed; (C) (c) mode; (D) (d) 5; (E) (a) mean; (F) (b) mid-range.

CHAPTER 11

Exercise 11.1
Home or away? Where to put your HQ
(A) *What are the elements in the description of this study?*
Location of their corporate HQ – where they put it, either home or overseas; location of business unit HQ – where they put it, either home or overseas; factors influencing location decisions – are they internal or external?
(B) *What are the variables?*
Dependent variable: location – home versus overseas.

Predictor variables: HQ – business unit versus corporate; source of influence factors – internal versus external.

(C) *How would you put these together into a formal model that could be tested?*

This research is about interactions between variables. It says that the relationship between influence factors and location depends on what kind of HQ we are talking about:

- For *business unit* HQ: internal factors → decision on whether to locate home or overseas
- For *corporate* HG: external factors → decision on whether to locate home or overseas

Should MNEs adapt their marketing strategy to each market or standardize across markets?

(A) *What are the elements in the description of this study?*

International marketing strategies of MNEs: either *adapt* your products and their marketing to the features of each market, or *standardise* across markets (sell the same products in the same way everywhere); fit to the market environment in a country; success – this is how we know that a strategy 'makes sense'.

(B) *What are the variables?*

Dependent variable: business success – how well the MNE performs in a country.

Predictor variables: marketing strategy – adaptation versus standardization; market environment – features of the country's market; fit – between strategy and environment.

(C) *Putting it all together*

Like the previous study, this research is about interactions between variables, though this is stated using the idea of 'fit' between the strategy and the environment where the MNE applies the strategy. The study concludes that there isn't just one best way of approaching a new market. Standardizing will sometimes be successful, but not always – it depends on how well the approach fits with what a specific market is like.

GLOSSARY

1-tailed test refers to a directional alternative hypothesis relative to the null hypothesis; a prediction of a positive association between variables, or that one group mean will be bigger than another

2-tailed test refers to a non-directional alternative hypothesis relative to the null hypothesis; association between variables may be either positive or negative, or that the means of two groups will differ in either direction

academic theory explicit ideas developed through exchanges between researchers to explain and interpret scientific and social phenomena

action research an approach to research which seeks understanding through attempting to change the situation under investigation

alternative hypothesis (H_1) position adopted during hypothesis testing if the evidence from data is strong enough to reject the null hypothesis (see also null hypothesis)

analysis of covariance (ANCOVA) a form of test of group differences on a continuous dependent variable which also includes continuous variables as predictors (covariates)

analysis of variance (ANOVA) a form of hypothesis test for comparing the means of two or more groups which may be classified on the basis of other variables

analytic theory a conceptual framework which seeks to explain *why* things happen

applied research studies that focus on tackling practical problems in organizations where the desired outcome will be knowledge about how to solve the problem

argument analysis an approach to the analysis of natural language data that identifies the data used in making claims, the premises made and the conclusions drawn by individuals about issues of relevence

association two variables are associated where knowing a value on one variable carries information about the corresponding value

on the other; can be measured by a correlation coefficient

Atlas.ti a software package that assists in the building and testing of theories through the creative assembly of qualitative analysis of textual, graphical and audio/visual data. Available from http://www.atlasti.com

auto-ethnography a form of insider research often conducted by those studying in the organization in which they work

axial codes codes that specify categories or sub categories where the dimensions are specified

bar chart a form of graphical summary for category scales, with bars whose length indicates the frequency of responses for each category

best practice research this seeks to identify practices in the most successful companies, which might be adopted in other companies.

beta weight see standardized regression weight

bias in sampling design, a biased sample is one which does not represent the features of the population from which it is drawn (see representativeness)

binomial distribution a form of reference distribution; the distribution of entities which are binary (present/absent, success/failure)

bootstrap a way of forming a reference distribution by repeated sampling from a specific dataset; used in hypothesis testing

CAQDAS computer assisted qualitative data analysis software

category scale a form of measurement scale where responses are recorded in a small number of discrete units, for example makes of car purchased (cf. continuous scale)

causal model(ling) a class of multivariate models of the causal relationships among a set of variables which can be fitted to data

chi-square distribution a form of reference distribution; the distribution of variances used for testing hypotheses about spread

chi-square test a form of hypothesis test for testing association between two variables measured on nominal category scales classical management theory a normative view of management which stresses the functions that managers need to perform assumes that human behaviour

cluster analysis a general term for a range of statistical methods that serve to group data with similar properties into categories

cluster sampling a modification of random sampling where the population is first divided into convenient units, called clusters, and then all entities within a cluster are selected

congnitive mapping a method of spatially displaying data in order to detect patterns and by so doing better understand their relationship and significance

common factors a class of latent variables in a measurement model which are assumed to account for the covariances among a set of observed variables (see also specific factors)

competency theory a normative theory of management which concentrates on the range of skills and abilities required by managers to perform their work effectively

confirmatory factor analysis (CFA) a multivariate method for testing measurement models of the relationship between a set of observed variables and a hypothesized set of latent variables (see also exploratory factor analysis)

content analysis a relatively deductive method of analysis where codes (or constructs) are almost all predetermined and where they are systematically searched for within the data collected

contingency theory theoretical models which propose that variables have different effects depending on the context

continuous scale a form of measurement scale where responses are recorded in a large number of discrete units, for example age recorded in months (cf. continuous scale)

convenience sampling a form of non-probability sampling design where entities are included in a sample on the basis of their ease of access

conversational analysis an analysis of natural language data used with naturally occurring conversations to establish linguistic patterns through the detailed examination of utterances

covariance a measure of association between two continuous variables expressed in the units of the measurement scales of the variables; its square root is the correlation coefficient

covariates variables measured on continuous scales which are included as predictors in analysis of group differences

critical discourse analysis the analysis of natural language data which emphasizes the power relations and ideologies that are both created and conveyed

critical incident technique a method of teasing out information often employed within interviews which go to the heart of an issue about which information is sought

critical management theory a perspective on management research which concentrates on power relations, and particularly on the less powerful members of organizations

critical theory a philosophy which critiques the structures and outcomes of capitalist society, and examines how powerful members of society maintain their dominance over the less powerful members

Cronbach's alpha coefficient an index of the internal consistency of a composite variable formed by combining a set of items; a common measure of reliability

cross-sectional surveys these usually involve selecting different organizations, or units, in different contexts, and investigating the relationships between a number of variables across these units

curvilinear relationship a relationship between two variables whose form changes according to the level of values on one variable; usually used to describe relationships which are positive in one part of the range and negative in another part (cf. linear relationship)

decision explorer a software program for collecting, conveying and managing ideas and other kinds of qualitative information that surround complex and uncertain situations. It is available from Banxia software (http://www.banxia.com)

decision theory a rational theory of management which assumes that optimum (if not ideal) decisions can be made through analysis of factual data, and this will lead to corporate success

degrees of freedom (df) the value that defines the shape of a standard reference distribution in hypothesis testing; for example, in testing association, df = sample size minus one

dependent variables the factors that research is trying to predict (see independent variables) descriptive theory seeks to provide an accurate view of what actually takes place in organizations and the work that managers do

discourse analysis the analysis of natural language data that takes into account the broader social context in which the interview takes place

efficiency the extent to which a summary measure captures all the information within the data which is relevant to what is summarized

eigenvalues the term used in exploratory factor analysis for the summary measure of the amount of variance in the observed variables accounted for by a factor

embedded case a case within a larger case, for example the Accident and Emergency Department within a hospital which was the primary case

emic insights into communities, societies or organizations as seen from the perspective of insiders

enlightenment model an approach to social policy formulation which engages those likely to be affected by the policy both in the research process and in determining its consequences

epistemology views about the most appropriate ways of enquiring into the nature of the world

ethnography approaches to research and data collection that emphasize gaining access to the perspectives and experiences of organizational members

etic insights into communities, societies or organizations as seen from the perspective of outsiders

everyday theory the ideas and assumptions we carry round in our heads in order to make sense of everyday observations

exogenous variables those variables which are part of a multivariate model, but whose causal influences are taken as given and do not form part of the model itself

exploratory factor analysis (EFA) a multivariate method for fitting measurement models which describes the covariances among a set of observed variables in terms of a set of latent variables (see also confirmatory factor analysis)

exploratory surveys these are similar to cross-sectional surveys, but tend to focus on identifying patterns within the data through the use of factor analysis or principal component analysis (see Chapter 11)

external validity whether the results of the research can be generalized to other settings or contexts

factor loading the weight allocated to the path between a latent variable and an observed variable in a measurement model

factual surveys involve collecting and collating relatively 'factual' data from different groups of people

falsification a research design that seeks evidence to demonstrate that the current assumptions or hypotheses are incorrect

f-distribution a form of reference distribution; the distribution of ratios of variances used for testing hypotheses about group differences in means

feminism a philosophy which argues that women's experiences and contributions are undervalued by society and by science; also an emancipatory movement to rectify these inequalities

financial databases archives of records about companies or other entities which contain financial data, such as income data, cash flow, profit & loss, share prices

focused codes codes that are directed, conceptual and analytical

frequency distribution a summary representation of a sample of data containing the number of responses obtained for each alternative on the measurement scale

generalizability the extent to which observations or theories derived in one context can be applicable to other contexts

generalized linear models a class of multivariate statistical models within which the relationships between DVs and PVs are linear, and DVs can be expressed through a transformation called a link function; it includes multiple regression analysis, ANOVA and logistic regression

goodness of fit a summary measure of the discrepancy between observed values and the fitted values derived from a hypothesized model

grand theory a coherent set of assumptions intended to explain social or physical phenomena. May or may not be empirically testable

grounded analysis the linking of key variables (theoretical codes) into a more holistic theory that makes a contribution to knowledge in a particular field or domain

grounded theory an open (and inductive) approach to analysis where there are no a priori definitional codes but where the structure is derived from the data and the constructs and categories derived emerge from the respondents under study hermeneutics a philosophy and methodology about the interpretation of texts. Stresses that textual materials should be understood in the context within which they are written

hierarchical regression a form of multiple regression analysis which involves entering predictor variables sequentially in blocks

histogram a form of bar chart for continuous scales, where scale points are first grouped together and the length of bars indicates the frequency of responses for each category

human relations theory assumes that performance of both individuals and organizations is dependent on the commitment and involvement of all employees, and hence managers need to foster positive relationships with, and between, employees

hypothesis testing the process of making inferences about populations based upon data drawn from samples

identifiability the characteristic of a hypothesized model defined by the relationship between the number of parameters in a model to be estimated and the information available to do it; a model is identified if there are fewer parameters to be estimated than there are items of information available

independent variables the factors that are believed to cause the effects that are to be observed (see dependent variable)

in-depth interview an opportunity, usually within an interview, to probe deeply and open up new dimensions and insights

inference drawing conclusions about a population based on evidence from a sample

inferential surveys surveys that are aimed at establishing relationships between variables and concepts

interaction effects where the effect on a variable depends on the context defined by another variable

internal validity assurance that results are true and conclusions are correct through elimination of systematic sources of potential bias

interquartile range see mid-range

interval scale a form of continuous scale which has no true zero point, so that ratio calculations are not meaningful, for example temperature (cf ratio scale)

interview bias occurs when the process of questioning influences the interviewees response

Kruskal–Wallace test a form of hypothesis test for comparing two or more groups which uses rank-order data

Lagrange multiplier test a form of modification index in SEM which indicates the value of a fixed parameter if it were to be set free

latent variables a class of variables within a multivariate model which are not measured directly but are inferred from observed variables

leading question a form of wording of a question which leads the respondent to give the answer preferred by the questioner

learning theory assumes that organizational competitiveness is linked to learning capacity, and hence a key role for managers is to foster learning processes

likelihood ratio chi-square an index of the overall quality of a model fitted by the maximum likelihood method; used in logistic regression analysis

Likert scale a form of ordinal category scale for measuring attitudes from very positive to very negative

linear relationship a relationship between two variables where as values on one variable increase there is a proportional increase in values on the other (cf. curvilinear relationship)

local knowledge ideas and principles which are relevant to the setting of a particular organization or social setting, but which may not apply in other contexts

location a characteristic of a set of data which summarizes where the data are located on the measurement scale; measured by the mode, median, mid-mean or mean

logistic regression a form of multivariate analysis of causal relationships among observed variables where the dependent variable is measured on a binary category scale

Mann–Whitney U test a form of hypothesis test for comparing two groups which uses rank-order data

mean a summary measure of location which uses all the values in a dataset in its calculation; the sum of all data points divided by the sample size

measurement model a multivariate model for the relationship between observed variables and latent variables

median a summary measure of location which uses the ranks of all the values in a dataset in its calculation; the middle value in an ordered set of data points mediational model a form of causal model in which the causal influence of a predictor variable on a dependent variable is indirect, operating through an intermediary variable (called a mediator)

methodological contribution this is achieved where an academic report or paper develops new methods of inquiry, or extends existing methods into new contexts

middle-range theory a set of ideas and concepts relevant to explaining social or physical phenomena within relatively specific contexts. Normally empirically testable

mid-mean a summary measure of location; the mean of the middle half of the data

mid-range a summary measure of spread; the range of the middle half of the data (also called the interquartile range)

mode 1 research the generation of theoretical knowledge through detached scientific research

mode 1½ research the generation of useful knowledge through combining scientific research methods with practical engagement

mode 2 research the generation of practical knowledge through direct engagement with practice

mode a summary measure of location; the most frequently occurring value in a dataset

modification index an estimate in SEM of the change in goodness of fit of a fitted model if a fixed parameter were allowed to become free

multiple regression model a multivariate method which includes a single dependent variable measured on a continuous scale and a set of predictor variables which may be measured on continuous or category scales

multistage sampling a process of dividing up a population into hierarchical units, such as countries, regions, organizations, work groups, and applying random sampling at each level

multivariate analysis of covariance (MANCOVA) a class of statistical methods for testing group differences for two or more dependent variables simultaneously, which also includes one or more continuous variables as predictors

multivariate analysis of variance (MANOVA) a class of statistical methods for testing group differences for two or more dependent variables simultaneously

multivariate methods a class of statistical methods which analyses the covariances among a number of variables simultaneously

multivariate test a test of a study hypothesis which involves consideration of several dependent variables simultaneously

narrative methods ways of conducting research that concentrate on collecting the stories told among organizational members

nodes these represent ideas or concepts linked to passages of text. Nodes can be recognized and reorganized during analysis without affecting the coding structure

nominal scale a form of category scale where the scale units have no natural ordering, for example makes of car purchased (cf. ordinal scale)

nominalism an ontological view that objects in the world are 'formed' by the language we use and the names we attach to phenomena

non-experimental designs positivist research conducted through comparing groups for which the members have not been assigned at random. Similar to quasi-experimental designs

non-normed fit index an incremental index in SEM of the goodness of fit of a hypothesized causal model relative to the null model

non-parametric test a form of hypothesis test which uses a reference distribution derived from all possible permutations of study outcomes using the ranking of data (cf parametric test)

non-probability sampling designs sampling designs where the likelihood of each population entity being included in the sample cannot be known

non-proportional stratified random sampling a form of sampling where the population is divided into subsets (called strata) and different sampling proportions are used for each stratum for selecting a sample

normal distribution a form of standard reference distribution; the distribution of the sum of independent measures where the standard deviation of the reference distribution is known (its shape is sometimes called the bell-curve)

normative theory describes how organizations *should* be structured and managed

null hypothesis (H_0) the initial position adopted during hypothesis testing which may be modified on the basis of evidence from data; for tests involving comparing groups, the null hypothesis is that the groups are nothing but random samples from a single population (see also alternative hypothesis) null model a model within structural equation modelling which assumes that all the covariances among the observed variables are zero; used as the baseline for calculating incremental fit indices

NVivo a software package that assists in the building and testing of theories by classifying, sorting and arranging information. Available from ORS International http://www.qsrinternational.com

observational methods ways of collecting data that involve direct sampling of aspects of behaviour

observed variables a class of variables in a multivariate model which are directly measured; they can be used to estimate latent variables

observer effects influences on behaviour which results from study participants knowing that they are being observed

odds ratio the relative likelihood of the two possible outcomes for a binary category variable; used to form the dependent variable in logistic regression analysis

ontology views about the nature of reality

open codes relatively indiscriminate codes, which derive from sampling, individuals or occurrences

ordinal scale a form of category scale where the scale units have a natural ordering, for example social class (cf. nominal scale)

paradigm a consensual pattern in the way scientists understand, and inquire into, the world

parametric test a form of hypothesis test which uses a standard reference distribution derived from probability theory whose form is defined by a small number of parameters (cf non-parametric test)

parsimony the extent to which a fitted model in SEM can account for observed data with fewer parameters

partial correlation a correlation between two variables which is adjusted to remove the influence of a third variable

participant observation a form of ethnography where there is close involvement in the organization in order to gain a detailed understanding of other peoples realities

permutations all possible ways of rearranging a set of entities; used in forms of nonparametric testing of hypotheses

phi coefficient a test of association between two variables measured on binary category scales

Poisson distribution a form of standard reference distribution; the distribution of the sum of independent measures where the standard deviation of the reference distribution is known (its shape is sometimes called the bell-curve)

population the set of entities about which a researcher wishes to draw conclusions

positivism the key idea of positivism is that the social world exists externally, and that its properties should be measured through objective methods

postal questionnaire survey a form of survey distribution which involves postal distribution, and relies on respondents to complete a survey themselves and return it to the researcher

postmodernism a collection of philosophies which are opposed to realism, and are generally critical of scientific progress

pragmatism a philosophical position which argues that knowledge and understanding should be derived from direct experience

precision the level of confidence that the researcher has in estimating characteristics of the population from evidence drawn from a sample; it depends on sample size but not on the sampling proportion

primary data new information that is collected directly by the researcher

principal component analysis a mathematical procedure that assists in reducing data and by so doing indicates possible relationships between a number of uncorrelated variables. The first principal component accounts for as much of the variability in the data as possible, successive components (of which there may be two, three or four) account for as much of the remaining variability as possible

probability sample designs sampling designs where the likelihood of each population entity being included in the sample is known

probe a device used as an intervention technique to improve and sharpen the interviewees response

product-moment correlation a test of association between two variables measured on continuous scales

proportional stratified random sampling a form of sampling where the population is divided into subsets (called strata) and within strata the same sampling proportion is used for selecting a sample

pure research research for which the primary objective/output is the development of theory

purposive sampling a form of non-probability sampling design where the criteria for inclusion in a sample are defined, and entities are first screened to see whether they meet the criteria for inclusion; those entities which meet the criteria are included in the sample

QASPS qualitative analysis software packages

quota sampling a form of non-probability sampling design where the population is divided into units and a target sample size (quota) is defined for each unit; entities which meet the criteria for a specific unit are added to the sample until the target sample size for the unit is achieved

random assignment where the objects of the experiment (e.g. people) are assigned at random to either the experimental treatment or to the control (nontreatment) groups

range a summary measure of spread; the difference between the largest and smallest data values

rank-order correlation a test of association between two variables measured on ordered category scales

ratio scale a form of continuous scale which has a true zero point, so that ratio calculations are meaningful, for example height (cf interval scale)

realism an ontological position which assumes that the physical and social worlds exist independently of any observations made about them

reference distribution the distribution of all alternatives values of a test statistic based on the assumption that the null hypothesis is true; used in hypothesis testing

reflexivity where researchers think about the effects they have had or may have on the outcome and process of research

regression weight the value of the independent contribution of a predictor variable to predicting a dependent variable in multiple regression analysis

relativism an ontological view that phenomena depend on the perspectives from which we observed them. Also an epistemological position that observations will be more accurate/credible if made from several different perspectives

reliability the consistency of measurement in a composite variable formed by combining scores on a set of items; can be measured by Cronbach's alpha coefficient

repertory grid a tool for uncovering an individual's (or group's) view of the world based on the constructs they develop and hold

representationalism. an ontological view that concrete phenomena exist, but cannot be observed directly, hence researchers should seek close correspondence between phenomena and the measures or words we use to describe them

representativeness in sampling design, this refers to how much the characteristics of a sample are the same as the characteristics of the population from which the sample is drawn

residual the value of that portion of the variance of a dependent variable which cannot be accounted for by a set of predictor variables

RMSEA (root mean squared error o approximation) an index in SEM of the goodness of fit of a hypothesized causal model adjusted for the complexity of the fitted model

robustness the extent to which a summary measure is sensitive to disturbances in data quality

sample size the number of entities included in a sample

sample a subset of the population from which inferences are drawn based on evidence

sampling distribution a form of reference distribution derived from probability theory based on repeated sampling from a theoretical population; used in hypothesis testing

sampling frame the list of all of those eligible to be included in a sample

sampling proportion the size of a sample relative to the size of a population

scholarship this is a term given to the development of high levels of knowledge about a particular issue or topic, largely on the basis of secondary data

search engine a program that will find text relating to the word(s) input

secondary data research information that already exists in the form of publications or other electronic media which is collected by the researcher

semi-concealed research a form of ethnography where there is negotiated access with research agendas that the researchers are not always willing to reveal to all those they meet

simple random sampling a form of sampling where every entity in the population has an equal chance of being included in the sample

snowball sampling a form of non-probability sampling design where the criteria for inclusion in a sample are defined; entities which meet the criteria are included in the sample and then asked whether they know others who also meet the criteria

Social Science Citation Index provides access to current and retrospective bibliographical information in the Social Sciences in the world's leading journals social constructionism the idea that 'reality' is determined by people rather than by objective and external factors, and hence it is most important to appreciate the way people make sense of their experience

social desirability where people adjust their answers to a survey in order to project a positive image of themselves to the interviewer

social engineering an approach to social policy formulation which relies on the research and analysis of expert scientists to determine the best course of action

specific factors a class of latent variables in a measurement model which is assumed to account for idiosyncratic aspects of an observed variable (see also common factors)

spread a characteristic of a set of data which summarizes how much the data vary around a measure of location; measured by the range, mid-range or standard deviation

squared multiple correlation an overall measure of the quality of a multiple regression model; the proportion of variance in a dependent variable accounted for by a set of predictor variables

standard deviation a summary measure of spread; based on the average deviation of scores around the mean

standard error the standard deviation of a sampling distribution used in hypothesis testing; estimated from the standard deviations and the sample size within groups in a sample

standardization the process of transforming a variable in order to express it on a scale with a mean of zero and a standard deviation of one; often carried out for variables measured on interval scales (with no true zero point) so that regression weights can be compared between predictor variables

standardized regression weight the value of the independent contribution of a predictor variable to predicting a dependent variable in multiple regression analysis after the predictor and dependent variables have been standardized; also called a beta weight

statistical control a way of simplifying inference about the relationships among variables by adjusting for their covariance with another variable

stepdown F-test the test statistic in a multivariate analysis of variance of group differences, where the DVs are tested singly in turn in a sequence decided upon by the researcher holding constant DVs earlier in the sequence

stepwise regression a form of multiple regression analysis where predictor variables are automatically entered or dropped sequentially on the basis of the extent of their independent contribution to predicting the dependent variable

stratified random sampling a form of sampling where the population is divided into subsets (called strata) and within strata every entity in the population has an equal chance of being included in the sample

stress survey a sample survey about the prevalence of causes of stress within the workplace and the extent of symptoms within employees

structural equation model a multivariate model of the hypothesized causal relationships among a set of variables which may include both observed and latent variables

structuration theory an epistemology which assumes that social structure and individual behaviour are interlinked, and that each is produced and reproduced by the other

structured interview surveys a form of survey where an interviewer locates each participant, and completes the survey face-to-face by asking structured questions

structured interviews where the interviewer follows a prescribed list of questions each of which may have predetermined response categories

substantive contribution this is achieved when the research throws new light onto the subject of study, whether it is a particular kind of organization or aspects of employee or managerial behaviour

summarizing describing a characteristic of a dataset such as location or spread based on aggregating data from all respondents

symmetry a balanced distribution of data points around a central value

synergy a form of interaction between variables, where their joint effect is different from the sum of their individual effects

systematic random sampling a process of random sampling where every nth entity from the population is selected

systematic review a means of synthesizing research on a topic or within a field in such a way that is both transparent and reproducible

t-distribution a form of standard reference distribution; a form of the normal distribution where the standard deviation of the reference distribution is estimated from sample data

telephone interview surveys a form of survey where an interviewer locates each participant, and completes the survey by telephone by asking structured questions

testing effect where changes observed in individual behaviour or attitudes over time are caused by the measures having been made in the first place

theoretical codes codes that derive from an understanding of how substantive codes relate one with another

theoretical contribution this is achieved when new concepts are developed, or existing concepts are extended, in order to understand or explain behaviour and organizational phenomena

topic guide a prepared list of areas (rather than specific questions) that need to be covered during the course of an interview

triangulation using different kinds of measures or perspectives in order to increase the confidence in the accuracy of observations

trimmed mean a family of summary measures of location where a proportion of the largest and smallest values are ignored in calculating a mean; the mid-mean is a 25% trimmed mean, the median is a 50% trimmed mean

t-test a form of hypothesis test for comparing means scores of two groups

type I error a false conclusion from a hypothesis test involving a claim that an effect exists (an association between variables or a group difference) when there is no such effect in the population

type II error a false conclusion from a hypothesis test involving a claim that no effect exists (an association between variables or a group difference) when there is an effect in the population

unit of analysis the main level at which data is aggregated: can be individuals, groups, events, organizations, etc. Within relativist studies researchers look for relationships between attributes which vary across different units of analysis

univariate F-test the test statistic in multivariate analysis of variance for group differences in a single dependent variable ignoring others

univariate test a test of a study hypothesis which involves consideration of a single dependent variable

universal theories theories that may be derived in one social organizational setting, and which are applicable in any other setting or context

validity the extent to which measures and research findings provide accurate representation of the things they are supposed to be describing

variance a summary measure of spread used in calculating the standard deviation; the average deviation of scores around the mean

verification a research design that seeks evidence to demonstrate that the current assumptions or hypotheses are correct

visual metaphors an approach to eliciting the views of individuals or groups with the notion of metaphors in order to get individuals (or groups) to draw and describe issues or events as they currently see them or would like to see them in the future

Wald test the test statistic in logistic regression analysis expressing the independent contribution of a predictor variable

Web of Science a database that provides a single route to journals in the Social Science Citation Index

web-based surveys a form of survey where a web site link is sent to each potential participant, respondents complete the survey by recording their answers on online; answers may be checked for consistency and then stored on a database for analysis

Wilks' lambda the test statistic in multivariate analysis of variance for group differences in a set of two or more dependent variables

work activity school this describes the nature of managerial work in practice. Although it does not assume that these work patterns are desirable, or undesirable, it does imply that training programmes need to prepare managers to cope with this 'reality'

Zetoc a current awareness service for Higher Education Institutions in the United Kingdom. The service gives access to the British Library's table of contents database and a Zetoc alert can provide users with information on the contents of new journals as soon as they are issued

BIBLIOGRAPHY

Abrahamson, M. (1983) *Social Research Methods*. Englewood Cliffs, NJ: Prentice Hall.

Agar, M.H. (1986) *Speaking of Ethnography*. Beverly Hills, CA: Sage.

Ahmed, S. (1998) *Differences that Matter: Feminist Theory and Postmodernism*. Cambridge: Cambridge University Press.

Aiken, H.D. (1956) *The Age of Ideology*. New York: Mentor.

Alvesson, M. (1990) 'Organization: from substance to image', *Organisation Studies,* 11: 373–94.

Alvesson, M. (1998) 'Gender relations and identity at work: a case study of an advertising agency', *Human Relations*, 51 (8): 969–1005.

Alvesson, M. (2003) 'Beyond neopositivists, romantics, and localists: a reflexive approach to interviews in organisation research', *Academy of Management Review* 28:11 13–33.

Alvesson, M. and Deetz, S. (2000) *Doing Critical Management Research*. London: Sage.

Alvesson, M and Skoldberg, K. (2000) *Reflexive Methodology: New Vistas for Qualitative Research towards a Reflexive Methodology*. London: Sage.

Amis, J. and Silk, M.L. (2008) 'Understanding quality: the philosophy and politics of quality in qualitative organizational research', *Organizational Research Methods*, 11 (forthcoming).

Anderson, M.L. (1993) 'Studying across difference: race, class and gender in qualitative research', in J.H. Stanfield and R.M. Dennis (eds): *Race and Ethnicity in Research Methods*. London: Sage. pp. 39–52.

Ashton, D.J.L. and Easterby-Smith, M. (1979) *Management Development in the Organisation*. London: Macmillan.

Astley, W.G. and Zammuto, R.F. (1992) 'Organisation Science, managers, and language games', *Organisation Science,* 3: 443–60.

Austin, J.H. (1978) *Chase, Chance and Creativity*. New York: Columbia University Press.

Baker, S. (1996) 'Consumer cognitions: mapping personal benefits relating to perfume purchase in the UK and Germany', 207th ESOMAR Seminar, Capturing the Elusive Appeal of Fragrance: Techniques, Experiences, Challenges. Amsterdam.

Baker, S. and Knox, S. (1995) 'Mapping consumer cognitions in Europe', in M. Bergadaa (ed.): *Marketing Today for the 21st Century*. Proceedings of 24th EMAC Conference, Cergy-Pontoisse, France. 1: 81–100.

Bales, R.F. (1950) *Interaction Process Analysis*. Cambridge, MA: Addison-Wesley.

Bales, R.F. (1970) *Personality and Interpersonal Behavior*. New York: Holt, Rinehart & Winston.

Bales, R.F. (1988) 'A new overview of the SYMLOG system: measuring and changing behavior in groups', in R.B. Polley, A.P. Hare and P.J. Stone (eds): *The SYMLOG Practitioner*. New York: Praeger. pp. 319–44.

Bales, R.F., Cohen, S.P. and Williamson, S.A. (1979) *SYMLOG: A System for the Multiple Level Observation of Groups*. New York: The Free Press.

Banks, M. (1995) 'Visual research methods', *Social Research Update*, 11. Guildford: University of Surrey.

Bannister, D. and Fransella, F. (1971) *Inquiring Man: The Theory of Personal Constructs*. Harmondsworth: Penguin.

Barley, S.R. (1986) *The Innocent Anthropologist: Notes from a Mud Hut*. Harmondsworth: Penguin.

Bartunek, J.M. and Louis, M.R. (1996) *Insider/Outsider Team Research*. Thousand Oaks, CA: Sage.

Barwise, P., Marsh, P., Thomas, K. and Wensley, R. (1989) 'Intelligent elephants and part-time researchers', *Graduate Management Research,* Winter: 12–33.

Bazeley, P. (2007) *Qualitative Data Analysis with NVivo*. London: Sage.

Bell, E. and Bryman, A. (2007) 'The ethics of management research: an exploratory content analysis', *British Journal of Management*, 18 (1): 63–77.

Bennis, W.G. and O'Toole, J. (2005) 'How business schools lost their way'. *Harvard Business School*, 83 (5): 1–9.

Bentler, P.M. and Dudgeon, P. (1996), Covariance structure analysis: statistical practice, theory and direction', *Annual Rev. Psychology*, 47: 563–92.

Berger, P.L. and Luckman, T. (1966) *The Social Construction of Reality*. London: Penguin.

Berghman, L., Matthyssens, P. and Vandenbempt, K. (2006), Building competences for new customer value creation: an exploratory study', *Industrial Marketing Management*, 35 (8): 961–73.

Berman, S.L., Wicks, A.C., Kotha, S. and Jones, T.M. (1999) 'Does stakeholder orientation matter? The relationship between stakeholder management models and firm financial performance', *Academy of Management Journal*, 42 (5): 488–506.

Bessant, J., Binley, S., Cooper, C., Dawson, S., Gernard, J., Gardiner, M., Gray, A., Jones, P., Mayer, C., Magee, J., Pidd, M., Rowley, G., Saunders, J., Stark, A. (2003) 'The state of the field in UK management research: reflections of the Research Assessment Exercise (RAE) Panel', *British Journal of Management* 14: 51–68.

Bettis, R.A. and Prahalad, C.K. (1995) 'The Dominant Logic: Retrospective and Extensions', *SMJ*, 16 (1): 5–14.

Beynon, H. (1973) *Working for Ford*. Harmondsworth: Penguin.

Beynon, H. (1988) 'Regulating research: politics and decision making in industrial organisations', in A. Bryman (ed.), *Doing Research in Organisations*. London: Routledge. pp. 21–33.

Bhaskar, R. (1989) *Reclaiming Reality: A Critical Introduction to Contemporary Philosophy*. London: Verso.

Billig, M. (1988) 'Review of: *Murderous Science: Elimination by Scientific Selection of Jews, Gypsies and Others. Germany 1933–1945*'. B. Muller-Hill, Oxford: OUP, *The Psychologist*, December: 475–6.

Billig, M. (1991) *Ideology and Opinions: Studies of Rhetorical Psychology*. London: Sage.

Birkinshaw, J., Braunerhjelm, P., Holm, U. and Terjesen, S. (2006) 'Why do some multinational corporations relocate their headquarters overseas?', *Strategic Management Journal*, 27 (7): 681–700.

Blaikie, N. (1993) *Approaches to Social Enquiry*. Cambridge: Polity Press.

Bloom, B.S. and Krathwohl, D.R. (1956) *Taxonomy of Educational Objectives*. London: Longman.

Boissevain, J. (1974) *Friends of Friends*. Oxford: Blackwell.

Boje, D. (2001) *Narrative Methods for Organisational and Communication Research*. London: Sage.

Boje, D.M. (1995) 'Stories of the story-telling organization: a postmodern analysis of Disney as "Tamara-land"', *Academy of Management Journal*, 38 (4): 997–1035.

Boje, D.M. (2001) *Narrative Methods for Organizational and Communication Research*. London: Sage.

Borgatti, S.P., Everett, M.G. and Freeman, L.C. (2002) *Ucinet for Windows: Software for Social Network Analysis*. Harvard, MA: Analytic Technologies. Available at: http://www.analytictech.com/

Bowey, A.M. and Thorpe, R. (1986) *Payment Systems and Productivity*. Basingstoke: Macmillan.

Box, G.E.P., Hunter, S.J. and Hunter, W.G. (2005) *Statistics for Experimenters: Design, Innovation, and Discovery*, 2nd edn. John Wiley & Sons.

Boyacigiller, N.A. and Adler, N.J. (1991) 'The parochial dinosaur: organizational science in a global context', *Academy of Management Review*, 16: 262–90.

Boyatzis, R.E. (1982) *The Competent Manager: A Model for Effective Performance*. New York: Wiley.

Brandi, U. and Elkjaer, B. (2008) 'Pragmatism', in R. Thorpe et al. (eds), *Sage Dictionary of Qualitative Management Research*. London: Sage. pp. 169–171.

Brewer, J.D. (2000) *Ethnography*. Buckingham: Open University.

Brouthers, K.D. and Brouthers, L.E. (2003) 'Why services and manufacturing entry mode choices differ: the influence of transaction cost factors, risk and trust', *Journal of Management Studies*, 40(3): 1179–204.

Brouthers, K.D., Brouthers, L.E. and Werner, S. (2003) 'Transaction cost-enhanced entry mode choices and firm performance', *Strategic Management Journal*, 24 (12): 1239–48.

Brown, S.L. and Eisenhardt, K.M. (1998) *Competing on the Edge: Strategy as Structured Chaos*. Boston, MA: Harvard University Press.

Bryman, A. and Bell, E. (2007) *Business Research Methods*, 2nd edn. Oxford: Oxford University Press.

Bryman, A. and Cramer, D. (2004) *Quantitative Data Analysis with SPSS 12 and 13: A Guide for Social Scientists*. London: Routledge.

Buchanan, D. (1980) 'Gaining management skills through academic research work', *Personnel Management*, 12 (4): 45–8.

Buchanan, D.A. (1999) 'The role of photography in organisation research: a re-engineering case illustration', *Journal of Management Inquiry*, 10: 151–64.

Buchanan, D. and Badham, R. (2008) *Power, Politics and Organizational Change: Winning the Turf Game*, 2nd edn. London: Sage.

Buchanan D.A., Boddy, D. and McCalman, J. (1988) 'Getting in, getting on, getting out, getting back: the art of the possible', in A. Bryman (ed.), *Doing Research in Organisations*. London: Routledge. pp. 53–67.

Buchanan, D. and Bryman, A. (2007) 'Contextualizing methods choice in organizational research', *Organizational Research Methods*, 10 (3): 483–501.

Bulmer, M. (1988) 'Some reflections upon research in organization', in A. Bryman (ed.). *Doing Research in Organizations*. London: Routledge. pp. 151–161.

Burgess, R.G. (1982) *Field Research: A Source Book and Field Manual*. London: Allen and Unwin.

Burgoyne, J. and James, K. T. (2006) 'Towards best or better practice in corporate leadership development: operational issues is Mode 2 and design science research', *British Journal of Management*, 17: 303–16.

Burgoyne, J. and Stuart, R. (1976) 'The nature, use and acquisition of managerial skills and other attributes', *Personnel Review*, 15 (4): 19–29.

Burrell, G. (1993) 'Eco and the Bunnymen', in J. Hassard and M. Parker (eds), *Postmodernism and Organizations*. London: Sage. pp. 71–82.

Burrell, G. and Morgan, G. (1979) *Sociological Paradigms and Organisational Analysis*. London: Heinemann.

Buzan, T. (2004) *Mind Maps: How to Be the Best at Your Job and Still Have Time to Play*. New York: Plume.

Calder, A. and Sheridan, D. (1984) *Speak for Yourself: A Mass-Observation Anthology 1937–49*. London: Cape.

Castells, M. (2000) *The Rise of the Network Society*, 2nd edn. Oxford: Blackwell.

Charmaz, K. (2000) 'Grounded theory: objectivist and constructivist methods', in N.K. Denzin and Y.S. Lincoln (eds), *Sage Handbook of Qualitative Research*, 2nd edition. London: Sage. pp. 509–35.

Charmaz, K. (2006) *Constructing Grounded Theory: A Practical Guide Through Qualitative Analysis*. London: Sage.

Chia, R. (2008) 'Postmodernism', in R. Thorpe et al. (eds), *Sage Dictionary of Qualitative Management Research*. London: Sage. pp. 162–3.

Churchill, J. (1990) 'Complexity and strategic decision making', in C. Eden and J. Radford (eds), *Tackling Strategic Problems: The Role of Group Decision Support*. London: Sage. pp. 11–17.

Clarke, J. (2007) 'Seeing entrepreneurship: visual ethnographies of embodied entrepreneurs', unpublished PhD thesis, University of Leeds.

Coch, L. and French, J.R.P. (1948) 'Overcoming resistance to change', *Human Relations* 1: 512–33.

Coffey, A. and Atkinson, P. (1996) *Making Sense of Qualitative Data*. London: Sage.

Cohen, W.M. and Levinthal, D.A. (1990) 'Absorptive capacity: a new perspective on learning and innovation', *Administrative Science Quarterly*, 35: 128–52.

Collier, J. and Collier, J. (1986) *Visual Anthropology: Photography as a Research Method*. Albuquerque, NM: University of New Mexico.

Collins, H.M. (1983) 'An empirical relativist programme in the sociology of scientific knowledge', in K.D Knorr-Cetina and M. Mulkay (eds), *Science Observed: Perspectives on the Social Study of Science*. London: Sage.

Collinson, D.L. (1992) *Managing the Shop Floor: Subjectivity, Masculinity, and Workplace Culture*. New York: de Gruyter.

Collinson, D.L. (2002) 'Managing humour', *Journal of Management Studies*, 39: 269–88.

Comte, A. (1853) *The Positive Philosophy of Auguste Comte* (trans. H. Martineau). London: Trubner and Co.

Cook, S.D.N. and Brown, J.S. (1999) 'Bridging epistemologies: the generative dance between organizational knowledge and organizational knowing', *Organization Science*, 10 (4): 381–400.

Cooper, R. (1992) 'Formal organization as representation: Remote Control, Displacement and Abbreviation', in M. Reed and M. Hughes (eds), *Rethinking Organization*. London: Sage.

Cooper, R. and Burrell, G. (1988) 'Modernism, postmodernism and organizational analysis: an introduction', *Organization Studies*, 9 (1): 91–112.

Cornelissen, J. P. (2004) *Corporate Communications: Theory and Practice*. London: Sage.

Cotterill, P. (1992) 'Interviewing women: issues of friendship, vulnerability and power', *Women's Studies International Forum*, 15 (5/6): 593–606.

Cotterill, S. amd King, S. (2007) 'Public sector partnerships to deliver local e-government: a social network study', *Sixth International EGOV Conference, Regensburg (Germany)*, 3–7 September. Available at: http://www.springerlink.com/content/a646737037n18g70/

Couper, M.P., Traugott, M.W. and Lamias, M.J. (2001) 'Web survey design and administration', *Public Opinion Quarterly*, 65 (2): 230–53.

Coyle-Shapiro, J. and Kessler, I. (2000) 'Consequences of the psychological contract for the employment relationship: a large scale survey', *Journal of Management Studies*, 37 (7): 903–30.

Crawford, S.D., Couper, M.P. and Lamias, M.J. (2001) 'Web surveys: perceptions of burden', *Social Science Computer Review*, 19(2): 146–62.

Cresswell, J.W. (2003) *Research Design: Qualitative, Quantitative and Mixed Methods Approaches*. London: Sage.

Crotty, M. (1998) *The Foundations of Social Research: Meaning and Perspective in the Research Process*. London: Sage.

Cryer, P. (2000) *The Research Student's Guide to Success*. Buckingham: Open University Press.

Cunliffe, A.L. (2001) 'Managers as practical authors: reconstructing our understanding of management practice', *Journal of Management Studies*, 38: 351–71.

Cunliffe, A.L. (2002) 'Reflexive dialogical practice in management learning', *Management Learning*, 33 (1): 35–61.

Cunliffe, A.L. (2003) 'Reflexive inquiry in organizational research: questions and possibilities', *Human Relations*, 56 (8): 983–1003.

Curran, J. and Downing, S. (1989) 'The state and small business owners: an empirical assessment of consultation strategies', paper presented at the 12th National Small Firms Policy and Research Conference, Barbican, London.

Cyert, R.H. and March, J.G. (1963) *A Behavioral History of the Firm*. Englewood-Cliffs NJ: Prentice-Hall.

Czarniawska, B. (1998) *A Narrative Approach to Organization Studies*. London: Sage.

Daft, R.L. and Lengel, R.H. (1986) 'Organisational information requirements, media richness and structural design', *Management Science*, 32: 554–71.

Daiute, C. and Lightfoot, C. (2004) *Narrative Analysis: Studying the Development of Individuals in Society*. London: Sage.

Dalton, M. (1959) *Men Who Manage: Fusion of Feeling and Theory in Administration*. New York: Wiley.

Dalton, M. (1964) 'Preconceptions and methods in *Men Who Manage*', in P. Hammond (ed.), *Sociologists at Work*. New York: Basic Books.

Davies, G., Chun, R., Da Silva, R. and Roper, S. (2002) *Corporate Reputation and Competitiveness*. London: Routledge.

Davila, C. (1989) 'Grounding management education in local research: a Latin American experience', in J. Davies, M. Easterby-Smith, S. Mann and M. Tanton (eds), *The Challenge to Western Management Development: International Alternatives*. London: Routledge.

Deem, R. and Brehony, K. (1997) 'Research students' access to research cultures: an unequal benefit?', paper presented at Society for Research in Higher Education Conference, University of Warwick.

Denzin, N.K. and Lincoln, Y.S. (2006) *Sage Handbook of Qualitative*, 3rd edn. London: Sage.

Dewey, J. (1916) *Democracy and Education*. London: Collier Macmillan.

Dhanaraj, C., Lyles, M.A., Steensma, H.K. and Tihanyi, L. (2004) 'Managing tacit and explicit knowledge transfer in IJVs: The role of relational embeddedness and the impact on performance', *Journal of International Business Studies*, 35 (5): 428–43.

Dillman, D.A. (2000) *Mail and Internet Surveys: The Tailored Design Method*, 2nd edn. New York: John Wiley & Sons.

Ditton, J. (1977) *Part-time Crime*. London: Macmillan.

Dobson, A.J. (2001) *Introduction to Generalized Linear Models*, 2nd edn. London: Chapman and Hall.

Douglas, J.D. (ed.) (1976) *Investigative Social Research*. Beverly Hills, CA: Sage.

Duggan, F. (2006): 'Plagiarism: prevention, practice and policy', *Assessment & Evaluation in Higher Education*, 31 (2): 151–4.

Dyer, J.H. and Hatch, N.W. (2006) 'Relation-specific capabilities and barriers to knowledge transfers: Creating advantage through network relationships', *Strategic Management Journal*, 27 (8): 701–19.

Easterby-Smith, M. (1994/1986) *Evaluation of Management Education, Training and Development*. Aldershot: Gower.

Easterby-Smith, M. (1997) 'Disciplines of organizational learning: contributions and critiques', *Human Relations*, 51 (9): 1085–116.

Easterby-Smith, M. and Ashton, D. (1975) 'Using repertory grid technique to evaluate management training', *Personnel Review*, 4 (4): 15–21.

Easterby-Smith, M., Graca, M., Antonacopoulou, A. and Ferdinand, J. (2008) 'Absorptive capacity: a process perspective', *Management Learning* (forthcoming).

Easterby-Smith, M. and Lyles, M. (2003) *Handbook of Organizational Learning and Knowledge Management*. Oxford: Blackwell.

Easterby-Smith, M. and Malina, D. (1999) 'Cross-cultural collaborative research: toward reflexivity', *Academy of Management Journal*, 42 (1): 76–86.

Easterby-Smith, M., Thorpe, R. and Holman, D. (1996) 'The use of repertory grids in management', *Journal of European Industrial Training*, 20 (3): 1–30.

Eden, C (1990) 'Strategic thinking with computers', *Long Range Planning*, 23 (6): 35–43.

Eden, C. and Ackermann, F. (1998) *Making Strategy: The Journey of Strategic Management*. London: Sage.

Eden, C. and Huxham, C. (1996) 'Action Research for Management Research', *British Journal of Management*, 7 (1): 75–86.

Eden, C. and Huxham, C. (2002) *Essential Skills for Management Research*. London: Sage.

Eden, C. and Huxham, C. (2007) 'Action research and the study of organisations', in S. Clegg, C. Hardy and W. Nord (eds), *Handbook of Organisation Studies*. London: Sage. pp. 526–42.

Eden, C., Jones, S. and Sims, D. (1983) *Messing About in Problems: An Informal Structured Approach to Their Identification and Management*. Oxford: Pergamon Press.

Eesley, C. and Lenox, M.J. (2006) 'Firm responses to secondary stakeholder action', *Strategic Management Journal*, 27 (8): 765–81.

Eisenhardt, K.M. (1989) 'Building theories from case study research', *Academy of Management Review*, 14 (4): 532–50.

Eisenhardt, K.M. and Graebner, M.E. (2007) 'Theory building from cases: opportunities and challenges', *Academy of Management Journal*, 50 (1): 25–32.

Engeström, Y. (1999) 'Activity theory as a framework for analysis and redesigning work', *Ergonomics*, 43 (7): 960–74.

Engestrom, Y. (2000) 'Activity theory and the social construction of knowledge: A story of four imports', *Organisation* 7(2): 302–310

ESRC (2001) *Postgraduate Training Guidelines*, 3rd edn. Swindon: ESRC.

Evers, F.T. and Rush, J.C. (1996) 'The bases of competence: skill development during the transition from university to work', *Management Learning*, 27 (3): 275–300.

Fairclough, N. and Hardy, G. (1997) 'Management learning as discourse', in J. Burgoyne and M. Reynolds (eds), *Management Learning: Integrating Perspectives in Theory and Practice*. London: Sage. pp. 144–160.

Fairhurst, E. (1983) 'Organisational rules and the accomplishment of nursing work on geriatric wards', *Journal of Management Studies*, Special Issue, 20(3): 315–32.

Fayol, H. (1916/1950) *Administration Industrielle et Generale*. Paris: Dunod.

Fielding, N.G. and Fielding, J.L. (1986) *Linking Data*. Beverly Hills, CA: Sage.

Filatotchev, I. (2006) 'Effects of executive characteristics and venture capital involvement on board composition and share ownership in IPO firms', *British Journal of Management*, 17, 75–92.

Flanagan, J.C. (1954) 'The critical incident technique', *Psychological Bulletin*, 1: 327–58.

Fournier, V. and Grey, C. (2000) 'At the critical moment: conditions and prospects for critical management studies', *Human Relations*, 52 (1): 7–32.

Freeman, R.E. (1984) *Strategic management: a stakeholder approach*. London: Pitman.

Gadamer, H.-G. (1989) Truth and Method, 2nd rev. edn (trans. J. Weinsheimer and D.G. Marshall). New York: Crossroad.

Gash, S. (2000) *Effective Literature Searching*. Aldershot: Gower.

Geary, L., Marriott, L. and Rowlinson, M. (2004) 'Journal rankings in business and management and the 2001 Research Assessment Exercise in the UK', *British Journal of Management* 15: 95–141.

Gergen, K.J. (1995) 'Relational theory and discourses of power', in D.-M. Hosking, H.P. Dachler and K.J. Gergen (eds), *Management and Organization: Relational Alternatives to Individualism*. Aldershot: Avebury. pp. 29–49

Gibbons, M. L., Limoges, C., Nowotny, H. Schwartman, S., Scott, P. and Trow, M. (1994) *The New Production of Knowledge: The Dynamics of Science and Research in Contemporary Societies*. Sage: London.

Giddens, A. (1984) *The Constitution of Society: Outline of the Theory of Structuration*. Cambridge: Polity Press.

Glaser, B.G. (1978) *Theoretical Sensitivity*. Mill Valley, CA: Sociological Press.

Glaser, B.G. (1992) *Basics of Grounded Theory Analysis: Emergence versus Forcing*. Mill Valley, CA: Sociological Press.

Glaser, B.G. (1998) *Doing Grounded Theory: Issues and Discussions*. Mill Valley, CA: Sociology Press.

Glaser, B.B.G. and Strauss, A.L. (1967) *The Discovery of Grounded Theory: Strategies for Qualitative Research*. New York: Aldine.

Gold, J., Hamblett, J. and Rix, M (2000) 'Telling stories for managing change: a business/academic partnership', *Education through Partnership*, 4 (1): 36–46.

Gold, J., Holman, D. and Thorpe, R. (2002) 'The role of argument analysis and story telling in facilitating critical thinking', *Management Learning*, 33 (3): 371–88.

Gold, J., Thorpe, R. and Holt, R. (2007) 'Writing, reading and reason: the "Three rs" of manager learning', in R. Hill and J. Stewart (eds), *Management Development: Perspectives from Research and Practice*. Abingdon: Routledge.

Goldacre, M.J., Davidson, J.M. and Lambert, T.W. (2004) 'Country of training and ethnic origin of UK doctors: database and survey studies', *British Medical Journal*, 329 (11): 597–600.

Golden-Biddle, K. and Locke, K. (1993) 'Appealing work: an investigation of how ethnographic texts convince', *Organisation Science*, 4 (2): 595–616.

Golden-Biddle, K. and Locke, K. (2007) *Composing Qualitative Research*, 2nd edn. London: Sage.

Grey, C. (2005) *A Very Short, Fairly Interesting and Reasonably Cheap Book about Studying Organizations*. London: Sage.

Guba, E.G. and Lincoln, Y.S. (1989) *Fourth Generation Evaluation*. London: Sage.

Gubrium, J.F. and Silverman, D. (eds) (1989) *The Politics of Field Research*. London: Sage.

Gummerson, E. (1992) *Case Study Research in Management: Methods for Generating Qualitative Data*. Stockholm: Stockholm University.

Gummesson, E. (1988/1991) *Qualitative Research in Management*. Bromley: Chartwell-Bratt.

Gunn, H. (2002) 'Web-based surveys: changing the survey process', *First Monday*, 7 (12).

Habermas, J. (1970) 'Knowledge and interest', in D. Emmett and A. Macintyre (eds), *Sociological Theory and Philosophical Analysis*. London: Macmillan.

Habermas, J. (1971) *Towards a Rational Society*. London: Heinemann.

Hair, J.F., Black, B., Babin, B., Anderson, R.E. and Tatham, R.L. (2005) *Multivariate Data Analysis*. Upper Saddle River, NJ: Prentice-Hall.

Hales, C.P. (1986) 'What do managers do? A critical review of the evidence', *Journal of Management Studies*, 23 (1): 88–115.

Handy, C. (1996) *Beyond Certainty: The Changing Worlds of Organizations*. London: Arrow Books.

Hanneman, R.A. and Riddle, M. (2005) *Introduction to Social Network Methods*. Riverside, CA: University of California. Available at: http://faculty.ucr.edu/~hanneman/

Hardy, C. (1996) 'Understanding power: bringing about strategic change', *British Journal of Management*, 7 (Special Issue): S3–S16.

Harper, D. (1989) 'Visual sociology: expanding sociological vision', in G. Blank et al. (eds), *New Technology in Sociology: Practical Applications in Research and Work*. New Brunswick, NJ: Transaction Books. pp. 81–97.

Harper, D. (1994) 'On the authority of the image: visual methods at the crossroads', in N.K. Denzin and Y.S. Lincoln (eds), *Handbook of Qualitative Research*. Thousand Oaks: Sage. pp. 403–12.

Harvey, C., Morris, H. and Kelly, A. (eds) (2007) *Association of Business Schools Academic Journal Quality Guide*. London, The Association of Business Schools.

Harzing, A.-W. (ed.) (2007) *Journal Quality List*, 27th edn. Available at: http://www.harzing.com/

Hassard, J. and Parker, M. (eds) (1993) *Postmodernism and Organizations*. London: Sage.

Hatch, M. J. (1996) 'Irony and the social construction of contradiction in the humor of a management team', *Organization Science*, 8 (3): 275–388.

Hayano, D.M. (1979) 'Auto-ethnography paradigms, problems and prospects', *Human Organisation*, 38: 99–104.

Hayes, R.H. and Abernethy, W.J. (1980) 'Managing our way to economic decline', *Harvard Business Review*, 58: 67–77.

Heath, C. and Hindmarsh, J. (2002) 'Analyzing interaction: video, ethnography and situated conduct', in T. May (ed.), *Qualitative Research in Action*. London: Sage. pp. 99–122

Heisenberg, W (1927) 'Über den anschaulichen Inhalt der quantentheoretischen Kinematik und Mechanik', *Zeitschrift für Physik*, 43: 172–98. [English translation: J. A. Wheeler and H. Zurek (1983) *Quantum Theory and Measurement*. Princeton, NJ: Princeton University Press. pp. 62–84.]

Heron, J. (1996) *Co-operative Inquiry: Research into the Human Condition*. London: Sage.

Herzberg, F., Mausner, B. and Snyderman, B.B. (1959) *The Motivation to Work*. New York: Wiley.

Hickson, D.J. (1988) 'Ruminations on munificence and scarcity in research', in A. Bryman (ed.), *Doing Research in Organizations*. London: Routledge.

Hofstede, G. (1980) *Culture's Consequences: International Differences in Work-Related Values*. Beverly Hills: Sage. [Abridged edn, 1984.]

Hofstede, G. (1991) *Cultures and Organizations: Software of the Mind*. Maidenhead: McGraw-Hill.

Holman, D. (1996) 'The experience of skill development in undergraduates', PhD thesis, Manchester Metropolitan University.

Hong, J., Easterby-Smith, M. and Snell, R. (2006) 'Transferring organizational learning systems to Japanese subsidiaries in China', *Journal of Management Studies*, 43 (5): 1027–58.

Howell, D. (2001) *Statistical Methods for Psychology*, 5th edn. Wadsworth.

Howell, D. (2007) *Fundamental Statistics for the Behavioral Sciences*, 6th edn. Wadsworth.

Hsiu-Fang, H. and Shannon, S.E. (2005) 'Three approaches to qualitative content analysis', *Qualitative Health Research*, 15 (9): 1277–88.

Huczynski, A.A. (1996) *Management Gurus: What Makes Them and How to Become One*. London: International Thomson Business Press.

Huff, A.S. (1999) *Writing for Scholarly Publication*. London: Sage.

Huff, A.S. (2000) 'Changes in organizational knowledge production', *Academy of Management Review*, 25 (2): 288–93.

Humphreys, M. and Brown, A.D. (2008) 'Narratives of corporate social responsibility: theorising identity at a bank', *Journal of Business Ethics*, forthcoming.

Huxham, C. (2003) 'Action research as a methodology for theory development', *Policy and Politics*, 31 (2): 239–48.

Hyder, S. and Sims, D. (1979) 'Hypothesis, analysis and paralysis: issues in the organisation of contract research', *Management Education Development*, 10: 100–11.

Irwin, A. (1994) 'Science's social standing', *The Times Higher*, 30 September: 17–19.

Jaccard, J. and Wan, C.K. (1996) *LISREL approaches to interaction effects in multiple regression*. Thousand Oaks, CA: Sage.

Jackson, P.R. (1986) 'Robust methods in statistics', in A.D. Lovie (ed.), *New developments in statistics for psychology and the social sciences*. London: The British Psychological Society & Methuen. pp. 22–43.

Jackson, P.R. (1989) 'Analysing data', in G. Parry and F.N. Watts (eds), *Behavioural and Mental Health Research: A Handbook of Skills and Methods*. London : Lawrence Erlbaum Associates. pp. 55–79.

Jackson, P.R. (2004) 'Employee commitment to quality: its conceptualisation and measurement', *International Journal of Quality & Reliability Management*, 21 (7): 714–30.

Jackson, P.R. and Parker, S.K. (2001) *Change in Manufacturing: How to Manage Stress-related Risks*. London: HSE Publications.

Jensen, J.P., Van den Bosch, F.A.J. and Volberda, H.W. (2005) 'Managing potential and realised absorptive capacity: how do organizational antecedents matter?', *Academy of Management Journal*, 48 (6): 999–1015.

Jobber, D. and Horgan, I. (1987) 'Market research and education: perspectives from practitioners', *Journals of Marketing Management*, 3 (1): 39–49.

Johnson, G., Scholes, K. and Whittington, R. (2008) Exploring Corporate Strategy, 7th edn. London: Prentice-Hall.

Jones, O. (2006) 'Developing absorptive capacity in mature organizations: the change agent's role', Management Learning, 37 (3): 355–76.

Jones, S. (1985) 'The analysis of depth interviews', in R. Walker, *Applied Qualitative Research*. Aldershot: Gower. pp. 56–70.

Kalaitzidakis, P., Mamuneas, T.P. and Stengos, T. (2001) *Ranking of Academic Journals and Institutions in Economics*. Available at: http://www.le.ac.uk/economics/research/rankings/econ-rankings.html

Katsikeas, C.S., Samiee, S. and Theodosiou, M. (2006) 'Strategy fit and performance consequences of international marketing standardization', *Strategic Management Journal*, 27(9): 867–90.

Kelly, G.A. (1955) *The Psychology of Personal Constructs.* New York: Norton.

King, N. (2004) 'Using templates in the thematic analysis of text', in C. Cassell and G. Symon (eds), *Essential Guide to Qualitative Methods*, 2nd edn. London: Sage. pp. 118–34.

Knorr-Cetina, K.D. (1983) 'The ethnographic study of scientific work: towards a constructivist interpretation of science', in K.D. Knorr-Cetina and M. Mulkay (eds), *Science Observed: Perspectives on the Social Study of Science.* London: Sage.

Kolb, D.A. (1984) *Organisational Psychology: An Experimental Approach to Organisational Behaviour.* Englewood Cliffs, NJ: Prentice-Hall.

Kolb, D.A. (1986) *Experiential Learning.* Englewood Cliffs, NJ: Prentice-Hall.

Kotter, J. (1982) *The General Managers.* Glencoe, IL: Free Press.

Krech, D., Crutchfield, R.S. and Ballachey, E.L. (1962) *Individual in Society.* London: McGraw-Hill.

Kuhn, T.S. (1962) *The Structure of Scientific Revolution.* Chicago, IL: University of Chicago Press.

Kvale, S. (1996) *InterViews.* London: Sage.

Labov, W. (1972) *Language in the Inner City.* Oxford: Blackwell.

Latour, B. (1988) 'The politics of explanation; an alternative', in S. Woolgar (ed.), *Knowledge and Reflexivity: New Frontiers in the Sociology of Knowledge.* London: Sage.

Latour, B. and Woolgar, S. (1979) *Laboratory Life: The Social Construction of Scientific Facts.* Beverly Hills, CA: Sage.

Law, J. (1994) *Organizing Modernity.* Oxford: Blackwell.

Lawrence, P.R. (1986) *Invitation to Management.* Oxford: Blackwell.

Lawrence, P.R. and Lorsch, J.W. (1967) *Organisational Environment: Managing Differentiation and Integration.* Boston, MA: Division of Research, Graduate School of Business Administration, Harvard University.

Lawrence, T.B., Mauws, M.K.. Dyck, B. and Kleysen, R.F. (2005) 'The politics of organizational learning: integrating power into the 4I framework', *Academy of Management Review*, 30 (1): 180–91.

Leask, B. (2006) 'Plagiarism, cultural diversity and metaphor – implications for academic staff development', *Assessment & Evaluation in Higher Education*, 31 (2): 183–99.

Lee, F.S. (2007) ' The Research Assessment Exercise, the state and dominance of mainstream economics in British universities', *Cambridge Journal of Economics* 31: 309–25.

Lee, R.M. (2000) *Unobtrusive Methods in Social Research.* Buckingham: Open University Press.

Legge, K. (1984) *Evaluating Planned Organisational Change.* London: Academic Press.

Lewin, K. (1948) 'Frontiers in group dynamics', *Human Relations*, 1: 5–41, 143–53.

Locke, K. (1997) 'Re-writing the discovery of Grounded Theory after 25 years?', *Journal of Management Inquiry*, 5: 239–45.

Locke, K. (2001) *Grounded Theory in Management Research.* London: Sage.

Lowe, A. (1998) 'Managing the post merger aftermath by default remodelling', *Management Decision*, 36 (2): 102–10.

Lu, Y. and Heard, R. (1995) 'Socialised economic action: a comparison of strategic investment decision-making in China and Britain', *Organization Studies*, 16: 395–424.

Luff, P., Hindmarsh, J. and Heath, C. (eds) (2000) *Workplace Studies: Recovering Work Practice and Informing System Design.* Cambridge: Cambridge University Press.

Luo, X. and Bhattacharya, C.B. (2006) 'Corporate social responsibility, customer satisfaction, and market value', *Journal of Marketing*, 70 (4): 1–18.

Lupton, T. (1963) *On the Shop Floor: Two Studies of Workshop Organization and Output.* New York: Macmillan.

Lyles, M.A. and Salk, J.E. (1996) 'Knowledge acquisition from foreign parents in international joint ventures: an empirical examination in the Hungarian context', *Journal of International Business Studies*, Special Issue, 27: 877–903.

Lyotard, J.-F. (1984) *The Postmodern Condition: A Report on Knowledge.* Manchester: Manchester University Press.

McClelland, D.A. (1965) 'Achievement and enterprise', *Journal of Personal Social Psychology*, 1: 389–92.

McClellend, D.A. (1967) *The Achieving Society.* Princetown: Van Nastrand.

McCullagh, P. and Nelder, J. (1989) *Generalized Linear Models.* London: Chapman and Hall.

McLaughlin, H. and Thorpe, R. (1993) 'Action Learning – a paradigm in emergence: the problems facing a challenge to traditional management education and development', *British journal of Management*, 4: 19–27.

Macfarlane, G. (1985) *Alexander Fleming: The Man and the Myth.* Oxford: Oxford University Press.

Mackinlay, T. (1986) 'The development of a personal strategy of management', Master of Science Degree, Manchester Polytechnic, Department of Management.

Maclean, D., Macintosh, R. and Grant, S. (2002) 'Mode 2 Management research', *British Journal of Management*, 13: 189–207.

Macpherson, A. (2006) 'Learning to grow: the evolution of business knowledge in small manufacturing firms', PhD thesis, Manchester Metropolitan University.

Mangham, I.L (1986) 'In search of competence', *Journal of General Management*, 12 (2): 5–12.

Marshall, C. (2000) 'Policy discourse analysis: negotiating gender equity', *Journal of Education Policy*, 15 (2): 125–56.

Marshall, S. and Green, N. (2007) *Your PhD Companion: A Handy Mix of Practical Tips, Sound Advice and Helpful Commentary to see you through your PhD*, 2nd edn. Oxford: Cromwell Press.

Mason, J. (1996) *Qualitative Researching*. London: Sage.

Mauch, J.E. and Birch, J.W. (1983) *Guide to the Successful Thesis and Dissertations: A Handbook for Students and Faculty*. New York, Marcel Dekker.

Mayo, E. (1949) *The Social Problems of an Industrial Civilisation*. London: Routledge and Kegan Paul.

Mehrabian, A. (1981) *Silent Messages: Implicit Communication of Emotions and Attitudes*, 2nd edn. Belmont, CA: Wadsworth.

Miles, N.B. and Huberman, A.M. (1984) *Qualitative Data Analysis: A Sourcebook of New Methods*. London: Sage.

Miller, D. (1993) 'The Architecture of Simplicity', *AMR*, 18 (1): 116–38.

Mintzberg, H. (1973) *The Nature of Managerial Work*. London: Harper and Row.

Mintzberg, H. (2005) *Managers Not MBAs: A Hard Look at the Soft Practice of Managing and Management Development*. San Francisco: Berrett-Koehler.

Moingeon, B. and Edmondson, A. (1997) *Organizational Learning and Competitive Advantage*. London: Sage.

Moser, C.A. and Kalton, G. (1971) *Survey Methods in Social Investigation*, 2nd edn. London: Heinemann.

Murray, R. (2002) *How to Write a Thesis*. Milton Keynes: Open University Press.

Nguyen, P. (2005) 'Public opinion polls, chicken soup and sample size', *Teaching Statistics*, 27 (3): 89–91.

Nonaka, I. (1988) 'Toward middle-up-down management: accelerating information creation', *Sloan Management Review*, Spring: 9–18.

Nonaka, I. and Takeuchi, H. (1995) *The Knowledge-Creating Company: How Japanese Companies Create the Dynamics of Innovation*. Oxford: Oxford University Press.

Nor, S.M. (2000) 'Privatisation and changes in organization: a case study of a Malaysian privatised utility', PhD thesis, Lancaster University.

Norman, M. (2006) 'Student teachers' perceptions of becoming teachers and their experiences of confidence during their transition to teaching', PhD thesis, University of Manchester.

Park, C. (2003) 'In other (people's) words: plagiarism by university students – literature and lessons', *Assessment & Evaluation in Higher Education*, 28 (5). pp. 471–88.

Patriotta, G. (2003) *Organizational Knowledge in the Making*. Oxford: Oxford University Press.

Pears, D. (1971) *Wittgenstein*. London: Fontana.

Peters, T.J. and Waterman, R.H. (1982) *In Search of Excellence: Lessons from America's Best Run Companies*. New York: Harper and Row.

Pettigrew, A.M. (1985a) *The Awakening Giant: Continuity and Change in Imperial Chemical Industries*. Oxford: Blackwell.

Pettigrew, A.M. (1985b) 'Contextualist research: a natural way to link theory and practice', in E.E. Lawler (ed.), *Doing Research that is Useful in Theory and Practice*. San Francisco, CA: Jossey Bass.

Pettigrew, A.M. (1990) 'Longitudinal field research on change: theory and practice', *Organization Science*, 1 (3): 267–92.

Phillips, E.M. (1984) 'Learning to do research', *Graduate Management Research*, 2 (1): 6–18.

Phillips, E.M. and Pugh, D.S. (2005) *How to get a PhD: A Handbook for Students and their Supervisors*, 4th edn. Maidenhead: Open University Press.

Pike, K.L. (1954) *Language in Relation to a Unified Theory of the Structure of Human Behavior*. Glendale, CA: Summer Institute of Linguistics.

Pink, S. (2001) *Doing Visual Ethnography: Images, Media and Representation in Research*. London: Sage.

Platt, J. (1976) *Realities of Social Research: An Empirical Study of British Sociologists*. Brighton: Sussex University Press.

Popper, K. (1959) *The Logic of Scientific Discovery*. London: Hutchinson.

Porter, L.W. and McKibbin, L.E. (1988) *Management Education and Development: Drift or Thurst into the 21st Century?* New York: McGraw-Hill.

Potter, J. and Wetherell, M. (1987) *Discourse and Social Psychology Beyond Attitudes and Behaviour*. London: Sage.

Potter, J. and Wetherell, M. (1988) *Social Psychology and Discourse*. London: Routledge.

Prieto, I.M. and Easterby-Smith, M. (2006) 'Dynamic capabilities and the role of organizational knowledge: an exploration', *European Journal of Information Management*, 15: 500–10.

Pugh, D.S. (1983) 'Studying organisational structure and process', in G. Morgan (ed), *Beyond Method*. Beverly Hills: Sage.

Pugh, D.S. (1988) 'The Aston research programme', in A. Bryman (ed), *Doing Research in Organisations*. London: Routledge. pp. 123–35.

Pugh, D.S. and Hickson, D.J. (1976) *Organisation Structure in its Context: The Aston Programme*. Farnborough: Saxon House.

Punch, M. (1986) *The Politics and Ethics of Fieldwork*. Beverly Hills, CA: Sage.

Punch, K.F. (1998) *Introduction to Social Research: Qualitative Approaches*. London: Sage.

Putnam, H. (1987) *The Many Faces of Realism*. La Salle: Open Court.

Ralston, D.A., Terpstra-Tong, J., Terpstra, R.H., Wang, X.L. and Egri, C. (2006) 'Today's state-owned enterprises of China: Are they dying dinosaurs or dynamic dynamos?', *Strategic Management Journal*, 27 (9): 825–43.

Rappoport, R.N. (1970) 'Three dilemmas in action research', *Human Relations*, 23 (4): 499–513.

Reason, P. (1988) *Human Inquiry in Action*. London: Sage.

Reason, P. and Bradbury, H. (2006) *Handbook of Action Research: Participative Inquiry and Practice*. London: Sage.

Ricoeur, P. (1981) 'What is a text? Explanation and understanding', in J.B. Thompson (ed.), *Paul Ricoeur, Hermeneutics and the Human Sciences*. Cambridge: Cambridge University Press. pp. 145–64.

Roethlisberger, F.J. and Dickson, W.J. (1939) *Management and the Worker*. Cambridge, MA: Harvard University Press.

Rouleau, L. (2005) 'Micro-practices of strategic sensemaking and sensegiving: how middle managers interpret and sell change every day', *Journal of Management Studies*, 42(7): 1413–41.

Roy, D. (1952) 'Quota restriction and goldbricking in a machine shop', *American Journal of Sociology*, 57: 427–42.

Roy, D. (1970) 'The study of Southern labour union organising campaigns', in R. Haberstein (ed.), *Pathway to Data*. New York: Aldine.

Rugg, G. and Petre, M. (2004) *The Unwritten Rules of PhD Research*. Maidenhead: Open University Press.

Ryave, A.L. and Schenkein, J.N. (1974) 'Notes on the art of walking', in R. Turner (ed.), *Ethnomethodology: Selected Readings*. Harmondsworth: Penguin.

Said, E. (1978) *Orientalism*. London: Routledge and Kegan Paul.

Sapsford, R. (2006) *Survey Research*, 2nd edn. London: Sage.

Saunders, M., Lewis, P. and Thornhill, A. (2006) *Research Methods for Business Students*, 4th edn. Harlow: Pearson Education.

Sayer, A. (2000) *Realism and Social Science*. London: Sage.

Scarbrough, H. (ed.) (2008) *The Evolution of Business Knowledge*. Oxford: Oxford University Press.

Scarbrough, H. and Swan, J. (1999) 'Knowledge management and the management fashion perspective', Proceedings of British Academy of Management Conference, Manchester, Vol II: 920–37.

Schmitt, N. and Stults, D.M. (1985), Factors defined by negatively keyed items: the results of careless respondents?', *Applied Psychological Measurement*, 9 (4): 367–73.

Schon, D.A. (1983) *The Reflective Practitioner: How Professionals Think in Action*. London: Maurice Temple Smith.

Scoble, R. and Israel, S. (2006) *Naked Conversations: How Blogs Are Changing the Way Businesses Are Talking to Customers*. Hoboken: NJ: John Wiley & Sons.

Seale, C. (2000) 'Using computers to analyse qualitative data', in D. Silverman (ed.), *Doing Qualitative Research: A Practical Handbook*. London: Sage.

Secrist, C., Koeyer I., de, Bell, H. and Fogel, A. (2002) 'Combining digital video technology and narrative methods for understanding infant development', *Forum: Qualitative Social Research* [online journal], 3 (2). Available at: http://www.qualitative-research.net/fqs-texte/2-02/2-02secristetal-e.htm

Selvin, H.C. and Stuart, A. (1966) 'Data-dredging procedures in survey analysis', *American Statistician*, 20: 20–3.

Senge, P. (1990) *The Fifth Discipline: The Art and Practice of the Learning Organization*. London: Century.

Shadish, W.R., Cook, T.D. and Campbell, D. T. (2002) *Experimental and Quasi-Experimental Designs for Generalised Causal Inference*. Houghton-Mifflin.

Shotter, J. (1993) *Conversational Realities*. London: Sage.

Shotter, J. (1995) 'The manager as a practical author: a rhetorical-responsive, social constructionist approach to social-organizational problems', in D. Hosking, H.P. Dachler and K.J. Gergen (eds), *Management and Organization: Relational Alternatives to Individualism*. Aldershot: Avebury. pp. 125–47.

Siggelkow, N. (2007) 'Persuasion with case studies', *Academy of Management Journal*, 50 (1): 20–4.

Silver, M. (1991) *Competent to Manage*. London: Routledge.

Silverman, D. (1993) *Interpreting Qualitative Data: Methods for Analysing Talk, Text and Interaction*. London: Sage.

Silverman, D. (2000) *Doing Qualitative Research: A Practical Handbook*. London: Sage.

Simon, H.A. (1959) *Administrative Behaviour*, 2nd edn. London: Macmillan.

Sims, D. (1993) 'Coping with misinformation', *Management Decision*, 3: 18–21.

Simpson, B. (1995) Unpublished MSc dissertation 'A University an organisation for learning but a learning NC Organisation. Manchester Metropolitan University.

Slater, D. (1989) 'Corridors of power', in J.F. Gubrium and D. Silverman (eds), *The Politics of Field Research*. London: Sage.

Smeyers, P. and Verhessen, P. (2001') 'Narrative analysis as philosophical research, bridging the gap between the empirical and the conceptual', *International Journal of Qualitative Studies in Education* (QSE), 14 (1): 71–84.

Snell, R.S. (1993) *Developing Skills for Ethical Management*. London: Chapman and Hall.

Spector, P.E. (1992) *Summated rating scale construction: An introduction*. Newbury Park, CA: Sage.

Sprigg, C.A. and Jackson, P.R. (2006) 'Call centers as lean service environments: well-being and the mediating role of work design', *Journal of Occupational Health Psychology*, 11 (2): 197–212.

Stake, R.E. (2006) 'Qualitative case studies', in N.K. Denzin and Y.S. Lincoln (eds), *Sage Handbook of Qualitative Research*, 3rd edn. London: Sage. pp. 443–66.

Starbuck, Bill (2004) *Journals Ranked by Citations per Article*. Available at: http://pages.stern.nyu.edu/~wstarbuc/

Starkey, K. and Tiratsoo, N. (2007) *Business Schools and the Bottom Line*. Cambridge: Cambridge University Press.

Steenkamp, J.-B.E.M. and Geyskens, I. (2006) 'What drives the perceived value of web sites? A cross-national investigation', *Journal of Marketing*, 70 (3): 136–50.

Steers, R.M., Bischoff, S.J. and Higgins, L.H. (1992) 'Cross-cultural management research: the fish and the fisherman', *Journal of Management Inquiry*, 1 (4): 321–30.

Steinbeck, J. (1970) *Journal of a Novel: The East of Eden Letters*. London: Pan Books.

Stewart, R. (1967) *Managers and their Jobs*. Maidenhead: McGraw-Hill.

Stewart, R. (1982) *Choices for the Manager: A Guide to Managerial Work and Behaviour*. London: McGraw-Hill.

Stewart, V., Stewart, A. and Fonda, N. (1981) *Business Applications of Repertory Grid*. Maidenhead: McGraw-Hill.

Stokes, D. and Bergin, R. (2006) 'Methodology or "Methodolatry"? An Evaluation of Focus Groups and Depth Interviews', *Qualitative Market Research: An International Journal*, 9 (11): 26–37.

Strauss, A.L. (1987) *Qualitative Analysis for Social Scientists*. Cambridge: Cambridge University Press.

Strauss, A.L. and Corbin, J. (1990) *Basics of Qualitative Research: Grounded Theory Procedures and Techniques*. Thousand Oaks, CA: Sage.

Strauss, A.L. and Corbin, J. (1998) *Basics of Qualitative Research: Techniques and Procedures for Developing Grounded Theory*, 2nd edn. Thousand Oaks, CA: Sage.

Tabachnick, B.G. and Fidell, L.S. (2006) *Using Multivariate Statistics*, 5th edn. Boston, MA: Allyn & Bacon.

Taylor, F.W. (1947) *Scientific Management*. London: Harper and Row.

Taylor, S.J. and Bogdan, R. (1984) *Introduction to Qualitative Research Methods*. New York: Wiley-Interscience.

Teagarden, M.B., von Glinow, M.A., Bowen, D.E., Frayne, C.A., Nason, S., Huo, Y.P., Milliman, J., Arias, M.E., Butler, M.C., Geringer, J.M., Kim, NM., Scullion, H., Lowe, K.B. and Drost, E.A. (1995) 'Toward a theory of comparative management research: an ideographic case study of the best international human resources management project', *Academy of Management Journal*, 38: 1261–87.

Thomas, W.I. and Thomas, D.S. (1928) *The Child in America: Behavioural Problems and Progress*. New York: Knopf.

Thompson, E.E. (2004) 'National competitiveness: a question of cost conditions or institutional circumstances?', *British Journal of Management*, 15: 197–218.

Thorpe, R. (1980) 'The relationship between payment systems, productivity and the organisation of work', MSc thesis, Strathclyde Business School.

Thorpe, R. and Cornelissen, J. (2003) 'Visual media and the construction of meaning', in D. Holman and R. Thorpe (eds), *Management and Language: the Manager as Practical Author*. London: Sage. pp. 67–81

Thorpe, R. and Holloway, J. (2008) Performance Management: Multidisciplinary perspectives. Houndsmill: Palgrave Macmillan NC.

Thorpe, R., Holt, R., Macpherson, A. and Pittaway, L. (2005) 'Knowledge within small and medium-sized firms: a review of the evidence', *International Journal of Management Reviews*, 7 (4): 257–81.

Todd, D.J. (1979) 'Mixing qualitative and quantitative methods: triangulation in action', *Administrative Science Quarterly*, 24: 602–11.

Todorova, G. and Durisin, B. (2007) 'Absorptive capacity: valuing a reconceptualization', *Academy of Management Review*, 32 (3): 774–86.

Toulmin, S. (2001) *The Uses of Argument*. Cambridge: Cambridge University Press.

Tranfield, D. (2002) 'Formulating the nature of management research', *European Management Journal*, 20 (4): 378–82.

Tranfield, D., Denyer, D. and Marcos, J. (2004) 'Co-producing management knowledge', *Management Decision*, 42 (3/4): 375–86.

Tranfield, D., Denyer, D. and Smart, P. (2003) 'Towards a methodology for developing evidence-informed management knowledge by means of systematic review', *British Journal of Management*, 14 (3): 207–22.

Tranfield, D. and Starkey, K. (1998) 'The nature, social organization and promotion of management research: towards policy', *British Journal of Management*, 9: 341–53.

Tsang, E.W.K. (1997) 'Learning from joint venturing experience: the case of foreign direct investment by Singapore companies in China', PhD thesis, University of Cambridge.

Tsang, E.W.K. (1999) 'Internationalisation as a learning process: Singapore MNCs in China', *Academy of Management Executive*, 13 (1): 91–101.

Tsang, E.W.K. (2002) 'Acquiring knowledge by foreign partners from international joint ventures in a transition economy: learning-by-doing and learning myopia', *Strategic Management Journal* 23, 835–54.

Tsoukas, H. and Hatch, M.J. (1997) 'Complex thinking, complex practice: the case for a narrative approach to organisational complexity', Paper Presented to the American Academy of Management.

Turner, B.A. (1988) 'Connoisseurship in the study of organisational cultures', in A. Bryman (ed.), *Doing Research in Organisations*. London: Sage. pp. 108–21

Ullman, J.B. (2006a) 'Structural equation modeling', in B.G. Tabachnick and L.S. Fidell (eds), *Using Multivariate Statistics*. Boston, MA: Allyn & Bacon. pp. 653–771.

Ullman, J.B. (2006b) 'Structural equation modeling: reviewing the basics and moving forward', *Journal of Personality Assessment*, 87 (1): 35–50.

Von Bertalanffy, L. (1962) 'General systems theory – a critical review', *General Systems*, VII: 1–20.

Walker, G.B. and Sillars, M.O. (1990) 'Where is argument? Perelman's theory of values in *Perspectives on Argumentation* (ed. R. Trapp and J. Schuetz). Illinois: Waveland Press.

Walker, R. (1985) *Applied Qualitative Research*. Aldershot: Gower.

Wall, T.D., Jackson, P.R. and Davids, K. (1992) 'Operator work design and robotics system performance: A serendipitous field experiment', *Journal of Applied Psychology*, 77: 353–62.

Wall, T.D., Kemp, N.J., Jackson, P.J. and Clegg, C.W. (1986) 'Outcomes of autonomous workgroups: a long-term field experiment', *Academy of Management Journal*, 29 (2): 282–304.

Walsh, G. and Beatty, S.E. (2007) 'Customer-based corporate reputation of a service firm: scale development and validation', *Journal of the Academy of Marketing Science*, 35(1) 127–143.

Walsh, G., Mitchell, V.-W., Jackson, P.R. and Beatty, S.E. (in press) 'Examining the antecedents and consequences of corporate reputation: a customer perspective', *British Journal of Management*.

Warr, P.B., Cook, J.D. and Wall, T.D. (1979) 'Scales for the measurement of some work attitudes and aspects of psychological well-being', *Journal of Occupational sychology*, 52: 129–48.

Watson, T.J. (1994) *In Search of Management: Culture, Chaos and Control in Managerial Work*. London: Routledge.

Watzlawick, P. (ed.) (1984) *The Invented Reality*. London: Norton.

Weick, K.E. (1995) *Sense-making in Organisations*. London: Sage.

Weick, K.E. (2001) 'Theory construction as disciplined imagination', *Academy of Management Review*, 14 (4): 516–31.

Wertsch, J.V. (1991) *Voices of the Mind: A Socio Cultural Approach to Mediated Action*. Cambridge, MA: Harvard University Press.

Whitley, R., Thomas, A. and Marceau, J. (1981) *Masters of Business?* London: Tavistock.

Winter, S.G. (2003) 'Understanding dynamic capabilities', *Strategic Management Journal*, 24: 991–5.

Wittgenstein, L. (1953) *Philosophical Investigations*. Oxford: Blackwell.

Wright, R.P. (2006) 'Rigor and relevance using repertory grid technique in strategy research', *Research Methodology in Strategy and Management*, 3: 295–348.

Yin, R.K. (2002) *Case Study Research: Design and Methods*, 3rd edn. London: Sage.

INDEX

ABI Inform, 40
absorptive capacity, research on, 105–8
abstract concepts, 98
abstracts of research, 40–1, 47, 316
academic research, nature of, 14–18
Academy of Management (American), 32, 41, 121, 132
   Conference of, 316
   Journal, 123
access to sources of research material
   primary sources, 7, 102, 114–17, 129–32, 149, 153, 157–61
   secondary sources, 33–7
action learning, 18, 206
action learning sets, 127
action research, 9–10, 93, 145, 165–7, 204
   definition of, 9
activity sampling, 152, 222
Advanced Institute of Management, 47
Agar, M.H., 94
agency, 77
agricultural research, 84
alignment between research context and methodology, 35
Allen, Woody, 307
alpha-rated research proposals, 119
Alvesson, M., 5, 106, 168
Amis, J., 96
AMOS software package, 296, 299
analysis of covariance (ANCOVA), 285, 291–2
analysis of variance (ANOVA), 257, 272
anecdotalism, 96
Antonacopoulou, A., 129
appraisal interviews, 100
archival data, use of, 219, 223–5, 254
argument analysis, 183
Ashton, D.J.L., 86–7
Aslib Index to Theses, 41

association between variables, testing of, 260–7
Atlas.ti software package, 186, 191–6
attitudes, measurement of, 229–30
Austin, J.H., 18–19, 25
authenticity, 96
autism, 255
autobiographical accounts of research, 115
autonomous workgroups, research on, 89
average values, 244–5
axial codes, 179–80, 192

Baker, S., 147, 204
Baker Library, 39
Bales, R.F., 223
bar charts, 240
Barclays Bank, 184
Bartunek, J.M., 95
Barwise, P., 118
Beatty, S.E., 235
behaviour change, 93
Bell, E., 132–5, 155
Berger, P.L., 58
Berghman, L., 221
Berman, S.L., 282
beta (β) weights, 287
Beynon, H., 117, 128, 131
Bhaskar, R., 61–2
Bhattacharya, C.B., 235
Bibliographic Index Plus, 38–9
bibliographic information, 34, 38–9, 45–6
'Big Brother', 222
Billig, M., 119
binomial distribution, 253
Birkinshaw, J., 235
Blair, Tony, 51
Bloom, B.S., 314
'blue sky' research, 119
Bogdan, R., 134
Boissevain, J., 115
books
   publication of, 136, 317
   use of, 38–9, 42
bootstrap distributions, 254
Bottin Administratif, 42
Bowey, A.M., 153

Box, G.E.P., 254
Bradford University, 127
British Academy of Management (BAM), 32, 41, 121, 132
British Lending Library, 39
British Library, 34, 39–41
British Publications Current Awareness Scheme, 42
Brouthers, K.D. and L.E., 270–1
Brown, A.D., 96
Brown, S.L., 271
Bryman, A., 132–5, 155
Buchanan, D., 12, 129, 136, 162
Bulletin Board for Libraries, 39
Bulmer, M., 136
Burgess, R.G., 144
Burgoyne, J., 23
Burrell, G., 70, 121
business schools, 3–5, 14–15, 40–1, 72, 129, 135
Business Source Premier, 40
Buzan, T., 48–50

Cadbury's, 242
call centres, research on, 279, 295
case study methodology, 84, 93, 97–100, 103, 123, 127
cataloguing of concepts, 178–9
category scales, 228, 255, 265
causal models, 275, 279–85
   analysis of, 284–5
   appropriate form for, 284
   rationale for, 279–82
   specification of, 281–3
causal relationships, 58, 281
Center for Research in Security Prices (CRSP), 224
Chain, Ernest, 319
charities, 119
Charmaz, K., 101–2, 178–9
China, 68, 100, 104, 114, 117, 235
China-British Business Council, 129
chi-squared (χ²) distribution, 253
chi-squared (χ²) index (in SEM), 299
chi-squared (χ²) tests, 263, 300
citations and citation indexing, 44–5, 122, 307

classification schemes for books, 38
cluster analysis, 92, 198
cluster sampling, 216–17
codes of ethics, 132–5
coding of data, 188–94, 221, 223
coding software, 47
cognitive mapping, 202–8
Cohen, W.M., 108
cold calling, 129
cold fusion, 255
collaborative research, 70
Collins, H.M., 62
Collinson, D.L., 156, 160
colloquialisms, 227
combination of samples, 250
common factors in measurement models, 276–8
competencies, managerial, 70
complete participation, 156–60
complexity in statistical models, pros and cons of, 282, 299
computer-aided qualitative data analysis software (CAQDAS), 185–93
Comte, Auguste, 57
concentration camps, research in, 119
conceptual diagrams, 186
conceptualization of research topics, 21, 178
conclusions of research, 312
conferences, 17–18, 120–2, 125, 316–18
confidence in statistical tests, 255–7
confidentiality, 134, 144–5, 150, 166, 214, 223
confirmatory factor analysis (CFA), 278–81, 300–1
conflict methodology, 128
constant comparison, principle of, 96
constructionism see social constructionism
'contaminated' research, 124
content analysis, 173–5, 180
context of research, 126
contingency tables, 263–4
contingency theories, 271
continuous scales, 228, 230–1, 255–7, 265

contradictory findings, 99
contributions to knowledge:
 substantive, theoretical
 and methodological, 315
control, statistical, 273–4
control groups, use of, 84–7
convenience sampling, 217–19
conversation analysis, 183
co-operative inquiry, 94
Copac, 39
Corbin, J., 102, 179–80
corporate social responsibility,
 research on, 96, 235
correlation coefficients, 265–7,
 284; see also partial
 correlation
Coyle-Shapiro, J., 274
creativity in research, 19
Cresswell, J.W., 71
critical discourse analysis, 182
critical examination of data, 21
critical incident technique,
 150–1
critical management
 studies, 160
critical realism, 62, 73
critical theory, 5–6, 74, 108
Cronbach's alpha (α), 277
cross-sectional research
 designs, 90–1, 105
Cunliffe, A.L., 168
Curran, J., 152
curvilinear relationships, 267
Czarniawska, Barbara, 131

Daft, R.L., 162
Dalton, Melville, 68–70, 86,
 116, 135–6
Dartington Hall Trust, 136
database packages, 45
databases, 224–5
Datastream, 42, 224
Davila, C., 127
Dawkins, Richard, 61
Decision Explorer
 software, 194, 204–5
decision theory, 4–6
Deetz, S., 5, 106
degrees of freedom, 260,
 265, 299
dependent variables, 91, 274,
 286
derived measures, 227
Derrida, J., 76
Dewey, John, 76
Dewey Decimal System, 38
dialogic thought, 182
diary studies, 152–4
disciplined imagination, 20
discourse analysis, 182–5
discovery, sources of, 18–19
discussion groups, 32

dissemination of research
 results, 306, 317–19
Dissertation Abstracts
 International, 41
dissertations, 314–15
distanciation, 75
distributions, shapes of, 239–41
Ditton, J., 134
doctoral research, 10, 12,
 14–17, 24–6, 32, 107,
 120–1, 127, 315–18
doctorates, professional, 120–1
DOGE, 41
Douglas, J.D., 128
Downing, S., 152
Doyle, Arthur Conan, 56
drawing out technique, 148
dress codes, 121–2
drug testing, 84–5, 133–4
Dyer, J.H., 235

Easterby-Smith, Mark
 (author), 32, 72, 86–7,
 98, 105, 117, 123, 129,
 131–2, 186, 200
eclectic methods of research,
 7–8, 56, 99
Economic and Social Research
 Council (ESRC), 11–12,
 119–20, 126
 Guidelines for Management
 Research Training, 23
 Newsletter (The Edge), 41
Eden, C., 206
Editions Ytem, 42
Eesley, C., 235
efficiency of summary
 measures, 248, 257
eigenvalues, 278
Einstein, Albert, 57–8, 88, 98
Eisenhardt, K.M., 99, 104, 271
embedded cases, 104
Emerald database, 40
emic perspective, 95
empathy, 146
Engeström, Y., 187
Engineering and Physical
 Sciences Research
 Council, 126
enlightenment model of
 research, 137–8
epistemology, 57, 60–4, 75–7,
 82–4, 95–7, 102, 108–10
 and methodology, 62–4,
 83–4
EQS program, 278, 296
equivocality, 162
ethical issues, 2, 86, 119, 132–5,
 166, 222
Ethnograph program, 186
ethnographic research, 83–4,
 94–5, 117, 142, 155–61

etic perspective, 95
European Academy of Man-
 agement (EURAM), 32
evaluation research, 10
experimental research
 designs, 84–7, 93, 104
exploratory factor analysis
 (EFA), 277–8, 280
exploratory surveys, 92
expressive studies, 97–8
external examiners, 121, 315
extreme values, 247–8, 257, 284

F-distribution, 253
F-tests, 287
 univariate, 292
facilitators, 166
Factiva database, 43
factor analysis, 66, 92; see also
 confirmatory factor
 analysis; exploratory
 factor analysis
factor loadings, 276–9, 297
factorial designs, 272
factual surveys, 90
fashions in research, 125
Fairhurst, Eileen, 159, 161
falsification of theory, 105–6
familiarization with data, 178
Fayol, H., 3
feminism, 74–5, 104
Fielding, N.G. and J.L., 71
Filatotchev, I., 270–1
financial data on businesses,
 42–3, 224
financial markets, research
 on, 88–9, 96
Financial Times, 42–3
Flanagan, J.C., 150–1
Fleming, Sir Alexander, 19,
 318–19
Florey, Howard, 319
focus groups, 151–2
focused codes, 178–9
focusing of research, 33
Foucault, Michel, 76
frequency distributions, 239
funding bodies for research, 10,
 118–20, 124, 133–4

Gadamer, H.-G., 75, 183
Gagnon, Suzanne, 102
Galileo, 57–8, 114
generalization of research, 21,
 58–9, 87, 97, 100, 104–5
generalized linear models, 284
Geyskens, I., 235
Gibbons, M.L., 8–9
Giddens, Anthony, 77
Glaser, B.G., 100–2, 175–80
Gold, J., 184
Goldacre, M.J., 228

Golden-Biddle, K., 96, 123,
 309–11
goodness of fit, 282, 298–9
Google Scholar, 44, 317
government publications, 42
grand theories, 107–8
grant holders, 117–18
grounded analysis, 173
grounded theory, 7, 76, 84, 93,
 96–7, 100–5, 175, 186
group-based research
 projects, 18
group maps, 204–5
groups, comparisons
 between, 257–60
Gubrium, J.F., 138
Gummesson, E., 165

Habermas, J., 58–9
Handy, C., 3
Hatch, M.J., 182–3
Hatch, N.W., 235
Hayano, D.M., 160
Health amd Safety
 Executive, 242
Hedge, Nicki, 312
Heisenberg, Werner, 61
Hemscott service, 42
hermeneutics, 75
Hickson, David, 127
hierarchical regression, 289–91,
 300
histograms, 240–1, 251
Hofstede, G., 66, 92, 272–3
holism in research, 105
'house styles' of academic
 departments, 121
Huberman, A.-M., 174–5
Huczynski, A.A., 25
Huff, A.S., 306
human relations school of
 management, 4, 6
human resource management
 (HRM), research
 on, 66–8
Hume's problem of
 induction, 106
Humphreys, M., 96
Huxham, C., 165–7, 206
Hyder, S., 117
hypotheses, 58, 84, 91, 99
 testing of, 249–57, 267,
 291–2

IBM, 129–30
ICI, 98
identifiability of structural
 equation models, 298
impact factors for individual
 journals, 122–3, 316
incentive schemes, research
 on, 154

independence model (in SEM), 299
Indeterminacy Principle, 61
Index Translationium, 39
indexing services, 40
inference, 212, 217, 234
inferential surveys, 90–1
informed consent, 222
in-jokes , 94–5
'insider' researchers, 117, 158, 160
Institute for Small Businesses and Entrepreneurship, 32
Institute of Chartered Accountants, 39
instrumental studies, 97–8
interaction effects, 271
interaction process analysis (IPA), 223
interactive methods of research, 142
interdependence in quantitative analysis, 271–5
internal realism, 61, 102
International Journal of Management Reviews, 47
Internet resources, 43–4, 50, 220
interquartile range, 245–6
interrupted involvement, 159–60
interval scales, 230–1
interviews, 95, 99, 131, 142–52
    group-based, 151
    in-depth, 144–5, 147, 151, 178
    non-directive, 143–4
    qualitative, 144
    recording of, 150
    skills needed for conducting of, 145–6
    structured and unstructured, 143–4, 219–20
    telephone-based, 145, 220
    see also appraisal interviews
introductions to research reports, 310–12
investigative model of research, 128, 136
ISI Web of Knowledge, 122
iSoft, 234

Jackson, P.R., 254, 279, 287, 289, 293, 295
JAI Press, 32
James, William, 76
jargon, 227
Jessop, Robin, 85
Johnson, G., 306
joint ventures, research on, 91
Jones, S., 142–4, 148–9
Journal of Management Studies, 122

Journal of Marketing, 32, 235
journals, 9, 30–2, 39–40, 107, 118, 122–3, 136, 316–18
Julius Caesar, 173
just-identified models, 298

Kalton, G., 219
Katsikeas, C.S., 235
Kendall's rank order correlation, 254, 265–7
Kessler, I., 274, 281
key elements in research reports, 311
key informants, 132
keywords, use of, 34–8, 41–2, 46
KIM project, 126–7
King, N., 173
Knorr-Cetina, K.D., 61
knowledge transfer, research on, 91, 235
Knox, S., 204
Kolb, D.A., 76
Kompass directory, 42
Kruskal-Wallace test, 254, 257
Kuhn, T.S., 57
Kvale, S., 144

laddering, 146–7, 204
Lagrange multiplier (LM) tests, 300
Lancaster University, 124, 129
language used in research, 149
latent variables, 274–9, 296–8
Latour, B., 19, 61
Law, J., 19–21
leadership, 145–6, 167
leading questions, 228
learning cycle theory, 76
Leask, B., 50
Lee, Raymond, 43–4
Lengel, R.H., 162
Lenox, M.J., 235
Levinthal, D.A., 108
Lewin, K., 93–4, 107
Lexis-Nexis database, 43
librarians, 34
Library of Congress, 39
library resources, 33–45
likelihood ratios, 294
Likert scales, 228, 230
LISREL software package, 296
literary theory, 95
literature reviews, 11, 19–20, 27, 30–52
    contents of, 30–1
    time needed for, 33
local knowledge, 104
localization of research, 127
Locke, K., 96, 101, 123, 178, 309–11
logistic regression analysis, 285, 292–6

longitudinal studies, 173
Louis, M.R., 95
Luckman, T., 58
Luo, X., 235
Lupton, Tom, 16
Lyles, M.A., 91, 105
Lyotard, Jean-François, 75–6

McClelland, D.A., 145
Mackinlay, T., 197
McPherson, A., 187
macro-politics, 131
Mafia, Sicilian, 115–16
Malaysia, 104
Malina, D., 123, 186
management
    as a cadre and as an activity, 3
    classical theory of, 3–4
    critical views of, 4–5
    definition of, 114
    nature of, 3–6, 11
management research
    distinctiveness of, 6–8, 11, 114–15
    getting started on, 24–6
    levels and outcomes of, 8–11
    organization of material for, 45–6
    philosophical foundations of, 2, 56, 64–77
    political factors in, 2, 111
    qualitative and quantitative methods of, 2
    role of, 2
    trans-disciplinary approach to, 7
managers
    actual behaviour of, 3–4, 68–70
    definition of, 3
    education and qualifications of, 7–8, 149
Manchester University, 212
Mangham, I.L., 145
Mann-Whitney U test, 254, 257
Marshall, C., 182
Mason, J., 135
mass-observation studies, 152
matrix structures of management, 3
maximum likelihood estimation, 299
MBAs, 4–5, 7, 117, 123, 314
mean values, 244–8
measurement models, 275–8, 296–7
    analysis methods for, 277–8
    rationale for, 275–6
    structure of, 276–7
measurement scales, 228–31
media relations, 318

median values, 242–8
mediational models, 290
medical research, 84–7, 133–4
Mehrabian, A., 221–2
Mencius, 3
mentoring, 118
mergers
    economic logic of, 271
    micro-politics of, 130
    research on, 225
middle-range theory, 107–8
mid-mean values, 244–8
mid-range of data, 245–6
Midvale Steel Company, 116
Miles, M.B., 174–5
military model of research, 127–8, 136
Milo (company), 70, 116
mind maps, 24, 50, 307–10
Mintzberg, H., 317
mirroring, 148
modal values, 242, 247
Mode 1 and Mode 2 research, 8–9, 314
moderators, 151
modification indices, 300
Morgan, G., 70
Moser, C.A., 219
motivations
    for interviewees, 145
    for researchers, 14, 117
multinational enterprises, research on, 235
multi-stage sampling, 217
multivariate analysis, 270–1, 274–87
    of causal models, 279–87
    of measurement models, 275–9
multivariate analysis of covariance (MANCOVA), 285, 292
multivariate analysis of variance (MANOVA), 285, 292–4
multivariate regression analysis (MRA), 285–91

narrative methods of research, 95–6, 182–3
national cultures, research on, 66
National Front, British, 71
National Health Service, 234
natural language data
    analysis of, 172
    collection of, 142–55, 172
natural settings for research, 150
network diagrams, 193–7
networking, 18, 32, 115–16, 120, 123, 316
Newton's laws of motion, 87–8, 98

Nguyen, P., 214
nominal scales, 228
nominalism, 61–2, 83, 102
Nonaka, I., 137
non-normed fit index
    (NNFI), 299
non-parametric tests, 246,
    255, 257
non-probability sampling, 217–19
non-response, 213
Nor, S.M., 104
normal distribution, 253, 255
Norman, M., 191–2
NUD*IST package, 186
'nuisance' factors, 274
null hypotheses, 252, 254, 258,
    260, 263, 287
null models (in SEM), 299
NVivo package, 186–93

objectivism, 96, 101
objectivity, 93, 167, 307
observation alone, 160
observational data
    collection of, 221–3
    questions answered by, 224
observed variables, 274–8,
    284–5, 298
observer effects, 222
official publications, 42
Oliver, Jamie, 248
one-tailed tests, 258
online catalogues and online
    databases, 38–9, 44
ontology, 57–63, 67–71, 76–7,
    83, 93–5, 102, 111
open questions, 147
open systems of thought, 21
operationalization of
    concepts, 58
opinions, measurement of, 214,
    229–30
opportunistic research, 128–9
ordinal scales, 228, 230, 257,
    265
Organization for Economic
    Co-operation and
    Development
    (OECD), 42
organizational structure,
    research on, 65
organizational theory, 76
outputs from research, 313
over-identified models, 298

paradigms, 57–8, 64
parameters, 253
parametric tests, 246, 253–7
Park, C., 51–2
partial correlation, 273–4
participant observation, 95,
    134, 152–60, 221

participative research, 166
partisan research, 96
Patriotta, G., 36
payment systems, research
    on, 174
Pearson product-moment
    correlation, 265–6
peer review, 46, 108, 122
penicillin, discovery of, 19,
    318–19
percentages, 238–9
Perfect Analysis, 42
periodicals see journals
permutation distributions, 254
personal construct theory,
    107–8, 197, 202
Peters, T.J., 317
Pettigrew, Andrew, 98
PhD qualifications, 14–15,
    25–6, 136
Phillips, E.M., 14–16, 21
philosophy of science, 60–1
photography, use of, 162
Pike, Kenneth, 95
pilot studies, 24
Pink, S., 155
plagiarism, 50–2
Platt, J., 117
plausibility, 96
policy-orientated research, 137
politics, definition of, 114;
    see also research:
    political influences on
Popper, Karl, 105–6
populations, 212–13, 215
positivism, 56–73, 76, 146,
    172, 175, 307
positivist research designs,
    82–99, 103–10, 115
    validity of, 87–90
post-colonial theory, 104
postmodernism, 5, 75–6
Potter, J., 182
power relationships, 104, 114,
    138
PowerPoint®, 307–9, 317
pragmatism, 76
precision in sampling, 214, 218
predictor variables, 91, 274,
    284–7
prepared minds of successful
    researchers, 19
presentations, 317
press releases, 318
pre-test/post-test comparisons,
    86–7
pre-understanding of a research
    topic, 165
Prieto, I.M., 98
primary data, 11, 219
principal components
    analysis, 198–202

private agent model of
    research, 127–8, 136–7
privatization, 104
probability sampling, 216–17
probes used in interviewing,
    147–8
process-based research, 145
professional associations, 129,
    132–3
proxy variables, 275–6
psychoanalysis, 107
Public Affairs Information
    Service Bulletin, 40
publication of research
    results, 9, 315–19
publication rights, 136–7
Pugh, D.S., 14, 21, 65, 127
Punch, Maurice, 136, 192
purposive sampling, 218
pyramiding, 204

qualitative research, 24, 115
    analysis of, 172–93
    data sources for, 219–27
    methods of, 2, 4, 71–2, 82,
        93, 96, 103, 142–69
    reporting on, 309
    research questions addressed
        by, 234
quasi-experimental designs for
    research, 86–9
questionnaires, 143, 214
    postal, 219
questions, wording of, 227–9,
    231
quota sampling, 218
quotations, use of, 309–10

Ralston, D.A., 235
random assignment of research
    subjects, 84–7
random sampling, 216
range of data, 245
rank order correlation co-
    efficient, 254, 265–7
Rappoport, R.N., 9
ratio scales, 230
realist philosophy, 61–2, 73,
    76–7, 83, 99, 102
real-time research, 145
Reason, P., 106
reciprocity in research, 130
record cards, use of, 45
reductionism, 57–8, 102, 105
refereeing process, 39, 316
reference books, 42
reference distributions, 252–4,
    260
reflexivity 63, 70, 75, 115, 125,
    135, 138, 148, 162,
    166, 168, 178, 307
refutability of theory, 96, 106

regression analysis see hier-
    archical regression;
    logistic regression
    analysis; multi-variate
    regression analysis;
    stepwise regression
regression weights, 286–7, 290,
    297
relativism, 61–3, 66–8, 73, 76
relativist research designs, 82–3,
    90–2, 97–105, 109–10
relativity, theory of, 88
relevance of research, 166
repertory grids 175–81, 185,
    197–202
representationalism, 61–2
representativeness in
    sampling, 213–15
reputation, corporate, research
    on, 235–8
research
    as an explicit role, 158–9
    political influences on,
        114–28
    pure and applied forms
        of, 9–10
    styles of, 18–20
    see also management
        research
research councils, 10, 26, 118
research design, 272
    constructionist, 93–7
    positivist, 84–90
    quantitative, 234
    templates for, 108–9
    see also relativist research
        designs; social
        construction-ism in
        research designs
research proposals, 25–6, 31,
    108, 119
research reports, 307–14
response rates, 213–14
Ricoeur, P., 75
Rigdon, Ed, 301
robustness of summary
    measures, 247
role-play, 13
roles for researchers, 161
root mean squared error of
    approximation
    (RMSEA), 299
Roy, Donald, 156
Ryave, A.L., 125

Salk, J.E., 91, 105
sample size, 59, 73, 90, 105,
    214–15, 234, 253–4,
    258–60, 284, 299
sampling design, 212–19, 231
sampling distributions, 253
sampling frames, 213

Sarbanes-Oxley Act (US, 2002), 226
Scarbrough, H., 125
Schenkein, J.N., 125
Schmitt, N., 228
Science Citation Index, 45
scientific advances, 58, 115
scientific laws, 77
scientific management, 116
scientific method, 69, 93, 104
SDC Platinum database, 224
search engines, 44, 50
searches, electronic, 34–5
secondary data, 11, 219, 223–4
Secrist, C., 153
self-awareness, 27, 138
self-ethnography, 160
self-reflexivity, 21
Selvin, H.C., 34
semi-concealed research, 160–1
SEMNET, 301
Shotter, J, 58, 182
Siggelkow, Nikolaj, 98
significance levels, 260
significance tests, 217, 246, 253–7, 263–5
Silk, M.L., 96
Silverman, D., 30–1, 96, 138, 183
Simpson, B., 163–4
Sims, D., 117
Singapore, research on, 68
skewness of data, 247
skills
    managerial, 15
    needed for research, 21–4, 166
    of writing, 306–12, 319
Skoldberg, K., 168
Skype, 92
Snell, R.S., 135
snowball sampling, 218
social constructionism, 5, 56–63, 68–73, 82–4, 93–111, 160, 172, 307
    in research designs, 93–7
social engineering model of research, 137–8
Social Sciences Citation Index, 45
Socrates, 114
special interest groups, 32, 41
specific factors in measurement models, 276
sponsors of research, 125–6, 137–8
sponsorship of organizational research, reasons for, 130

spread in data, measures of, 245
Sprigg, C.A., 279, 295
Stake, Robert, 97, 99
stakeholders, 123–4, 282–3
standard deviation, 246, 253
standard error, 258–60
standard error of difference (in SPSS), 258
standardized variables, 287
Stationery Office, 42
statistics, access to, 42
Steenkamp, J.-B.E.M., 235
Steinbeck, John, 307
stepdown tests, 292
stepwise regression, 291, 296, 300
Stewart, V. and A., 200
story-telling, 182
Strategic Management Journal, 235
strategy development process 204, 206
stratified random sampling, 216
Strauss, A.L. 100–2, 105, 175–80, 192, 194
stress, research on, 60, 212, 295
structural equation modelling (SEM), 91, 296–301
Structural Equation Modelling (journal), 301
structuration theory, 77, 108
Stuart, A., 34
Stuart, R., 23
Stults, D.M., 228
summary measures of data, 234, 247–8
supervisors of research, 15–18, 21, 118, 120, 124–6
support sets in research communities, 16–17
surveys, 83–4, 90–2, 219–21
    by telephone, 220
    web-based, 220
Swan, J., 125
symmetry in data, 247–8
synergy, 117, 271
system closure, 186
System of Multiple Level Observation of Groups (SYMLOG), 223
systematic random sampling, 216
systematic reviews, 46–8

t-distribution and *t*-tests 253, 257–60
tacit knowledge and skills, 21, 76
Tanton, Morgan, 72

Taylor, Frederick, 3, 116
Taylor, S.J., 134
Teagarden, M.B., 66–7, 127
team-based research, 117, 128, 136–7
telephone interviews and surveys, 145, 220
templates
    for research designs, 108–9
    for research reports and papers, 309–10, 319
testing effects, 87
theory
    building of, 20, 107–8
    as distinct from practice, 121
    evaluation of, 100
    everyday and academic, 107
    falsification of, 105–6
    importance in relation to data analysis, 300, 302
theses, 108, 120, 315, 318
    access to, 40–1
Thomas, W.I. and D.S., 206
Thomson Financial, 225
Thorpe, R., 32, 47–50, 150–3, 157–9
3M (company), 137
time management , 152
time sampling, 222
titles for research, 312
topic guides, 143, 151
Toulmin, S., 183
Toyota, 235
Tranfield, D., 47
transcendental realism, 61
transcription symbols, 183–4
transcripts, analysis of, 172–85
transitional economies, 104
transparency, 97
triangulation, 66, 68
triple MMR vaccine, 255
triticale yields, 85
trust, 137, 147–8, 161
Tsang, E.W.K., 68
Tsoukas, H., 182–3
Turner, B.A., 21, 24
Turnitin, 50
two-tailed tests, 258
Type I and Type II errors, 254–5, 260

Ullman, J.B., 278, 296
under-identified models, 298
units of analysis, 102–4
universalist theories, 104
university libraries, 40

University of Paris-X, 41
usefulness of research, 119
utilization of research, 135–8

validity, 87–90, 92, 96–7, 108, 143
    internal and external, 87–8, 92, 104
'value-free' criteria, 58
variance, 246
verification of theory, 105–6
video recording, use of, 153–5
virtual teams, 3, 92
visual metaphors, 163–5
voice over Internet protocol (VIP), 220
VoVici software package, 220

Wald test, 294–5, 300
Walford, A.J., 42
Walker, R., 151
Wall, T.D., 89, 225
Wall Street Journal, 42–3
Walsh, G., 235
Warwick Business School, 129
Waterman, R.H., 317
Watson, Tony, 68, 70, 155
Watzlawick, P., 58
web-based surveys, 220
websites, 43
Weick, Karl, 20
Wertsch, J.V., 182
Wetherell, M., 182
Wharton Research Data Service (WRDS), 224
Who Owns Whom, 42
why-type questions, 146–7
Wikipedia, 44
wildcards, 37
Wilks' lambda (λ), 292–4
Wittgenstein, Ludwig, 57
Woolgar, S., 19, 61
work activity view of manage-ment, 4–6
workplace studies, 153
World Wide Web, 43
Wright, Sir Almroth, 319
writing
    skills of, 306–12, 319
    structures for, 307–9

Yin, Robert, 97, 99

Zetoc Alert, 39–41
ZTC Ryland (company), 70